Safavid Government Institutions

Safavid Government Institutions

Willem Floor

MAZDA PUBLISHERS, Inc. ◆ Costa Mesa, California ◆ 2001

Funding for the publication of this volume was provided in part by a grant from the Iranica Institute, Irvine California.

Mazda Publishers, Inc.
Academic Publishers since 1980
P.O. Box 2603
Costa Mesa, California 92626 U.S.A.
www.mazdapublishers.com

Library of Congress Cataloging-in-Publication Data

Floor, Willem M.
Safavid Government Institutions/ Willem Floor.
p.cm. Includes bibliographical references and index.

ISBN: 1-56859-135-7
(Softcover, alk. paper)

1. Iran—Politics and government. 2. Iran—History—Safavid dynasty, 1501-1736. I. Title.
JQ1785.F56 2001
320.455'09'03—dc21
2001044454

CONTENTS

FOREWORD

There is a trend in the writing of the history of Iran, as well as of other geographical areas, to provide new insights and theoretical contributions to the so-called intellectual discourse rather than to provide a solid foundation of the understanding of the basic socio-economic and political functions and institutions, the changes therein, and how these systems operated. These new insights may be indeed refreshing and innovative, but the reader is often left guessing what the societal building blocks are made of, and whether the actors and organizations referred to actually are one and the same under different shahs and/or timeframes. This predilection with new insights and comparative studies, brought about by the pressure on scholars to broaden their scope of analysis and avoid narrow approaches such as practiced in this book, may actually lead to analyses that, if viewed from a longer historical timeframe, are not tenable, require more nuances, or more often than not, are just plainly wrong. Now I do not want to discourage this kind of intellectual risk-taking. However, comparative studies that analyze and synthesize knowledge across regions and cultural systems require that the material that the authors work with is sound, which in the case of Iranian studies often is not the case. Therefore, more dry, narrow, and in-depth scholarship is needed to make this kind of necessary comparative studies possible, but only on a sound intellectual and factual basis. In these comparative studies what is common to these societies is often stressed, though one could also argue it is the differences that matter.

Therefore, in this study the use of Persian technical terms is not avoided, for the fact is that the devil is in the detail. It certainly helps that the author of these comparative studies shows that [s]he knows what [s]he is writing about and does not assume that the readers actually know what, for example, a *vakil*, a vizier, or a *darugheh* is in the Safavid era. In fact, they do not, because our understanding of these institutional matters is highly imperfect. Studies in this area have been greatly neglected so far, including by myself. Partly out of the need to correct my own ignorance I started this book as a commentary to the English translation of the Safavid State manual, the *Dastur al-Moluk*, which I have translated in collaboration with Mohammad Faghfoory. It became soon clear to me, that the size of the commentary would far outweigh that of the translated text. This meant that the size of this commentary might overshadow the importance of the *Dastur al-Moluk* as a text in its own right. I therefore decided to transform this commentary as a book that would stand alone and deal with the government and court organization of the Safavid State. The size of the resulting work was such that I have significantly reduced it by taking out the section of the organization of the court and of the judicial system as well as some other subjects which will be published separately. Part of the size of this book is due to the fact that since Minorsky made the first serious effort to put this subject on the map in 1943, many Persian texts have become available as well European (especially British, Dutch, French) archival source material, which both offer much new information. Also, much further analytical pioneering work has been done by Klaus Röhrborn, but this is still only available in German. Also, the important work by Jean Aubin (in French) is less accessible. Thus, only the various studies by Roger Savory could guide the English reader to the Safavid state institutions. This study of Safavid government institutions makes their analyses and materials available to the English reader. It is therefore clear that this work robustly rests on the work done by these earlier scholars, though it takes their analyses further or corrects them, where necessary.

Chapter one, dealing with the central government organization, clearly owes much to Röhrborn, Aubin and Savory. Nevertheless, much new information has been added to the subject of the state's high offices and chancellery procedures. In chapter two, which discusses the provincial government, though in broad terms following Röhrborn 's earlier analysis, adds many new data, in particular on the function of the *darugheh* and vizier. Neither of these two chapters discusses fiscal issues as I have dealt with those in a separate book. Chapter three offers most of the new available information. It deals with the Safavid army; how it was formed, what reforms took place and how these were given form and with what results. The discussion does not limit itself to organization of the various army corpses, but also describes the arms they used, the tactics and battle formation they applied and how battles and sieges were won. In all chapters, where sufficient material was available to do so, a list of the known office holders has been inserted in the text. Finally, this study shows that there was major shift in the power structure in the Safavid state after 1600, when the Qezelbash tribes had to share power with the new kids on the block, the royal slaves or *gholam*s, who were later joined by the eunuchs. This dissipation of power reinforced the Crown's executive power, but ultimately, paralyzed the state due to the impossibility of strong statesmen to lead the country. The lack of a guiding principle or ideology reinforced this trend and finally led to the demise of the Safavid dynasty.

CHAPTER ONE

Organization of the Central Government

Introduction

IN THIS CHAPTER an analytical overview is given of the key functions in the central government organization in Safavid Persia. In most cases the Persian terminology has been retained, for it would not make much sense to use the generic word 'governor', for example, where in Safavid Persia a variety of terms was used to denote a provincial governor, which different terms reflected his relative standing in the administrative hierarchy. Also, to better understand their importance and changes over time it necessary to see these functions and institutions in their contemporary context. In particular, one needs to realize that Safavid Persia was a pre-capitalistic state whose economy was mainly agrarian. Communications were underdeveloped, and the population was diverse in language, ethnicity, and religion. Also, outside the cities, which may have housed 15% of the population, the people were either sedentary, living in villages, or nomadic, migrating annually in tribal groups. The nomadic population probably constituted at least one-third of the population and increased in size during unsettled times.[1]

Safavid Persia's political system was patrimonial. That is the shah was the sole source of political power. His will was executed through a civil bureaucracy and, if need be, by an army. Both were loyal to the shah rather than to the political system. Hence, political rule, relations, and responsibilities were highly personalized. Put another way, the inner circle (civil, religious, and military) surrounding the shah derived their influence and power from their proximity to the shah. Thus, it was not so much their function and responsibilities that gave them power but the knowledge for those lower on the social ladder that they held that function for the shah.

Because of the underdevelopment of the communication system and the high cost of an absolutist central rule, the shah exercised selective

---

[1] J.Aubin, "Chiffres de population urbaine en Iran occidentale autour de 1500", *Moyen Orient & Océan Indien*, vol. 3, 1986, pp. 37-54; G. Gilbar, "Demographic developments in late Qajar Persia, 1870-1906", *Asian and African Studies* 11 (1976), pp. 125-56.

control only. That is, provincial, local, and other leaders were delegated with responsibility, but not with authority. This served to minimize initiative, to foster obedience, and, above all, to maximize uncertainty. To reduce the risk of the rise of local independent power bases, governors usually were rotated annually, sometimes even more, towards the end of the 17th century. The shah aimed to increase his hold on the local rulers also through the judicious use of military force and other coercive measures. Various local rulers were therefore permitted to continue to exercise their traditional role in a precisely circumscribed way, which served to formalize their submission to the center. This decentralization of power, however, did not mean that the center relinquished its sovereignty; rather, it served to underscore that sovereignty, because the center could intervene locally whenever it wished to do so.

This system, combined with the legitimacy that the Safavids enjoyed, allowed for great political stability. For the shah was and remained the pivot of the universe throughout the period that the dynasty held power. His authority was never called into question and never did anyone else develop a serious power base independent of, or in opposition to, the shah. As a result political opposition and infighting only took place between members of the power elite, both the military, religious and administrative leaders. However, one of the constants of Safavid political life was that the grand vizier as the executive arm of the shah's authority was and remained the dominant political figure throughout the entire Safavid period. The fact that there were other contenders for power and the shah's favor does not invalidate what has been said about the pre-eminence of the grand vizier's position. On the contrary, it confirms it, for the man to beat, so to speak, was the grand vizier, not the shah. Therefore, there was a constant challenge of the grand vizier's position by royal favorites and other powerful lords, who would try and weaken the grand vizier's powers. They might even be successful at times in doing so, but it was a temporary gain. For eventually the grand vizier would prevail, as long as he enjoyed the shah's trust.

In 1722, Jan Oets, the director of the Dutch East Indies Company in Safavid Persia, wrote, based on 20 years of personal experience with Safavid government institutions and four grand viziers, that: "The shah having entrusted his power and authority to the grand vizier it is easy to understand that this minister is the foremost and most important one to whom one addresses oneself to make requests for the Hon. Company. It is his favor that one has to seek, for although occasionally one or another favorite has the shah's ear and he for a short time directs the affairs according to his liking, one often observes that this is only of short duration after which the power returns again to its first origin and source, namely, the grand vizier."[2]

---

[2] *ARA*, KA 1891, f. 245.

Nevertheless, there were changes in the power structure of the Safavid bureaucracy over time, but these did not concern the grand vizier's position, but rather that of other important officials. The royal household (*khasseh*) staff gained ground at the cost of their state bureaucratic (*mamalek*) colleagues. This was epitomized by the growth in importance of, for example, the function of the *mostoufi-ye khasseh* and the *majles-nevis* as against the marginalization of that of the keepers of the seal (*mohrdar*) and the *monshi al-mamalek*. This change was a function of the growth of the relative size of *khasseh* lands at the expense of the *mamalek* lands and therefore the number of 'independent' governors as against dependent royal viziers decreased. It also meant that compared with the 16th century the balance of power had moved from the Qezelbash emirs to those who were in charge of the *khasseh* administration in the 17th century. For the grand vizier this meant no change in working conditions, only a change in the composition of the constraints on his powers.

Further, the incorporation of the Qezelbash tribal force into the administrative structure of the country was concluded successfully, though not without pain and struggle. The Qezelbash emirs were from the beginning of the Safavid state governors of large and small governates, but they were held in check by the traditional class of Tajik bureaucrats. In the military area, their oligopoly of military power was countervailed by the increased role of Iranic forces, formalized by the creation of the *gholam* corps. This meant that henceforth power had to be shared with the *gholam*s as well as the Tajik class of bureaucrats. The relative political importance of the Qezelbash received an additional blow by the growth of the *khasseh* lands which generally were not governed by Qezelbash emirs. The severing of the direct ties between Qezelbash emirs and Qezelbash clans also meant the end of a unified Qezelbash political and military force. For henceforth Qezelbash emirs when appointed governors usually were not appointed in their 'homeland' thus weakening their nuisance value and making them more dependent on the central government. Finally, initial Qezelbash-*gholam* rivalry, consciously fostered by 'Abbas I, grew into co-habitation, as is clear from the way the murder of the powerful grand vizier Mirza Taqi in 1645 was handled by the two groups. Also, Qezelbash leaders became grand viziers as of 1669 thus signaling that they had become part of the Tajik bureaucratic culture.

As a consequence of these changes and developments the power and role of the Crown grew, though not that of the shah. For the shah already had, and continued to hold, absolute power, but the scope and size of, and control over, his executive means and instruments had grown considerably over time. However, rather than the shah's position it was that of the various contending officials of the *khasseh* administration and other high officials who tried to use these new increased powers for their own use that grew in importance. Also, the fact that towards the end of the Safavid regime the power elite depended on the Crown for its financial position, which hold was enhanced by the increased rotation of office holders, diminished the elite's power. This resulted in more dispersal of power among the elite, led to more in-fighting between the weakened leading political and military leaders, in particular in challenging the grand vizier. All this did not endanger the position of the shah who had withdrawn from political life, for all practical purposes since the 1670s. This situation, however, led to political stagnation due to lack of decision making at the government level. For the contending parties were very effective in thwarting each other's plans so that nobody really won and consequently paralysis rather than action characterized the latter days of the Safavid state. The fall of this state, that was unable to even take the most elementary steps against the early 18th century revolts and marauding, was but the logical end of this process.

Geographical Extent of the Kingdom

The geography of Safavid Persia is still only known sketchily. Röhrborn, so far, has given the best broad outline of the Safavid possessions. The Safavid kingdom reached its largest size under its founder Esma'il I (r. 907/1502-930/1524). It included modern day Iran as well as much of 'Iraq-e 'Arab (Baghdad, Diyarbekr), the western part of Afghanistan (Herat, Qandahar), parts of Trans-Caucasia (Georgia, Armenia, Azarbaijan and Daghestan) and of Transoxiania (Marv). Both western and north-eastern possessions were challenged by Ottoman (to whom Baghdad and Diyarbekr were lost in 1516) or Uzbeg forces (who regularly infested Herat). His successors, Tahmasp I (r. 930/1524-984/1576) and Esma'il II (r. 984/1576-985/1577), were more or less able to hold on to these borders. However, under Khodabandeh (r. 985/1577-995/1587) and the early years of 'Abbas I (r. 995/1587-1038/1629) large parts (including Tabriz and Herat) were lost to the Ottomans and the Uzbegs. 'Abbas I was able to retake all of the lost possessions, but his successor, Safi I (r. 1038/1629-1052/1642) had to abandon 'Iraq-e 'Arab entirely to the Ottomans in 1049/1639. Safi I's successors were able to consolidate their borders. The danger, however, came from within, for the Safavids lost control over Qandahar in 1715 due to a rebellion by the local Ghalza'i tribe. It was Mahmud Khan, the son of the leader of the Qandahar rebellion, who in 1135/1722 would bring down the Safavids by his conquest of Isfahan.[3]

From a fiscal point of view the administration still followed the ancient Sasanid model of dividing the country into four areas (North, West, South, East). This is clear, for example, from the fact that there were four *avajareh-nevis*, accountants, who kept the records as to agricultural and

---

[3] For more detailed information see Röhrborn, Klaus-Michael. *Provinzen und Zentralgewalt Persiens im 16. und 17. Jahrhundert* (Berlin 1966) pp. 3-18. For a contemporary account by Du Mans see Richard, Francis (editor) *Raphael du Mans, missionnaire en Perse au XVIIe s.* 2 vols. (Paris 1995) vol. 2. pp. 4-7.

other natural resource revenues. It is also confirmed by Chardin.[4] However, in practice Safavid Persia was divided into five administrative regions: Khorasan, Fars, Azerbaijan, Gilan-Mazandaran, and 'Iraq-e 'Ajam. This fivefold division followed the ancient fourfold one and added the central arid province of 'Iraq-e 'Ajam as the center-piece.[5] Some sources have it that Persia was divided into 7 regions, which basically meant that Shirvan (or Transcaucasia) was a separate jurisdiction from Azerbaijan, and that Kerman was also considered a separate region.[6] These four or five administrative regions did not correspond to provinces or to administrative jurisdictions, however. For Safavid Persia was divided into about 50-70 jurisdictions, which were governed by a varying number of *vali*s (vice-roys), *begler-begi*s (governor-generals), *hakem*s (senior-governors), *soltan*s or *qul-begi*s (junior-governors), *darugheh*s (superintendents) and viziers (administrators). Their number, geographic designation and land area, changed over time as a function of political and military vicissitudes. But before we discuss the organization of the provincial administration we will first review that of the central government.

Organization of the Central Government

By 1580, according to Minadoi, the hierarchy of the Safavid state was as follows: "This is then the order of the States of the kingdome: First the Sahha, then the Miriza and Mirize, the Chan and Sultan, the Mordar, the Defterdar, the Caddi, the Mustaed-Dini, and the Calife."[7]

The Sahha or shah, of course, was at the top of the pyramid and he was followed by the Miriza or *mirza*s. With this term Minadoi refers to the Safavid princes, who all bore this title after their name, such as 'Abbas Mirza.[8] Apart from being a personal title, the term was also used to refer to a function as in the case of 'Abbas Mirza, who was appointed by his father, Shah Khodabandeh, as prince-governor of Herat or *mirza-ye Herat*.[9] Because 'Abbas Mirza was still an infant at that time his tutor held

---

4 Chardin, Jean. *Voyages*, ed. L. Langlès, 10 vols., Paris 1811, vol. 5, p. 439.

5 Minadoi, John-Thomas. *The History of the Warres betwen the Turkes and the Persians* (London 1595 [1976]), p. 48; Kaempfer, Engelbert. *Am Hofe des persischen Grosskönigs (1684-85). Das erste Buch der Amoenitates exoticae in deutscher Bearbeitung*, hrsg. v. Walter Hinz (Leipzig 1940) (henceforth cited as *Am Hofe*), p. 127; Nasiri, Mohammad Ebrahim b. Zein al-'Abedin, *Dastur-e Shahriyan*. ed. Mohammad Nader Nasiri Moqaddam (Tehran 1373/1995), p. 18.

6 Isfahan; Shiraz; Khorasan; Azerbaijan; Mazandaran; Shirvan; and Gilan; Berchet, Guglielmo. *La Repubblica di Venezia e la Persia* (Torino 1865 [1976]), pp. 290-1.

7 Minadoi, p. 68.

8 See on this subject John Perry, "Mirza, Mashti and Juja Kabab: Some Cases of Anamolous Noun Phrase Word Order in Persian" in Ch. Melville ed., *Persian and Islamic Studies in Honour of P.W. Avery* (Cambridge 1990), pp. 213-28.

9 Molla Jalal al-Din Monajjem, *Ruznameh-ye 'Abbasi ya Ruznameh-ye Molla Jalal*, ed. Seifollah Vahidniya, Tehran 1366/1967, p. 22; Khodabandeh Mirza had himself

the function of princely tutor (*mansab-e dedegi-ye mirza'i*).[10] Missing from Minadoi's list is the function of the *vakil*, about which later, as well as that of the grand vizier, unless the term 'Mirize' is meant to convey this, which is likely. Traditionally, people from the administrative class bore the honorific *mirza* in front of their names, e.g. Mirza Salman. The function of the keeper of the seal (*mohrdar*) and the financial comptroller (*daftardar*) will be discussed in chapter two. The listing of the khan and *soltan* by Minadoi refers to the ranks held by the governors, who played a vital administrative and military role in governing the country. Because their role (as well as that of prince-governors) belongs to the section of the provincial government it will be discussed at its proper place. The role of the 'Caddi' or qadi and of the 'Calife' or *khalifeh al-kholafa* will be dealt with in separate publications.

Vakil

The position of *vakil* or regent was not a creation of the Safavids, because it existed already under the Aq-Qoyunlus. After the death of Shah Ya'qub (r. 886-96/1478-90) the young Aq-Qoyunlu princes Baysunghur (r. 1490-92), Rustam (r. 1492-97) and Alvand (r. 1497-1505) were too young as yet to rule themselves and therefore a *vakil* took care of the affairs of state.[11] Under Esma'il I the *vakil* seems to have had a similar role, although he was competent enough to rule himself. However, Esma'il I was not interested in the daily drudgery of governing (*molk va mali*), which he left to his Tajik *vakils*.[12] Princes were not the only ones who had *vakils*, in fact all important Turkoman emirs had one, invariably a Tajik, who managed their financial and other non-military affairs for them as well. But even military affairs were sometimes entrusted to the *vakil*.[13]

---

also been appointed Mirza-ye Khorasan. V. Minorsky transl., *Calligraphers and Painters. A treatise by Qadi Ahmad, Son of Mir-Munshi (circa A.H. 1015/A.D. 1606)* (Washington 1959), p. 91; Montazer-Saheb, Asghar (ed.) *'Alamara-ye Shah Esma'il* (Tehran, 1349/1970), p. 452.

[10] Qomi, Qadi Ahmad ibn Sharaf al-Din al-Hosein al-Hoseini. *Kholasat al-Tavarikh*, 2 vols., ed. Ehsan Eshraqi. (Tehran, 1363/1984), vol. 1, p. 164.

[11] Alvand Mirza: Khvandamir. *Habib al-Seyar*, 4 vols. ed. Mohammad Dabir-Siyaqi. (Tehran, 1362/1983 [3rd. ed.]), vol. 4, p. 455; Ross, Denison E. "The Early Years of Shah Isma'il, Founder of the Safavi Dynasty" *Journal of the Royal Asiatic Society* (1896), pp. 299, 304; Woods, John E. *The Aqquyunlu. Clan, Federation, Empire* (Minneapolis 1976), p. 291, n. 119; Morad Mirza: Rumlu, Hosein Beg. *Ahsan al-Tavarikh*. ed. 'Abdol-Hosein Nava'i. (Tehran 1357/1978), p. 28.

[12] See for an excellent analysis of Esma'il I's role, both as spiritual and government leader Aubin, Jean. "L'Avènement des Safavides reconsiderée" (Etudes Safavides III), *Moyen-Orient et Océan Indien*, 5 (1988), pp. 1-130. The contemporary term Tajik rather than the modern day term Persian is used in this study to denote those who spoke an Iranic language and originated from that part of the population who were not Qezelbash Turkomans. The latter also used the term Tat to refer to the same group, but this word had a deragotary meaning.

[13] Aubin, "L'Avènement", p. 112, n. 456.

Also, regional rulers such as the *malek al-moluk* (king of kings) of Seistan had a *vakil*. The office of the regency (*vekalat*) of Seistan was in the hands of the *miran*, a group of hereditary local chieftains, often that of the Emir Mohammad Mahmud family. The *vakil* was in charge of all matters of state (*mahammat-e kolli va jozvi-ye mamlakat*), and as such he had the right to seal all documents. Sometimes, the *vakil* of Seistan was refered to as the independent regent (*vakil-e mostaqell* or *vakil-e motlaq al-'enani*). Under Tahmasp I, the *vakil* of Seistan, who was appointed by the shah, had the right to collect so-called regent fees (*rosum-e vakil*) and had been assigned four of the 14 *boluk*s of Seistan (as *teyul* or revenue assignment), while the remainder were assigned to the traditional local ruler (*malek*). The latter did not like this and fled his country.[14] The rulers of Gilan, Mazandaran and Georgia also had the institution of *vakil*, who sometimes also was the ruler's tutor or *laleh*, in case the ruler was a minor.[15]

There is as yet no consensus on the extent of the *vakil*'s authority. Savory argues that the *vakil* was the *alter ego* of the shah, which he believes included the spiritual aspect of the shah's position as spiritual leader (*morshed-e kamel*) of the Safavid order.[16] Aubin, however, considered the *vakil* as nothing but the deputy or *locum tenens* (*janeshin*) of the shah, who took care of those affairs in which the shah took no direct and daily interest. The shah did not act differently from his Turkoman emirs who also delegated the administration of all non-military affairs to Tajik *vakil*s.[17]

From the textual evidence, available from contemporary chancery documents and chronicles, it would seem that the *vakil* indeed was nothing but the deputy of the shah, who derived his power and authority from the shah and not from the function itself. However, the occurrence of

---

14 Seistani, Malek Shah Hosein b. Malek Ghayath al-Din Mohammad b. Shah Mahmud. *Ehya al-Moluk*. ed. Manuchehr Setudeh. (Tehran 1344/1966) pp. 138-9, 147, 144, 147-8, 154, 157, 161, 164, 185, 318, 428-9. For a history of the dynasty of the *malek*s of Seistan see C.E. Bosworth, *The History of the Saffarids of Sistan and the Maliks of Nimruz (247/861 to 949/1542-3)* (Costa Mesa 1994).

15 Eskander Beg Monshi, *History of Shah 'Abbas the Great*, tr. R.M. Savory, 2 vols. (Boulder 1978), vol. 1, pp. 183, 312, 395; vol. 2, p. 1087 (henceforth cited as Savory, *History*); Valeh Esfahani, Mohammad Yusef. *Khold-e Barin*. ed. Mir Hashem Mohaddeth. (Tehran 1372/1993), pp. 631, 645.

16 Savory, Roger M. "The Principal Offices of the Safawid State During the Reign of Isma'il I. (907-30/1501-24)", *BSOAS* 23 (1960), pp. 93-99; Ibid. "The Principal Offices of the Safawid State During the Reign of Tahmasp I. (930-84/1524-76)", *BSOAS* 24 (1961), pp. 77-78.

17 Aubin, L'Avènement, pp. 112-6. Röhrborn, K. "Regierung und Verwaltung Irans unter den Safawiden" in Idris, H.R. & Röhrborn, K. *Regierung und Verwaltung des Vorderen Orients in Islamischen Zeit* (Handbuch der Orientalistik) (Leiden 1979) basically agrees with Aubin.

the title of *vakil-e nafs-e nafis-e homayun*, as Savory has argued, seems to indicate that the *vakil* was more than a secular, temporal regent and that he also was the shah's deputy as to spiritual affairs and authority. This term was conferred for the last time on Emir 'Abd al-Baqi who died at the battle of Chaldiran in 1514.[18] Because Esma'il I was both temporal and spiritual ruler (*nazem-e manazem-e din va doulat*) his *vakil* was also referred to as his deputy (*qa'em-maqam*) for these same functions.[19] But this did not necessarily mean that the *vakil* deputized for both the worldly and the religious aspects of Esma'il I's kingship. The term, *vakil va janashin-e morshed-e kamel*, used by Najm-e Thani to refer to himself, also seems to suggest that there was may be more to the regency than just a secular administrative function.[20] However, it was just another way of saying "I am the shah's deputy", or *janeshin-e shah-e din-e panah* (the deputy of the king, the refuge of religion), a normal and recurring term to refer to the king. However, Najm-e Thani was talking to hostile sufi emirs (*omara-ye sufi*) and to try to get them to agree to his point of view he appealed to their allegiance to their spiritual leader, the *morshed-e kamel*, who had become shah, whom he represented. Also, there were two other officials who contrary to the *vakil* did indeed have an explicit religious and even spiritual function and had a better claim to the alleged religious deputyship. First there was the *sadr*, and second, the *khalifeh al-kholafa*. The fact that the latter, in 1576, refused to accept the function of *vakil-e nafs-e nafis-e homayun*, because he considered his authority as *khalifeh* to be greater than that of the *vakil*, is telling within this context. The title *nafs-e nafis-e homayun* was not conferred anymore on any person after 1514, though it was offered to Hoseinqoli Rumlu, the *khalifeh al-kholafa*, in 1576. It was mentioned once more in 1612 when Mohammad Amin, the former *mir jomleh* (chief minister) of the Qotbshahi ruler, wanted to become Shah 'Abbas I's vizier and *vakil-e nafs-e homayun*. The last time I have come across the term *nafs-e nafis* was in 1730 when it was used to refer to Tahmasp II (r. 1724-32).[21]

The function of the Safavid *vakil* was first held by a Qezelbash emir. He was in fact the shah's tutor, Hosein Beg Laleh Shamlu, with the title of *vakil-e nafs-e nafis*.[22] As of 914/1509 till 920/1514 Tajiks, (other) sufis of Lahejan, i.e. members of the fellowship who had followed Esma'il I in his exile to Lahejan, held the function. For Hosein Beg Shamlu was dismissed in 913-14/1508 as *vakil*. In his place as *vakil* and *emir al-omara*, a Tajik

---

18 Khvandamir, vol. 4, pp. 526, 527.

19 Khvandamir, vol. 4, p. 598, 468.

20 Montazer-Saheb, p. 317.

21 Savory, *History*, vol. 2, p. 1098; Mervi, Mohammad Kazem. *Tarikh-e 'Alamara-ye Naderi*, 3 vols. ed. Mohammad Amin Riyahi. (Tehran, 1369/1990 [2nd. ed.]), vol. 1, p. 85.

22 Khvandamir, vol. 4, p. 468; Valeh Esfahani, p. 123; he was also referred to as *vakil-e shah-e din-e panah*.

was appointed, viz. Emir Najm al-Din Mas'ud Gilani, a goldsmith and notable from Resht, who was an early convert to Esma'il I's cause, whom he had joined for his quest for the throne in 906/1500-1. Najm al-Din "sealed the royal orders on the backside above the seals of the emirs and took charge of the financial administration. He did not allow any interference by the Turkoman emirs in financial affairs. He also became powerful in administrative (*molki*) affairs."[23] Khvandamir wrote: "within a short time Emir Najm al-Din acquired a position of trust and authority, and... was promoted to the office of *vekalat-e nafs-e nafis-e homayun*, and undertook the conduct of *administrative and financial affairs* with full independence; his power and position surpassed that of all the great emirs and *moqarrabs*."[24] Khvandamir used the term *nafs-e nafis*, which as I have argued, is just another way of saying *shah din-e panah* and nothing more. It is not surprising that Khvandamir did not say anything about a spiritual role for Najm al-Din, but rather stipulated, and explicitly so, that his function was a purely administrative one (*molk va mali*).

When Najm al-Din died in 915/1509-10, Esma'il I conferred the office of *vakil* on another Tajik and sufi of Lahejan, Emir Yar Ahmad Khuzani with the title Najm-e Thani. He also was placed two degrees (*payeh*) above all the other emirs and officials and was entrusted with the handling of the country's administrative and financial affairs.[25] Najm-e Thani is referred to as *vakil-e motlaq*, *vakil-e koll-e ekhtiyar*, or as *vakil al-saltaneh*, which latter term would remain in use for over one century.[26] No mention is made of Najm-e Thani being the *alter ego* of the shah. Rather he is said to be an independent *vakil* and in charge of *hall va naqd va zabt va rabt-e omur-e saltanat*,[27] i.e. of the management of the material side of governing the country. Najm-e Thani gathered much wealth; he surpassed all emirs and *soltans* in importance and his retainers (*molazem*) numbered 5,000 horsemen.[28]

The Qezelbash resented the fact that they had to serve under a peasant (*rusta'i*)[29], a Tajik, who, moreover, did nothing to make himself agreeable.

---

[23] Kvandamir, vol. 4, p. 491; Efendiev, O.A. *Obrazovanie Azerbaidzhanskogo Gosudarstva Sefevidov v natsale XVI veka* (Baku 1961), f. 246 b; Qom:, vol. 1, p 96.

[24] Khvandamir, vol. 4, p. 491. The italics are mine. His title was *vakil-e nafs-e homayun*, and his seal was placed above that of all other emirs. Valeh Esfahani, pp. 167-8.

[25] Khvandamir, vol. 4, p. 501; Qomi, vol. 1, p. 100; Nasiri, Mirza 'Ali Naqi. *Alqab va mavajeb-e doureh-ye salatin-e Safaviyeh* ed. Yusef Rahimlu (Mashhad 1371/1992), p. 32, also stresses the pre-eminent position of the *vakil*.

[26] Montazer-Saheb, pp. 315, 391; Valeh Esfahani, pp. 178, 210 (*vakil-e 'alahezrat-e jahanbani*)

[27] Khvandamir, vol. 4, p. 501, 527; Valeh Esfahani, p. 214; he had "*koll-e ekhtiyar-e molki va mali-ye sarkar-e sharifeh*" and wore the seal of the *vekalat* around his neck. Montazer-Saheb, p. 386.

[28] Valeh Esfahani, p. 214; Montazer-Saheb, p. 387.

[29] Aubin, "L'Avènement", p. 117; Montazer-Saheb, pp. 319, 431, 433, 440, 461.

As a result of this friction the Persian army was defeated and the *vakil* lost his life in November 918/1512. If Najm-e Thani would have had religious authority as the *alter ego* of the shah it is doubtful that the Qezelbash emirs would have acted so unruly and disobedient to the shah's *vakil*. Also, in chancery documents none of the *vakil*s is referred to as *vakil*, but rather by more mundane terms such as sheikh, Rokn al-Douleh, (Najm-e Thani), and 'Azud al-Douleh, Nezam al-Douleh (Mir 'Abd al-Baqi).[30]

Despite the disastrous defeat against the Uzbegs in 1512, Esma'il I appointed again a Tajik to the function of *vakil*, Mir 'Abd al-Baqi, who had been *sadr* (head of the religious institution) as well as vice-regent (*na'eb-e vakil*) in Najm-e Thani's absence.[31] He was, however, assisted by Mohammad Beg Sofrehchi Ostajalu, who was his deputy for military affairs.[32] When Mir 'Abd al-Baqi died in 1514 (at Chaldiran), he was succeeded by another Tajik, Mirza Shah Hosein Esfahani, who held the function of *vakil al-saltaneh* with the title of E'temad al-Douleh. However, the shah now divided the office of *vakil* in two parts, one with an administrative and one with a military function. To placate his Qezelbash emirs, Esma'il I appointed a military man to be responsible for military affairs after the devastating defeats in 1512 and 1514 which had decimated Safavid military strength. Such a division of labor was not unusual. It existed for other high ranking functions too, such as in case of the *sadr*. The new military *vakil*, who at the same time held the office of *emir al-omara* (see below), was Mohammad Beg Sofrehchi Ostajalu, who was given the new name of Chayan Soltan. He was a minor Qezelbash emir, who was not even promoted to the rank of khan, for the shah clearly did not want to create too powerful a military commander. Chayan Soltan remained in function from 920/1514-5 till 930/1523-4 when he died, preceding Esma'il I by a few months. He was succeeded by his son Bayazid Soltan Ostajalu, also a minor emir, who died a few days later.[33] The latter's son, Eyghut Mirza, tried to claim his father's function, but after a few days died as well.[34]

As of 920/1514, the office of the administrative *vakil* was also referred to as *nezarat-e divan* [-*e a'la*]. In fact, a few sources state that the *vakil* had been appointed to the *vezarat va nezarat-e divan-e a'la*.[35] But

---

[30] Aubin, "L'Avènement", p. 114.

[31] Mir 'Abdu'l-Baqi appointed as *vakil* and *emir al-omara* in 919/1513. Qazvini Ghaffari, Qadi Ahmad. *Tarikh-e Jahanara*. (Tehran 1343/1964), p. 276. There is no evidence for Eskander Beg Monshi's report that Emir Gayath al-Din Mohammad Mirimiran, was *sadr*, *vakil* and *emir-al omara*. Savory, *History*, vol. 1, p. 340, n.12.

[32] Khvandamir, vol. 4, p. 542; Ross, "Early Years", f. 224b.

[33] Yahya b. 'Abd al-Latif al-Hoseini al-Qazvini, *Lobb al-Tavarikh*. ed. Sayyed Jalal al-Din al-Qazvini (Tehran 1314/1935), p. 258.

[34] Sam Mirza, *Tadhkareh-ye Tohfat-e Sami*. ed. Rokn al-Din Homayunfarrokh (Tehran n.d.), p. 441.

[35] e.g. Ghaffari Qazvini, pp. 277, 282; Rumlu, pp. 242, 247.

whatever the wording, the administrative *vakil* still enjoined very great power, much to the envy of the Qezelbash emirs.[36] The new *vakil*, Mirza Shah Hosein Esfahani, in fact was the more powerful of the *vakil*-duo, despite the fact that the Qezelbash emirs referred to him as a peasant (*rusta'i*).[37] For he had "absolute power in the affairs of the kingdom and government, and authority over all emirs, magnates, viziers and notables."[38] Emir Khan Mousellu, when he was dismissed from his governorship of Khorasan realized that Mirza Shah Hosein was the real power in the state when he said: "What have I done to Mirza Hosein that he takes it out on me?"[39] Despite the existence of the military *vakil*, it was Mirza Shah Hosein, not Chayan Soltan, who created the new corps of musketeers (*tofangchis*) in 1516.[40] Mirza Shah Hosein also showed his power when he ordered his former master, Durmish Khan Shamlu, (whose vizier and deputy he had been in Isfahan), to go to Herat to take up his governorship rather than to remain at court. This insult to the most distinguished of Qezelbash emirs was the cause of the *vakil*'s death. For after a few failed murder attempts the emirs were able to kill Mirza Shah Hosein in 929/1523. The new *vakil* again was a Tajik, Khvajeh Jalal al-Din Mohammad Tabrizi.[41] In their thirst for power the Qezelbash emirs were at first constrained by Khvajeh Jalal, whom they therefore killed. With the approval of the Ostajalu emirs, who had been left out of the power structure by the Rumlu faction, Qadi Jahan Qazvini was appointed *vakil*. He soon fell victim to court intrigues and was dismissed and replaced by Mir Ja'far Savaji.[42]

---

[36] Mirza Shah Hosein *vakil* and *nazer*, Valeh Esfahani, p. 268, (*vakil al-saltaneh*) pp. 271, 275; (*nazer-e divan-e a'la* and was charged with the management of the *omur-e jomhur*), p. 243.

[37] Montazer-Saheb, pp. 617, 619, 620.

[38] Khvandamir, vol. 4, p. 549; Qomi, vol. 1, p. 151; Ross, "Early Years", p. 254b.

[39] Rumlu, p. 228; Qomi, vol. 1, p. 149.

[40] Bacqué-Grammont, Jean-Louis. *Les Ottomans, les Safavides et leurs voisins.* (Leiden 1987), p. 158. Also other Tajiks were given military tasks and/or ranks. Khvandamir, vol. 4, p. 576.

[41] Khvandamir, vol. 4, p. 598; although some sources only refer to him as vizier; Bidlisi, Sharaf Khan. *Cherefnama ou Histoire des Kourdes*, publiée par V. Veliaminof-Zernof, 2 vols. (St. Petersburg 1860-62), vol. 2, p. 167.

[42] Qadi Jahan al-Hasani was *vakil al-saltaneh*. Qomi, vol. 1, p. 254.

Table 1.1 List of *vakil*s

1. Hosein Beg Laleh Shamlu[43] *vakil* + *emir al-omara*   907/1501-2
2. Mir Najm Zargar Gilani[44]   914/1509
3. Mir Yar-Ahmad Khuzani Najm-e Thani[45]   915/1509-10
4. Sayyed Mir 'Abd al-Baqi Ne'matollahi[46]   919/1513-4 -
                                                                  920/1514
5. Mohammad Beg Sofrehchi Ostajalu (Chayan Soltan)[47]   920/1514-5
6. Bayazid Soltan Ostajalu[48] son of 5.   930/1523-4
6.a Eyghut Mirza,[49] son of 6   930/1523-24
7. Div Soltan Rumlu[50]   930/1523-4
8. Div Soltan Rumlu + Mostafa Soltan (Kepek Soltan) Ostajalu[51]
                                                                  930/1524
9. Div Soltan Rumlu + Choqa Soltan Tekellu[52]   932/1526
10. Choqa Soltan Tekellu[53]   933/1527
11. Hosein Beg Shamlu + 'Abdollah Khan Ostajalu[54]   937/1531-
                                                                  940/1533-4

vacancy?

12. Ma'sum Beg Safavi[55]   960/1553 –
                                                                  976/1568
13. Hamzeh Mirza[56]   985/1577-8 - 994/1586

---

[43] Valeh Esfahani, p. 123; Rumlu, p. 164; Röhrborn, *Regierung*, p. 23, n. 17. According to al-Qazvini, *Lobb*, p. 394, Hosein Beg Laleh and Abdal Beg Dedeh were both appointed as *emir al-omara* and *saheb-e ekhtiyar*.

[44] Valeh Esfahani, pp. 167-8; Khvandamir, vol. 4, p. 514, 527; Röhrborn, *Regierung*, p. 23, n. 18.

[45] Montazer-Saheb, pp. 315, 391; Khvandamir, vol. 4, p. 527; Qomi, vol. 1, p. 100. Röhrborn, *Regierung*, p. 23, n. 20.

[46] Qazvini Ghaffari, p. 376; Röhrborn, *Regierung*, p. 23, n. 22.

[47] He was replaced in his function by his *na'eb* or deputy, Jalal al-Din Mohammadi Tabrizi. Vahid Qazvini, Mohammad Taher. *'Abbasnamah*. ed. Ebrahim Dehgan (Arak 1329/1950), p. 280; Khvandamir, vol. 4, p. 542; Qomi, vol. 1, p. 152-3; Mohammad Khan *sepahsalar* Ostajalu. Montazer-Saheb, pp. 363, 524 (in 916/1510/11); Röhrborn, *Regierung*, p. 23, n. 24.

[48] Röhrborn, *Regierung*, p. 24, n. 26; al-Qazvini, p. 258.

[49] Sam Mirza, p. 344, for a few days only.

[50] Qomi, vol. 1, p. 152-3; Montazer-Saheb, p. 623; Savory, *History*, vol. 1, p. 152-3; Röhrborn, *Regierung*, p. 24, n. 28.

[51] Qomi, vol. 1, p. 364; Qazvini Ghaffari, p. 382; Valeh Esfahani, pp. 331, 334; Röhrborn, *Regierung*, p. 24, n. 29.

[52] Savory, *History*, vol. 1, pp. 78, 81, 89; Röhrborn, *Regierung*, p. 24, n. 31.

[53] Savory, *History*, vol. 1, pp. 82, 83; Röhrborn, *Regierung*, p. 24, n. 32.

[54] Röhrborn, *Regierung*, p. 24, n. 34.

[55] Qomi, vol. 1, p. 406, 559; Shamlu, p. 89; Savory, *History*, vol. 1, p. 168.

[56] Savory, *History*, vol. 1, p. 338; Astarabadi, Sayyed b. Morteza Hoseini. *Az Sheikh Safi ta Shah Safi*, ed. Ehsan Eshraqi (Tehran, 1364/1985), p. 104; Qomi, vol. 2, p. 662.

Table 1.1 (continued)

14. Abu Taleb Mirza[57]	995/1586-7
15. Morshedqoli Khan Ostajalu[58]	995/1586-7 - 996/1588
16. Zeinal Khan Shamlu[59]	1038/1629 to 1039/1630
17. Mohammad 'Ali Khan[60]	1135/1722
18. Mirza 'Abdallah[61]	1136/1724
19. Fath 'Ali Khan Qajar[62]	1139/1726
20. Tahmaspqoli Khan Afshar	1142-45/1730-32

When Shah Esma'il I died in 1524, "Among the emirs and the principal officers of state, disputes occurred in regard to the office of [military] *vakil* and these disputes, fanned by tribal rivalries, ended in civil war. Every few minutes, another great emir or elder of state took charge of the office of [military] *vakil* and administered the affairs of state with full authority. During the early part of his reign, Tahmasp, because of his tender years, for a while neglected the affairs of state."[63] When Tahmasp I ascended the throne in 930/1524, the office of military *vakil* was in the powerful hands of Div Soltan Rumlu, who had become *emir al-omara* after Bayazid Soltan Ostajalu and his son, Eyghut Mirza, had died. He initially (in 930/1524) shared the regency with Mostafa (or Kepek) Soltan, brother of Chayan Soltan Ostajalu,[64] who wanted to become sole *vakil* and therefore started to quarrel with Div Soltan. The latter was able to hold on to the function for three years, but usually had to share power with other contenders, such as Kepek Soltan.[65] Div Soltan initially gave in, and Kepek Soltan Ostajalu became *mir divan* and *vakil al-saltaneh*.[66] But after having dealt with the Uzbegs, Div Soltan asked the emirs to support him against Kepek Soltan to get the regency back, in which he was successful.[67] In 934/1527-8, Div Soltan was slain by Chuqa Soltan, the

[57] Qomi, vol. 2, p. 847; Monshi, vol. 1, p. 131.

[58] Monshi, vol. 1, pp. 305, 385; Qomi, vol. 2, p. 869.

[59] Yusef, p. 279; Esfahani, Mohammad Ma'sum b. Khvajegi. *Kholaseh al-Siyar*, ed. Iraj Afshar. (Tehran n.d. [1992]), pp. 34, 40, 47, 55.

[60] Mostoufi, Mohammad Mohsen. *Zobdat al-Tavarikh*. Ed. Behruz Gudarzi (Tehran 1375/1996), p. 141.

[61] Mostoufi, p. 145. He was grand vizier at the same time.

[62] Mervi, vol. 1, p. 65; Nasiri, *Alqab*, p. 33.

[63] Savory, *History*, vol. 1, p. 76; also Qomi, vol. 1, p. 172.

[64] Qazvini Ghaffari, p. 382; al-Qazvini, *Lobb*, p. 259; Div Soltan was appointed as *emir al-omara* and was charged with ordering the country's affairs. Valeh Esfahani, p. 326.

[65] Savory, *History*, vol. 1, p. 77; Qomi, vol. 1, p. 152-3; (*vakil-e motlaq*) Montazer-Saheb, p. 623. Valeh Esfahani, p. 331, together *vakil*, p. 334.

[66] Qomi, vol. 1, p. 364.

[67] Savory, *History*, vol. 1, p. 78.

doyen of the Qezelbash emirs, who then became *vakil*.[68] After his death, Olama Tekellu wanted to become *vakil* and *mokhtar al-saltaneh* in his stead, but he failed in his bid for power, and fled to the Ottomans.[69] The new military *vakil* became Hosein Beg [Khan] Shamlu, who shared the function with 'Abdollah Khan Ostajalu; both were nephews of Esma'il I. They remained in that function till 940/1533-34. Thereafter, the division of the function of *vakil* was discontinued.

After Tahmasp I had been able to put an end to the civil war among the Qezelbash and assert his royal authority in 1534, he appointed Qadi Jahan as grand vizier and *vakil*. Qadi Jahan first shared that function with two other Tajiks, but as of 942/1535 he held both functions alone. Qadi Jahan remained 11 years in function, when he retired because of his advanced age. Tahmasp I however said to him that as long as Qadi Jahan lived he would not appoint another *vakil*. When Qadi Jahan died in 960/1552-3, Tahmasp I did not immediately appoint a new *vakil*.[70] Ma'sum Beg Safavi, of the lateral line of the Safavid family, became *vakil al-saltaneh* in 960/1553-54 and remained in that function for 15 years.[71] After his death Tahmasp II did not appoint another *vakil* for the remainder of his reign.

His successor, Esma'il II (r. 1576-7), did not appoint a *vakil* at all.[72] It was only when Esma'il II got into a power conflict with Hoseinqoli Rumlu, the *khalifeh al-kholafa*, that he offered the latter the *vekalat-e divan-e a'la* and the *niyabat-e nafas-e homayun* on condition that Hoseinqoli would step down as *khalifeh*. The latter refused, was outmaneuvered by Esma'il II, and lost everything.[73] When Esma'il II died in Ramazan 985/November 1577, one of the emirs, Vali Soltan, suggested that Esma'il II's baby son be his successor. The other emirs refused to accept this suggestion, alleging that Vali Soltan merely wanted to become *vakil al-saltaneh* and thus exact obedience from the rest of the Qezelbash. "How could an eight month old infant be a suitable king of Iran?" they countered. It was then decided to give their allegiance to Tahmasp I's eldest son, Mohammad Khodabandeh (r. 1577-87).[74] When Khodabandeh succeeded Esma'il II, he appointed his eldest son, Hamzeh Mirza, *vakil-e divan-e a'la*. He was authorized to put his seal on all royal decrees, on the

---

68 Savory, *History*, vol. 1, pp. 81, 89.

69 Savory, *History*, vol. 1, pp. 83, 110.

70 He was appointed as *vakil-e divan-e a'la* in 941/1534-5. Qomi, vol. 1, pp. 254, 337, 363. Ahmad Beg Nur Kamal, grand vizier in 938/1531, also was referred to as occupying the function of *vakil*. Minorsky, *Calligraphers*, p. 76.

71 Qomi, vol. 1, pp. 406, 559; (*vakil-e shah din-panah*), Shamlu, Valiqoli b. Da'udqoli. *Qesas al-Khaqani*, vol. 1, ed. Hasan Sadat Naseri. (Tehran, 1371/1992), p. 89; Savory, *History*, vol. 1, p. 168.

72 Monshi, Eskander Beg. *Tarikh-e 'Alamara-ye 'Abbasi*, 2 vols. ed. Iraj Afshar. (Tehran, 1350/1971), vol. 1, p. 223 (henceforth cited as Monshi).

73 Valeh Esfahani, p. 522.

74 Savory, *History*, vol. 1, p. 328.

inside, above that of the grand vizier.[75] After Hamzeh Mirza's death in Dhu'l-Hijjah 994/November 1586, Khodabandeh decided not to appoint another regent (*nayeb-e divan-e a'la*) and to undertake the burdens of state affairs himself.[76] In reality, 'Aliqoli Khan Fathoghlu Khanlarkhan, a favorite of Hamzeh Mirza, was *vakil* in all but name, and it was he and his supporters who forced Khodabandeh to appoint Abu Taleb Mirza as *vakil* and crown-prince (*vali-'ahd*) one month later.[77]

These developments were not to the liking of the supporters of Khodabandeh's third son, 'Abbas Mirza. His tutor, Morshedqoli Khan, therefore made himself *vakil* with full powers in the service of 'Abbas Mirza. Meanwhile, 'Aliqoli Khan Fathoghlu had been raised to a position of the highest authority in the supreme *divan*. He exercised control over both the affairs of state and the shah and considered himself a king maker par excellence; he was also well aware that he and Morshedqoli Khan could not co-exist.[78] The conflict was resolved by 'Abbas Mirza's forces being able to rout 'Aliqoli Khan Fathoghlu. 'Abbas Mirza acceded to the throne (r. 1587-1629) and put his father and brother under house arrest. Shah 'Abbas I's position was still weak and he had to give Morshedqoli Khan absolute authority in the affairs of government. Morshedqoli Khan had quarters in the royal palace. Morning and evening, the emirs, viziers, and principal officers of state assembled in his presence and all *divan* business, of whatever importance, was concluded in accordance with his judgement. After a few days he moved to a house next to the palace that had belonged to a daughter of Tahmasp I.[79] Morshedqoli Khan also took the *khasseh* province of Isfahan for his own use, which always had been for reserved for princes, which was his first mistake, commented Eskander Monshi.[80]

The other was the *vakil*'s highhanded behavior. Therefore a conspiracy was organized against him by those who were envious of him. Their grievances were that they were important officers of state to whom the *vakil* did not delegate enough greater authority. Further "he has been taking decisions on matters of state without consulting Your Majesty. He has used the royal seals, which are affixed to administrative documents and which open the door to the treasury, to achieve his own ends. Morshedqoli Khan must surrender control of these seals to Your Majesty, and they should be deposited for safekeeping in the harem, as was the practice in the time of Shah Tahmasp. The *vakil* also should be required to convene the council of emirs twice per week. All the great emirs .....

[75] Astarabadi, p. 104; with Isfahan as his *teyul*. Qomi, vol. 2,p. 662; Savory, *History*, vol. 1, p. 338.
[76] Savory, *History*, vol. 1, pp. 486-7, 493.
[77] Qomi, vol. 1, p. 489.
[78] Savory, *History*, vol. 1, p. 496, see also pp. 508, 510 [*vakil al-saltaneh*].
[79] Savory, *History*, vol. 2, pp. 548, 505.
[80] Savory, *History*, vol. 2, p. 549.

should have a say in decisions affecting their tribal fiefs and military obligations, so that the *qurchi bashi* may be able to maintain his prestige among the *qurchi*s, and the tribal chiefs in their respective tribes."[81] The coup proved to be abortive, after which Morshedqoli Khan held the office of *vakil-e divan-e a'la* with full powers. The *vakil* allowed the shah no say in the matters of the state, and therefore 'Abbas I wanted him killed.[82] This time the conspiracy was successful and the *vakil* was killed in 997/1589-90. 'Abbas I who wanted to put an end to all sedition among the Qezelbash and bolster his own authority therefore also had other contenders for the office of regent killed.[83]

For the same reason 'Abbas I also decided not to appoint a *vakil* anymore.[84] He further ordered that Mirza Shokrollah, the *mostoufi al-mamalek*, would henceforth put the seal of the chancellery (*divan-e a'la a'la*) on the back of the royal decrees and that the *dushakollat-e vakil* (the *vakil*'s chancellery's fees) would be used for the royal household (*khasseh*) department.[85] Although 'Abbas I did not appoint a *vakil* during his entire reign this did not mean that the function of *vakil* was done away with altogether. His emirs, as well as local rulers, continued to appoint *vakil*s.[86] Even his successor used a *vakil*. On the accession to the throne by the 11 year old Safi I in 1629 Zeinal Khan was appointed as *sepahsalar* and *vakil al-saltaneh* and was put in charge of state affairs (*rateq va fateq-e omur-e saltanat*). His period in office lasted one year and it was the penultimate time that a *vakil* was appointed by a Safavid shah.[87] The only vestige of the function's existence was the collector for the *vakil*'s chancellery's fees, which were collected on behalf of the royal household (*khasseh*) treasury till the fall of Isfahan in 1722.[88] Tahmasp II (1723-32), who had fled Isfahan and set up court first in Azerbaijan and then in Khorasan, was driven by desperate need, and appointed a number of *vakil al-doulehs* such as Fath 'Ali Khan Qajar, a rather powerful, but lukewarm supporter,

---

[81] Savory, *History*, vol. 2, p. 553.

[82] Savory, *History*, vol. 2, pp. 555, 576-7.

[83] Savory, *History* vol. 2, p. 578.

[84] That this was on purpose is clear from the *Rouzat al-Safaviyeh*, quoted by Röhrborn, *Regiering*, p. 19, n.6; see also Nasiri, *Alqab*, p. 16, whom bluntly states that it had been 'Abbas I's explicit intention to ensure that the *gholam*s were a check on the unruly behavior of the *qurchi*s.

[85] Qomi, vol. 1, p. 587. This custom would be continued till 1722; Minorsky, V. ed. and tr. *The Tadhkirat al-Muluk, A Manual of Safavid Administration*. London 1943 (reprint Cambridge 1980), p. 77 (henceforth cited as TM).

[86] Mohammad Baqer Mirza became governor of Hamadan with Ogurlu Soltan Bayat as his *vakil*. Savory, *History*, vol. 2, p. 614; two factions in Gilan had traditionally filled the offices of *vakil al-saltaneh* and *saheb-ekhteyar*. Ibid., vol. 2, p. 634; *vakil* of Soltan Hosein Mirza. Ibid., vol. 2, p. 652.

[87] Yusef, Mohammad. *Dheil-e Tarikh-e 'Alamara-ye 'Abbasi*, ed. Soheil Khvonsari (Tehran 1938), p. 279.

[88] TM, p. 77.

in 1726. The latter was not able to capitalize on his promotion, because his main rival, Tahmaspqoli Khan Afshar, was able to have him beheaded in that same year. Although Tahmaspqoli Khan only was promoted to *qurchi-bashi*, he nevertheless became *vakil* in 1730 and it took him only two years before he deposed Tahmasp II and another four before he proclaimed himself Nader Shah (r. 1736-47).

Emir al-Omara or Sepahsalar

The Qezelbash emirs did not vie for the function of grand-vizier. However, when they could they claimed the office of regent (military *vakil*), which was combined with that of the office of *emir al-omara*. The holder of that office thus held significant military and political power, in particular when the shah was a minor or weak. The function was known as *emir al-omara* (-ye Iran) or *sepahsalar* (-e Iran). The function of *sepahsalar* existed already under the Sasanids.[89] Under the Seljuqs the function also existed and was known as *esfahsalar* or *sepahsalar*.[90] The function, meaning army chief, also occurred under the Safavids and was the same function as that of *emir al-omara*, which title was more commonly used in the pre-'Abbas I period. Div Soltan for example was appointed as *vakil*, *sepahsalar-e Iran* and *begler-begi* of Diyarbekr,[91] while in other texts Div Soltan is reported to be the *emir al-omara*. The *emir al-omara* (in the 17th century usually styled as *sepahsalar*) was the chief military commander of the Qezelbash troops, and therefore, it was a function that was held by a Qezelbash emir in the 16th century. In addition to military authority over the other emirs, the *emir al-omara* also had considerable influence in political and administrative matters. The function was combined with that of the regent or *vakil* from 907/1501-2 till 940/1533. Because of the considerable power that had been yielded by the military *vakil-emir al-omara* Tahmasp I not only did not re-appoint anyone to the office of military *vakil*, but he also reduced the office of *emir al-omara* in importance. As of the late 1530s, the *emir al-omara* was not the national *primus inter pares* among the Qezelbash emirs anymore. For Tahmasp I created the function of *begler-begi* (governor-general), who at the same time was *emir al-omara* in his province only, with authority only over his provincial emirs. As a result there was not one national *emir al-omara* anymore, but more than 10, which diminished the power of the Qezelbash emirs, but strengthened that of the Crown. However, it would appear that there was still one *emir al-omara* who had more prestige than his colleagues, viz. the *emir al-omara* and *begler-begi*

---

[89] Roger M. Savory, "The Office of Sipahsalar (Commander-in-Chief) in the Safavid State", in Bert G. Fragner et alii, *Proceedings of the Second European Conference of Iranian Studies* (Rome 1995), p. 599, n. 10.

[90] Horst, H. *Iran unter der Horezmshahs und Gross-seljuqen* (Wiesbaden 1956), p. 42.

[91] Montazer-Saheb, pp. 181, 319, 575.

of Azerbaijan, who is mentioned under Tahmasp I in 975/1567-8. The holder of this function remained one of the most prominent *emirs al-omara* throughout the Safavid reign. This was also enhanced by the fact that the combination of these two functions became almost regular in the 17th century.[92]

The title of *sepahsalar-e koll-e lashkar-e Iran* is mentioned in the early 1600s.[93] It would seem that this title was introduced by 'Abbas I, but not, as Savory has it, "to be a supreme commander superior in status to both the *qurchi-bashi* and the *qollar-aghasi*."[94] Savory's argument that the *sepahsalar* commanded armies which consisted of both Qezelbash and other units is not convincing, because this also held true for other officers. Neither is his argument convincing that, according to the DM and the TM, the salary of the *sepahsalar* was about 10 times higher than that of the *qurchi-bashi*, who was superior in rank, according to these same sources. The confusing factor here is that Savory only refers to the direct income of the *qurchi-bashi* and not to the indirect income that he also received in the form of a share of the payments made to other officials.[95] It is my opinion that, after 1540, the *emir al-omara/sepahsalar* was only the commander of a major army group or military campaign, who was at first the equal, but later as of the first decade of the 17th century, subordinate to the *qurchi-bashi* and the *qollar-aghasi*, who were more powerful political players at the same time. Because of the importance of the function and other posts such as governor, that the *sepahsalar* held, he also had a deputy (*na'eb*) and a vizier.[96] Rostam Beg was even simultaneously *sepahsalar*, *divan-begi*, and *tofangchi aghasi* in the 1630s.[97] According to Nasiri, the *sepahsalar* had the supreme command of the army, whether the royal army or the provincial levies, in time of war. It was his task to choose the battle ground and to put the army in battle order. Nobody was allowed to interfere with his decisions and those who did were liable to be punished and dismissed from their function.[98]

Savory is also wrong when he, following Falsafi, ascribed this function to leading generals such as Allahverdi Khan and Jani Khan Shamlu. There is no historical evidence that either of these two men actually bore this title.[99] After 1654, when 'Aliqoli Beg was dismissed, no *sepahsalar* was

---

[92] The combination of *emir al-omara* (or *sepahsalar*) with that of *begler-begi* of Azerbaijan is not always true, see e.g. Vahid Qazvini, pp. 48, 138 (Mortezaqoli Khan, Pir Budaq Turkoman). The first *emir al-omara* also was governor of Tabriz.

[93] Monshi, vol. 2, p. 904; Savory, *History*, vol. 2, pp. 1119-20; Yusef, p. 31.

[94] Savory, "Sipahsalar", p. 612.

[95] Savory, "Sipahsalar", p. 601-02; Nasiri, *Alqab*, pp. 12, 15. See on this issue Willem Floor, *Fiscal History*, p. 55.

[96] Yusef, pp. 215, 248; Mostoufi, p. 176.

[97] Yusef, p. 149, also p. 166.

[98] Nasiri, *Alqab*, p. 14.

[99] Savory, "Sepahsalar", pp. 603-05, 609.

appointed. Chardin reports that the function of *sepahsalar* existed under previous shahs, but not at present. He adds that in case of war the shah would appoint a *sardar*.[100] For example, in 1665, Sheikh 'Ali Khan was appointed as *sardar* to put a stop to the Uzbeg incursions into Khorasan.[101] Chardin does not mention the *sepahsalar* either among those present at Soleiman's coronation. However, Kaempfer writes that Hajji 'Ali Khan was governor of Azerbaijan and general, and was called field marshall.[102] It would indeed seem that under Soleiman (r. 1666-94) the function was reinstated again, for Kaempfer states that: "Nowadays when the army takes the field it is customary to appoint a *sepahsalar* for each of the three corpses and to dismiss them when campaign is over. In case of one campaign only a *sardar* is appointed and at the end dismissed."[103] However, Chardin writes that under Soleiman the function was not filled.[104] In this and other cases it would seem that the title *sepahsalar* equaled that of the provincial *emir al-omara*, who was in charge of all troops within a particular province, as is clear in the case of Zaman Beg, who was *sepahsalar-e Khorasan*, or for a particular campaign.[105] The title of *sepahsalar-e Iran* indeed seems to have been reinstated only towards the end of Soleiman's reign in 1104/1692, when Rostam Khan was appointed *sepahsalar*.[106] The *qurchi-bashi*, *qollar-aghasi* and *tofangchi-bashi* were neither under the *sepahsalar* nor under a *sardar*, as Le Bruyn has it. "They are now under a Seraer [sic; *sardar*] only, a chief appointed for any particular expedition, after which he is discharged and rewarded for his extraordinary service."[107]

Towards the end of the Safavid dynasty the *sepahsalar* was one of the council emirs and the most important military official after the *qurchi-bashi*. However, du Mans creates the impression that the *sepahsalar* was the most important commander, though he may have indeed only referred to the militia.[108] The dismissal and change of governors was contingent

---

100 Jean Chardin, *Les Voyages*, 10 vols. Ed. L. Langlès. (Paris 1811), vol. 5, pp. 321-2. See however, 'Aliqoli Khan. Ibid, vol. 10. pp. 68-70.

101 Richard, vol. 2, p. 265.

102 Kaempfer, *Am Hofe*, p. 68.

103 Kampfer, *Am Hofe*, p. 74.

104 Chardin, vol. 5, p. 322.

105 Zaman Beg, *sepahsalar-e Khorasan*. Yusef, p. 26; Savory, "Sipahsalar", p. 600, n. 16, 17.

106 Nasiri, *Dastur*, pp. 58, 100; Gemelli-Careri, *Voyage du Tour du Monde*. 6 vols. (Paris 1727), vol. 2, p. 39, 107. According to Bardsiri, Mir Mohammad Sa'id Moshizi. *Tadhkereh-ye Safavi*, ed. Ebrahim Bastani Parizi (Tehran, 1369/1990), p. 626, he was appointed, however, in Safar 1104/October 1692. Rostam Khan was the son of Safiqoli Khan and grandson of Rostam Khan, who also was *sepahsalar* and *begler-begi* of Azerbaijan.

107 Le Bruyn, Cornelius. *Travels into Moscovy, Persia and part of the East-Indies*, 2 vols. (London, 1737), vol 1, p. 205.

108 Richard, vol. 2, pp. 117, 287.

upon his approval. Any decision involving military operations had to involve him. He was by that time usually also governor of Tabriz and Moghan and some other regions in Azerbaijan.[109] Nevertheless, the function of *sepahsalar-e Iran*, despite its high-sounding title and prerogatives, did not amount to much. There was no money to pay for the troops and so the Dutch commented in February 1715, that all that the function amounted to was "that you have 200 musketeers go in front of you and 200 *qollar*s behind you."[110] When Vakhtang Mirza was appointed as *sepahsalar* he also was handed a marshal's baton. This is the first time, as far as I know, that such an item, distinct for a field marshal, is mentioned in historical records. Andersen in 1649, observed a Persian soldier with a regiment's staff in his hand, which may have been a mace.[111] If this marshall's baton really existed it may have looked like the kind that, in 1817, preceded the *sardar* of Erivan carried by an officer who had "on his shoulder a silver axe, the emblem of the *sardar*'s power over life and death."[112] Such a baton was still in use, in 1915, when it is reported that the Vali-ye Posht-e Kuh "rode before us with his silver staff."[113] The fact that maces that belonged to high-ranking commanders were "entirely covered with gold, blue enamel, turquoises and rubies" may indeed support the identification of the marshal's baton with a mace.[114]

Table 1.2 List of *emirs al-omara ~ sepahsalars*

1. Hosein Beg Laleh Shamlu[115]	907/1501-2
2. Mir Najm Zargar Gilani[116]	914-1509
3. Mir Yar-Ahmad Khuzani Najm-e Thani	915/1509-10
4. Sayyed Mir 'Abdol-Baqi Ne'matollahi[117]	919/1513-4
5. Mohammad Beg Sofreji Ostajalu[118]	920/1514-5

---

109 Mirza Rafi'a, *Dastur al-Moluk*. ed. Mohammad Taqi Daneshpazhuh. Zamimeh-ye shomareh-ye 5 va 6 sal-e 16 Majalleh-ye Daneshkadeh-ye Adabiyat va 'Olum-e Ensani (Tehran 1347/1967), pp. 49-50 (henceforth cited as DM); Nasiri, *Alqab*, p. 14.

110 Floor, Willem. *Bar Oftadan-e Safaviyan va Bar Amadan-e Mahmud Afghan*, Tehran 1365/1987, p. 24-5; or the English version, Ibid. *The Afghan Occupation of Safavid Persia 1721-1729* (Paris 1998), pp. 26.

111 Jürgen Andersen und Volquard Iversen, *Orientalische Reisbeschreibungen in den Bearbeiting von Adam Olearius*. (Schleswig 1669 [Tübingen 1980]), p. 160. For pictures of maces see Zdzislaw Zygulski Jr. "Islamic weapons in Polish collections and their provenance", in Robert Elgood ed. *Islamic Arms and Armour* (London 1979), pp. 213-38.

112 M. von Kotzebue, *Narrative of a Journey into Persia .... in the year 1817* (London 1819), p. 105.

113 H. Erdman, *Im Heiligen Krieg* (Berlin 1918), p. 118.

114 Zygulski, p. 215.

115 Qazvini Ghaffari, p. 266; Valeh Esfahani, p. 178.

116 Qomi, vol. 1, p 96.

117 Qomi, vol. 1, p. 125; Qazvini Ghaffari, p. 276.

Table 1.2 (continued)

6. Bayazid Soltan Ostajalu[119] son of 5.	930/1523-4
7. Div Soltan Rumlu[120]	930/1523-4
8. Div Soltan Rumlu +	
Mostafa Soltan (Kepek Soltan) Ostajalu	930/1524
9. Div Soltan Rumlu + Choqa Soltan Tekellu	932/1526
10. Choqa Soltan Tekellu	933/1527
11. Hosein Beg Shamlu and	
12. 'Abdollah Khan Ostajalu[121]	937-40/1531-34
vacant for some years?	
13. Shahqoli Soltan Ostajalu[122]	975/1567-8
vacant	
14. *Qarchiqay Khan[123]	1025-34/1616-26
vacant	
15. Zeinal Khan Shamlu[124]	1038-39/1629-30
16. *Rostam Khan[125]	1040-52/1631-43
17. Mortezaqoli Khan Qajar[126]	1059/1649
18. *'Aliqoli Beg[127]	1060-64/1650-54
vacancy?	
19. Hamzeh Khan[128]	till 1102/1690
20. 'Aliqoli Khan Zanganeh[129]	1077-1103/1666-91

---

[118] Otherwise named Chayan Soltan. Valeh Esfahani, p. 243; Qomi, vol. 1, pp. 100, 132.

[119] Qomi, vol. 1, p. 153; al-Qazvini, *Lobb*, p. 258.

[120] Qomi, vol. 1, p. 153; Valeh Esfahani, pp. 318, 326.

[121] Qomi, vol. 1, p. 215; Savory, *History*, vol. 1, p. 83.

[122] Röhrborn, *Regierung*, p. 24, n. 41.

[123] Monshi, vol. 2, pp. 904, 1040; *sepahsalar-e Iran*, Savory, *History*, vol. 2, p. 1120; Yusef, p. 71.

[124] Rokn al-Douleh Mobarez al-Din Zeinal Khan Shamlu became *sepahsalar-e koll-e lashkar-e Iran*. Yusef, pp. 31, 38 41; he was at the same time *ishik aghasi-bashi*. Esfahani, p. 68. When he became *sepahsalar* he occupied himself with all matters, small and large, of the kingdom. Yusef, pp. 266, 279.

[125] Rostam Beg, *sepahsalar-e Iran*. Yusef, pp. 66, 103, 114; 'Aliqoli Beg brother and *na'eb* of Rostam Khan. Ibid., p. 181; Rostam Khan *sepahsalar va begler-begi-ye Azerbaijan*. Ibid., p. 182, 215; 'Isa Beg *yasavol-sohbat*, brother and *na'eb* of Rostam Khan *sepahsalar*. Ibid., p. 215, 248; Rostam Beg *gholam sepahsalar* in 1039, Shamlu, p. 212; became khan p. 282; Esfahani, pp. 116.

[126] He was an old *khanehzad*, previously governor of Mashhad, and became *sepahsalar-e Iran* and *begler-begi* of 'Ali Shekar (= Hamadan) and not of Azerbaijan; Vahid Qazvini, p. 89, 107, 138; Shamlu, pp. 292, 326, 345, 429.

[127] Vahid Qazvini, pp. 138, 164, 180. He was *sepahsalar-e Iran*, khan of Tabriz and *begler-begi* of Azerbaijan.

[128] Mostoufi, p. 114. He was *sepahsalar* and *begler-begi* of Qandahar.

[129] Chardin, vol. 9, pp. 558-62, 572; Ibid., vol. 10, pp. 4ff, 69-70; Hajj 'Ali Khan Kaempfer, *Am Hofe*, p. 68 brother's son of Sheikh 'Ali Khan Zanganeh, whose older brother also was *sepahsalar*. Kroell, Anne ed. *Nouvelles d'Ispahan 1665-1695* (Paris

Table 1.2 (continued)

21. *Rostam Khan[130]	1104/1692
22. *Shahnavaz II[131]	1115/1703
23. *Khosrou Khan[132]	1121/1709
24. Mohammad Zaman Khan Shamlu[133]	1124/1712
25. Mansur Khan[134]	1127/Feb. 1715
26. Safiqoli Khan[135]	as of Feb. 1715
27. Mohammad 'Ali Khan[136]	1128/June d. 1716
28. Fath 'Ali Khan Turkoman[137]	1128/October 1716
29. *Hoseinqoli Khan Vakhtang[138]	1128/end 1716
30. Lotf 'Ali Khan Daghestani[139]	1130-33/1718-20
31. Esma'il Khan[140]	1133/Dec. 1720
32. Shamir 'Ali[141]	April 1721
33. Mohammad Beg Shamlu[142]	September 1721
34. *Vakhtang Mirza[143]	June 1722

* means that the person is a gholam, not a Qezelbash.

1979), p. 29 mentions him in 1691 at the *noruz* ceremony. He was army commander, governor of Tabriz and head of the infantry (*tofangchi aghasi*).

[130] Nasiri, *Dastur*, p. 58; Qarakhani, Hasan. "Buq'eh-ye Ayyub Ansari dar Takab - faramin-e shahan-e Safavi dar bareh-ye mouqufat-e an", *BT* 9 (1353/1974), doc. 5, dated Safar 1106/September 1694; Bardsiri, p. 626; Gemelli-Careri, vol. 2, p. 39, 107.

[131] Lockhart, L. *The Fall of the Safavid Dynasty*, Cambridge 1958, pp. 88, 87; Röhrborn, *Regierung*, p. 88.

[132] Lockhart, *Fall*, pp. 88, 90; Mostoufi, p. 117.

[133] Lockhart, *Fall*, p. 91; Mostoufi, p. 117.

[134] Dismissed in February 1715. Floor, *Bar Oftadan*, p. 24; Ibid., *Afghan Occupation*, p. 26.

[135] He was *divan-begi* and was also governor of Tabriz. *ARA*, KA 1740 (13/4/1715), f. 2375; KA 1789 (22/1/1717), f. 272; Floor, *Bar Oftadan*, p. 24; Floor, *Afghan Occupation*, p. 26; Mervi, pp. 18, 22-3, 83, 99.

[136] He was governor of Shirvan-Tabriz and died in June 1716. He was replaced by his 8 year old son, whose name has not been reported. Floor, *Bar Oftadan*, p. 27; Ibid., *Afghan Occupation*, p. 26.

[137] Lockhart, *Fall*, p. 97. He was also *mir-shekar bashi*.

[138] *ARA*, KA 1789 (30/11/1716), f. 14; Ibid (22/1/1717), f. 272; Krusinski, [Judasz Tadeusz]. *The History of the Late Revolutions of Persia*. London 1740 [1973], p. 143.

[139] Lockhart, *Fall*, p. 112; Mostoufi, pp. 125-6.

[140] Röhrborn, *Regierung*, p. 28, n. 80; Mostoufi, p.175.

[141] Puturidze, V.S. *Persidskie istoricheskie dokumenty v knigoxraniloshchax Gruzii*, 4 vols., (Tiflis 1961; 1962; 1965; 1977). Year 1965, doc. 37 dated Rajab 1133/April 1721.

[142] Also governor of Azerbaijan. Floor, *Bar Oftadan*, p. 39; Ibid., *Afghan Occupation*, p. 36; Musavi, Mamad Taqi. *Orta asr Azarbaijan tarikhina dair fars dilinda jazymysh sanadlar*. Baku 1965, doc. 19 confirms Mohammad Khan Begdeli Shamlu's appointment as *begler-begi* of Azerbaijan in a document dated 1131/24 August 1721.

[143] Also governor of Azerbaijan on 19/6/1722. Floor, *Bar Oftadan*, p. 177; Ibid., *Afghan Occupation*, p. 138.

In addition to the Safavid *sepahsalars* there were also *sepahsalars* who were appointed by local rulers such as those of Gilan, Mazandaran,[144] and Seistan. The first thing that the rebellious Gharib Shah did in 1629 was to appoint *sepahsalars* and emirs.[145] In Seistan the *malek al-moluk* had a *sepahsalar-e a'zam* in addition to *sepahsalaran-e sarhadd*, who had the task of guarding the border.[146] Other terms to refer to the *sepahsalar* were *sepahbod* and *lashkar-kesh*.[147] The office of *espahsalaran-e sarhadd* was a hereditary function in one Seistani clan.[148]

As pointed out above, when there was no *emir al-omara* or *sepahsalar* the function of *sardar*, or commander, occurred frequently. This official was charged with a specific task and carried this title for its duration only and more often than not there was more than one *sardar* at the same time, operating in different parts of the kingdom. It is not always clear whether the *sardar* had the command of an entire army, because many times the chronicles inform us that an army was led by emirs and *sardars*, thus in the plural.[149] The title *sardar* usually refers to a senior commander or a commander of a tribal unit.[150] We seem to be on firmer ground when a person has been appointed as *sardar* of Khorasan or *sardar* (of the troops) going to Khorasan. Here it is clear that the *sardar*, and no one else, was in charge of these troops. When an official was appointed as *sardar-e lashkar* it would seem that his command was valid for the entire army.[151]

Grand Vizier

The grand vizier (*vakil, vazir* or *nazer-e divan-e a'la*, or *vazir a'zam*)[152] was one of the pillars of the state (*arkan-e douleh*), but the only one with the title E'temad al-Douleh. This title already occurs among the early Safavids to refer to the *vakil-vazir*, who then was the most important

---

144 *Sepahsalar-e Mazandaran va nayeb-e u.* Montazer-Saheb, p. 377; Amir Shah Mansur *sepahsalar-e Leshteh-nesha va Deilaman.* Valeh Esfahani, p. 352; Rumlu, p. 561; Qomi, vol. 1, p. 472; *sepahsalar-e Biyapas*, Qomi, vol. 1, pp. 468, 471; see also Savory, "Sipahsalar", p. 599-600.
145 Yusef, p. 16.
146 Seistani, pp. 128, 185, 203, 317. Pir Mohammad Khan *sepahsalar* of Malek Mahmud of Tun va Tabas. Mostoufi, p. 148.
147 Seistani, pp. 206, 235.
148 Seistani, pp. 436, 472; *sepahsalaran-e sarhadd va tamami-ye jonud-e Seistan.* Ibid., p. 311; *va jami'-ye marzbanan-e Seistan*, Ibid., p. 406; *sar-kheilan-e sarhadd* and *sepahsalaran-e anja.* Ibid, p. 472.
149 Qomi, vol. 1, p. 172; group of *sardaran-e* Qezelbash, Ibid., vol. 1, p. 241; *sardaran*, Ibid., p. 268; two governors were ordered to leave with a group of *sardaran*, Ibid., vol. 1, p 275
150 Qomi, vol. 1, pp. 44, 89.
151 Yusef, pp. 200, 205, 208, 259; Shamlu, p. 238, 241, 343; Mostoufi, p. 128.
152 Molla Jalal, pp. 44, 311 (*vazir-e koll*); Natanzi, Mahmud b. Hedayatollah Afushteh-ye. *Naqavat al-athar fi dhekr al-akhyar*, ed. Ehsan Eshraqi. (Tehran, 1350/1971), pp. 29, 53, 65 (*vazir-e khasseh*).

government official. Mirza Shah Hosein Esfahani, who was *vakil al-saltaneh* between 1514-1523, already held the title of E'temad al-Douleh. Subsequent *vakil-vazir*s also held the title.[153] Another honorific that the grand vizier was entitled to was that of *'alijah*, which was the most important honorific an official could acquire. Some of the *'alijah*s were not even khan or emir, and some were not Qezelbash. For example, in 970/1562-63, 'Isa Khan, son of Lavand Mirza, was given the title of *'alijah* in the royal council, which gave him precedence over the emirs, a governorship and gifts to the amount of 6,000 tomans and a robe of honor.[154] However, by the end of the Safavid dynasty the exclusivity of the title *'alijah* had been somewhat eroded, as was the case with other similar titles. Both the DM and TM still distinguish between emirs who had the title *'alijah* and those who did not and were only *moqarrab al-khaqan*. However, by then all governors enjoyed the title *'alijah*, thus more than the 14 that the TM and DM indicate.[155] By the mid-19th century it was still an honorific sought after by the elite. It still required a royal decree to be thus honored.[156] However, by the end of the Qajar period the importance of the term *'alijah* had been totally eroded, when, according to Minorsky, it became a term for the lowest ranking officials such as village chiefs and messengers.[157]

In the 16th century, when the shah's powers were strong, those of the grand vizier likewise were strong. In the 17th century, with the weakened power of the Qezelbash emirs, and the more divided and dispersed nature of power elite (*gholam*s, Qezelbash, Tajiks, eunuchs, royal women) the power of the main contender for control of the state, that of the grand vizier grew significantly. Surviving appointment diplomas do not provide information about his tasks.[158] The only description of the grand vizier's tasks is from the end of the Safavid period in the DM and TM and what some European contemporary sources write about this official. In the beginning of the Safavid period the power of the grand vizier was not more limited than that of the 17th century grand vizier. The fact that the reign of the various shahs in the 17th century seems to have been dominated by their grand viziers, whilst those in the 16th seemingly were

---

[153] Natanzi, pp. 85, 142, 551; Valeh Esfahani, pp. 271, 275; *vekalat-penah* E'temad al-Douleh Ma'sum Beg Safavi. Seistani, p. 171.

[154] Astarabadi, p. 88.

[155] The Dastur-e Shariyan mentions the following officials with the honorific of *'alijah*: the *eshik aghasi bashi*, the *nazer-e boyutat*, the *majles-nevis*, the *divan-begi*, the *hakem* of Orumi, the *na'eb-e nazir*, two *sardar*s, the *hakim-bashi*, the *mostoufi al-mamalek*, four *begler-begi*s and two other governors. Nasiri, *Dastur*, pp. 20; 34, 44, 51, 54-6, 107, 110, 114-5, 146, 160, 193, 200-01, 273, 296; Röhrborn, *Provinzen*, p. 23.

[156] Mo'asseseh-ye pazuhesh va motale'at-e farhangi, *Farmanha va raqamha-ye doureh-ye Qajar* (Tehran 1371/1992), vol. 1, p. 97.

[157] TM, p. 114.

[158] Röhrborn, *Regierung*, p. 20, n. 9.

not (with few exceptions) is the result that the latter had no European observers to write about them. Also, early Safavid shahs such as Tahmasp I and 'Abbas I, were more active administrators, who claimed much of the attention that the grand-viziers received in the 17th century. True, the powers of the grand vizier in most of the 16th century were checked by those of the important Qezelbash emirs. But in the waning years of the 16th and the entire 17th century till the end of the dynasty, the grand vizier's powers were checked by leading members of the power elite such as the steward of the royal court (*nazer-e boyutat*), the secretary-general of the royal secretariat (*nazer-e daftar-e homayun*), the treasurer-general (*mostoufi al-mamalek*), the military commanders, or by one or more of the shah's favorites, and not to forget the harem inmates.[159] However, if the grand vizier enjoyed the shah's favor none could stand against him and he would control all other courtiers.[160]

The function of grand vizier existed independently as of 907/1501 till 915/1509-10. Thereafter the function was subsumed by the *vakil*, who, at the same time, also was *emir al-omara* till 920/1514. Between 920/1514 and 930/1524 the function of grand vizier was held by the administrative *vakil*, and was also referred to as *nazer-e divan a'la*. This title (*nazer-e divan*) is also used after 1524, but fell into disuse after the 1530s.[161] The grand vizier and other administrative officials, who, in the 16th century, were all Tajiks and not Qezelbash, often clashed with the latter. These opined that the grand viziers had to limit themselves to purely administrative and fiscal affairs. Governing the country and managing the military was a Qezelbash affair. The Tajik bureaucracy's only role was to provide the Qezelbash with the means to do so. Nevertheless, the grand vizier not only was in charge of administrative affairs and revenue administration in the 16th century. He also had influence in matters of appointments outside the military sector and that of governance. Foreign relations also were under his jurisdiction.

This meant that the 16th century viziers indeed made their influence felt. The broad powers of the vizier-*vakil* under Esma'il I have already been mentioned. Under the long reign of Tahmasp I the influence of his longest serving (11 years) grand viziers, Qadi Jahan, and the shah's own kinsman, Ma'sum Beg Safavi (15 years), who both had special ties to the shah, had grown beyond that of a traditional vizier. During Tahmasp I's reign no other strong viziers manifested themselves, which was also due to the short terms of office of the other viziers as well as the tight control over the state by Tahmasp I after 1532. In fact, at the time of Tahmasp I's

---

159 Rudi Matthee, *Politics and Trade in Late-Safavid Iran: Commercial Crisis and Government Reaction Under Shah Solayman (1666-1694)* (Ph.D. dissertation UCLA 1991), pp. 153-59.
160 Richard, vol. 2, p. 295; Chardin, vol. 5, p. 347-8 and vol. 9, p. 518-9.
161 Savory, *History*, vol. 1, pp. 98, 102; al-Qazvini, p. 257; Ghaffari Qazvini, pp. 277, 282; Rumlu, pp. 197, 242, 320; Valeh Esfahani, pp. 326, 443.

death, "no one from among the 'men of the pen' held the office of *vazir-e divan-e a 'la*. Prior to this, twelve men (as far as I have been able to make out) held the office of vizier during the reign of Shah Tahmasp" wrote Eskander Beg Monshi.[162] This fact, combined with the perceived paramount role and powers of the *vakil* during the 16th century, probably explains why a late Safavid source submits that the *vazir-e divan* was not an important function at all. He was only in charge of the *maliyat-e divan-e dakheli* (taxes set aside for the divan) and had further no role in the country's administration.[163] However, reality was, as we have seen, somewhat more nuanced and complicated.

Tahmasp's successor, "Esma'il II increased [his grand vizier] Mirza Salman's power. He ordered that the [grand] vizier not need rise from his place to salute any emirs, no matter how eminent in rank. After the shah's death he was reappointed [grand] vizier and E'temad al-Douleh with independent authority."[164] However, those grand viziers who were not circumspect in their dealings with the Qezelbash emirs and went beyond the unwritten boundaries did so at their own risk. Two cases in this respect are telling. Esma'il I had appointed Mirza Shah Hosein Esfahani as *vakil* in 908/1514. The new *vakil* was the former vizier of Durmish Khan one of the most important Qezelbash emirs. His high handed behavior towards his former employer cost him his life in 929/1523. Likewise, 50 years later the Qezelbash revolt against Mirza Salman was caused by similar sentiments. "He was a Tajik. He was only expected to look after the accounts and *divan* business. It did not fall within his province to have an army at his disposal and to interfere in state affairs on his own behalf, and thus become the cause of discord and rebellion."[165]

An active and hands-on shah, such as 'Abbas I, directed much of the management of government affairs himself. He "occupied himself with the despatch of much business all the rest of the day. He arranged many things, despatched divers men and divers letters; and he received many letters, all of which Agamir [Aqa Mir Taher, the *majles-nevis*] read to him openly and loudly, so that we all heard."[166] But one thing is clear, as of the beginning of the 17th century "the highest official is the grand vizier, chair of the royal council, first of the pillars of the state, and the shah's deputy. His title is E'temad al-Douleh or *vazir-e a'zam*. Nothing can be done without his say-so, both with regards internal and external relations and affairs. His influence is also felt in the provinces, the governors may not take any action without his endorsement, which he

---

[162] Savory, *History*, vol. 1, p. 251.

[163] Nasiri, *Alqab*, p. 4.

[164] Savory, *History*, vol. 1, p. 257.

[165] Savory, *History*, vol. 1, p. 419.

[166] Della Valle, Pietro. "Extract of the Travels of Della Valle", in John Pinkerton, *A General Collection of Voyages and Travels*, (London, 1811), vol. 9, p. 65.

supervises."[167]

On his appointment the grand vizier received, for the duration of his term in office, a special gem-studded pen and ink holder, which was kept in the treasury. He also received rich robes of honor, and, probably only members of the Qezelbash, a resplendent hat (*taj-e vahhaj*), with an aigrette and a baton (*tumar*).[168] It was the grand vizier's task to approve all appointments, all revenues and expenditures, including those managed by the *sadr*s (head of the religious institution), (which required his counterseal) as well as the correct implementation of policy and existing rules. No appointment or expense could be made without his endorsement, even when the decree had been sealed by the shah. In most cases the grand vizier did not ask the shah at all for his decision for appointments.[169] He further was the superior of all central and provincial administrative government staff. He also carried on all negotiations with foreign nations, but did not effect the signing of treaties.[170]

According to Chardin, under Soleiman the shah was only for show, for the real king was the grand vizier,[171] which is an opinion contradicted by du Mans. The latter rightly observed that the grand vizier's power was totally dependent on the shah's favor and implied that without this favor his enemies would bring him down.[172] The grand vizier had control over the chancellery (*daftar-khaneh*) and the finance department, for both the *mamalek* and *khasseh* sectors, or in words of the TM "the sums sent to the Treasury and other *Boyutat* from the whole of the *mamalek* and from the capital of Isfahan"[173] All documents committing the state to anything had to be sealed and approved by the grand vizier.[174] In financial matters, the grand vizier did not act without consulting the *mostoufi al-mamalek*, the *mostoufi-ye khasseh*, and the *nazer-e boyutat*, but he could act totally

---

[167] Kaempfer, *Am Hofe*, p. 62.

[168] DM, pp. 44-7; TM, pp. 44-46; Richard, vol. 2, p. 269. This was after 1669, when Sheikh 'Ali Khan Zanganeh was appointed grand-vizier, the first member of a Qezelbash tribe to be thus honored. For other Qezelbash grand-viziers see Table 1.3.

[169] TM, pp. 44-5.

[170] Kaempfer, *Am Hofe*, p. 62; Hotz, A. *Reis van de gezant der O.I. Compagnie Joan Cunaeus naar Perzië in 1651-1652* (Amsterdam, 1908), pp. 159-317; Floor, Willem. *Commercial Conflict between Persia and the Netherlands 1712-1718* (University of Durham Occasional Paper Series no. 37-1988) chapters 1 and 5.

[171] Chardin, vol. 5, p. 430, which is not borne out by the facts, see Matthee, *Politics*; and Ibid. "Administrative Stability and Change in Late-17th-Century Iran: The Case of Shaykh 'Ali Khan Zanganah", *IJMES* 1994, pp. 77-98.

[172] Richard, vol. 2, pp. 10, 268, 295.

[173] TM, p. 116.

[174] Chardin, vol. 5, 339-40; Kaempfer, *Am Hofe*, p. 62; Olearius, Adam. *Vermehrte newe Beschreibung der moscowitischen und persischen Reyse*, ed. D. Lohmeier (Schleswig, 1656 [Tübingen, 1971]), p. 670; Raphael Du Mans, *Estat de la Perse*. ed. Ch. Schefer (Paris 1890), p. 14; Busse, H. *Untersuchungen zum islamischen Kanzleiwesen*. Karo 1959, p. 96.

independent from these officials. They played only an advisory role and had no formal authority to interfere with the grand vizier's decisions.[175] The grand vizier and the secretary of the shah both submitted a monthly statement of the country's expenditures to the *mostoufi al-mamalek*, together with an account of the money that they had withdrawn from the financial department. However, this should not be explained, as Chardin did, that this meant a lack of control by the *divan* over the treasury.[176] The same holds for the alleged control that some officials had over the management of the financial affairs of certain areas. For example, in 1682, Mirza Razi, the *mostoufi-ye khasseh*, was solely in charge of the Dutch silk payments to the court. However, this should not be explained that he had more authority over financial affairs than the grand vizier. This was just a division of labor, which continued to be the standard bureaucratic practice under strong grand viziers.[177]

The grand vizier spent most of his time in the hall at the entry of the palace, awaiting the shah's orders. During that time he dealt with all business that was presented to him, in terms of decisions, reports, and writing orders and letters.[178] According to Kaempfer, he seldom spoke the shah, for he received his orders via the eunuchs, i.e. the treasurer or the chamberlain (*mehtar*). At council meetings he sat close to the shah, on his left side. At that occasion he presented petitions for decisions, and reported on current affairs. If the shah went riding, usually in the evening, then the grand vizier accompanied him.[179] The grand vizier tried to contain opposition against him and to deny his detractors access to shah; further to give the shah a sense of well-being, and to keep all bad news from him.[180] He earned at least 20,000 tomans, some greedy ones even 30,000 tomans by way of normal pay and graft.[181]

The Role of the Royal Council

As his title indicates the grand vizier was the vizier of the royal council or the *divan-e a'la*. This council was the bureaucratic institution in charge of

---

[175] See e.g., the role played by the *mostoufi-ye khasseh* and other officials in the negociations with the various Dutch embassies. Matthee, *Politics*, o.c.; Floor, *Commercial*, chapters 1 and 5.

[176] Chardin, vol. 5, p. 430.

[177] Matthee, "Administrative Stability", p. 89; for the situation thereafter see Floor, *Commercial*, o.c. and Ibid, *Bar Oftadan*, chapter one; Ibid., *Afghan Occupation*, chapter one.

[178] See also TM, p. 46. The grand vizier was not always accessible, see Rudi Matthee, "The Career of Mohammad Beg. Grand Vizier of Shah 'Abbas II (r. 1642-1666)", *IS* 24 (1991), p. 31.

[179] Kaempfer, *Am Hofe*, p. 63; Sanson, *The Present State of Persia* (London, 1695), p. 63.

[180] Kaempfer, *Am Hofe*, p. 65. This could also back fire, as in the case of Mohammad Beg, see Rudi Matthee, "Career", pp. 33-34.

[181] Kaempfer, *Am Hofe*, pp. 67; see also Richard, vol. 2, p. 10; DM, p. 47; TM, p. 86.

governing the country as the main executive branch of government directed by the grand vizier. In addition, there was a smaller inner or privy council, the *janqi*, where membership was limited to the most important state officials. Both councils were presided over by the shah. Royal council meetings took place regularly, and membership was larger than that of the *janqi*. In both cases, the members, only had an advisory voice, not a decisive one. However, during the periods of civil war (1525-32 and 1577-82) the *vakil* and other important Qezelbash leaders were the *de facto* rulers of the state.

The royal council (*janqi*, *divan*) meetings only took place during the time that the shah was unable to take charge of state affairs himself, because of his youth, according to Röhrborn.[182] For example, "At Erzanjan, after taking council, Esma'il decided to invade Shirvan."[183] When Tahmasp I was still a minor, he accordingly, consulted his emirs.[184] The leading Qezelbash emirs demanded shortly after 'Abbas' I accession to the throne "The *vakil* also should be required to convene the council of emirs twice per week. All the great emirs ..... should have a say in decisions affecting their tribal fiefs and military obligations."[185] An important feature was that during the unsettled periods of the 16th century the composition of the council was tribal in nature rather than that the various state functions were presented. For example, just after Esma'il II's death "Each tribe chose a trusted elder to present it and agreed to follow his counsel."[186] This did not mean that state officials, such as the *emir al-omara*, did not have a seat on the council. However, their membership was dictated by their tribal affiliation not by their function, which was incidental. All these council meetings took place when the shahs concerned were minors and inexperienced, and seem to support Röhrborn's conclusion. However, such council meetings also took place when these same shahs had taken firm control of the state apparatus.[187] Under Tahmasp I, as soon as he was able to get control of the state the royal council regularly met. These meetings were held till the very end of his reign.

According to the Venetian d'Allesandri:

> The Council is really one body, in which the king is the sole President, with the intervention of twelve Sultans, men of long experience in affairs of State. It is remarkably well

---

182 Röhrborn, *Regierung*, p. 18.
183 Savory, *History*, vol. 1, p. 43.
184 Savory, *History*, vol. 1, p. 88.
185 Savory, *History*, vol. 2, p. 553.
186 Savory, *History*, vol. 1, p. 333, also p. 410.
187 Montazer-Saheb, pp. 329, 392, 428, 494, 520; the shah held a *janqi* with his *omara*, *yuzbashiyan* and *qurchiyan*, Qomi, vol. 1, p. 217.

attended by those Sultans who from time to time come to the Court, and who all enter the Council, which is held every day except when the king goes to the bath, or has his nails cut; the time of this council in summer as well as in winter is from the twenty-second hour of the day, and according to matters in hand, continued till the third, fourth, and sixth hour of the night. .... The Sultan's Councilors, who are four in number, named viceroys, sit in front. The king introduces the subjects, and discourses about them, asking their opinions from the Sultans, and each one as he states his opinion, rises and comes near the king, speaking aloud, that he may be heard by his colleagues. If, in the course of the argument, the king hears anything which strikes him, he has it noted by the Grand Councilors, and very often takes a note of it with his own hand; and thus in their order in which the king inquires of them, the Sultans give their opinions. When the king has no doubt about the matter in question, it is settled at the first Council; and if he has doubts, he hears the arguments of the full Council, and then settles it after private consideration. In the number of the consulting Sultans is included the Curzibassa [*qurchi-bashi*], chief of the king's guard, although he may not be a Sultan. The grand Councilors have no vote, and can say nothing unless they are called upon by the king; they, although of great dignity, cannot rise to the rank of Sultan, nor to any other appointments belonging to the military service, even if they are nobly born.[188]

Under 'Abbas I the influence of the Qezelbash tribes was eliminated and the royal council came under the control of bureaucratic managers hand-picked by the shah. Sherley observes that "The Vizir sitteth every morning in council about the general state of all the King's provinces, accompanied with the King's Counsel, Advocates resident, and Secretaries of State. There are all matters heard, and the opinions of the council written by the Secretaries of State; then after dinner the council - or such a part of them as the King will admit - present those papers, of which the King pricketh those he will have proceed, and the rest are cancelled; which being done, the council retire them again to the Vizir, and then determine of the particular business of the King's house. ..... The King himself every Wednesday sitteth in the council publicly, accompanied with all those of

---

188 *Travels to Tana and Persia by J. Barbaro and A. Contarini*, (ed) Lord Stanley, Hakluyt no. 49, 2 vols. in one, (London 1873), part 2, p. 220-1. The grand councilors were, of course, non-Qezelbash administrators such as the grand vizier, *monshi al-mamalek* and *mostoufis*. For a slightly different version of this report see Anonymous, *A Chronicle of the Carmelites in Persia and the Papal mission of the seventeenth and eighteenth centuries*, 2 vols. (London, 1939) [henceforth cited as Carmelites], vol. 1, p. 49.

his council and the aforesaid Advocates. Thither come a flood of all sorts of people, rich and poor, and of all nations without distinction; and speak freely to the King in their own cases, and deliver everyone of his own several bill which the King receiveth; pricketh some and rejecteth others to be better informed of. The Secretaries of State presently record in the King's book those which he hath pricked, with all other acts then by him enacted; the which book is carried by a Gentleman of the Chamber into his chamber where it ever remaineth; and woe be to his Vizir if after the King hath pricked bill or supplication it be again brought the second time."[189]

But 'Abbas I could not take care of all business himself. Therefore his grand vizier, like his other officials, worked with the same diligence in dispatching business as the shah himself. The grand vizier, "who has charge of all the royal revenues, the dispatch of ambassadors, and all other affairs, and who is the first person after the Shah, used to dispatch 200 petitions in a morning, and after having sat and given a hearing for six or seven hours would go out as serene, as if he were coming from taking his horse for a walk."[190] 'Abbas I, despite being the absolute autocrat that he was, also was in the habit in consulting his main councilors, who in 1608, were comprised of Allahverdi Khan, Hatem Beg the grand vizier, the *qurchi-bashi*, and an unnamed person who was his 'governor' and preceptor, probably the *majles-nevis*.[191] For example, when the Carmelites were discussing a papal Note Verbale with 'Abbas I he had it read aloud to him by the grand vizier, "and then had a brief discussion with him and his councilors, then he told me to sign it."[192] This does not mean, of course, that 'Abbas I was not the absolute ruler that he was, but it shows that he was in the habit of taking counsel, which he might or might not follow.

Thus, Röhrborn is wrong in stating that when the shah himself took the reins of power the royal council seldom met, as is clear from the both Tahmasp I and 'Abbas I's behavior. It may be true that, according to Fendereski, 'Abbas II's decisions were very arbitrary, an argument adduced by Röhrborn to make his point. We do not have confirmation for this behavior from other sources, but even if it is true, it confirms what Röhrborn contests, viz. that the royal council regularly met.[193] Kaempfer

---

189 *Sir Anthony Sherley and his Persian adventures.* ed. Sir Denison Ross (London 1933), p. 230.

190 Carmelites, vol. 1, p. 159.

191 Carmelites, vol. 1, p. 159.

192 Carmelites, vol. 1, p. 127.

193 Röhrborn, "Staatskanzlei und Absolutismus im safawidischen Persien", *ZDMG* 127 (1977), pp. 316-17; Ibid, "Regierung", p. 18, quoting the *Tohfat al-'Alam*, f. 219. Chardin, vol. 5, p. 231-2 also mentions 'Abbas II's arbitrariness, but he makes it clear that this only held for the shah's behavior towards his courtiers, and that outside that circle he knew of no single instance of arbitrary behavior by the shah.

holds the view that there was not a privy council to give advice to the shah. The grand vizier arranged for everything in accordance with the wishes of the shah, his mother and the chief eunuchs, he wrote. In difficult cases the grand vizier took counsel with the *nazer*, the *majles-nevis* or the military commander, the latter especially for military decisions. At times he also took counsel with the *divan-begi* or the *ishik aghasi* and the *mostoufi*s, with the guild leaders or other officials, as the occasion required.[194]

Chardin took a similar position when he wrote that there was no royal council in Persia such as exists in Europe. However, he added that the magnates discussed all state affairs in the guardhouse (*keshik-khaneh*) of the royal palace. The shah sent the petitions that he received to this council to be advised what he should respond as well as on business matters to get their opinion. Chardin also noted that this procedure was interfered with by the other unofficial council, to wit that of the queen mother, the favorite wives and the principal eunuchs.[195] Chardin further wrote that the *janqi* only was convened in case of war (see however below) when auguries were taken from the book "Karajamea which Sheikh Safi, the founder of the Safavid order, allegedly had written." There was only one copy of the book which was kept in the royal treasury.[196] Sanson agreed with Chardin when he stated that there was a privy council "which is compos'd of the principal Eunuchs. In this Council are determin'd the most important Affairs of State. The chief Minister, and the other Lords know nothing of what is transacted there."[197] However, Sanson also stated that all decisions were taken in the royal council and that only after ample reflection and deliberation.[198] He also gave examples that the power of the eunuchs was not unfettered and that influential councilors, such as Saru Khan Sahandlu, the *qurchi-bashi*, could get their way despite the strong enmity of the eunuchs.[199]

From what we know of some of the practical side of government in Safavid Persia it would seem that the royal privy council or *janqi* was indeed in charge of governing the country. When in 1652, the Dutch ambassador Cuneaus negotiated a new trade agreement he was received by the royal council to discuss its terms. From the list of participants to

---

[194] Kaempfer, *Am Hofe*, p. 87.

[195] Chardin, vol. 5, pp. 237-40; Kaempfer, *Am Hofe*, p. 165 also confirms the parallel council meetings in the guard-house. See also Vahid Qazvini, p. 220.

[196] Chardin, vol. 5, p. 237. This is a reference to the *Qara-majmu'ah*. For information on this book see TM p. 113, n. 6. Kaempfer, Englebert. *Amoenitatum Exoticarum. Fasciculi V, Variae Relationes, Observationes & Descriptiones Rerum Persicarum.* Lemgo 1712 [1976], p. 12, who states that this book (*kara dsjelde: qara juldeh*) was neither opened nor read (*hactenus nondum apertus, nondum lectus*).

[197] Sanson, M. *The Present State of Persia* (London, 1695), p. 104.

[198] Sanson, p. 99-101.

[199] Sanson, p. 89. For the council meeting on Soleiman's succession see Kaempfer, *Am Hofe*, pp. 39, 45; see also Chardin, vol. 9, pp. 425-67.

that discussion it is clear that the *janqi* is meant rather than the full royal council. Present were: the grand vizier, who presided over the meetings, the *qurchi-bashi*, the *sepahsalar*, the *ishik aghasi-bashi*, the *nazer*, the *divan-begi*, the *tofangchi-aghasi*, the shah's secretary (*majles-nevis*) and some less important officials, probably secretaries. The composition of this group was not fixed and changed somewhat during the negotiations, depending on the availability of each councilor.[200] This list, more or less, tallies with whom we know to have belonged to the pillars of state under 'Abbas II: the grand vizier, the *qurchi-bashi*, the *qollar-aghasi*, the *ishik aghasi-bashi*, the *divan-begi*, and those emirs required to examine judicial complaints raised against high-ranking emirs at the indication of the shah.[201] At the end of Safavid period the following pillars of state (*arkan-e douleh*) were members of the *janqi*: the grand vizier, the *qurchi-bashi*, the *qollar-aghasi*, the *eshik aghasi-bashi*, the *tofangchi-aghasi*, the *divan-begi*, and the *majles-nevis*. When military affairs were discussed the *sepahsalar* also participated.[202] Under Shah Soltan Hosein the royal council met regularly to discuss matters of state and import, usually leading to no effective decisions, due to the weathervane character of the shah. The various factions in the council therefore tried to fight one another rather than being responsible and fight the internal and external threats to the security of the state and its citizens. At one occasion the enmity between the councilors even lead to threats uttered in the council meeting. Whereas in the past this would have led to the execution of the councilors involved now only bruised egos were the result.[203]

The order of precedence as well as who was a member of the council was originally based on a Safavid protocol referred to as *tartib-e moqarrar va ayin-e ma'hud-e Qezelbash*. Both the membership and order of precedence changed over times as a function of the prestige of the office and the relationship with the shah.[204] As to its membership, Sanson's statement that "His Councilors of Religion, the Sword, and the Gown are of an equal number"[205] is not borne out by the DM and TM. The order of precedence in the royal council and in the *keshik-khaneh* was the same.[206] It was of great importance to one's standing in society where one was positioned in comparison with one's competitors. This even affected the representatives of the Europeans in Persia. There was a constant jockeying by the Dutch and English East Indies Companies' Agents in Isfahan to be better placed or treated than the other. This kind of behavior even

---

[200] Hotz, pp. 163, 184, 218.
[201] Vahid Qazvini, p. 57.
[202] DM, p. 49.
[203] Floor, *Commercial*, p. 20.
[204] See Chardin, vol. 9, p. 423-4 with the seating arrangement in the council during the discussion of Solaiman's succession.
[205] Sanson, p. 99.
[206] DM, p. 46.

continued during the Afghan occupation (1722-1729) when they had more important issues to worry about such as their lives and property.[207]

Who were the grand viziers?

According to Chardin and Kaempfer the vizier was constantly in danger of his life.[208] However, when we observe the record, the facts do not bear out this statement. Of all the grand viziers only Mirza Mohammad (996/1588), Mirza Taleb Khan (1041-1044/1631-34) and Fath 'Ali Khan Daghestani (1128-33/1715-20) were executed at the shah's orders. Mirza Salman fell victim to machinations of the Qezelbash emirs, but he was not executed at the shah's orders. Usually, a grand-vizier was simply dismissed, or at worst was ordered to retire to some shrine.[209] It also happened that a grand vizier occupied the office twice as was the case with Qadi Jahan, Mirza Abu Taleb, Khalifeh Soltan and Sheikh 'Ali Khan. Many of the grand viziers were from bureaucratic administrative families, and were career bureaucrats themselves.[210] Others were recruited from the religious class, many had a military background, and some had made the *hajj*, or were even related to the royal house. In this respect the office of grand vizier did not differ from other government functions, where people, from whatever professional background, shifted from one position (e.g. military) to the other (e.g. civil). Apart from the eunuchs and special favorites, the grand vizier was the man who had most contact with the shah after 1666. It was normal that the grand vizier was close to the shah, also when he went out riding, to discuss matters of state or otherwise.[211] Sometimes a courtier through a special relationship would even wield more power than the grand vizier such as in the case of 'Abbas II, when the *nazer*, Mohammad Beg, wielded more power than the grand vizier. Also, Allahverdi Khan, the *emir shekar-bashi* had extraordinary influence over 'Abbas II.[212]

Neither Mirza Taqi, Mohammad Beg (Khan) nor Sheikh 'Ali Khan were of low social origin as some scholars have asserted.[213] Mirza Taqi's father and uncle were educated people and belonged to "the class, that were the normal recruiting grounds for government and religious officials."[214] The fact that Mohammad Beg's father was chief-tailor at the

---

[207] Floor, *Bar Oftadan*, p. 231; Ibid. *Bar Takhtegah-ye Esfahan* (Tehran 1366/1987), pp. 12, 26; Ibid., *Afghan Occupation*, pp. 186, 253-5.

[208] Chardin, vol. 5, p. 235; Kaempfer, *Am Hofe*, p. 64.

[209] Chardin, vol. 5, p. 340.

[210] E.g. Mirza Salman was a *dabir* (clerk), and a scion of a bureaucratic family. Qomi, vol. 2, p. 648; Mirza Mohammad, *mostoufi al-mamalek*, became *vazir-e divan-e a'la*. Qomi, vol. 2, p. 847.

[211] Kaempfer, *Am Hofe*, p. 63.

[212] Chardin, vol. 5, p. 348; *ARA*, VOC 1236 (2/9/1660), f. 9.

[213] See e.g. Matthee, *Politics*, p. 153; Ibid, "Career", p. 20; Ibid., "Sheikh 'Ali Khan"; Röhrborn, *Regierung*, p. 22, n. 15.

[214] Floor, Willem. "The rise and fall of Mirza Taqi, the eunuch grand vizier (1043-

royal court was not an indication of a humble origin, but rather that he held a very much sought after high court function. Sheikh 'Ali Khan was an important Qezelbash- Kurdish tribal leader, whose family had held many important court functions throughout the 16th and 17th century.

A very interesting development is the trend that as of 1079/1669 the grand vizier was usually a tribal leader (Kurdish/Zanganeh, Turkoman/Shamlu) of Qezelbash rather than of Tajik origin. The loss of power by the military Qezelbash elite was thus partly regained through the back door. The reason for this "usurpation" of what traditionally had been an exclusive Tajik function[215] was the fact that the grand vizier had become by then more than ever the uncontested chief of the central bureaucracy; he had become the real *vakil* without the title.[216] It also signaled the assimilation of the Qezelbash in the administrative structure of the Safavid state and their acquiescence in the reality of having to share power with the *gholams*.

Table 1.3 List of grand viziers

1. Emir Shams al-Din Zakariya Tabrizi Kajuji[217]	907/1501-2
2. Mahmud Khan (Jan) Deilami Qazvini[218]	909/1503-04
3. Mir Yar-Ahmad Khuzani	914-5/1508-10
4. Aqa Kamal al-Din Hosein Monshi Qomi[219]	915-20/1509-14
5. Khvajeh [or Mirza] Shah Hosein Esfahani[220]	920/1514
6. Khvajeh Jalal al-Din[221]	929-30/1523-24
7. Qadi Jahan Seifi Hoseini[222]	930/1524
8. Mirza Ja'far Savaji[223]	931/1525
9. Ahmad Beg Nur Kamal[224]	938/1531

55/1634-45)", *Studia Iranica* 26 (1997), pp. 237-66.

[215] Chardin, vol. 5, p. 334 even states that the function of grand vizier can only be given to a Persian of ancient stock (Tajik); see also Nasiri, *Alqab*, pp. 5-6.

[216] TM, p. 115. This is also the conclusion that Nasiri, *Alqab*, p. 5 drew.

[217] Qazvini Ghaffari, p. 266; Röhrborn, *Regierung*, p. 23, n. 19.

[218] Malek Mohammad Deilami, one of the Deilami magnates, who had been vizier for the Turkoman kings for years, was made *vazir-e divan-e a'la* and partnered (*sharik*) with Mir Zakariya Kehaji. Qomi, vol, 1, p. 80; Valeh Esfahani, p. 133; Rumlu, p. 110.

[219] Qomi, vol. 1, p. 119.

[220] Valeh Esfahani, pp. 243, 317; Rumlu, p. 197 (*nazer-e divan*); Röhrborn, *Regierung*, p. 23, n. 25.

[221] Valeh Esfahani, pp. 326, 443, *nazer-e divan-e a'la*. Khvajeh Jalal al-Din Mohammadluleh Tabrizi became *vazir-e divan-e a'la* in 929/1523, Qomi, vol. 1, p. 152; Röhrborn, *Regierung*, p. 24, n. 27.

[222] *Vazir* and *saheb-e ekhtiyar*. Valeh Esfahani, pp. 318, 326, 334, 340, 443; *nazer-e divan*, Rumlu, p. 242; Röhrborn, *Regiering*, p. 24, n. 30.

[223] Valeh Esfahani, p. 340, till 938. Ibid., p. 444 (Amir Kamal al-Din Ja'far Savaji, *nazer-e divan*), Rumlu, pp. 247, 258; Monshi, vol. 1, p. 160; Röhrborn, *Regierung*, p. 24, n. 33.

[224] Valeh Esfahani, p. 444; (*nazer-e divan*) Rumlu, p. 320; Minorsky. *Calligraphers,*

Table 1.3 (continued)

10. Khvajeh Sa'd al-Din 'Enayat Khuzani and
Khvajeh Mo'in Yazdi[225]   940/1534-5
11. Khvajeh Sa'd al-Din 'Enayat Khuzani with
Qadi Jahan[226]   941/1535
12. Qadi Jahan[227]   942-57/1535-51
The function of grand vizier was shared between various individuals
between 1551 and 1553
13. Khvajeh Emir Beg [Tabrizi] [Mohrdar] and
Khvajeh Ghayath al-Din 'Ali and   958/1551
Aqa Mohammad Farahani Kajaji[228]
14. [Khvajeh] Mirza Beg [Sabaqi] Abhari and
Khvajeh Seif al-Moluk Tehrani.[229]   959-60/1552-53
15. Ma'sum Beg Safavi[230]   960-76/1553-68
16. Emir Sayyed Sharif-e Thani[231]   976/1568-9
After Ma'sum Beg's death no vizier with independent authority was
appointed for a number of years.[232]
17. Mir Sayyed Hosein Farahani and
Khvajeh Kamal al-Din 'Ali[233]   981-2/1573-4
vacancy
18. Mirza Shokrollah[234]   984/1576

---

p. 76; Röhrborn, *Regierung*, p. 25, n. 35. According to Qomi, vol. 1, 235 his brother Mir Ghayath al-Din Mahmud also was vizier.

[225] Mir 'Enayatollah Khvari and Khvajeh Ghayath al-Din 'Ali Sabzavari. Valeh Esfahani, p. 444; Qomi, vol. 1, p. 236; Röhrborn, *Regierung*, p. 24, n. 36.

[226] Rumlu, p. 482; Qomi, vol. 1, p. 364.

[227] Valeh Esfahani, p. 444; Monshi, vol. 1, p. 160; Rumlu, p. 482; Röhrborn, *Regierung*, p. 24, n. 37.

[228] Valeh Esfahani, p. 444; Rumlu, p. 457. Agha Moh. Farahani replaced Emir Beg when he resigned.

[229] Valeh Esfahani, p. 444; Röhrborn, *Regierung*, p. 24, n. 38.

[230] Valeh Esfahani, p. 444; Rumlu, p. 483; Monshi, vol. p. 161. [Amir] Saraj al-Din ['Ali] Qomi acted as his substitute. Valeh Esfahani, p. 445. According to Rumlu, p. 481 his substitute was Khvajeh Jalal al-Din Mohammad.

[231] Monshi, vol. 1, p. 161; Röhrborn, *Regierung*, p. 25, n. 40.

[232] Valeh Esfahani, p. 445.

[233] They were joint viziers for one year, then dismissed and not replaced. Savory, *History*, vol 1, p. 251-4; Monshi, vol. 1, pp. 159, 161; Sayyed Hosein Farahani and Khvajeh Jamal al-Din 'Ali Tabrizi were vizier in 981/1573-4. Valeh Esfahani, pp. 373, 455; Rumlu, p. 591 with a salary of 500 tomans each. Tahmasp I dismissed Mir Hasan Farahani and Khvajeh Jamal al-Din Marmari from the *vezarat-e divan-e a'la* in 982/1574-5.

[234] Savory, *History*, vol. 1, p. 255; Valeh Esfahani, p. 448 [*vazir-e a'zam*], p. 536, 556 [dismissed 985/1577-8 on 6 Rabi' al-avval] after 11 months; Rumlu, p. 639. Mirza Shokrollah first was one of the *motafarreqeh-nevisan*, then he became *mostoufi-ye baqaya*, then *mostoufi al-mamalek*; then vizier; then *motavalli* of Mashhad. Valeh Esfahani, p. 448. Mohammadi Beg Tabrizi Kejaji was in the days of Abu Taleb Mirza

Table 1.3 (continued)

19. Mirza Salman Jaberi[235]	985-91/1577-83
20. Mirza Hedayatollah[236]	991-4/1583-6
21. Mirza Mohammad [Kermani][237]	994/1586
22. Mirza Shah Vali[238]	995/1587
23. Mirza Lotfi[239]	995/1587
24. Mirza Mohammad [Kermani][240]	996/1588
25. Mirza Lotfollah Shirazi[241]	997-1000/1589-91
26. Hatem Beg Ordubadi[242]	1000-19/1591-1610
27. Mirza Abu Taleb Ordubadi[243]	1019-30/1610-21
28. Salman Khan[244]	1030-3/1621-24
29. Sayyed 'Ala' al-Din Hosein (Khalifeh Soltan)[245]	1033-41/1624-32
30. Mirza Abu Taleb Beg Ordubadi[246]	1041-44/1632-34
31. Mirza Taqi (Saru Taqi)[247]	1044-55/1634-45
32. Khalifeh Soltan[248]	1055-64/1645-54
33. Mohammad Beg (Khan)[249]	1064-70/1654-60
One year vacancy	
34. Sayyed Mirza Mohammad Mehdi[250]	1071-77/1661-69
35. Sheikh 'Ali Khan Zanganeh[251]	1080-84/1669-73

---

vazir-e divan. Valeh Esfahani, p. 452.

[235] Savory *History*, vol. 1, p. 315, 333 reconfirmed, 383 also vizier of Hamzah Mirza. Valeh Esfahani, pp. 449, 556; Qomi, vol. 2, p. 648.

[236] E'temad al-Douleh, Savory, *History*, vol. 1, p. 259; Qomi, vol. 2, p. 748.

[237] E'temad al-Douleh, Savory, *History*, vol. 1, p. 489, 493; Qomi, vol. 2, p. 847; Minorsky, *Calligraphers*, p. 97.

[238] Monshi, vol. 1, p. 385, vol. 2, p. 1090; Qomi, vol. 2, p. 869.

[239] Savory, *History*, vol. 1, p. 512.

[240] Qomi, vol. 2, pp. 868, 883; Minorsky, *Calligraphers*, p. 97; Monshi, vol. 1, p. 401; Savory, *History*, vol. 2, pp. 578, 581.

[241] Qomi, vol. 2, pp. 627, 889; Monshi, vol. 2, p. 1090.

[242] Monshi, vol. 2, p. 1090.

[243] He was Hatem Beg's son. Monshi, vol. 2, p. 1091.

[244] Monshi, vol. 2, pp. 904, 1091 (he was a brother-in-law to 'Abbas I and grandson of Tahmasp I through his mother).

[245] Monshi, vol. 2, pp. 1013, 1022. He was *sadr* and son-in-law of 'Abbas I and also known as Khalifeh Soltan.

[246] A.k.a. Taleb Khan. Yusef, p. 260; Esfahani, pp. 124, 127, 184, 187-8. This was his second time as grand-vizier.

[247] For a biography see Floor, "Mirza Taqi".

[248] Ibid.; Vahid Qazvini, p. 170; Matthee, "Career", p. 21, n. 15. This was his second time as grand vizier.

[249] Vahid Qazvini, pp. 171, 298; for a biography see Matthee, "Career".

[250] Vahid Qazvini, pp. 298-300; (he had been *sadr*). Matthee, "Sheikh 'Ali Khan", p. 81. He was appointed on March 10, 1661 and died in 1081/1670-1, shortly after his dismissal from office. Richard, vol. 2, p. 268, n. 21.

[251] He was appointed as grand vizier in June 1669 and dismissed in October 1689. Matthee, *Politics*, p. 200 and Ibid. "Administrative Stability". Röhrborn, *Regierung*, p.

Table 1.3 (continued)

From March 1673 till June 1674 there was no grand vizier.[252]

36. Sheikh 'Ali Khan Zanganeh[253]	1085-99/1674-89

One and half year vacancy, October 1689-March 1691[254]

37. Mirza Taher Vahid Sharif Qazvini[255]	1102-10/1691-99
38. Mohammad Mo'men Khan Shamlu[256]	1110-19/1699-1707
39. Shahqoli Khan Zanganeh[257]	1119-28/1707-15
40. Fath 'Ali Khan Daghestani[258]	1128-33/1715-20
41. Mohammadqoli Khan Begdeli Shamlu[259]	1133-34/1720-21
42. Rajab 'Ali Beg[260]	?
43. Mohammad 'Ali Khan Mokri[261]	1135/1722
44. Mortezaqoli Khan[262]	1135/1723
45. Mirza 'Abdol-Karim[263]	1136/1724
46. Farajollah Khan 'Abdollu[264]	?
47. Mirza Mohammad Hosein[265]	?

---

[27] is wrong to list Sayyed Mirza Abu Taleb (referencing Nasrabadi, p. 78) as grand vizier and immediate predecessor of Sheikh 'Ali Khan.

[252] Sheikh 'Ali Khan was in disgrace from March 1673 till June 1674, or for 14 months. During that time "three of the chief Officers of the Crown discharg'd his Duty," which was without precedent. Sir John Chardin, *Travels in Persia 1673-1677* (London 1927 [1988], pp. 6, 8 (henceforth cited as John Chardin). For the dates of the dismissal period see Matthee, *Politics*, pp. 178-9.

[253] He was appointed as grand vizier in June 1669 and dismissed in October 1689. Matthee, *Politics*, p. 200. Röhrborn, *Regierung*, p. 27 is wrong to list Sayyed Mirza Abu Taleb (referencing Nasrabadi, p. 78) as grand vizier.

[254] From October 1689 till March 1691, the post of grand vizier remained vacant. Matthee, Sheykh 'Ali Khan, p. 93 (1102/March 1691).

[255] Nasiri, *Dastur*, p. 90; according to Dutch sources he was a weak man and not much respected, in fact, he was hated by all, and he loved presents. *ARA,* VOC 1507, 19/1/1693, f. 474; see also Gemelli-Careri, vol. 2, p. 135.

[256] Nasiri, *Dastur*, p. 235; *ARA,* VOC 1763, f. 75, 135.

[257] He was appointed in June 1707 and died on July 22, 1715. Floor, *Commercial*, pp. 4, 20.

[258] He was Shahqoli Khan's son-in-law and was appointed on July 25, 1715 and he was deposed in December 1720. Floor, *Commercial*, p. 20; Ibid, *Bar Oftadan*, p. 38.

[259] He was appointed in December 1720 and was dismissed at the fall of Isfahan in October 1722. Floor, *Bar Oftadan*, pp. 38, index; Ibid., *Afghan Occupation*, pp. 24, 29, 36, 40

[260] Nasiri, *Alqab*, p. 8. He had been *qurchi-bashi* and joined Tahmasp II in Azerbaijan and was appointed grand-vizier

[261] Nasiri, *Alqab*, p. 8. He had been *tofangchi-aghasi* and joined Tahmasp II in Azerbaijan. He had been grand-vizier for 10 days only when he died. Mostoufi, p. 141.

[262] On the accession to the throne Tahmasp II made him a khan and appointed him as *vakil al-douleh* or grand vizier. Mervi, pp. 63-4.

[263] Mostoufi, p. 143.

[264] Nasiri, *Alqab*, p. 8. He had been *qurchi-bashi* and was appointed grand-vizier after Mokri's sudden death, whose deputy he was.

Table 1.3 (continued)

48. Mirza 'Abdollah[266]	1136/1724
49. Mirza Mo'men Qazvini[267]	1137/1725
50. Mirza Mohammad Rahim[268]	1141-43/1728-30
51. Rajab 'Ali Khan[269]	1144/1731

What the above shows is that the Safavid political system was a relative open one and that managerial talent, though drawn mainly from the traditional class of Tajik bureaucrats, was a multivaried one (ethnic, religion, social). Grand viziers with different backgrounds served, though all were selected because of their administrative qualities in addition to whatever other plusses they might have had. The usurpation of the exclusive Tajik role by Qezelbash grand viziers after 1669 is a testimony to the successful absorption of the Turkomans into the Persian administrative culture, and also underscores the persistence of bureaucratic and administrative tradition. Many of the grand viziers held and exercised real power and this was not something that all of sudden emerged in the 17th century when weak shahs were on the political scene. One difference is that the strong grand viziers of the 16th century exercised real power whether there were strong shahs or weak-willed ones, and when the survival of the regime was at stake. The other difference is that towards the end of the Safavid period there was no idealogy that provided a common bond between the contenders for power. This was due to the emasculation of Safavid idealogy, which as yet had not been replaced by Shi'i idealogy. Imamite Shi'ism, which was in the process of trying to eliminate the traditional, more sufi-oriented brand of Shi'ism, was as yet a divisive force. Therefore, there was nothing that really provided a binding element between the power elite, beyond the competition for power. The precariousness of the grand vizier's life did not change either. He held his position by the grace of the shah's will and that did not change. Grand viziers therefore held their power for as long as

---

[265] Nasiri, *Alqab*, p. 8. He had been *mostawfi al-mamalek* and joined Tahmasp II in Azerbaijan and was appointed grand-vizier

[266] Nasiri, *Alqab*, p. 9. He had been *motavalli* of the Imam Reza shrine in Mashhad. He became grand-vizier in the Astarabad period. Mostoufi, p. 145.

[267] He was the son of Mirza Qavam. Mostoufi, pp. 147-8.

[268] *ARA*, VOC 2253 (1/10/1730), f. 659; Nasiri, *Alqab*, p. 9 notes that from the beginning of Tahmasp II's accession to the throne till now, which was in 1141/1728 or seven years in all, Mirza Mohammad Rahim had been grand vizier. It is not known when the persons numbered 41, 45-46, whom Nasiri also lists as having been Tahmasp II's grand vizier, actually held the function of grand vizier, if at all. It may have been that Mirza Mohammad Rahim held the function during the 1720s intermittently.

[269] Mervi, pp. 120, 213-4, 217-8f. He was a former *divan-begi* who had fled with Tahmasp Mirza from Isfahan during the siege. Floor, *Bar Oftadan*, p. 173; Ibid., *Afghan Occupation*, p. 135.

the shah considered his continuation in his interest. The change in the balance of power between the *khasseh* and *mamalek* part of the administration had no real impact on the position of the grand vizier. What it meant was that instead of having to deal with powerful Qezelbash emirs the grand vizier now had to cope with powerful administrators of the *khasseh* branch of government. These included Qezelbash, *gholams*, Tajiks, and harem inmates. So, the players had changed, who moreover were more divided among themselves, but the game remained the same.

The Divan-e a'la or Royal Chancellery

The grand vizier was assisted by a large bureaucratic institution, known as the *divan-e a'la*. The latter was subdivided into a *daftar[khaneh]-ye [homayun-e] a'la*, which was in charge of fiscal affairs, and a *dar al-ensha*, which was in charge of all administrative correspondence. The Qezelbash and *gholams* (royal slaves) dominated most court functions, but this was initially not the case in the *divan-e a'la*. Here, Tajiks dominated, who either held those functions because of family tradition and/or because of technical competence. The latter factor was above all important for those who held functions in the *daftar-khaneh*.[270] However, gradually members of the Qezelbash clans were absorbed by the bureaucracy and became holders of important administrative functions, thus turning into 'men of the pen.' A notable example is Eskander Beg Turkoman Monshi, the noted historian, who held important functions in 'Abbas I's bureaucracy. The staff serving the *vakil*, when that function still existed, served in the so-called *divan-e vekalat* and was separate from the staff working in the *dar al-ensha*.[271]

The most important bureaucrats were six viziers according to Sanson. They were, in order of importance: "[1] the *mostoufi-ye mamalek* or the comptroller-general of the revenues. He is seated directly behind the six principal ministers [2] the *mostoufi-ye khasseh* or the comptroller of the king's household and the government of Isfahan, he is seated behind nr. 1 [3] the *darugheh-ye daftar* or the keeper of the general register of the revenues, he is seated amongst the *valis* [4] *vazir al-molki* the keeper of the register of the government of Isfahan and is seated among the governors, [5] the *vazir-e khasseh* the keeper of the accounts of the king's household and is seated near the secretary of state, and [6] the *kalantar* or the chief provost of the merchants of Isfahan is seated among the foreign princes who are royal pensioners. They do their business everyday in the king's palace. The grand vizier is further assisted by two *saheb-raqams* or secretaries who dispatch all orders of the court."[272]

From this list it is clear that the function of vizier was more important than that of *mostoufi*. The grand vizier or vizier of the supreme *divan* was

---

270 Richard, vol. 2, p. 264.
271 Minorsky, *Calligraphers*, p. 98.
272 Sanson, p. 19.

assisted by two *mostoufi*s of the same *divan*. This also holds true for all other departments, which had both a vizier and a *mostoufi*. Eskander Monshi reports that "Malek Beg was first *mostoufi* of the *qurchi*s and then was promoted to *vazir* of the *qurchi*s."[273] However, it was not the function, but the holder of the function (his personality, his connections, etc.) that determined the extent of its influence. For example, 'Aliqoli Beg of the 'Arabgirlu clan of the Shamlu tribe held the office *vazir-e qurchiyan*, which office had been vested in his family since early Safavid times. Mirza Fathollah was *mostoufi-ye qurchiyan*, to which office he was appointed at an early age, and actually had more influence among the *qurchi*s [household troops] than the *vazir-e qurchiyan*.[274]

The Daftar-khaneh

According to Minadoi the first *soltan*, referring to the *emir al-omara*, was in charge of military affairs. "The other two [Sultanes] gather up all the revenues, and keepe a diligent reckoning thereof: which two may be rather called Treasurers then anything els, such as the Turkes call Defterdar."[275] The treasurers referred to were the *mostoufi al-mamalek* and the *mostoufi-ye khasseh*.

The *daftar-khaneh* was managed by the *mostoufi-ye mamalek* or the comptroller-general of the revenues. He was in charge of the entire financial administration of the kingdom, more in particular of the *mamalek* or state domains. His salary was 600 tomans per year.[276] The finances of the crown or *khasseh* properties were managed by the *mostoufi-ye khasseh*, though the *mostoufi-ye mamalek* continued to have a controlling function over his colleague. The DM states unequivocally that "Scribes of the *khasseh* department did not have a senior officer other than the *mostoufi al-mamalek*." In fact, no payment or tax collection could be made without his approval, for "No document is registered in the *divani* books, or becomes operative, without his knowledge or writ."[277] There is only one contemporary source that ranks the *mostoufi-ye khasseh* higher than his alleged superior, the *mostoufi-ye mamalek*.[278]

---

[273] Savory, *History*, vol. 2, p. 1061; also Ibid, vol. 2, p. 1295.

[274] Savory, *History*, 1, p. 258.

[275] Minadoi, pp. 67-8; there were three viziers: the first for the palace's entrance [the *ishik aghasi bashi* is meant]; the second for the correspondance [the *monshi al-mamalek*], and the third for the treasury [the *khazinehdar*], Berchet, p. 287.

[276] Richard, vol. 2, pp. 18, 139, 271; see further DM, p. 64; TM, p. 90, and in particular Nasiri, *Alqab*, p. 45, which has much detailed information.

[277] TM, p. 54-55. It is interesting to note that the TM does not even describe the function of *mostoufi-ye khasseh*, which must be an omission because the DM, pp. 77-8, does as does Nasiri, *Alqab*, p. 47.

[278] Petro Bedik, *Cehil Sutun seu explicatio utriusque celeberrisimi, ac pretiosissimi theatri quadriginta columnarum in Perside Orientis* (Vienna 1678), p. 18.

Table 1.4 List of *mostoufiyan al-mamalek*

Moulana Shams al-Din Esfahani[279]	907/1501-02
Yar Mohammad Khuzani Esfahani[280]	till 915/1509
Ahmad Soltan[281]	919/1513-14
Mir Sayyed Sharif Shahrestani[282]	919-30/1514-23
Mir Mas'ud Golpaigani[283]	930-38/1524-32
Khvajeh Shah Hosein [Saruqi][284]	938/1531-2
Khvajeh Ghayath al-Din 'Ali[285]	till 958/1551.
Khvajeh Qasem Natanzi[286]	958/1551
Khvajeh Malek Mohammad Esfahani[287]	960s/1560s
Mir Ghayath al-Din Mahmud Shahrestani Esfahani[288]	981/1573
Mirza Shokrollah Esfahani[289]	981-4/1573-6
Mirza Shah Ghari[290]	984-5/1576-77
Mirza Hedayatollah[291]	985-91/1577-83
Mirza Mohammad[292]	991/1583
Khvajeh Mohammad Baqer Mervi[293]	?
Hatem Beg Ordubadi[294]	till 1000/1591
Qavama Mohammada[295]	1000/1591

---

[279] al-Qazvini, *Lobb*, p. 407; Qomi, vol. 1, p. 94; Aubin, Jean. "Révolution chiite et conservatisme. Les soufis de Lahejan, 150-1514 (Etudes safavides II)", *Moyen Orient & Océan Indien* 1 (1984),[henceforth cited as Aubin, "Soufis"], p. 30, n. 115.

[280] Montazer-Saheb, p. 315. In 915/1509 he became *vakil* with the title of Najm-e Thani.

[281] Qazvini Ghaffari, p. 276.

[282] Savory, *History*, vol. 1, p. 256; Monshi, p. 263.

[283] During the reign of Tahmasp I (1524-76) there were seven *mostoufis al-mamalek* of which he was one. Monshi, pp. 162; Savory, *History*, vol. 2, pp. 254-5; Valeh Esfahani, p. 445.

[284] Monshi, pp. 162; Savory, *History*, vol. 2, pp. 254-5; Valeh Esfahani, p. 445; Qomi, vol. 1, p. 218.

[285] He was known as Ghayath-e Kahreh and became grand vizier in 958/1551. Monshi, pp. 162; Savory, *History*, vol. 2, pp. 254-5; Valeh Esfahani, p. 445.

[286] Monshi, pp. 162; Savory, *History*, vol. 2, pp. 254-5; Valeh Esfahani, p. 445; Qomi, vol. 1, p. 428. He was *mostoufi al-mamalek* for 30 years. He died in 969/1561-2.

[287] Monshi, pp. 162; Savory, *History*, vol. 2, pp. 254-5; Valeh Esfahani, p. 445.

[288] Monshi, pp. 162; Savory, *History*, vol. 2, pp. 254-5; Valeh Esfahani, p. 445.

[289] Monshi, pp. 162; Savory, *History*, vol. 2, pp. 254-5; Valeh Esfahani, p. 373, 445 (in 981/1573-4).

[290] Valeh Esfahani, pp. 536, 614.

[291] Qomi, vol. 2, p. 748.

[292] Valeh Esfahani, p. 808; Qomi, vol. 2, pp. 816, 868. He was the son of Mirza Shokrollah Esfahani.

[293] Astarabadi, p. 113

[294] Monshi, pp. 166, 1091.

[295] Yusef, p. 274.

Table 1.4 (continued)

Mirza Qasem[296]	?
Mirza Abu'l-Hosein Beg Ordubadi	1038-41/1629-32
Mirza (Mohammad) Sa'id[297]	1041-71/1632-62
Mirza Sadr al-Din Mohammad Jaberi[298]	1071-77/1662-66
?	
Mirza Sadeq[299]	1084/1673
Mirza Ebrahim[300]	d. 1102/1690-91
For some time nobody filled this post[301]	
Mirza Abu'l-Hasan[302]	1105-06/1693-1695
?	
'Ali Reza Khan[303]	1124-26/1712-14
Mirza Mohammad Khan[304]	1126/1714
Mirza Mohammad Hosein[305]	1128/1715-16
Mirza Abu Taleb[306]	1132-35/1720-22
Mirza Mohammad Rahim[307]	1135/1722
Mirza Mohammad Hosein[308]	1136/1724
?	
Mirza Esma'il[309]	1129/1730

The *mostoufi-ye khasseh,* as his title suggests, was in charge of the accounts of all *khasseh* or crown properties and some special revenues such as seignorage and import and export duties. The latter was one of the reasons why the Europeans had so many dealings with him and why he seemed to acquire a more important role than the comptroller-general.[310]

---

[296] Vahid Qazvini, p. 23 (the grandfather of Mirza Sa'id?)

[297] He was the grand son of Khvajeh Qasem Natanzi. Yusef, p. 282; Vahid Qazvini, p. 300.

[298] Vahid Qazvini, p. 300.

[299] Matthee, "Sheikh 'Ali Khan", p. 84; Ibid. *Politics*, p. 73, n. 53 for particulars about him and his brother who succeeded him. *ARA*, VOC 1360 (4/3/1679), f. 1909 vs.

[300] Khatunabadi, p. 547. He was the brother of Mirza Sadeq.

[301] Kroell, p. 46.

[302] He was the son of the former *mostoufi al-mamalek*. Nasiri, *Dastur*, p. 57.

[303] *ARA*, KA 1710 (12/1/1713), f. 394; KA 1726 (23/4/14), f. 2630; KA 1778, 9/9/1715, f. 209; Floor, *Commercial*, p. 13 (Jan. 1713).

[304] *ARA*, KA 1740 (27/8/1714), f. 2266 vs.

[305] Daneshpazhuh, Mohammad Taqi. "Amar-e Mali va nezami-ye Iran dar 1128". *FIZ* 20, p. 296; Nasiri, *Alqab*, p. 8; Mostoufi, p. 145.

[306] *ARA*, KA 1856, 1/1/1721, f. 205.

[307] Nasiri, *Alqab*, p. 9; Mostoufi, p. 144.

[308] Mostoufi, pp. 145, 149. He had held the same function in 1715-16.

[309] *ARA*, VOC 2253 (1/10/1730), f. 660; VOC 2168, f. 576. He was at the same time *mostoufi-ye khasseh*.

[310] DM, pp. 77-8; TM, pp. 25, 45, 123; Floor, *Commercial*, chapter 1. There were also several *vazir-e mahall-e khasseh*, who were in charge of specific royal properties.

This function existed already under Esma'il I. Bairam Beg, Esma'il I's first *divan-begi*, was at the same time in charge of the *divan-e qalamru-ye khasseh-ye sharifeh*, which was also known as the *divan-e foqara*.[311] The function was taken over by Mohammad Sofrehchi Ostajalu, the military *vakil* or regent.[312] Natanzi reported that his ancestor, Amir Abu Torab, was Esma'il I's *mostoufi-ye khasseh* and *daftardar-e khasseh*, who gave him the title of "Amin-e man".[313] That this function was an important one, is not only clear from the involvement of important courtiers such as Bairam Beg and Mohammad Sofrehchi Ostajalu, but also from the existence of extensive *khasseh* lands under Esma'il I.[314] Mention is also made of the *motasaddiyan-e vojuhat-e khasseh* (administrators of the *khasseh* revenues) in Isfahan in 1511 and of a *vazir-e khasseh* of Khorasan in 1510.[315] The function was clearly not a temporary one, for in 973/1565-6, we learn, that 'Abdi Beg Shirazi, the *mostoufi-ye khasseh* resigned, which implies the uninterrupted continuation of the function.[316] Mirza Ahmad Kofrani was *mostoufi-ye mahall-e khaleseh-ye Fars* about the same period, and it shows that the *khasseh* administration was already well developed having provincial branches since the beginning of the dynasty.[317] The *moustoufi-ye khasseh* was not only in charge of the records of the royal domains (*daftar-e khasseh*), but also of the *dafater-e amval-e sunk*, i.e. the records that listed all confiscated and conquered land and property.[318] As is usual, the *mostoufi-ye khasseh* also had a *na'eb* or deputy.[319] With the growth in *khasseh* property the importance of this function grew, though it never overtook that of the *mostoufi al-mamalek*, such as happened in other areas, e.g., in the *dar al-ensha*.

(e.g. Mirza Ahmad Nazer-e Esfahani Qomi, vol. 2, p. 748). This official was not the *vazir-e khasseh* who logically would have been the higher ranking function in the *khasseh* administration, this in fact was the grand vizier.

[311] Aubin, "Soufis", p. 5, n. 47; see also Qomi, p. 83; Rumlu, p. 106; and Montazer-Saheb, p. 127. Naseri, *Alqab*, p. 47 maintains that the function was created by Shah 'Abbas I.

[312] Aubin, "Soufis", p. 12, n. 130.

[313] Natanzi, p. 15.

[314] Aubin, "L'Avènement", pp. 80, 87, 97.

[315] Aubin, "Soufis", p. 14, n. 166, p. 16, n. 183, p. 20, n. 228. See also Khvandamir, vol, 4, p. 507; Qomi, p. 109; Rumlu, p. 151, and Honarfar, Lotfollah. *Ganjineh-ye athar-e tarikhi-ye Esfahan*. (Tehran 1350/1971 [2nd. ed.]), p. 86-7.

[316] Shirazi, 'Abdi Beg. *Takmeleh al-Akhbar*, ed. 'Abdol-Hosein Nava'i (Tehran, 1369/1990), p. 127.

[317] Valeh Esfahani, p. 447; Qomi, vol. 1, p. 446. In Kerman, which was a *khasseh* province, the *khaleseh* administration around 1670, had a staff of 300 men, of which 50 were *safar-kesh*. Bardsiri, p. 290.

[318] Qomi, vol. 2, 1032. In 981/1573-4, there also was a *nazer-e amval-e sunk*. Ibid., p. 582. On the term *sunk* see Floor,*Fiscal History*.

[319] *ARA*, KA 1726, 28.3.13, f. 236.

Table 1.5 List of *mostoufiyan-e khasseh*

Amir Abu Torab[320]	around 916/1510
?	
?	
'Abdi Beg Shirazi[321]	till 973/1565-6
?	
?	
Aqa Abu'l-Fath Esfahani[322]	1020/1602
?	
?	
Mirza Qasem Esfahani[323]	till 1038/1629
Mirza Hashem Beg Tehrani[324]	1038-42/1629-33
Mirza Mohsen Esfahani[325]	1043-52/1634-42
?	
?	
Mirza Yahya[326]	?
Mirza Razi[327]	till 1095/1684
Mirza 'Ali Akbar[328]	1095-/1684
Mirza Mahmud[329]	1106/1695
Mirza Da'ud[330]	1109/1697-98.
Mirza Rabi'a[331]	1114-15/1701-03
Rajab 'Ali Beg[332]	?
Mirza Mohammad 'Ali [Khan][333]	1124-32/1712-14
'Ali Reza Khan[334]	1126/1714
Mirza Mohammad[335]	1126-32/1714-19

---

320 Natanzi, p. 15.

321 Sam Mirza, p. 95; Shirazi, p. 127.

322 *Mostoufi-ye khasseh* and *avajareh nevis-e 'Eraq*. Molla Jalal, p. 430.

323 Yusef, p. 282.

324 Esfahani, p. 164; Yusef, p. 283.

325 Vahid Qazvini, p. 84; Yusef, pp. 171, 203, 283; Esfahani, p. 198.

326 *bagh-e mostoufi-ye khassseh*. Nasiri, *Dastur*, p. 30.

327 He died in 1684. *ARA*, VOC 1416, f. 1609 v-10 r (20 Oct. 1684); already in function in 1682. VOC 1364, f. 390 v (7 Sept. 1682).

328 DM, p. 42.

329 Miersa Mhamoet Jenae. *ARA*, VOC 1549, f. 593 [17.6.1695].

330 Nasiri, *Dastur*, p. 218.

331 *ARA*, VOC 1679, f. 103-4 (12/8/1702); He want on the *hajj* in the summer of 1703. VOC 1694, f. 169 [4/10/1703].

332 *ARA*, KA 1856, 20/2/1721, f. 428 mentioned as the former *mostoufi-ye khasseh*.

333 Floor, *Commercial*, p. 12; *ARA*, KA 1735 (1/6/1712), f. 47 mentions him as the new appointee. KA 1710 (12/1/1713), f. 394.

334 *ARA*, KA 1726 (12/5/1714), f. 2685 vs; he was shortly thereafter dismissed. KA 1740 (27/8/1714), f. 2266 vs.

335 *ARA*, KA 1778 (24/3/1716), f. 6; dismissed in May 1719, KA 1839, 25/11/1719, f. 45.

Table 1.5 (continued)

Mirza ['Abdol-] Karim[336]	1132-3/1719-20
Mirza Mohammad 'Ali[337]	1133-34/1720-22
Nurallah Khan[338]	1134/June 1722
Mirza Mohammad 'Ali[339]	1134/June 1722
?	
Mirza Esma'il[340]	1142/1729-30

Further assistance was provided by the comptroller of the endowments (*mostoufi-ye mouqufat*)[341], the *mostoufi-ye baqaya* (comptroller of the arrears), and the *mostoufi-ye kholaseh* (comptroller of the consolidated accounts). The function of *mostoufi-ye baqaya* was abolished in the late 1650s, and was replaced by that of the *mostoufi-ye kholaseh* in 1659, which function only lasted till 1670. Thereafter, these functions were collapsed into that of the *baqaya* or arrears scribe; a function that previously already existed when there still was a *mostoufi-ye baqaya*. The function was revived for some time under Shah Soltan Hosein, but thereafter abolished again.[342]

Table 1.6 List of *mostoufiyan-e baqaya*

Mir Hedayatollah Maqtul	930/1524
Mir Moh. Ma'muri his brother	?
Mir Shah Ghari Esfahani[343]	till 984/1576
?	
Mir Shah Mirakeh[344]	989/1581
?	

---

336 *ARA*, KA 1839, 25/11/1719, f. 45; Nasiri, *Alqab*, p. 8.

337 Floor, *Bar Oftadan*, pp. 39, 99; Ibid., *Afghan Occupation*, pp. 36, 108, 147; KA 1856, 24/2/1721, f. 196.

338 Floor, *Bar Oftadan*, p. 174; Ibid., *Afghan Occupation*, pp. 134, 136. He was appointed on 11/6/1722. He was the former governor of Lar and Bandar 'Abbas.

339 He was reinstated on 28/6/1722; Floor, *Bar Oftadan*, p. 181; Ibid., *Afghan Occupation*, pp. 141, 165, 168

340 *ARA*, VOC 2253 (1/10/1730), f. 660; VOC 2168, f. 576. He was at the same time *mostoufi-ye mamalek*.

341 On this official see Willem Floor, "The *sadr* or head of the Safavid religious administration, judiciary and endowments and other members of the religious administration", ZDMG 2000, and Richard, vol. 2, p. 271.

342 DM, pp. 82-3; TM, p. 93; Esfahani, p. 276; Nasiri, *Alqab*, p. 62. For details about their tasks see Floor, *Fiscal History*, chapter three.

343 There were only three *mostoufiyan-e baqaya* under Tahmasp I. Monshi, vol. 1, p. 163; Valeh Esfahani, p. 446.

344 Qomi, vol. 2, p. 723. He also dealt with *sunki* property.

Table 1.6 (continued)

Mirza Ma'sum[345]	1039-43/1629-34
Mirza Abu'l-Fath[346]	1043-52/1634-42
Mirza Sadeq[347]	till 1655

These *mostoufi*s were assisted by the *nazer-e daftar*, the *darugheh-ye daftar*, the *saheb-toujih*, the *zabeteh-nevis*, and the *avarajeh-nevis*, who were all under the *mostoufi al-mamalek* and were appointed after his approval.[348] The *nazer* of the *divan* (or *daftar*) had two bosses. Chardin writes that the *nazer-e dafter* was appointed by the shah to serve the grand vizier as secretary. He also states that the other magnates also had such a *nazer*.[349] Chardin admits, however, that all the actions by the *nazer* of the royal secretariat had to be endorsed by the comptroller-general.[350] This is in agreement with the TM, which states that the *nazer* was under the *mostoufi al-mamalek*.[351]

The *nazer*'s task was to check and seal for approval all documents which granted employment, wages, tax exemption, pensions, and revenue assignments, in short all those documents that had financial implications for the state. In addition he had to clear the accounts of the various provincial revenue agents. He had 9 scribes to assist him in this task, eight of who registered and endorsed the various documents that were submitted for approval. The ninth scribe wrote the approval signature (*qalami shod*) on the document, so that the *nazer* could seal it. The *darugheh* had to keep order in the office and settle problems among the staff. He also had to put his seal for approval on the same documents. If approval was denied the *darugheh* had to pursue and investigate the matter and bring them to conclusion. To that end he could summon the taxpayers, or appoint any of the staff as tax collector to verify the accounts.[352]

The *lashkar-nevis* and the *sar-khatt nevis* were respectively vizier and

---

[345] Yusef, pp. 147, 161, 232; Esfahani, pp. 176, 183.

[346] Yusef, p. 161.

[347] Vahid Qazvini, p. 162.

[348] TM, p. 54; Nasiri, *Alqab*, pp. 49, 53, 57-9, 61.

[349] Chardin, vol. 5, p. 341. 'Ali Beg *darugheh-ye daftarkhaneh*. Valeh Esfahani, p. 514; *nazer-e daftarkhaneh*, Qomi, vol. 2, p. 623; 'Alikhan Beg Turkoman *darugheh-ye daftarkhaneh*, Qomi, vol. 2, p. 649; Oghurlu Beg, *nazer-e daftarkhaneh-e homayun*. Yusef, p. 147, 249.

[350] Chardin, vol. 5, p. 446. In 1714 the *nazer* was Mirza Khalil. *ARA*, KA 1740 (27/8/1714), f. 2268.

[351] TM, pp. 54, 71.

[352] DM, pp. 54-5; TM, pp. 73-4; Richard, vol. 2, pp. 137, 271. According to the DM, the *nazer*'s signature was "*behnazar rasid*" [submitted for review], not [*qalami*] *shod*. The *nazer* had an annual salary of 200 tomans in 1660. Richard, vol. 2, p. 18; see further DM, p. 97; TM, p. 90.

mostoufi of the department of *aqayan* or gentlemen-in-waiting.[353] As such they were under the orders of the *ishik aghasi-bashi*. Whenever the *ishik aghasi-bashi* mustered his subordinates or sent them on a mission, the *lashkar-nevis*, the *sar-khatt nevis* and the scribes of that department wrote the records of the muster (*noskhehjat-e san*) and the *lashkar-nevis* read them in the presence of the *ishik aghasi-bashi*, and whatever the latter ordered with regard to them the *lashkar-nevis* and the *sarkhatt-nevis* wrote under each person's name.[354]

The *aqayan*, roughly corresponding to the middle echelon of court personnel, also constituted a kind of military yeomanry (see chapter three).[355] They included the falconers (*qushchis*), ushers (*yasavol*) and door keepers (*qapuchi*) of both the *divan* and harem. However, the personnel that fell into this department's purview extended to groups that went beyond that of the *aqayan*, for it encompassed the following categories of staff: "the *moqarraban*, the *aqayan*, the *yasavolan-e sohbat*, the *ishik aqasis*, the *nazers*, the *darughehs*, the tax officials, the *mo'azzens* (prayer-callers), of the lower staff of the royal workshops, the buildings, and the gardens, the divisional chiefs, the entertainers, the physicians, the astrologers, the surgeons, the blood cuppers (*kahhal*), the holders of pensions, wages, and the fixed allowances for women ('*awrat*), the dog-keepers, the lion keepers, the hunting-feline groomers (*parschiyan*), the falconers, and other groups [such as] the Georgians, the Daghestanis, the Indians, the Anatolians, the Uzbegs, the Arabs and non-Arabs [Persians], and the castle guards who are not affiliated with any special unit."[356]

The *lashkar-nevis* approved and sealed all financial documents related to this staff as well as verified all financial and appointment documents of all high and low government staff, while he also wrote all employment orders for these same people.[357] He also kept the individual files of the emirs, governors and *soltans* of the frontier provinces. If the shah led the army, the *lashkar-nevis* had to be in attendance to keep note who would

---

[353] *Lashkar-nevis*. Qomi, vol. 1, p. 200; vol. 2, pp. 748, 872, 922, 1082. Ahmad Beg and Mohammad Beg, *lashkar-nevis*. Monshi, pp. 164; Nasiri, *Alqab*, pp. 56, 58.

[354] DM, p. 52; TM, p. 75.

[355] TM, pp. 75-6; Khvajeh Shokrollah, *sarkhatt-nevis*, and Khalifeh Soltan 'Ali, *lashkar-nevis* under Safi I. Yusef, p. 284.

[356] TM, p. 75; DM, p. 113.

[357] DM, p. 52, 113; TM, p. 75. According to the DM the *lashkar-nevis* wrote employment decisions of the said officials, but not for the emirs, *begler-begis*, governors, *soltans* and whatever is by oral order (*bel-moshafeheh*) which pertains to the *vaqaye'-nevis*. The TM, however, states that he wrote these orders for everybody, ranging from emirs to workmen of the royal workshops. It seems likely that the DM version is more in line with reality. It would seem that the rolls of the *yasaqis* also had to be sealed by the *lashkar-nevis*. Molla Jalal, p. 220.

be rewarded for valor.[358] When a *sepahsalar* or *sardar* left on a campaign the *lashkar-nevis* sent a deputy with him to keep the muster-roll, which was sent for action to the *divan*.[359]

The *sarkhatt-nevis*, as the accountant of the *aqayan* department, reviewed, confirmed, prepared, and recorded the various financial statements and files for each of the staff under the purview of his department and endorsed it.[360] In general, these two officials dealt with all military staff, except of the four corpses (*qurchi*s, *gholam*s, *tofangchi*s, and *tupchi*s), which were under the so-called *vozara-ye sarkarat-e kharj*.[361]

The *saheb-e toujih* was responsible to make all payments drawn upon the state, after these payment orders had been verified by the various departments, whether *khasseh* or *mamalek*, who requested the payment. It was only after he had approved the payment that the relevant documents were submitted to the *divan* hierarchy for endorsement. All new claims on revenues had to be registered at the *toujih* department. The *saheb-e toujih* had 12 scribes, each of whom kept the register for the claims (*talab*), the cash payments, the grants, the annual salaries, the revenue assignments, the tax exempt revenue grants (*soyurghal*s), and the exemptions of *begler-begi*s, governors, *soltan*s, and others.[362]

These high-ranking financial officials each had a number of *farrash*es, scribes, and clerks at their disposal. The *farrash*es were the lowest ranking staff, doing the menial work. The scribes (*nevisandeh, moharrer*, and *kateb*) dealt with the lower level administrative work, while the specialized clerks *(-nevis, monshi*) did the more complicated work and provided guidance to the other secretarial staff. Among these clerks there were the so-called *motafarreqeh-nevisan (-e divan)*, whose task it was to keep the records up to date of each and every single revenue source.[363]

---

358 DM, p. 92; Nasiri, *Alqab*, p. 56.

359 DM, p. 92; TM, pp. 75, 92-3; Nasiri, *Alqab*, p. 56. Mirza Fathollah *lashkar-nevis.* Valeh Esfahani, p. 446.

360 TM, p. 75; DM, pp. 93, 113. Ahmad Beg *zabet-nevis.* Valeh Esfahani, p. 446.

361 Yusef, p. 283. For their organization see Floor, *Fiscal History.*

362 DM, p. 111, also for his remuneration; TM, p. 92; Nasiri, *Alqab*, pp. 57-8. Moh. Yusef, the author of the *Dheil-e Tarikh*, was appointed as *[moharrer-e] toujih-e divan-e a'la.* Yusef, p. 232. Mir Abu Torab Natanzi *saheb-e toujih.* Valeh Esfahani, p. 446. The first *saheb-e toujih* under Safi I was Mirza Saleh, son of Mirza Baqer, who held this post for years under Abbas I. When his father died he took over and gave up the post of *mostoufi-ye khasseh.* In the year of the conquest of Erivan his younger brother Mirza Mohsen, the vizier of Emir Khan, the *qurchi-bashi*, took over this post. Yusef, p. 283.

363 Monshi, p. 162; Valeh Esfahani, p. 448; Qadi Ahmad b. Sharaf al-Din Hosein Monshi-ye Qomi. *Golestan-e Honar.* ed. Soheili Khvonsari, Ahmad. Tehran 1351/1972 [2nd. ed.], p. 35. Minorsky, *Calligraphers*, p. 78 gives the term as *tafriqeh-nevis.* Hedayat Beg Shirazi *avarajeh-nevis* of Azerbaijan and Shirvan. Valeh Esfahani, p. 446. Mirza Mohamad Shafi' *avajareh-nevis* of Iraq replaced his father as *vazir-e*

The *lashkar-nevis* and the *sarkhatt-nevis* were assisted by scribes known generically as *nevisandeh-ye lashkar*,[364] and by specialized clerks such as the *ishik-nevis*.[365]

Dar al-Ensha

Minadoi in listing the most important officials writes that: "Next unto them [the treasurers] there are at Casbin two great Chauncellours, whome the Persians call Mordar, whose office it is to write all the orders, Commaundementes, and letters concerning the governement of the kingdome: one of them keepeth the Seale, and the other the penne."[366] Here he refers to the *monshi al-mamalek* and the *mohrdar*.

Monshi al-Mamalek

All official government correspondence was prepared in the *dar al-ensha* or the royal chancellery. Given the intricate style of Persian letters, in particular of chancellery documents, a special class of professional bureaucrats had come into being to write, process and register them.[367] As to the style of the documents Chardin remarked: "The Compliments observ'd in Letters, Memoiers, and Petitions, are still longer and exacter than the Verbal ones, which are spoken in the Presence of Friends: But seeing that I shall have occasion to discourse on them elsewhere, I shall only say here, that they have a Book on Purpose, containing the Titles to be given to all Orders of Men, from the King to the Cobler. That Book is call'd Tenassour, i.e. Method or Rule. Men of Business have it by Heart."[368] One of the items that must have been mentioned in that book is that "All the Requests, Petitions, and Memorials, that are presented in Persia, are always concluded with these Words Amrala, the Sense whereof as the Persians give it, is, the Answer you shall make to my Petition, shall regulate my desires."[369]

Sometimes, the style of the documents was such that even old hands at this game, such as the grand vizier, were upset. Sheikh 'Ali Khan had a molla given 200 strokes on the soles of his feet, "because some Inferior Officers of the ordnance had presented Petitions to him, which this Doctor had written, and where the Sense was so confus'd and perplex'd with Compliments, and old Canting Stuff, that it was a difficult Matter to penetrate into the Meaning thereof.... Use a more simple and clear Style, or else do not write for the Publick; for otherwise I'll cause your Hands to

---

qurchiyan and his brother, Mirza Mohamad Baqer, replaced him, Yusef, pp. 229, 284.
364 Qomi, vol. 1, p. 218; vol. 2, pp. 617, 816.
365 'Emada Mohammad *ishik-nevisi*. Yusef, p. 148.
366 Minadoi, pp. 67-8; Berchet, p. 287.
367 For an appreciation of their skills and expertise see Minorsky, *Calligraphers*.
368 John Chardin, p. 192.
369 John Chardin, p. 67.

be cut off."[370]

The Safavid bureaucracy continued to function in the tradition of that of the preceding regimes, i.e. the Qara-Qoyunlu and the Timurids. In the 16th century, the chancellery or *dar al-ensha* was undivided under the *monshi al-mamalek*. He wrote the so-called *shajareh* appointment diplomas for the *khalifeh*s as well as the *neshan*s (decrees), either with or without an *intitulatio* (introductory formula) or *sözümiz* (see below).

Esma'il II decreed in 984/1576 the following rule in case of appointment of important government officials: the pillars of state had to approve a draft text, by putting their seal and sign (*khatt va mohr*) on it, and then to inform the *monshi al-mamalek* that he had to write a *parvancheh*. When that was done he had to submit it to the pillars of state for the drawing of the *toghra*. The *davatdar* and Hosein Beg Laleh sealed the document and forwarded it to the pillars of state. The *davatdar* and tutor would receive their chancellery fee (*haqq al-say'*), but should neither demand any other fee (*doshakol*) nor accept any presents in cash or kind. Thus, apart from those two nobody would receive any fee.[371]

The managers of the *daftar-khaneh* also trained the young clerks. For example, Shams al-Din, the *mostoufi al-mamalek* taught the computation ciphers (*siyaq*) to the young staffers of the financial department on Tuesday and Thursday.[372] This also held for non-clerical staff, such as the emirs, who were trained in the art of how to compose a proper letter by e.g. Khvajeh Malek Mohammad Yazdi, who was *monshi al-mamalek*. The emirs wrote orders with the introductory formula of *farman-e 'ali shod*, which, out of respect for the shah, they sealed at the bottom of the document.[373] The importance of the function was such that in case of a very effective *monshi al-mamalek* the shah was averse to fill the space that was left in case of his death. "Mir Zakariya, the *monshi al-mamalek*, had such a good public record, that after his death no one was appointed to the office of *monshi al-mamalek*."[374] According to Nasiri, the function of *monshi al-mamalek* had been in the Nasiri Ordubadi family since the foundation of the Safavid dynasty. Table 1.7, however, suggests otherwise. The Nasiri family clearly had a firm grip on the function for much of the 17th century, but had to share it with other families (such as the Jaberi Ansaris). Nevertheless, Nasiri, when discussing the remuneration of the *monshi al-mamalek*, mentions that part of his income was from being *darugheh* of the town of Ordubad. He also mentions that the traditional title for the *monshi al-mamalek* included the term *"be'l-erth va estheqaq"* (by right of inheritance and entitlement).[375]

---

370 John Chardin, p. 97.
371 Natanzi, p. 40.
372 Aubin, "Soufis", p. 30, n. 115.
373 Qomi, vol. 2, p. 816.
374 Savory, *History*, vol. 1, p. 263.
375 Nasiri, *Alqab*, p. 52.

The *monshi al-mamalek*'s position was challenged and later considerably weakened and overtaken by the increasingly important role that the *majles-nevis* played in government affairs after 1600. The function of *majles-nevis*, also known as *vaqaye'-nevis* or *vaqaye'-negar*, existed prior to the Safavid era.[376] Under Tahmasp I, Mirak Beg[377] and Mir Monshi Hoseini were *majles-nevis*, the latter till the end of Tahmasp I's reign.[378] The change in the importance of this function was initiated by Esma'il II, but formalized only under 'Abbas I, probably as of 1603, as part of a chancellory reform (see below). Mirza Mohammad Monshi was *majles nevis-e majles-e behesht-ayin* as well as private secretary to the shah or *monshi-ye khasseh-ye sharifeh*. He was confirmed in this position by Shah Esma'il II who placed him above all other secretaries and made him a close companion (*anis-e majles-e khass*). Mirza Mohammad Monshi further had to write the *toghra* (introductory formulas) on decrees (*parvanchehs*), which recorded the decisions taken by a special judicial tribunal created by Esma'il II. These *parvanchehs* were written by a scribe attached to this court, who was appointed by Mirza Mohammad Monshi.[379] He also was reported to have written Esma'il's II order to have 'Abbas Mirza killed, reason by Shah Mohammad Khodabandeh wanted to have him excuted when he acceded to the throne.[380]

Table 1.7 List of *monshi*s al-mamalek

Khvajeh 'Atiq 'Ali[381]	907/1501-02
Mir Mohammad Hadi Shirazi[382]	919/1513-4
?	
Mir Monshi Hoseini Qomi[383]	938-40/1531-34
Mir Zakariya[384]	940/1534

---

[376] Khvandamir, vol. 4, p. 219. In general see Hinz, Walther. "Die persische Geheimkanzlei im Mittelalter", im: *Westöstliche Abhandlungen. Festschrift für Rudolf Tschudi*. Wiesbaden 1954, pp. 342-54.

[377] Savory, *History*, vol. 2, p. 914.

[378] Minorsky, *Calligraphers*, p. 78. There was also a *vazir-e khasseh* and a *majles-nevis* in Seistan, who were also known as *razdar* and *moharrem-e ashraf*. Seistani, p. 446.

[379] Natanzi, pp. 29-30, 40. According to Nasiri, *Alqab*, p. 51 the function of *monshi al-mamalek* declined after 'Abbas I had created the functions of *majles-nevis* and *mostoufi-ye khasseh*. Although the latter part of information is clearly wrong Nasiri confirms that the decline was caused by the growth of the importance of the *khasseh* administration.

[380] Molla Jalal, p. 41.

[381] Glassen, p. 209.

[382] Montazer-Saheb, p. 496.

[383] Minorsky, *Calligraphers*, p. 76.

[384] "After his death no one was appointed to the office of *monshi al-mamalek*. "Savory, *History*, vol. 1, p. 263.

Table 1.7 (continued)

Kvajeh Mirak[385]	d. 943/1536
Mohammad Beg[386]	943/1536
Mirza Kafi[387]	d. 969/1561
Qadi 'Abdollah Joveini[388]	970s/1560s
Mohammad Beg[389]	d. 982/1574
Khvajeh 'Ala al-Din Mansur[390]	982-984/1574-1576
Mirza Mohammad [Kermani][391]	984-5/1576-85
Khvajeh Malek Mohammad Yazdi[392]	994/1585-6
?	
Mirza Abdo'l-Hosein Ordubadi Nasiri[393]	1017-52/1608-42
?	
Mirza Zein al-'Abedin Ordubadi Nasiri[394]	d.1090s/1680s
?	
Mirza Yahya Jaberi[395]	1126-27/1714-15
Mirza Rafi'a[396]	1127-35/1716-22
Mirza Rafi'a Jaberi[397]	1135/1722
?	
Mirza Taqi Shirazi[398]	1142-49/1729-36

---

[385] Minorsky, *Calligraphers*, p. 92.

[386] Kh. Mirak was succeeded by Mohammad Beg, d. 982/1574, according to Minorsky, *Calligraphers*, p. 92 which cannot be right. However, he was twice *monshi al-mamalek*. Qomi, vol. 1, p. 590.

[387] Savory, *History*, vol. 2, p. 913; Minorsky, *Calligraphers*, p. 93.

[388] Monshi, p. 167; Savory, *History*, vol. 1, p. 263.

[389] Kh. Mirak was succeeded by Mohammad Beg, d. 982/1574, according to Minorsky, *Calligraphers*, p. 92 which cannot be right. However, he was twice *monshi al-mamalek*. Qomi, vol. 1, p. 590.

[390] Minorsky, *Calligraphers*, p. 96. Savory, *History*, vol. 1, 263.

[391] He was *monshi al-mamalek* under Esma'il II and Khodabandeh. In 1587, he was appointed grand vizier. Savory, *History*, vol. 1, p. 263, 512; Minorsky, *Calligraphers*, p. 92

[392] Qomi, vol. 2, p. 816.

[393] Mirza 'Abdol-Hosein Adham Beg Ordubadi Nasiri, brother of Hatem Beg the grand vizier, was *monshi al-mamalek* during the entire reign. Savory, *History*, vol. 2, p. 1007; Yusef, p. 91, 282.

[394] Nasiri, *Dastur*, p. forty-eight; Nasrabadi, p. 72. He was the son of Mirza 'Abdo'l-Hosein, and brother to Mirza Mohammad Reza, *majles-nevis*.

[395] *ARA*, KA 1740 (27/9/14), f. 2265vs. He was not a friend of the VOC.

[396] Floor, *Bar Oftadan*, p. 100 where he is wrongly identified as his namesake and successor, the author of the DM.

[397] He died in 1728. Floor, *Bar Oftadan*, p. 100; Ibid., *Afghan Occupation*, p. 85.

[398] *ARA*, VOC 2168, f. 575. He had great influence over Nader Shah, whose deputy *nazer* he was at the same time. VOC 2416 (22/12/1735), f. 721. His own clerk and deputy was Aqa Ja'far Jaberi "who was the key to his head." VOC 2417 (12/9/1736), f. 1302.

According to Röhrborn the reason for the eclipse of the *monshi al-mamalek* by the *majles-nevis* was the need for secrecy. However, the *monshi al-mamalek* always had a close relationship with the shah as well. In fact, the DM states that the *monshi al-mamalek* "was always one of the close companions of the king and a confidant of his secret correspondence."[399] Secrecy therefore was not foreign to the *monshi al-mamalek*. Also, the argument that the shah wanted to keep his correspondence with the governors confidential is not convincing either. Before the *majles-nevis* was charged with that task it had been done by the *monshi al-mamalek*. Also, that correspondence had to be cleared by the grand vizier, who dispatched those documents and received the replies.[400] The more likely reason is the significant growth of the *khasseh* domains, which meant that the *majles-nevis* automatically had to play a larger role than before. For much of the correspondence, decision memos and decrees now referred to *khasseh* domains, whereas before they did mainly to *mamalek* lands. This is also suggested by 'Ali Naqi Nasiri (*majles-nevis* 1728-32), who argued that 'Abbas I created the function, because the traditional chancellery took too long in replying to the many petitions and documents that reached the shah, when the country was in turmoil. Whatever the case may be, under Shah 'Abbas I an administrative reform took place. This probably began in 1603, for the earliest known decrees showing these administrative changes bear this date. In the 16th century the correspondence between shah and governors took the form of *parvancheh*s, which were drawn up by the *monshi al-mamalek*. However, 'Abbas I gave this charge to the *majles-nevis*, who moreover, did not use the *parvancheh*, but a type of document called *raqam*. The *majles-nevis* specifically had to write the *toghra* or introductory formula: *hokm-e jahan-e mota' shod*, in black ink. The first such *raqam* is known from 1012/1603.[401]

Abu'l-Ma'ali was *majles-nevis* of 'Abbas I, who respected him so much that he said "my seal has no weight (*e'tebar*), but the writing of the *mir* does."[402] Yusef also states that he was the *majles-nevis* of 'Abbas I. Despite this influential position of Abu'l-Ma'ali, the *majles-nevis'* jurisdiction remained limited to the correspondence between shah and governors, however. In Safi I's days the drafting of the appointment letters for all higher officials (*vakil*; *nazer*; *vazir-e koll*; *mostoufi-ye mamalek*; *divan-begi*; *emir al-omara*) was still the prerogative of the *monshi al-*

---

[399] DM, p. 80.

[400] Röhrborn, *Regierung*, p. 30; Ibid., "Staatskanzlei", pp. 315-17. See e.g. Matthee, "Career", p. 34 where Mohammad Beg, the grand vizier, controlled the flow of information between the shah and the governors.

[401] Papaziyan, A.D. *Persidskie Dokumenty Matenadarana I, Ukazy, vypusk vtoroi (1601-1650)*, Erivan 1959, doc. 1; Nasiri, *Alqab*, pp. 27, 51.

[402] Nasrabadi, p. 70.

mamalek.[403] Nevertheless, the *monshi al-mamalek* is hardly mentioned by European travellers, who mention, however, his bureaucratic counterpart, the *majles-nevis* and emphasize the importance of that function. Olearius writes that the *majles-nevis* had to draft general edicts. He also had to countersign all income and expenditure documents.[404] These appointment diplomas continued to take the form of a *parvancheh* written by the *monshi al-mamalek* till at least in the 1650s. The earliest known *raqam*-appointment diploma, written by the *majles-nevis*, dates from 1071/1661, while after that date many more examples are known. The *monshi al-mamalek*'s role was thereafter limited to writing diplomas for provincial viziers and lower staff as well as correspondence to foreign powers. Henceforth, all correspondence with the governors was read by the *majles-nevis*, who recorded the shah's reaction to each point, and prepared a draft *raqam*, if this was required, based on these notes.[405] He had an annual salary of 200 tomans in 1660.[406] Another indication of the reduced importance of the *monshi al-mamalek* was the fact that towards the end of the Safavid reign he held a lower seat in the royal council than before. Those office holders, who had been seated below him, such as the *mostoufi-ye khasseh*, gradually had been placed higher than he. [407]

The *monshi al-mamalek*'s function generally consisted of the writing of the revenue assignment diplomas of the governors and the orders for the various modes of payments for the *divan* staff. Further, the caution-money orders that each person gave to the royal chancellery, decisions that were written on the inside of the precepts of the *sadr*s, the *shajarah* documents for the *kholafa*, "as well as orders, decrees and so on that were written by the scribes using the drafts of the *monshi al-mamalek* which he embellished and adorned (*mohalla*) by drawing different signatures (*toghra*s) in red ink and gold-ink, each of which was peculiar to [a type of] decree, command."[408]

Majles-Nevis

The *majles-nevis* was also known as *vazir-e chap*, because he sat on the left side of the grand vizier. The interpretation given by all scholars that he sat on the left side of the shah in the royal council, while the grand vizier sat on the right side (*vazir-e rast*), is incorrect, and is neither borne out by Chardin, Kaempfer and other observers nor by what we know of his place

---

[403] Esfahani, p. 47.

[404] Olearius, p. 671.

[405] Röhrborn, "Staatskanzlei", p. 315-7; Richard, vol. 1, p. 294 has a letter by du Mans of 1684 which stated that it was the *monshi al-mamalek*'s responsibility to write the foreign correspondance.

[406] Richard, vol. 2, p. 18. For more detailed information see Nasiri, *Alqab*, pp. 51, 65

[407] Nasiri, *Alqab*, p. 51.

[408] DM, p. 80; Nasiri, *Alqab*, pp. 50-53.

in the council.[409] Du Mans gives conflicting information on the subject. On the one hand he records that the *majles-nevis* sat on the left side, while elsewhere he writes that he was on the right side.[410] This confusion may have been caused by a mix-up by the contemporary observers whether they meant to the left of the shah, or to the left of the observer. The Dutch embassy in 1652 noted that the *majles-nevis* was seated on the same side as the grand vizier, who sat on the left, not the right, side of the shah.[411] He also was the deputy of the grand vizier for whom he acted in his absence. He had to keep the shah and the privy council informed of what occurred in the country. To that end there were provincial *vaqaye'-nevis*es who reported to him. He also was a kind a foreign minister, for he was the person to see to learn how relations were with other powers, what treaties there existed, etc. For this reason all foreigners, including ambassadors, made sure to see him and to leave their documents with him, which he filed. The *majles-nevis* further registered the time of their arrival, the purpose of their visit, the nature of their requests and what had been decided. He read the letters, which the grand vizier gave to him, to the shah in the public council.[412] The Dutch embassy in 1652 also noted that the *majles-nevis* played an important part in the negotiations and consequently they were much in contact with him.[413] His annual salary amounted to 1,000 tomans.[414]

Table 1.8 List of *majles-nevis*

Mirak Beg Ordubadi[415]	in the 1560s
Mir Monshi Hoseini[416]	till 984/1576
Mirza Mohammad Monshi	984-85/1576-77
Hatem Beg Ordubadi[417]	997/1588-9
?	
Mir Feizollah[418]	1018-19/1609-11

---

[409] Chardin, vol. 5, p. 343; TM, p. 53.

[410] Richard, vol. 2, pp. 13, 270, 295.

[411] Hotz, pp. 149-50. The order of precedence was grand-vizier, *qurchi-bashi*, *qollar-aghasi*, *nazer*, *mir akhor-bashi* and *majles-nevis*, who thus sat on the left side of the grand vizier.

[412] Chardin, vol. 5, p. 343-4; Richard, vol. 2, p. 270; Della Valle, Pietro. "Extract of the Travels of Della Valle", in John Pinkerton, *A General Collection of Voyages and Travels*, (London, 1811), vol. 9, p. 65.

[413] Hotz, pp. 148, 150, 163, 184, 207, 209, 218, 244, 255.

[414] Richard, vol. 2, p. 13.

[415] Savory, *History*, vol. 2, p. 914. He was a brother of Hatem Beg, one of his successors and later grand-vizier. Nasiri, *Dastur*, p. forty-five.

[416] Minorsky, *Calligraphers*, p. 78.

[417] Yusef, p. 143.

[418] He was *vazir-e qurchiyan* when he was appointed as *majles-nevis*, which office he continued to hold when he also was appointed *vazir-e gholam*an. Savory, *History*, vol.

Table 1.8 (continued)

Mir Mirza Taher[419]	till 1030/1621
Sayyed Emir Abu'l-Ma'ali[420]	1030-37/1621-27
Mirza Mohammad Tuyserkani[421]	1037-38/1627-29
Mirza Abu Taleb Ordubadi[422]	1038-40/1629-31
Mirza Mohammad Tuyserkani[423]	1040-43/1631-34
Mirza Ma'sum[424]	1043-52/1634-42
Abu'l-Fazl Mirza Moh. Taher Vahid[425]	1052-90/1642-79
Mirza Mohammad Reza Ordubadi Nasiri[426]	1090-1105/1679-93
Mirza Abu'l Qasem Nasiri[427]	1105-10/1693-98
Mirza Mohammad Ebrahim Nasiri[428]	1110/1698-99
Mirza Hayat[429]	till 1135/1722
Mirza Sadeq[430]	1135/1722
?	
Mirza 'Ali Naqi Nasiri[431]	1142-46/1729-32

This did not make the *majles-nevis* the rival of the grand vizier as Röhrborn has suggested. Nevertheless, the *majles-nevis* had become a very important state official, second to the grand vizier and *nazer*,[432] who was a member of the *janqi* and an *'alijah*. He, moreover, had the right of immediate access to the shah, whether he was in a private or public gathering. Despite the importance of the function contemporary observers do not ascribe to such a view. Kaempfer only had an inkling of the *majles-nevis*' responsibilities. He wrote, his main task "is to record in his diary the

---

2, p. 1035. Carmelites, vol. 1, p. 186.

[419] Nasrabadi, pp. 83-4.

[420] He was charged with the conversion of the Armenians living around Isfahan in 1030/1621-2. Savory, *History*, vol. 2, p. 1183, 1231 (his career); Yusef, p. 283; Carmelites, vol. 1, p. 249.

[421] Yusef, p. 161; Esfahani, p. 128.

[422] He became grand vizier. Esfahani, p. 40; Yusef, pp. 260, 274.

[423] Yusef, p. 161; Esfahani, p. 128.

[424] Esfahani, pp. 183, 276; Olearius, p. 671.

[425] Vahid Qazvini, p. 72; Shamlu, p. 427; Richard, vol. 1, p. 165, n. 73; vol. 2, p. 270.

[426] Bardsiri, p. 512; *ARA*, VOC 1410, (14/1/1685) (*vaqaye'- negar*); Nasiri, *Dastur*, p. forty-eight.

[427] Nasiri, *Dastur*, pp. 44, 55.

[428] He was the grandson of the former grand vizier Taleb Khan and still alive in 1126/1714. Nasiri, *Dastur*, pp. forty-nine, fifty-one, 273.

[429] *ARA*, VOC 2416, f. 948

[430] Mostoufi, p. 140. He fled with Tahmasp Mirza from Isfahan in June 1722.

[431] *ARA*, VOC 3168, f. 576; VOC 2168 (1/6/1730), f. 896; VOC 2255 (3/11/1731), f. 1814. He was one of the few grandees appointed, due to the lack of funds. The other grandees were the *divan-begi* and the *nazer-e boyutat*. VOC 2168 (30/3/1730), f. 199-200.

[432] TM, p. 54; Bedik, p. 17.

shah's decisions and remarks, the good wishes brought by ambassadors as well as decisions and replies to them."[433] Some 15 years later, Sanson had a better, but still limited, appreciation, when he wrote that "The Vaki-Anevis, who is the only Secretary of State, is always seated near the King, that he may the better take notice of his Orders. 'Tis he that keeps account of the Expences of which he must be responsible to the Etmadaulet [grand vizier]. He writes all the Orders and Letters which the King sends to foreign Princes. He is also the Historiographer of Persia. He makes a Journal of all that passes every Year, and reads it to the King and all the Court, the First Day of the ensuing."[434] The *majles-nevis* also read out in a loud voice the presents that a foreign ambassador had presented to the shah at the moment that these were submitted for general viewing.[435]

Persian sources confirm what contemporary travelers write about the *majles-nevis*, but expand on the latter's tasks. He and his staff wrote down all oral orders given by the shah and those written down in a *ta'liqeh* or instruction by the grand vizier or the leading magnates (*moqarrab*s). He also was responsible for writing all the appointment diplomas of the emirs, *begler-begis*, governors, *soltan*s, viziers and *mostoufi*s of the *khasseh* (royal household) department and whatever concerned the *khasseh*. To that end draft standard texts were used, which existed in the chancellory. He also had the exclusive right to draw the *toghra* in black and the selection of the titles. He was one of the *omara-ye janqi*, and he made a summary report of what said in the royal council meetings.[436] The *majles-nevis* therefore always was in the shah's presence and summarized petitions and reports sent to the shah, of which he also had to keep a register. He also wrote the shah's decisions and replies to these petitions, which he read out loud in the council, once these had been determined. Finally, he had the right to submit requests for stipends by seminary students and the needy to the shah. For those stipends that were granted and charged to the *khasseh* department he wrote the draft orders. When charged to the *mamalek* department this task was discharged by the *monshi al-mamalek*.[437]

The Staff of the Dar al-ensha

Both the *monshi al-mamalek* and the *majles-nevis* were assisted by the staff of the *dar al-ensha*, which consisted of at least 40 scribes in 1637. It was only under Soleiman that the *majles-nevis* was assigned as many as 30 persons. Prior to that period he had only three clerks. By that time he had totally eclipsed the office of *monshi al-mamalek*, who did not work

---

[433] Kaempfer, *Am Hofe*, p. 80.

[434] Sanson, p. 24.

[435] Valentijn, F. *Oud en Nieuw Oost-Indien* 5 vols. (Dordrecht-Amsterdam 1726), vol. 5, p. 277.

[436] DM, pp. 61-2.

[437] DM, p. 61-2; Chardin, vol. 5, pp. 450-1; Nasiri, *Alqab*, pp. 26-30.

anymore in the royal secretariat, but at his house.[438] At the lower end there were the *farrash*es and *'azab*s. These were under the *'azab-bashi*. It was his task to manage the operational records, i.e. those which had not yet been stored. It was further the responsibility of the *daftardar* to take care of all stored records. His task, at the end of the Safavid regime, does not appear to have been onerous, because the TM remarks that "the files of previous years were consulted only occasionally," which were stored separately, and from which he had to protect from mice and dust. However, every morning he had to come to the office before the secretariat's managers to have the various files that they would be working on were ready for them. He was also the last to leave and put away the files, so that no harm would befall them.[439] Higher in rank were the junior scribes, who were generically known as *moharrer*, *kateb* or *nevisandeh*. The more accomplished clerks were called *monshi*s, and they were specifically assigned to one or the other of the state secretaries.[440] For example, the *raqam*s were written by a clerk called the *raqam-nevis*.[441] Chardin states that one of the three secretaries who draw up diplomas is "the *raqam-nevis* who only deals with state matters."[442] The latter as well as eight other clerks were subordinates of the *majles-nevis*.[443] The third secretary mentioned by Chardin "is the *hokm-nevis*, i.e. the writer of decrees of all those that require the small seal, both for state and domain affairs.[444] The documents were written with a pen or *qalam* made of a small Indian reed.[445] In the 1630s, the villages of Dermen and Saru, in the Qazvin area, were famous for the good scribes they produced.[446]

Persian sources mention additional staff. The *monshi-ye divan* was a subordinate of the *monshi al-mamalek*. He wrote caution-money orders in accordance with the instructions of the grand vizier.[447] The *nameh-nevis* also was a subordinate of the *monshi al-mamalek*. He wrote the letters that were sent to foreign rulers. Another clerk was known as the *toghra-nevis*, who specialized in writing the *intitulatio* (*'onvan* and *toghra*) of the decrees.[448] In addition there were 26 *monshi*s who wrote all the *parvaneh*s and decrees at the instruction of the *mostoufi al-mamalek* and the *monshi*

---

[438] Olearius, p. 671; Nasiri, *Alqab*, p. 27, 53, 63.

[439] TM, p. 77; Nasiri, *Alqab*, pp. 62-3. These functions are not mentioned by the DM. The *'azab-bashi* is listed by Asaf, Mohammad Hashem. "Rostam al-Hokoma", *Rostam al-Tavarikh*, ed. Mohammad Moshiri (Tehran, 1348/1969), p. 101.

[440] Minorsky, *Calligraphers*, p. 97.

[441] DM, p. 115.

[442] Chardin, vol. 5, p. 451.

[443] DM, pp. 62, 115; Molla Jalal, p. 390.

[444] Chardin, vol. 5, p. 451.

[445] Richard, vol. 2, p. 120.

[446] Olearius, p. 671.

[447] DM, p. 116; *monshi-ye divan-e a'la*. Qomi, vol. 1, p. 263, 590 (important enough to mention his death; he held the rank of *beg*).

[448] Molla Jalal, p. 390; Qomi, vol. 1, p. 271; DM, pp. 81, 116.

al-mamalek. These clerks were different from the *kateb*s and *nevisandeh*s, who were lower ranking scribes.[449] Other clerks were attached to one of the pillars of the state such as the *saheb-raqam* or "the two secretaries of the E'temad al-Douleh, who dispatch all the orders of the court."[450] The *saheb-raqam* should not be confused with the *raqam-nevis*. In addition to these scribes we also find mention of the *ta'liq-nevis*, who undoubtedly wrote documents in the *ta'liq* style.[451] The *divan-nevis* was the clerk of the *divan*.[452] The *keshik-nevis* wrote the payment orders for the guards (*keshikan*) of the guardhouse.[453] The *methal-nevis* wrote precepts or *amtheleh* of the *sadr*.[454] Finally, there was the *parvanehchi* or *parvanchi* (secretary), who was in attendance to the shah or prince to write down his orders.[455]

Three Bureaucratic Administrative Procedural Periods.

It is of interest to note that even in the use of official documents the changes in political authority and in particular the shift in power from the state (*mamalek*) to the royal household (*khasseh*) administration is reflected. During the *first* period, in the beginning of the regime, the *neshan* document prevailed, which was partly replaced by the *parvancheh* after 1533. However, both were state (*mamalek*) administration documents and were gradually replaced by the *raqam*, which was a royal household (*khasseh*) document after 1603. The chancellery of Esma'il I, which was headed and staffed by former Aq-Qoyunlu viziers and clerks, reflected the practices of the previous regime.

The *second* period starts under Tahmasp I, when changes were made in administrative and bureaucratic practices reflecting his desire to exert greater control over the country's affairs. Stylistic formulas were introduced, with relevant change in corresponding seals, which set these new documents apart from preceding similar documents. The innovations were simply introductory formulas which gave the documents concerned only then authority when these formulas introduced the text. This formula was written down by the head of the administration after the text of the

---

[449] *kateb-e daftarkhaneh*. Qomi, vol. 1, p. 247; *nevisandeh-ye daftar*, Qomi, vol. 2, p. 617.

[450] Sanson, p. 20; Rumlu, p. 533; Yusef, p. 208.

[451] Valeh Esfahani, p. 469.

[452] Monshi, vol. 2, p. 1620.

[453] DM, pp. 115-6; Nasiri, *Alqab*, p. 67; Chardin, vol. 5, p. 374; Mirza 'Emad the *keshik-nevis* in 1043/1635, Astarabadi, p. 250.

[454] DM, p. 89.

[455] Membré, Michele. *Relazione*, ed. G.C. Scarcia (Rome, 1969). English translation A.H. Morton, *Mission to the Lord Sophy of Persia (1539-1542)* (SOAS; London, 1993), pp. 20, 21, 39; Shah Tahmasp, p. 23; Yusef, p. 249; Valeh Esfahani, p. 753. See on the *parvanehchi* prior to the Safavids: Roemer, Hans Robert. *Staatsschreiben der Timuridenzeit. Das Sharafnama des 'Abdallah Marwarid in kritischer Auswertung*, Wiesbaden 1952, p. 198.

document had been finalized and been submitted for his review. Also, the type of formula characterized a document and therefore its purpose could not be misunderstood.

Tahmasp's I innovations were introduced in November 1533/Jomada II 940 and heralded the imposition of his authority on the Qezelbash emirs after ten years of tutelage. It is during that month that documents with the two new formulas *farman-e homayun shod* and *farman-e homayun sharaf-e nafadh yaft* were introduced for the first time. Although documents issued by Esma'il I also sometimes have this formula, its intent was a different one than of those after November 1533, for there is no misunderstanding the purpose of the royal documents bearing these formulas after that date. These introductory formulas were used till the end of the Safavid reign. In accordance with the rules (*dastur al-'amal*) laid down by Tahmasp I, which (with some exceptions) were still valid and being applied down to the end of the Safavid dynasty, the diplomas (*manashir*) and decrees (*ahkam*) were of three types, to wit: the *neshan*, the *parvancheh*, and the *raqam*.

[a] The *neshan* was especially used for the granting of tax exemptions (*soyurghals*), and appointment diplomas for shrine managers (*motavallis*) and other high state functions (*makhsus-e soyurghal va touliyat va manaseb*). For the latter appointments, later also the *parvancheh-ye sharaf-e nafadh* was used, certainly until the reign of Esma'il II. Both the *neshan* and the *parvancheh* were written in the office of the *monshi al-mamalek*.

Because the *mohrdars* were entitled to chancellory fees (*doshallek*) they put their contra-seal on the backside of the document once they had received their fee. Up to the reforms of 'Abbas I, the shah would write *khutima* (it has been sealed) in the margin of the *neshan*.[456] Thereafter, diplomas for *soyurghals*, were usually made out as a *parvancheh*. Also in this case the contra-seal was put on the back of the document. The *neshan* was written in the *ta'liqeh* manner, i.e. the first two lines were written as half lines so as to make space for the seal under the *toghra* opposite the half lines.

The introductory formula (*toghra*) of the *neshan* was different from that of the *parvancheh* and read "*al-hokm lillah al-mo'aiyad min 'inda 'llah* [name shah] *sözümiz.*" This introductory formula (*toghra*) was written in such a way that the names of the 12 emams each fit into a separate field. Until some time in the reign of 'Abbas I this introductory formula was "*al-hokm lillah* [name shah] *sözümiz.*" Thus, the early Safavid correspondence continued to use the *sözümiz* formula, prominently displayed in the center on the top of the original documents. This formula was used up to the beginning of the 17th century. Under Safi I the term was persianized into *syozumiz*, while graphically it was depicted

---

456 The *mohr-e khutima* was used when the Shah wrote in the margin of a *neshan* "*khutima*".

as a quadrant, with the names of the 12 Shi'ite Emams. However, under 'Abbas II the *sözümiz* disappeared entirely. Its latest occurrence in Safavid usage, written as *suzom*, is in a decree by the *vali* of Georgia dated 1067/1657. This disappearance of the *sözümiz* formula undoubtedly was due to the fact that it was written on a *neshan* or a *parvancheh*, documents which after the 1650s were hardly used anymore.[457]

[b] The *parvancheh*, with the introduction formula *farman-e homayun sharaf-nafadh*, was used for the grants of revenue assignments (*teyul*s) to emirs, for the appointment to high office, for victory announcements (*fathnameh*s), and for orders (*ahkam*) that were sent to the emirs and magnates of the provinces. All were sealed by the *mohrdar*. The heading (*'onvan*) of the *parvancheh-ye sharaf-e nafadh* was like that of the *neshan*, but without the *bismillah* formula. Also, in case of a victory announcement (*fathnameh*) the heading (*'onvan*) was different.[458] The simple *parvancheh* had as heading (*'onvan*): "*huwa*" and "*al-mulk lillah*", while its introductory formula (*toghra*) was "*farman-e homayun shod*". It was used for the revenue and expenditure affairs of the chancellery, *barat*s (payment vouchers) and simple routine matters. The simple *parvancheh* was also used for the grants of a revenue assignment (*teyul*) or wages (*hamehsaleh*), and decisions concerning fiscal issues.

[c] the *raqam*, was originally only an instruction or decision memorandum. It was not written by the office of the *monshi al-mamalek*, but by the vizier of the issuing department. For example, the *vazir-e qurchi* or the *lashkar-nevis* would write a *raqam-e teyul* or *teyulnameh* (grant of a revenue assignment), from there it went to the secretariat (*daftar*), where accountants (*mostoufis*) would make a draft text (*mosavvadeh*) with the exact specification of the amount and allocation of the payment. Based on this draft a *parvancheh* would be made out, which was sent to the *monshi al-mamalek*. The *raqam* remained in the secretariat as a document of record (*sanad*). *Raqam*s for the payment of wages (*mavajeb*) of troops were written by the vizier of the relevant corps and handed to the recipient.[459] The *raqam* for the grant of a robe of honor (*khal'at*) was written by the bookkeeper (*moshref*) of the tailor department

---

[457] Puturidze, V.S. *Gruzino-Persidskie Istoriricheskie Dokumenty* (Tiflis 1955), doc. 117.

[458] The *inna fatahna* seal, which was used on documents dealing with the state treasury's revenues and expenditures. No examples are known. In Aq-Qoyunly times the *parvaneh* may have been of greater importance given the fact that under Ya'qub there was a separate *divan-e parvanehchi*. Woods, p. 11.

[459] The seal of expenditures and revenues or the *mohr-e dad o setad* was used on all royal orders that bore the *toghra* "*farman-e homayun shod*". On the circle band the names of the 12 emams were engraved. They came in both round, and round with arched (*mehrab*) forms. This seal was also used by Esma'il I on documents that had no *toghra* (see Busse, *Untersuchungen*, docs. 7 and 5; Qa'em-Maqami, Jahangir. *Moqaddameh'i bar shenakht-e asnad-e tarikhi az Jala'iriyan ta Pahlavi*, Tehran 1350/1971. p. 359). This document may be the forerunner of the simple *parvancheh*.

(*khayyat-khaneh*) and given to the recipient.[460] None of these *raqam*s (memoranda) displayed the introductory formula (*toghra*) and therefore may just have served the practical internal needs of the chancellery, while at the same time they signalled the completion of a particular bureaucratic process, such as the payment of wages to a particular person. These *raqam*s (for *teyul*s, salaries), therefore, were all sealed with the chancellery's draft seal (*mohr-e mosavvadeh*), with the exception of the *raqam-e khal'at*, which was sealed with the rectangular seal kept by the *mohrdar*.[461] The term *ta'liqeh* also was used to denote a decision memorandum or instruction by the grand vizier and other pillars of the state.[462]

In addition to the *neshan*, *parvancheh* and *raqam* there were also documents which had neither the *syozumiz* nor the other formulas, but simply started with formulas such as "*az ebteda*" or "*chun dar in*". These documents were standard texts, usually for the appointment to a low government function or assignment of an income. These documents did not carry the normal royal seals, but usually only the draft or *mosavvadeh* seal of the royal secretariat. Finally, there were the documents that were addressed to the *vakil* or regent and the *shajareh* appointment diplomas for the *khalifeh*s. In the former case the formula "*farman-e homayun*" was used. The latter were not sealed by the royal secretariat until 1603.[463]

A decision (*hokm*) in response to a petition ('*arzeh-ye divan*) was written above the petition's heading ('*onvan*), while the formula of "*hokm-e jahan mota' shod*" as introduction (*toghra*) was also used. However, the decision was sealed with the draft seal (*mohr-e mosavvadeh*). Leasing contracts (*shartnamehcheh-ye ejarat*) also had an introductory formula (*toghra*), but because they were written by *mostoufi*s and not by *monshi*s they were not classified as patents, diplomas, or decrees. The introductory formula (*toghra*) that the *monshi al-mamalek* would write over the lease contract was *Huwa al-ghani* with gold ink, or *min divani'l-a'la* by the chancellery staff in red ink.[464]

The **third** period began when 'Abbas I made changes in Tahmasp I's administrative procedures. Tax exemptions (*soyurghal*s) were not granted anymore per *neshan*, but per *parvancheh* with the introduction formula *farman-e homayun sharaf-e nafadh yaft*. Also, the *raqam* had become a much more widespread document by that time. The introduction of a new

---

460 The *mohr-e raqam-e khal'at*. This seal was also kept by the *mohrdar*. The *moshref* of the *khayyat-khaneh* wrote the *raqam* in *siyaq*. On the border of the seal the names of the 12 emams were written. It was quadrangular in form. See Busse, *Untersuchungen*, p. 51; Chardin, plate XXXI.

461 Röhrborn, "Staatskanzlei", pp. 335-36.

462 Röhrborn, "Staatskanzlei", p. 321.

463 Schimkoreit, Renate. *Regesten publizierter safawidischer Herrscherurkunden*. Berlin 1982, pp. 27-9.

464 Röhrborn, "Staatskanzlei", p. 337.

toghra or introduction formula: *hokm-e jahan-e mota' shod* which probably took place in 1603, was the result of this reform. It was a formula written in black ink by the *majles-nevis* only, who had become the head of the administration of the royal household (*khasseh*) part of the bureaucracy, while the state administration or *mamalek* part, was under the *monshi al-mamalek*.

By the end of the 'Abbas I's reign most of the *raqam*s or decision memoranda that were standard in the 16th century were not used anymore. The decision memorandum for the grant of a revenue assignment (*raqam-e teyul*) had fallen into disuse because a revenue assignment (*teyul*) was often attached to an office. The appointment decree or *raqam* invariably mentioned the office as well as the attached revenue assignment. A similar fate befell the salary decree (*raqam-e mavajeb*). The robe of honor decree (*raqam-e khal'at*) was henceforth drafted by the *majles-nevis* at the oral instruction by the shah. This meant that all the old-style *raqam*s or decision memoranda were replaced by the new style *raqam* that was written in the royal secretariat by the *majles-nevis* with the introductory formula (*toghra*) "*hokm-e jahan mota' shod*". This *raqam*, which came into being in 1603, was sealed with the royal signet seal (*mohr-e mobarak-e angoshtar-e homayun*). When the term "*hokm-e jahan mota' shod*" was used in documents which had been drawn up by the *divan-begi* it was written in red, and not black ink as was usual.[465] This introductory formula also remained in use till the end of the Safavid reign in 1736.

The subject matter of these new *raqam*s was limited however to specific subjects such as correspondence with governors till Safi's I reign. However, under 'Abbas II the *majles-nevis* also was given the prerogative to write the diplomas for appointments of governors and other important emirs, viziers, and *mostoufi*s. Henceforth, the *monshi al-mamalek* only wrote the diplomas for lower provincial officials. More documents (*raqam*s) with the formula "*hokm-e jahan-e mota' shod*" have survived than those documents (*parvancheh*) with the formula "*farman-e homayun*". This may suggest that the office of *majles-nevis* had indeed become more important than that of the *monshi al-mamalek* as the other available information also indicates.

Seals

The bureaucratic changes were also reflected in the seals that were used to 'officialize' and authenticate the documents concerned. Shah Esma'il I used two types of seals. i.e.: a simple, round seal and a simple pear-shaped seal. Tahmasp I used a traditional pear-shaped seal for some time, as well as two new types of seal to reflect the changes in bureaucratic procedures.

---

[465] See however Semsar, Mohammad Hasan. "Du farman va mohri tazeh as padeshahan-e Safaviyeh va Zandiyeh," *BT* 8 (1352/1973), p. 80f. where it seems that an official other than the *divan-begi* signed in red, because it dealt with a fiscal issue.

The main difference in form was that the two new seals had various sections. The seal used for the *farman-e homayun sharaf-e nafadh* documents was a round seal with a concentric circle and a roof-like top and was known as the *mohr-e sharaf-e nafadh*, or *mohr-e khasseh*.[466] This seal was larger if used for correspondence to foreign powers. The seal used for the *farman-e homayun shod* documents was round with a concentric circle and was known as *mohr-e homayun* or *mohr-ashraf*, and was used for appointment diplomas and the like.[467] However, Tahmasp I also used the small seal (*mohr-e kuchek*) to seal letters to foreign princes.[468] These seals continued to be used by Tahmasp I's successors, though there were changes. Under Esma'il II, the judgements and mandates of the court of justice were to be embellished with the endorsement "ratified by the supreme *divan*" and were to bear the imprint of the *mehr-athar* seal, which shah Esma'il II had allocated for this purpose, and on which had been engraved the formula "the seal of the supreme *divan*."[469]

The *mohr-e sharaf-e nafadh* was used on decrees which had the *toghra* "*farman-e homayun sharaf-e nafadh yaft*" and on *shajareh* appointment documents for *khalifehs*. On the side it had a poem by Sana'i; its form was round with an arched top. This seal with arched top was used for first time since 'Abbas I, previously it was round.[470] The *mohr-e neshan* was the same as the royal seal (*mohr-e homayun*). This seal was kept by the *mohrdar*. The seal was initially round, but later acquired an arched (*mehrabi*) top.[471] The great seal was also used for authenticating receipts of payments by the royal court.[472]

With the increased emphasis on the two-fold division of the administration (*khasseh* and *mamalek*, respectively under the *majles-nevis* and the *monshi al-mamalek*) the "*hokm-e jahan-e mota' shod*" documents, which were to dominate the administrative process in the 17th century, were sealed with the royal finger seal (*mohr-e angoshtar-e aftab-e athar*). It was also known as the *mohr-e kuchek* or small seal as well as *mohr-e thabti*; it was the royal signet-ring. This type of seal was small and mostly quadrangular or rectangular, with or without an arch. Only Shah Soleiman

---

[466] Qomi, vol. 2, pp. 668, 699.

[467] Schimkoreit, pp. 30-31, which is the best study on this subject. See also Moham-mad Hasan Semsar, "Farman-nevisi dar doureh-ye Safaviyeh", *BT* 3 (1), pp. 61-83. Natanzi, p. 37; he also mentions that this was in accordance with the *dastur al-'amal* of Tahmasp I.

[468] Afshar, Iraj ed. *'Alamara-ye Shah Tahmasp* (Tehran 1370/1991) , p. 143.

[469] Savory, *History*, vol. 1, p. 308; according to the *Khold-e Barin* this was a special seal with the text "*huwa al-'adel*". Valeh Esfahani, pp. 540, 546. No documents with these seals are known to have survived.

[470] This seal was used as of 930/1534-4. Qomi, vol. 1, p. 157; Busse, *Untersuchun-gen*, p. 49.

[471] Qa'em-maqami, *Moqaddameh'i*, p. 361; Papaziyan 1956, doc. 18.

[472] Hotz, pp. 342-3.

used, in addition to the angular seal, also a shield type seal.[473] This signet seal existed already under Tahmasp I. Eskander Monshi reports that the emirs alleged that Tahmasp I's testament had been written after his death, and his signet ring removed from his finger and the will sealed with it.[474] According to an *ensha* (administrative) manual from 1043/1634 this seal came only in regular use under Shah 'Abbas I and was rectangular, and later acquired an arch (*mehrab*).[475] The signet-ring certainly was used by 'Abbas I, who wore it either on his finger,[476] or around his neck.

Although 'Abbas I continued to use the old system he nevertheless introduced subtle changes. These reflected his policy to reduce his dependence on the Qezelbash (the *mohrdar*s were Qezelbash emirs) as well as the fact that the great seals had been kept from him by his regent (*vakil*), Morshedqoli Khan. Around 1590, we observe that the bestowal of a governorship with attached *teyul* was still done by issuing a *neshan*, but this document was now sealed with the signet seal (*mehr-e athar*), not the royal seal (*mohr-e homayun*).[477] Also, under 'Abbas I letters of amnesty were sealed with the *mehr-athar* seal.[478] An undertaking given by 'Abbas I in 1607 to the Carmelites to allow them to construct churches in each town that he took from the Turks, if the king of Spain would also take up arms against them, he also sealed with his small seal.[479] In 1618, della Valle reports that "the grand seal is not that which is in highest esteem in Persia, although it be affixed to all patents and emanations from royal authority, (it is kept by the mohurdar, or keeper of the seal,) but a small seal, which is worn in a ring by the shah himself; and which he uses in sealing all his letters to the princes and governors of provinces."[480] The small seal was used to seal a *raqam* after 'Abbas I's death to keep his demise a secret.[481] The same happened when Soleiman died, when Fazlollah Beg, the *davatdar*, took the blessed signet-ring (*angoshtar-e mobarak*).[482]

According to Chardin "The king has five different seals, three large and two small ones. The fifth one is round. The small square seal is a

---

[473] The seal that was introduced when Shah Soleiman was enthroned for the second time. It was round with an arch (*mehrabi*). It was often used on letters. Qa'em-Maqami, *Moqaddameh'i*, p. 370; Röhrborn, "Staatskanzlei", p. 340.

[474] Savory, *History*, vol. 1, p. 284.

[475] Röhrborn, "Staatskanzlei", p. 340; Busse, *Untersuchungen*, doc. 20; Qa'em-maqami, *Moqaddameh'i*, pp. 362, 364-5.

[476] Seistani, p. 516.

[477] Natanzi, p. 381.

[478] Savory, *History*, vol. 2, p. 832; he also gave the vizier unregistered rolls (*tavamer-e bayaz*) sealed with the *mehr-athar* seal authorizing him to issue orders for whatever he deemed necessary. Ibid., vol. 2, p. 968.

[479] Carmelites, vol. 1, p. 93.

[480] della Valle, p. 58.

[481] Esfahani, p. 34.

[482] Nasiri, *Dastur*, p. 20.

beautiful ruby, and is the most respected of the seals, it is the shah's own seal that hangs around his neck, which all shahs since 'Abbas I have done. The large seals are called *homayun*; the small ones *hokm-e jahan mota'* *shod.* The other small seal, is an emerald, and is kept by an eunuch who is guardian of the royal treasury. The large seals are engraved on thick turquoises, and are in use since 'Abbas I. The great square seal is put on decrees concerning the entire royal domains, the other one concerning the entire country such as treaties, letters to foreign countries, and patents. The third one, which is round, is used for military affairs. The small seals are used for financial and appointment, court, military wages matters, thus for all royal household (*khasseh*) matters."[483]

The seals were pretty much uniform as to the information they contained. A prayer starting with *allahuma* with the names of the 12 emams. Further, a legend, with various standardized words such as: *huwa allah*, *hasabi allah*, etc. Often, in the center of the seal, the words *bandeh-ye shah-e vilayat* [name reigning shah] to which sometimes the year was added. A number of shahs also used legends which were peculiar to them only, whilst others only used the uniform terminology. The *mosavvadeh* or draft chancery seals generally bore the words *bandeh-ye shah vilayat* [name of shah and year] *mohr-e mosavvadeh*-ye *divan-e a'la.* The seals were generally between 2,5 and 3,5 cm wide, although some could be larger.[484]

In addition to the royal seals there was also the chancellery's draft seal, the so-called *mohr-e mosavvadeh*-ye *divan-e a'la.* In a round form it occurred already under Tahmasp I. This seal was subdivided into three parts. Under Shah Soltan Hosein both round and quadrangular, with or without arch, *mosavvadeh* seals were used. The *mosavvadeh* seal was used on decrees which had the red ink *toghra hokm-e jahan mota' shod*; further on lease documents; on orders that were written in the margin of other documents; and on payment documents which remained as records in the accountancy department.

The counter-seal of the *homayun* seal or the *mohr-e thabt-e mohr-e homayun* was kept by the *mohrdar* and was put on the backside of (*soyurghal*, *ma'afi*, *teyul*, *hamehsaleh*) grants of the emirs and on appointment diplomas. Did this mean that the *mohrdar* did not keep any longer the original seals, and only the counter seals? The *Zobdat al-Tavarikh* reports that on the accession to the throne by Safi I the *mohrdar* was ceremoniously presented with the *mohr-e chap va rast* (the left and right seals). Were these the counter seals or the original ones? As we have seen, Chardin reported that the original seals were kept in the harem.[485] Thus, given their largely ceremonial role, it is likely that the keepers of the seal only held the counter seals in the 17th century.

---

[483] Chardin, vol. 5, pp. 451-62.

[484] For more detailed information see Schimkoreit, pp. 30-34.

[485] Chardin, vol. 5, p. 453.

At the death of the shah his successor had the name of his predecessor removed from the seal.[486] Safi II gave orders to remove the name of his father from the royal seals and if possible to engrave his own name, though he preferred to have new seals made. It was finally decided to destroy the old coin seals and make new ones.[487] Four hours after Safi II's re-enthronement, as Soleiman in 1666, new seals had been made.[488]

Mohrdar

To officialize documents they needed to be sealed. To that end the shah kept a *mohrdar* or a Keeper of the Seal. European observers describes the role of the Keeper of the Seal as follows. Membré, in 1540, writes that the *mohrdar*, "that is, he who seals the King's affairs."[489] Minadoi some 30 years later submits that "there are at Casbin two great Chauncellours, whome the Persians call Mordar, whose office it is to write all the orders, Commaundementes, and letters concerning the governement of the kingdome: one of them keepeth the Seale, and the other the penne."[490] He also writes that the *mohrdar* ranked higher in importance than other administrative staff and religious officials.[491] Sanson, writing in 1690, writes that the task of the keeper of seal is that he "assists at all Ceremonies with the King's Seal."[492] The TM still considers them to be among the leading *moqarrabs al-khaqan*. However, at the same time both the DM and the TM state that the rule to appose their seals on relevant documents had fallen into disuse, thus underlining the reduction to a mostly ceremonial role of the *mohrdars*.[493]

Initially there was only one *mohrdar*. In 1533, Tahmasp I appointed a second *mohrdar*, because a second type of document and a seal peculiar to it had been created in that year, the so-called "*sharaf-e nafadh*" decree. The new *mohrdar* was not a Qezelbash emir, but an 'Iraqi sayyed, Soleiman Beg Kamuna. He held this office (*mohrdar-e mohr-e sharaf-nafadh*) till the beginning of 'Abbas I's reign.[494] This innovation remained in force till the end of the Safavid dynasty. Although Chardin states that there were three keepers of the seal, of which one, an eunuch, who remained in the harem close to the shah, he in fact also confirmed that there were two keepers of the seal. These were also called *mohrdar-bashi*. "They only put the seal on the documents and have no other task or responsibility. One of them only seals commissions for the army and

486 Chardin, vol. 5, p. 456.
487 Kaempfer, *Am Hofe*, p. 43.
488 Kaempfer, *Am Hofe*, p. 46.
489 Membré, p. 20.
490 Minadoi, pp. 67-8.
491 Minadoi, p. 68.
492 Sanson, p. 25.
493 TM, p. 62; DM, pp. 75-7.
494 Monshi, vol. 1, pp. 141, 385, 630.

military affairs, and is therefore called *mohrdar-e qoshun.*"[495] The third *mohrdar*, added by Chardin, was not a real *mohrdar*. Chardin himself, when enumerating the staff dealing with diplomas, states that there were only two keepers of the seal. What Chardin meant to convey is that the third person, an eunuch, was a keeper of the seal in the literal, not in the bureaucratic sense, for he kept the seals for the shah in the harem.[496] It is also possible that the eunuch was both *mehtar-e rekab-khaneh* and *davatdar*. Such a combination is found at the court of the *begler-begi* of Astarabad, seemingly as a standard practice, because there existed a model *raqam* for this function.[497]

Thus, as of 1533, there were two keepers of the seal. One was the *mohrdar-e mohr-e homayun* or the keeper of the great seal, the other the *mohrdar-e mohr-e sharaf-nafadh* or the keeper of the small seal. The former had to seal all *teyul-nameh*s for emirs and governors as well as appointment diplomas for viziers, *kalantar*s, *mostoufi*s, and local tax officials (*'ommal*) as well as documents granting various tax exemptions (*soyurghal*s, *ma'afi*s, *mosallami*s and *eqta'-ye tamlik*).[498] The small seal was used to seal documents such "as the revenue assignment diplomas of the emirs, instructions (*parvanejat*) for the viziers, the *mostoufi*s and *kalantar*s and of those who belong to the group of the *'ommal.*"[499]

In the 1660-70s, the sealing of the documents by the *mohrdar*s still was a recognized and practised process. "Friday is the normal day for the sealing of documents. On that day all departments send their documents, properly sealed by the ministers or high officials, to the gate of the harem. In case the shah is abroad the box with seals goes with him. It is the task of the *mohrdar* to break the seal, after the shah's inspection, to get the seals, and while the documents are read to the shah to prepare the appropriate seal with ink, prepare the location on the document where the seal has to be put by lightly moistening it with his thumb, and thus present it to the shah, who puts the seal himself, or, what is more usual, who indicates that he can seal. If the shah does not leave the harem the sealing is postponed till the next day, or the shah has them brought into the harem where the eunuch keeper of the seal seals the documents."[500]

Both seals, large (*homayun*) and small (*sharaf-nafadh*), lost their importance due to the increased use of the *raqam*, which was authenticated with the royal signet seal. But the *mohrdar*s kept however

---

[495] Chardin, vol. 5, p. 452.

[496] Chardin, vol. 5, p. 451.

[497] Dhabihi, M. and Setudeh, M. *Az Astara ta Astarabad*, 10 vols., Tehran 1354/1975, vol. 6, p. 462.

[498] DM, p. 76-7.

[499] DM, p. 77.

[500] Chardin, vol. 5, p. 454; a similar situation existed under 'Abbas II in 1660. Richard, vol. 2, p. 15; Bedik, p. 17 still lists the keeper of seal among the most important officials.

the right to put their seal on the backside of relevant documents and to claim their chancery fee. When, under Soltan Hosein, the act of sealing by the *mohrdars* had fallen into disuse, there were those who tried to circumvent obtaining their seal and forgo paying the chancery fee. Though the sealing of documents itself may have lost its bureaucratic importance, the collection of its bureaucratic fees had not. Therefore, to accommodate the *mohrdars*, the payment or *toujih* department would pay the *mohrdars* their fee directly.[501] Though this was very helpful to the *mohrdars* it further weakened a function whose importance had already been reduced.

Who Were the Mohrdars?

Although the actual operation of the chancellery was mainly in the hands of Tajiks, only Qezelbash emirs, with two exceptions, were *mohrdars*. Because of the importance of the function and their close proximity to the shah the *mohrdars* often had a special relationship with the shah. During most of Tahmasp I's reign and shortly thereafter the function of keeper of the great seal (*mohrdar-e mohr-e homayun*) was hereditary in the Dhu'l-Qadr clan. This was the result of the promise Tahmasp I had made to Shahqoli *khalifeh-ye mohrdar* that after the latter's death the great seal would not be taken from his children and that his son 'Aliqoli would get the function of *mohrdar* and Qom as fief.[502] Although Esma'il II made his nephew Ebrahim Mirza *mohrdar* with the privilege of conversing with the shah, this did not break the hold of the Dhu'l-Qadrs on this post.[503] According to Röhrborn, in the 17th century, the office of *mohrdar* had become so unimportant that we do not even know their names.[504] This is not entirely true as is clear from the list of known *mohrdars*. The latter clearly lost in importance when the documents they were supposed to seal became obsolete or were less used. It is therefore no coincidence that the names of *mohrdars* after Safi I (d. 1642) are not known, for that was the period when the documents the *mohrdars* had to seal were eclipsed by the class of new documents (*raqams*) produced by the *majles-nevis*, which were sealed by the shah himself. The annual salary of the *mohrdar* in 1660 was 200-250 tomans.[505] Table 1.9 only lists the keepers of the great seal. The keepers of the *mohr-e sharaf-nafadh* seal are hardly mentioned

---

[501] TM, p. 62.

[502] Qomi, vol. 1, p. 396, in particular vol. 1, p. 119.

[503] Savory, *History*, vol. 1, p. 306.

[504] Röhrborn, *Regiering*, p. 32. Nasiri, *Alqab*, p. 34 referred to the function as the *emir-e mohr* and confirmed that his role was to seal documents such as *ahkam*, *manashir* and other documents that required the great seal to be affixed. He distributed these documents among the chancellery staff such as seal holders (*mohrdars*), inkpot holders (*davatdars*), and secretaries (*parvanchiyan*). He listed the function in the chapter dealing with once important officials, whose function had been abolished by Shah 'Abbas I.

[505] Richard, vol. 2, p. 15; DM, p. 76; TM, p. 89.

in Persian texts and thus their names are still mostly unknown.[506]

Table 1.9 List of *mohrdars*

Saru'Ali Tekellu[507]	907-12/1501-07
Emir Beg [Khan] Mousellu[508]	912-21/1506-15
Shahrokh Soltan *mohrdar* Afshar[509]	917/1511
Ebrahim Soltan[510]	921/1515
Qaytemes Beg, brother of Emir Beg Mousellu	?
Qasem Beg *mohrdar*[511]	928/1522
Kebe? Khalifeh Tekellu[512]	till 937/1531
Mahmud Beg Dhu'l-Qadr[513]	till 939/1532-33
Shahqoli Khalifeh-ye Qughlu Dhu'l-Qadr[514]	939-65/1532-59
'Aliqoli Khalifeh Dhu'l-Qadr, his son	965-66/1558-59
Mohammadqoli Khalifeh Dhu'l-Qadr[515]	984/1576
Quch Khalifeh Dhu'l-Qadr[516]	till 984/1576
Soltan Ebrahim Mirza[517]	984/1576-77

---

[506] For their remuneration see DM, p. 77; TM, p. 89. Sayyed Beg Kamuna (1533-158?). Sayyed Soleyman, known as Sayyed Beg Kamuna, was regarded with great favor by Tahmasp I, who made him one of the trusted emirs of the court and custodian of the Great Seal. Savory, *History*, vol. 1, p. 228; vol. 2, p. 555; Qomi, vol. 2, pp. 668, 699 [appointed in 976/1568-9]. The other keeper was Qujeh Beg. He was the brother's son of Yusef Agha and *mohrdar-e mohr-e sharaf-nafadh* and *emir shekar-bashi* and was dismissed when his uncle was killed. Yusef, p. 101; Esfahani, pp. 78, 124.

[507] Saru 'Ali Tekellu *mohrdar*, Valeh Esfahani, pp. 117, 128, 157. Saru 'Ali the *mohrdar* killed in 911/1505-06. Savory, *History*, vol. 1, p. 50; Rumlu, p. 83 (in 907/1501).

[508] Amir Khan became *mohrdar* and the seal was hung around his neck. Montazer-Saheb, p. 192; Amir Beg b. Golabi Beg Mousellu [Turkoman] *mohrdar*. Valeh Esfahani, pp. 160-1, 193; Rumlu, p. 125 [in 913]; Qomi, vol. 1, p. 90; Astarabadi, p. 45.

[509] With a detachment of seasoned troops in 1511, Savory, *History*, vol. 1, p. 65.

[510] Ebrahim Soltan *mohrdari-ye mohr-e homayun* appointed in Ramazan 924/1518. Valeh Esfahani, p. 287. He was the brother of Emir Beg Mousellu.

[511] Valeh Esfahani, p. 289.

[512] Röhrborn, *Regiering*, p. 32.

[513] Astarabadi, p. 61-2; Röhrborn, *Regiering*, p. 32.

[514] Shahqoli khalifeh-ye *mohrdar*, one of the emirs of Fars and governor of Darabjerd. Valeh Esfahani, p. 410. -khalifeh-ye *mohrdar*. Qomi, vol. 1, p. 180, 243, 266, 316; Shahqoli Kalifeh-ye *mohrdar* made a deal that after his death the seal would not be taken from his children and that his son 'Aliqoli would get the function of *mohrdar* and the *olka-ye* Qom. Qomi, vol. 1, p. 396. See in particular vol. 1, p. 119 (*mohrdar* with Kashan as *teyul*). Qomi, vol. 2, 642.

[515] Rumlu, p. 602; Valeh Esfahani, p. 410; Savory, *History*, vol. 1, p. 287.

[516] In 975/1567-8, Quch Khalifeh the *mohrdar*. Monshi, p. 112; Savory, *History*, vol. 1, p. 184; Valeh Esfahani, p. 353; Rumlu, p. 561; he replaced by Ebrahim Soltan Mirza who now held the *mohr-e bozorg*. Natanzi, p. 34; Rumlu, p. 630.

[517] Natanzi, p. 34; Ebrahim Soltan Mirza son Bahram Mirza became *mohrdar*,

Table 1.9 (continued)

Shamkhal Soltan Cherkes[518]	984-85/1576-78
Shahrokh Khan Tatioghli Dhu'l-Qadr[519]	985-93/1578-85
Eselmes Khan Dhu'l-Qadr[520]	993-95/1585-87
Shams Khan[521]	995/1587
'Aliqoli Soltan Dhu'l-Qadr[522]	996/1587
Eselmes Khan Dhu'l-Qadr[523]	996/1587 - 1000/1592
Badr Khan [Dhu'l-Qadr?][524]	1010/1601-02
Nadr Khan [Dhu'l-Qadr?][525]	1020-1/1611-13
Amir Khan Suklan Dhu'l-Qadr[526]	1037/1627
'Abdollah Beg Suklan Dhu'l-Qadr[527]	1041/1631-32
Rostam Beg Suklan Dhu'l-Qadr[528]	1047/1637-38
Geda 'Ali Beg[529]	till 1053/1642
Rostam Beg Mousellu[530]	1053/1643-44
?	

Where Were the Seals Kept?

According to Chardin, seals were mostly kept around the neck, though some people wore them as a signet ring. Because of fear of misuse, a seal only left a person's body in the baths. As to their size and the material it was made of, he writes, that normally seals were oval or square of form, made of cornaline, and of the size of a *denier*. Whether due to or in spite of the care taken with personal seals counterfeiting was rare, according to

---

Shamlu, p. 98.

[518] Rumlu, p. 633; Shamlu, p. 100.

[519] Natanzi, p. 85, 95; Valeh Esfahani, pp. 566, 615; Astarabadi, p. 104; Shahrokh Beg Tatioghlu Dhu'-l Qadr was released from prison, promoted to the rank of governor and khan, and appointed as *mohrdar* by Khodabandeh, he was part of the council of emirs as was the *qurchi-bashi* Qoli Beg. Savory, *History*, vol. 1, pp. 333-4, 339.

[520] Shahrokh Khan was taken prisoner by the Ottomans in 1585, his son Salmas Khan became *mohrdar*. Savory, *History*, vol. 1, p. 452; Valeh Esfahani, pp. 775, 828; Astarabadi, p. 142 mistakenly has Soleiman.

[521] Astarabadi, p. 127.

[522] Natanzi, p. 288; Savory, *History*, vol. 2, pp. 549, 551. Another son of Sharokh Khan Tatioghli.

[523] Monshi, p. 444; Savory, *History*, vol. 2, pp. 617.

[524] Astarabadi, p. 173.

[525] Savory, *History*, vol. 2, p. 1044.

[526] Monshi, vol. 2, p. 1084; Savory, *History*, vol. 2, p. 1310; Yusef, p. 99, also p. 259. He was *qurchi-bashi*, governor of Kerman and *mohrdar-e mohr-e homayun*; the latter function was transferred to his son.

[527] Yusef, p. 99, also p. 259. Son of Amir Khan.

[528] Yusef, p. 228; Rostam Beg, son of Emir Khan the *qurchi-bashi*, became *mohrdar* in 1047/1637. Esfahani, p. 258. He was 'Abdollah Beg's younger brother.

[529] Vahid Qazvini, p. 216.

[530] Shamlu, p. 283.

Chardin.[531] However, it did happen, even with the shah's seals, and culprits were arrested and punished.[532] Therefore precautions were taken, including in the area of diplomatic relations, to ensure that the seals were properly used. To make sure that the destinaries of his correspondence would be able to authenticate his letters, 'Abbas I gave Robert Sherley "the impression in ink of his private seal on a piece of paper as a countersign for his letters, which in the future he would write to Your Highness and the Christian princes."[533]

Around 1510, a Venetian merchant "met Amirbec [Emir Beg [Khan] Mousellu] the governor of Mosul-miniato, a great adherent of Ismael's, who wore two gold chains, covered with rubies and diamonds, round his neck, to which was attached the seal of Ismael, a mark of his greatest confidence."[534] Later the *mohr-e bozorg,* or great seal, continued to be held by the *mohrdar*s, around their neck,[535] as did the regent (*vakil*).[536] Shahqoli Khalifeh, the *mohrdar*, "carries his seals on his breast on golden chains with many jewels."[537] Later in his reign Tahmasp I kept the small seal (*mohr sharaf-e nafadh*) in the harem,[538] while he kept the *mehr-e athar* seal on his finger.[539] This was probably caused by the fact that during the first unruly decade of his reign one of the contending power hungry Qezelbash emirs, Dedeh Beg, had tried to rip off the *vakil*'s seal which hang around Tahmasp's neck.[540] The great seal or *mohr-e bozorg* or -*homayun* continued to be held by the *mohrdar*. This was also true under Esma'il II, who hang the great seal around the neck of his nephew, Soltan Ebrahim Mirza.[541] Under Khodabandeh, Soleiman Beg Kamuna kept the small seal (*sharaf-e nafadh*) with him.[542] D'Allessandri also mentioned that one of the *mohrdar*s "always carried the royal seal attached to his neck."[543] Hosein Beg, son of Khvajeh Shoja' al-Din Shirazi was appointed as Hamzeh Mirza's vizier and entrusted with the regent's seal (*mohr-e*

---

531 Chardin, vol. 5, p. 455.

532 Minorsky, *Calligraphers*, p. 186. The painter 'Abdol-'Aziz, a favorite and pupil of Tahmasp I, had forged the shah's seal and for that reason lost his ears and nose.

533 Carmelites, vol. 1, p. 127, also p. 125, n. 2.

534 *Travels to Tana*, part 2, pp. 197, 109. the seal "is made out of a diamond set in a beautifully worked ring of gold; it is about the size of a nut, and is engraved in minute letters with the name of Ismael surrounding the twelve sacraments of their sect." Ibid., p. 206.

535 Montazer-Saheb, p. 192.

536 Montazer-Saheb, p. 386; Nasiri, *Alqab*, p. 32.

537 Membré, p. 29.

538 Monshi, vol. 1, p. 383.

539 Valeh Esfahani, p. 491.

540 Afshar, *'Alamara-ye Tahmasp*, p. 31.

541 Valeh Esfahani, p. 536; *mohr-e bozorg*. Natanzi, p. 34.

542 Qomi, vol. 2, p. 668.

543 Carmelites, vol. 1, p. 49, n. 2.

vekalat).[544] Under 'Abbas I, when he was still under the tutelage of the *vakil*, Morshedqoli Khan, the latter kept the royal seals (*mohrha-ye mobarak-e ashraf*) around his neck to seal the royal orders.[545]

When 'Abbas I ruled without a *vakil*, decrees (*raqam*s) were sealed by the shah himself with his small seal. 'Abbas I wore the *mohr-e thabti* around his neck.[546] The great seals were kept in the harem in a box sealed with the shah's seal that he wore around his neck. Normally the shah's mother or sister kept this box.[547] Alternatively, the chamberlain (*mehtar*) had a small box around his waist in which he kept, amongst other things, some seal rings.[548] Throughout the 17th century the *mohrdar* still hung the great seal around their neck, "fix'd to a golden Chain enamell'd and garnish'd with precious Stones, and which goes over his Shoulder, and hangs just before his Breast. But it is however certain, that these Men [assistants of *mohrdar*] have not any seal of the King's Seals in their Custody, but that they are affix'd to Grants by a Matron in the Haram."[549] The DM reports that the keeper of the great seal (*mohrdar-e mohr homayun*) continued to display the seal around his neck in the royal council till the end of the Safavid regime in 1722.[550]

The Mohrdar's Staff

The *mohrdar* was assisted by a number of staff such as a vizier and a *davatdar* (literally, ink holder). These functions existed from the beginning of the Safavid reign.[551] According to Sanson "He has Five Under-keepers of Seal whose Business it is to present the King with all Petitions and Addresses, and to return 'em to the Suppliants when they are pass'd."[552] These five under-keepers were *mohrdar*s, who were not the same as the *davatdar*s, of whom there were only two. Chardin mentioned only one chief clerk or *davatdar*. "He is always close to the shah with a pencase in his belt and a role of paper in his breast to write down immediately the royal commands."[553] However, the *davatdar*, according to Persian texts, did not take down the shah's orders. This was the task of the clerical staff such as the *monshi al-mamalek* and the *majles-nevis*. Also, there were indeed two *davatdar*s. One for the great seal, the *davatdar-e*

---

544 Savory, *History*, vol. 1, p. 338.

545 Monshi, vol. 1, p. 383.

546 Esfahani, p. 34.

547 Richard, vol. 2, p. 15; Chardin, vol. 5, p. 452; Soleiman wore a secret seal around his neck. Kaempfer, *Am Hofe*, p. 48.

548 Kaempfer, *Am Hofe*, pp. 82, 184.

549 Sanson, pp. 25-6; Olearius, p. 672.

550 DM, p. 76.

551 Savory, *History*, vol. 1, p. 260; Valeh Esfahani, p. 447; Qomi, vol. 1, p. 224; Esfahani, p. 169.

552 Sanson, p. 26.

553 Chardin, vol. 5, p. 451; Nasiri, *Alqab*, p. 34. Bell, p. 305 even thought that the *davatdar* was the keeper of the seal.

arqam, ahkam va parvanehjat, the other for the small seal (*aftab-athar*). They kept, all orders and decrees (respectively [a] *parvanehjat, ahkam, neshan, shajareh* and [b] *bayazi* (unregistered), *daftari* (registered), and oral royal orders that were in final written form, readied respectively by the *monshi al-mamalek* and the *vaqaye'-nevis* for the shah's seal. After the documents had been sealed in the harem they put them in a small pouch and sent them to the addressee. The TM states that the *davatdar-e arqam*, as assistant to the *monshi al-mamalek*, was the representative of the oldest branch of the chancellery.[554]

The small pouch in which the official correspondence was transmitted was an innovation introduced by 'Abbas I.[555] "On receipt of a royal order, usually contained in a small pouch made of a rich fabric, the recipient to the highest rank, would drop to his knee, say a prayer, then press the seal that closed the pouch to his forehead, then to his eyes, then to his mouth. After having broken the seal and taken out the letter he would kiss the message, press it to his breast, and only then would he rise respectfully. Then the recipient would express a benediction such as: May God keep and spare the shah and give him the two-edged sword of 'Ali, so that he may subjugate all enemies. Then he would say: Allah akbar, and la illa'llah. I will remain the shah's slave. This ceremony was invariably, on pain of punishment, performed by all recipients of the shah's commands."[556]

The *davatdar*s were *qurchi*s, who, in addition to their chancellery function, usually also held other government functions such governor (*hakem*), superintendent (*darugheh*), deputy-governor, and tax collector. Like other government bureaucrats the *davatdar* also held military posts.[557] Whereas the *mohrdar*s and *davatdar*s belonged to the Qezelbash, the administrators of the keeper of the seal (*vazir-e mohrdari*), a function that also dated from the beginning of Safavid reign, typically were Tajiks.[558] This function is neither mentioned in the DM nor in the TM and may have been abolished by the end of the Safavid reign.

Apart from the shah a number of officials also had to seal the various documents *qualitate qua*. These persons, according to Chardin were refered to as *saheb-e hokkam*, those with the right to seal royal decrees. They had to return their seal when they were dismissed from their

---

[554] DM, pp. 102-03; TM, p. 63, 89. Vahid Qazvini, p. 338. Hasan Beg *davatdar* was killed by Shah Safi, and was replaced by Emir Guna Khan, governor of Erivan. Olearius, p. 672. The sealing of the documents was done with a kind of thick ink and not with wax, reason why the *davatdar* was one of the keeper of the seal's assistants.

[555] Carmelites, vol. 1, p. 125.

[556] Andersen, pp. 151-3; Montazer-Saheb, p. 397.

[557] Savory *History*, vol. 1, p. 434; Ibid. vol. 2, p. 1063, 1230; Yusef, p. 136.

[558] Monshi, pp. 164-5, 1010; Savory, *History*, vol. 1, p. 259; Ibid., vol. 2, p. 1232; Valeh Esfahani, p. 451; Nasiri, *Dastur*, p. 13 (*vezarat-e mohr*). Nasiri, *Alqab*, p. 34, whose ancestors held that function, lists the function as having been abolished by 'Abbas I.

function. The regent (*vakil*) as the most important official after the shah had the right to put his seal the documents above that of all other emirs.[559] When 'Abbas I did away with the function of *vakil* he instructed the *mostoufi al-mamalek* to put his seal on the inside of the royal orders.[560] The emirs were authorized to write royal orders with the text *farman-e 'ali shod* but out of respect for the shah put their seal at the bottom.[561] Khvajeh Seif al-Din Mozaffar Betekchi, was the first of the viziers who received the right to seal royal decrees (*ahkam-e mota'* and *farmans*).[562] Apart from the grand vizier, other administrative officials had to put their seals on royal orders to indicate that their contents had been recorded, verified and processed. These officials included the *saheb-e toujih*, the *avarajeh-nevis*, the *sar-khatt nevis*, the *mofredeh-nevis* and the *lashkar-nevis*, who all put their seal on the back of the royal orders.[563]

In addition to these bureaucratic checks, there were officials, who, because of political reasons or their special relationship to the shah, also received the right to seal these same documents. For example, Esma'ilqoli Khan, the *tovachi-bashi*, was allowed to affix his seal to *divan* documents and letters of appointment.[564] To conciliate the Ostajalus, Shah Khodabandeh appointed Dalman Khan, grandson of 'Abdollah Khan Ostajalu, to the office of *divan-bashi* and it was ordained that he should, like his illustrious grandfather, affix his seal to official documents.[565] Esma'il Khan was a *yuldash* and *qurchi-bashi*, who was permitted to seal inside the royal decrees (*ahkam-e mota'*) at the same level as the location for the regent's seal (*mohr-e vekalat*).[566] Irrespective of whoever sealed, no royal decree was valid without the counter-seal of the grand vizier.[567]

Local rulers such as the *malek* of Seistan also had a *mohrdar*.[568] In fact, all officials and important persons kept their own seal such as "the Cadi [who] calls for his Seal, which are words Engraven on Silver."[569] In 1048/1638, the *vali* of Georgia had his own *mohrdar*, who was *davatdar* at the same time. All officials were instructed to submit to the *mohrdar*

---

559 Rumlu, p. 141-2; Valeh Esfahani, pp. 167, 340; Rumlu, p. 247; Seistani, p. 318; Astarabadi, p. 104.

560 Qomi, vol. 1, p. 587.

561 Qomi, vol. 2, p. 816.

562 Valeh Esfahani, pp. 186-7.

563 Qomi, vol. 2, p. 816; for more information see Busse, *Untersuchungen*, and Floor, *Fiscal History*, chapter three.

564 Savory, *History*, vol. 1, p. 479.

565 Savory, *History*, vol. 1, p. 410.

566 Valeh Esfahani, p. 789.

567 Chardin, vol. 5, p. 339; see also DM, pp. 45; TM, p. 44.

568 Seistani, p. 318; Valeh Esfahani, p. 472, 704.

569 Fryer, John. *A New Account of East India and Persia Being Nine Years' Travels, 1672-1681*, 3 vols. (London, 1909-15) (Hakluyt Second Series), vol. 3, p. 109. Only after the qadi had sealed a document it became valid. Kaempfer, *Am Hofe*, p. 100. For the sealing of commercial documents. Chardin, vol. 6, pp. 70-72.

their documents (*sanad*), undertakings (*shartnamcheh*), payment vouchers (*barat*), etc. so that he could submit them for the vice-royal seal. Nobody was permitted to interfere in the execution of his function, while his fees were also specified, as follows:[570]

hokm-e deh	per house	1 qorush
hokm-e tarkhani	per *ra'yat* or taxpayer	2 marchil
	per *nokar* or servant	0.5 marchil
Salaries paid per *barat* and the like	per toman	5 dinars
an'am or gifts	per toman	200 dinars
Collector of *chupan-begi* (herd-tax)	lump sum	12,000 dinars
Kvadzepuri[571]	per *tahsildar* or tax collector	1 qorush
Collector of *darughegi-ye posht-e kuh*	lump sum	12,000 dinars
Sabalakhi-ye Gorjestan[572]	per *tahsildar*	1 qorush
Mafasa or quittance note	per toman	5 dinars
'alafkhvori (grazing tax)	from the collector	10 head [of sheep]
Georgian *savari* and *rosum* of the *baj* (customs) collectors	per toman	200 dinars
hokm-e darughegi	per 10 houses	3 marchil
hokm-e hameh-saleh	per toman	100 dinars
Shartnamcheh-ye zarrabi	lump sum	12,000 dinars
Ejareh-ye qapan va qassab-khaneh	per toman	1 shahi
Collection of *hameh-saleh* from Gilan	lump sum	3,000 dinars
Ejareh-ye zarrab-khaneh (Mint rent)	per toman	1 shahi

---

[570] Puturidze 1955, doc. 64; the Georgian keeper of the seal received a special fee known as *samordlo*. For the meaning of the various technical terms see Floor, *Fiscal History*.

[571] Probably a Georgian term derived from *kwadje*, an agglomeration of Circassian houses.

[572] The Georgian term *sabalaxe* means pasture right.

Conclusion

The shift in power from the *mamalek* to the *khasseh* administration, which we observed in the section dealing with the grand vizier, was also reflected in the changes that took place with regards to other high government positions. This not only held true for the finance department, which was only to be expected, but also for the chancellery. Though the position of the *mostoufi al-mamalek* was not totally surpassed by that of the *mostoufi-ye khasseh*, the latter nevertheless held a more visible and above all more influential position in the 17th century than in the preceding one. What is even more striking is that in the chancellery there was a shift in prominence, or rather an almost reversal of roles of the leading administrators. The *majles-nevis*, who is hardly mentioned in the 16th century, totally overshadowed the *monshi al-mamalek* in the 17th century. This did not only manifest itself in the increased powers that the *majles-nevis* enjoyed, but even more striking, it was reflected in bureaucratic procedures and documents. Concomitant with this change in administrative practice was the erosion of the once important function of keeper of the seal. Though this function continued to be held by important Qezelbash emirs, by the end of the 17th century, the function had become entirely ceremonial without any bureaucratic authority or meaning. The latter had been taken over by *khasseh* staff, in particular in the second half of the 17th century by eunuchs. This was just another function which underlined the growth of the influence of the harem community, and in particular of the eunuchs. In addition, eunuchs held functions such as *jabbehdar-bashi* (chief of the arsenal) and *nazer* (steward). The chief of the arsenal was a white eunuch as of Soleiman, which function, prior to that time, had been the prerogative of the Qezelbash emirs. The function of *jabbehdar-bashi* remained in the hands of the white eunuchs till the end of the dynasty. [573] The function of *nazer*, towards the end of the 17th century, was held by eunuchs for a considerable period. This meant an increase in the diversity of the make-up of the power elite. Also, that additional competitors for the same pie had to be accommodated which increased the tension between the various parties, for the pie had not become any bigger. As to the function of *sadr* (head of the religious institution) there was also some shift in power between the *sadr-e khasseh* and the *sadr-e mamalek*. For the *sadr-e khasseh* was considered to be more important than his colleague in the 17th century. Another phenomenon is that local rulers and governors copied both the bureaucratic offices and administrative procedures followed by the central government. Of course, there was not the same problem as with the

---

[573] TM, p. 56; DM, pp. 68-9. A white eunuch held the function in 1665. Richard, vol. 2, p. 267

khasseh and *mamalek* power shift, for the lands they governed were by definition in the *mamalek* domain.

CHAPTER TWO

The Organization of the Provincial Government

Introduction

T
O MANAGE the country the shah had divided the land into so-
called *mamalek* (*divan* or state) and *khasseh* (royal household)
areas. *Khasseh* land included the shah's personal property, those
lands that he governed directly and areas that had been confiscated or
conquered. The latter category of land was referred to as *khaleseh*. The
revenues of *khasseh* lands were remitted directly to the royal court and
were used by the shah as he saw fit. From the beginning of the Safavid
regime a *khasseh* administration was set up to manage *khasseh*
properties, such as in Azerbaijan, Khorasan and Kashan between 1507-
15.[1] Various governates were *khasseh* in the 16th century, for a longer,
shorter or intermittent period of time. These included Tabriz, Qazvin,
Isfahan, Kashan, Yazd, Aberquh, Semnan and Demavand. These same
areas remained, for the most part, *khasseh* under 'Abbas I and later
shahs, many down till the end of Safavid reign (see list). Thus, the
development of the *khasseh* administration is not something that started
under Safi I, as Chardin reported, but existed from the beginning of the
dynasty.

The *mamalek* lands the shah bestowed upon his Turkoman emirs and
their leading clansmen (*aqa*), or on those rulers that had submitted
themselves to him. These revenue assignments were known as *teyul*.
The revenues of these *teyul*s were used by the *teyuldar*s or *teyul* holders
to pay for the upkeep of the troops they had to maintain and for the
administration of their jurisdiction. The emirs only paid certain dues and
submitted presents to the court and paid no other imposts. They
constituted the military aristocracy of the Safavid State and were the
governors of most of the governates during the 16th century. The
Qezelbash emirs also held many other important political and military
functions. The subjugated local rulers, who had become vassals of the
shah, were usually called *vali*s and were allowed to continue to manage
their lands under certain conditions. The emirs were assisted in the
management of their governates by viziers. *Khasseh* governates were
under royal viziers, but were nominally mostly governed by princes till

---

[1] Aubin, "L'Avènement", pp. 80. 87, 97.

1580, after that time royal viziers were appointed as governors to those areas. Finally, in the *khasseh* areas special military governors or *darughehs* were also appointed. These could either be in charge of an entire jurisdiction or parts thereof. In the latter case they usually were subject to the viziers of that area.[2] Thus, we will discuss in this section the function and role of the *vali*, emir, *aqa*, vizier and *darugheh* as representatives of provincial government.

Vali

According to Sanson, writing about 1690, "The valis are Descendants from such Princes as have been conquer'd by the King of Persia, and whose Kingdom he leaves to their sole Governments."[3] In the 16th century, there were more *vali*s or subject rulers than there were in the 17th century. The main characteristic was that these *vali*s were quasi-independent, but paid tribute (often an annual nominal lump sum) and recognized the shah as their overlord. This was *inter alia* clear from the fact that in the *khotbah* the shah's name was read and the shah's name was on the coinage. Otherwise the *vali* was allowed to manage the internal affairs of his territory as he saw fit.

However, it is not always easy to determine whether the contemporary texts, when using the term *vali*, refer to an independent, though subject ruler, or just to a Safavid governor of a province. For, generally speaking, the term is used in both meanings by Safavid texts. In principle, the term *vali-ye an velayat* simply meant governor of that province.[4] Persian texts referring to the situation in the 16th century are confusing when they mention the existence of a *vali*, for the *vali* of a certain province is styled as a simple *hakem* later on in the same text. This is the case with, for example, the *vali* or *hakem* of Kerman and Marv.[5] In 17th century texts, governors, such as those of Herat, Erivan, Chokhur Sa'd, Tabriz and Bandar 'Abbas, are both and indiscriminately referred to as *vali* and *hakem* in the same text.[6] Other *vali*s that are mentioned include those of Shiraz, Kuhgilu, Khvar, Semnan, and Hormuz, areas of which we know that they never have constituted *vali*doms, and just were mostly minor governates.[7] The term *vali* was

---

[2] For a discussion of the fiscal aspects of *khasseh*, *khaleseh* and *mamalek* domains see Floor, *Fiscal History* and Röhrborn, *Provinzen*.

[3] Sanson, p. 30.

[4] Ben Khvandamir, Amir Mahmud. *Iran dar Ruzgar-e Shah Esma'il va Shah Tahmasp*, ed. Gholam Reza Tabataba'i, Tehran 1379/1991, p. 211. (henceforth cited as Ben Khvandamir).

[5] Valeh Esfahani, p. 357; Ben Khvandamir, p. 362, 392; Astarabadi, pp. 154, 197, 201.

[6] Nasiri, *Dastur*, pp. 96, 177, 214-5, 218, 273, 281.

[7] Nasiri, *Dastur*, pp. 95, 152-4, 181, 183; Valeh Esfahani, p. 541; Astarabadi, p. 172; Shirazi, p. 332; *vali* of Khvar and Semnan, Firuzkuh, Demavand, and Halbrud, Astarabadi, p. 37.

also used to refer to rulers of neighboring powers such as those of Khvarezm, Orgenj, Russia, Balkh, Kich-Mekran, and Badakhshan.[8] The same lack of rigor in terminology occurs in case of the real *valis*. The *valis* of 'Arabistan, Lorestan, Shirvan and Georgia, for example, were varyingly referred to as *vali, hakem* or *begler-begi*.

The reasons why the Safavids allowed scions of the former dynasties to continue to govern under their rule (as previous dynasties also had done) were: inaccessibility of the terrain (Mazandaran, Gilan, Lorestan) unattractive climatological conditions (Mazandaran, Gilan, Makran, Seistan), religious, cultural and linguistic differences ('Arabistan, Georgia); and nomadic lifestyle of the population (Kurdestan, Makran, Lorestan, Bakhtiyari). Also, most of these areas were border areas, which served as a buffer with the Ottoman empire (Georgia, Kurdestan, Lorestan, Daghestan). If no buffer state existed between the two countries (either a *vali*dom or a quasi-independent ruler as in some Kurdish principalities) it was agreed by the two parties to leave those areas as a kind of deserted and devastated no-man's land. This was the case with Qars after the treaty of 961-2/1554-5, and with Qotur, Maku and Maghadhberd after the treaty of 1049/1639.[9]

Thus, *valis* therefore, after having been subjugated, continued to hold their land as quasi-independent rulers, which the shah bestowed on them as *teyul*.[10] Eskander Beg called the governor of Kurdestan, Khan Ahmad Khan, who succeeded his father, governor of Ardalan, ruler of his hereditary domains, and *begler-begi* of Shahrezur.[11] With regards to Simon I of Kartli, Eskander Beg also stated that he held his inherited lands, and so did Rostam Khan *vali* of Kartli in 1067/1657.[12] The special position of the *valis* is also clear from the fact that they had a seat in the royal council just behind the six pillars of the state (*arkan-e douleh*). "They are consider'd of as Princes, and have those Privileges as the King's Guests have, which is to be Pensioners and Tablers during their stay at Court," which is confirmed by both the DM and the TM.[13] Another sign of their privileged position was their fiscal burden as compared with other governors. The *valis* had to pay tribute, but this often was but a nominal annual fixed amount and/or present. In the 16th century the usual term for the lump sum tribute was *mal-e ma'hud, mal-e moqarrari, maqta'*.[14] The tribute was usually called *savari* or *pishkesh*

---

[8] Valeh Esfahani, p. 379; Astarabadi, pp. 91, 155, 166, 170, 217, 248; Nasiri, *Dastur*, pp. 54, 87, 90, 189, 254; Yusef, pp. 249-50; Ben Khvandami*r*, pp. 175, 291; Shirazi, pp. 148-9.

[9] Monshi, vol. 2, p. 742; Carmelites, vol. 1, p. 43; Yusef, p. 222.

[10] DM, pp. 40-4; TM, pp. 44, 112-13.

[11] Savory, *History*, vol. 2, p. 1295; Monshi p. 1070.

[12] Monshi, vol. 1, p. 227; Puturidze 1955, doc. 106..

[13] Sanson, pp. 30-1.

[14] Qazvini Ghaffari, p. 279; the *vali* of Hormuz paid a *moqarrari* of 2,000 *ashrafis*

in the 17th century. Taxes were collected in the *vali*'s lands in accordance with local custom (*movafeq-e qanun va beh dastur al-'amal-e Gorjestan*).[15] When a *vali*dom was done away with, such as Gilan, then these local taxes were also abolished.[16] In exchange for this annual tribute the *vali*s were basically left alone. Occasionally they presented themselves at court, provided military support when required, and sent family members to court as hostage for their good behavior.

When appointed as *vali*, they, like other governors, were given the title of khan. The term *vali*, as local dynast, is only used since 'Abbas I. Before that time the *vali*s were usually referred to as *hakem*. After 'Abbas I, the terminology that is usually employed is the *vali* of Kartli, Kakheti and 'Arabistan, but the *begler-begi* of Kurdestan and Lorestan. At the end of the Safavid reign it was again simply *hakem* of Lorestan. The *vali*s were so-called *valiyan-e atraf*, which the other governors were not. All held the title of *'alijah*, followed by other high sounding titles.[17] The *vali*s of Kurdestan and Lorestan were only *begler-begi*s, though on occasion they were also referred to as *vali*. The investiture of a *vali* was a festive and rich occasion, which is typical for appointments of all high Safavid officials such as emirs.[18]

Only Georgian *vali*s played a major role in the Safavid court in the 17th century. Georgian princes often were *sepahsalar* of Iran, *qollar-aghasi*, *darugheh* of Isfahan, and they were sometimes adopted by the shah, either as son or brother. For example, in 967-8/1560-1, Jesse ['Isa] son of Leos, king of Kakht, converted to Islam and was elevated to the rank of *farzand*, or son, by the shah.[19] The first Moslem *vali* of Kartli, Davud Khan, also was adopted by the shah as his son at his investiture.[20] The Georgian *vali*s also issued decrees with typical princely introductory formulas, *intitulatio* or *toghra*, such as: Abu'l-Mansur

---

only. Jean Aubin, "Cojeatar et Albuquerque", *Mare Luso-Indicum* 1 (1971), p. 101; Pedro Teixera, *The Travels*. tr. William F. Sinclair, Hakluyt Society (London 1902 [1991]), p. 190, n. 4.

15 Puturidze 1955, docs. 20-27, 31-41, 44, 46-49, 52, 7, 81, 83, 88, 101, 109, 117, 121, 126, 129, 157.

16 Laheji, 'Ali b. Shams al-Din b. Hajji Hosein. *Tarikh-e Khani*, ed. Manuchehr Setudeh (Tehran 1352/1973), p. 321; Röhrborn, *Provinzen*, p. 60, n. 364; Monshi, vol. 1, p. 459.

17 For more details see Röhrborn, *Provinzen*, pp. 84-85.

18 For a discussion of the *khal'at* or robe of honor and all that was tied up with the investiture ceremony see Floor, Willem. *The Persian Textile Industry in historical perspective 1500-1925*, chapter three (Paris 1999).

19 Qomi, vol. 1, p. 409.

20 Brosset, Marie-Félicité. *Histoire de la Géorgie depuis l'antiquité jusq'au XIX siècle*. 2 vols. (St. Petersburgh 1849-58), vol. 2. p. 32. For other examples of Georgian princes adopted as son (*farzand*), brother (*baradar*) and uncle ('*ammu*) see Monshi, vol. 1, p. 227, vol. 2, pp. 718 (Luarsab II), 898; Yusef, pp. 155, 268, 289 (Rustam Khan); Brosset, vol. 2, p. 513 (Konstantin II = Mohammadqoli Khan).

Mahmud Khan Mirza *sozum*.[21] Although this adoption also occurred in cases of other rulers or emirs, the frequency is significantly less than in the case of the *valis* of Georgia.[22] Röhrborn has noted that there are no known cases of the bestowal of new names on Georgian *valis* at their investiture, a phenomenon that is a fixture for other governors. The fact that the *valis* of Georgia had to become Moslem to be confirmed in their position, which meant changing one's name, may explain this. In 1716, for example, Vakhtang Mirza was appointed as *vali* of Georgia, he also converted to Islam and received the new name of Hoseinqoli Khan.[23] The conversion to Islam sat very lightly on the shoulders of the Georgian *valis*. They promoted the Christian religion and were only nominally Moslem.[24] The Safavids required the conversion for political reasons to demonstrate their overlordship. However, if political expediency required it also Christian *valis* were appointed, when Safavid power was not strong enough.[25]

Already under Tahmasp I there was a trend to replace local dynasts with Qezelbash governors.[26] 'Abbas I was most successful in totally subjugating most of the *valis*. Those that held out longest were the buffer states on the Ottoman border: 'Arabistan, Georgia, Kurdestan and Lorestan. Chardin writes that the only *vali* was the ruler of Seistan,[27] which is neither borne out by Persian nor by other European sources. According to Kaempfer there were three *vali*doms: Georgia, 'Arabistan and Lorestan. He adds that the ruler of Daghestan also was considered a *vali*, but only as an honorific. "The shah has to appoint them, but he can only select someone from the reigning family."[28] According to Sanson, writing some 15 years later, there were 10 *valis*, to wit: the rulers of Georgia, Laurestan (Lar), Aviza (Hoveizeh), Bactria (Marv), Zeitoun Ardelan (Lorestan), Mazandran, Tcharkez (Daghestan), Herat, Kandahar, and Kerman. Soleiman had done away with the *vali* of Kerman at the end of the 1680s and also was considering measures against the others, including Georgia. In Lar, he also had replaced the *vali* with a governor, Sanson reports.[29] As we will see below, some of the areas indicated by Sanson never were *vali*doms, whilst others had

21 Puturidze 1955, doc. 9, 76; Papaziyan 1959, doc. 23; Röhrborn, *Provinzen*, p. 87.

22 See Röhrborn, *Provinzen*, p. 87 for the rulers of Gilan (twice) and two Uzbeg princes. Monshi, vol. 1, pp. 227, 598. see further section on 'emir'.

23 Floor, *Bar Oftadan*, p. 27; Ibid., *Afghan Occupation*, p. 29.

24 Lang, D.M. *The Last Years of the Georgian Monarchy*, (New York 1957), pp. 76-8, 82-4; Lockhart, *Fall*, pp. 84, 88.

25 Monshi, pp. 692, 709 (Theimurath I of Kakhet); Brosset, vol II/1, p. 51 (Luarsab II of Kartli).

26 Monshi, vol. 1, pp. 500, 460, 471, 681.

27 Chardin, vol. 5, p. 257.

28 Kaempfer, *Am Hofe*, p. 129-30.

29 Sanson. p. 30.

already been annexed by 'Abbas I around the turn of the 17th century.
Both the DM and the TM record that by the end of the Safavid dynasty
the royal court acknowledged four *valis*, to wit: the *valis* of 'Arabistan,
Lorestan, Georgia and Bakhtiyari, to which the DM adds the *begler-begi* of Kurdestan.[30]

Throughout the Safavid reign the following *vali*doms existed:

Lorestan: The Lor chiefs accepted the suzerainty of the Safavids
early in Esma'il I's reign (914/1508-09). The Lor *valis* generally
speaking remained loyal allies, although there were several revolts in
the 16th century, sometimes occasioned by adventurers who played on
the religiosity of the Lors.[31] Tahmasp I therefore had divided Lorestan in
two parts and assigned them to two Ardalan brothers.[32] Because of the
inaccessibility of Lorestan with its rugged mountains it was cheaper and
more effective for the Safavids to allow the Lor chiefs considerable
leeway in local affairs. Nevertheless, Safavid control was increased as
of 1005-06/1597-98. The *vali* briefly retook control under Soleiman
(1077/1667 to 1105/1694), when the shah had appointed a *vali* who was
not of the ruling family.[33] However, when Soleiman appointed
Shahverdi Khan, a Georgian, as *vali*, this led to a revolt. He, his wife
and children were sent packing in their shirt.[34] The *vali* of Lorestan was
often simply referred to as *hakem*.[35]

Georgia: The united medieval kingdom of Georgia had gradually
been dissolved by 1480. The core lands of the kingdom had fallen apart
into seven contending principalities, the most important of which were:
Kartli in central and northern Georgia with Tiflis as capital; Kakheti,
north of the Kura with the capital at Gremi; and Imereti, west of the
Suram mountains with the capital at Kutais. In addition, there were in
the north-west the small principalities of Mingrelia and Abkhazia;
Samtskhe (Mezkhetia) in the south-west and Guria between Samtskhe
and Imereti. Georgia was never entirely under Safavid control. Masq
(Mezkhetia) was only intermittently subject to Safavid rule (958/1551 -
990/1582) and some years after 1022/1613-4. Finally it was ceded to the
Ottomans in 1049/1639. The Georgian kings of Kartli, Imereti and

---

[30] TM, p. 44; DM, p. 39-44; the *hakem* of the Bakhtiyari. Nasiri, *Dastur*, pp. 252,
257. Du Mans only lists three *valis*, excluding Kurdestan. Richard, vol. 2, p. 283.

[31] However, at times one of the *valis* was rebellious and refused to pay tribute. *Don
Juan of Persia, a Shi'ah Catholic 1560-1604*, tr. G. le Strange (London, 1926), p.
216.

[32] Monshi, vol. 1, p. 141.

[33] Kaempfer, *Am Hofe*, p. 129.

[34] Chardin, vol. 5, p. 206; Kaempfer, *Am Hofe*, p. 165; Richard, vol. 2, p. 283.

[35] *Vali* of Lur-e kuchek and *ra'is* of that tribe. Nasrabadi, pp. 32-3. *vali* of Lurestan.
Valeh Esfahani, p. 175; *hakem* of Lorestan. Ibid, p. 500; Ahmad Khan Ardalan *vali*.
Yusef, p. 40; Hosein Khan *begler-begi* of Lorestan. Ibid, p. 48, 288; Hosein Khan
hakem-e Lorestan was succeeded by his son Shahverdi Khan. Ibid., p. 77; *hakem* of
Lurestan. Astarabadi, p. 226; *hakem* of Lorestan-e Feili. Nasiri, *Dastur*, p. 60.

Kakheti had a running battle with the Safavids throughout the 16th century. Initially, Safavid rule only extended to Tiflis. Also, the king of Kakheti pursued a more accommodating policy towards the Safavids than his kinsman of Kartli. Nevertheless, the Safavids were able to impose themselves, as a result of which "the governors of all seven districts of Georgia were appointed by the shah and became his subjects, contracted to pay the poll-tax and the land tax, and were instructed to have the name and exalted titles of the shah included in the khotbah and stamped on the coinage."[36] But intermittently the Georgian kings tried to maintain their independence. Luarsab I of Kartli refused to acknowledge the suzerainty of the shah and pay tribute to him.[37] However, each and every time, the Safavids were able to impose themselves. The result was that Georgian princes promised to pay tribute and gave sons as hostage for good behavior.[38] Occasional Ottoman occupation (985/1577-1014/1606-7) also constituted an unstable factor in Georgian-Persian relations. It was only in the early 17th century, after having been thoroughly defeated by 'Abbas I, who forcefully deported a large part of the population of Georgia to the various corners of Persia, that the Georgian kings acquiesced in Safavid rule. Instead of regularly challenging the Safavids the Georgians valis became staunch supporters, who often held, either themselves or their kinsmen, important state functions. Whereas in Kartli Georgian valis ruled, most of the time Qezelbash emirs were appointed as governors in Kakheti, which in particular had suffered from 'Abbas I's punitive expeditions. Although the valis of Georgia at occasion also were referred to as hakem, in general, they were invariably styled as vali, and sometimes as soltan (salatin).[39]

'Arabistan: The other Shi'ite dynasty in Persia was that of the Arab Mosha'sha' family who ruled over Khuzestan.[40] This included Hoveizeh, their capital, Dezful and Shushtar. The Mosha'sha' were defeated by Esma'il I in 914/1508-09. The Safavids accepted the fealty of the local ruler, who was allowed to run the internal affairs of Hoveizeh. Thus, Sayyed Shoja' al-Din Badran Mosha'sha'i the ruler of

---

[36] Savory, History, vol. 1, p. 139-40.

[37] Savory, History, vol. 1, p. 147.

[38] Savory, History, vol. 1, p. 399-400; The Georgian kings sent one of their sons to court, a custom known as nava to serve as hostage. Valeh Esfahani, p. 636.

[39] For more information see Röhrborn, Provinzen, pp. 75-8; and Lang, The Last Years. vali of Gorjestan. Valeh Esfahani, pp. 263, 355, 378; hakem of Gorjestan. Ibid, p. 281; salatin-e Gorjestan. Ibid, p. 596; Salim Khan Shams al-Dinlu vali of Gorjestan. Yusef, p. 165; Aleksander vali-ye Gorjestan was subjected to 2 years' kharaj or taxes. Shamlu, p. 106; hakem-e velayat-e Gorjestan (Qezelbash governor), Ben Khvandamir, pp. 291, 410. vali of Kartil, Astarabadi, p. 190; hakem-e Gorjestan, Nasiri, Dastur, pp. 157-8; vali of Gorjestan, Ibid., p. 59.

[40] In general see Morteza Modarresi Chahardehi, "Mosha'sha'iyan", BT 12/6 (2536/1977), pp. 149-88.

Hoveizeh, was confirmed in his position.[41] Dezful and Shustar, however, were henceforth governed by other local magnates, while as of 948/1541-42, Shushtar was governed by a Qezelbash governor till the end of Safavid reign.[42] Occasionally, the *vali*s of Hoveizeh challenged Safavid rule, but finally under 'Abbas I accepted what seemed to be inevitable. By that time the *vali* also held sway over Duraq (for some time) and later in the second half of the 17th century also over Ahvaz, and for a while over Basra.[43] Towards the end of Soleiman's reign there were once again local troubles. As a result, in 1108/1696-7, 2.000 tomans revenue from Hoveiza were set aside to pay for the 1.200 *tofangchi*s that were stationed as a garrison in Hoveiza to prevent further uprisings by aspiring *vali*s.[44] Fights among local dynastic contenders for the *vali*dom broke out again in the early 18th century, one of whom, Sayyed 'Abdollah Khan, played a rather ignominious role during the Afghan siege of Isfahan in 1722.

Kurdestan: The relationship with Kurdestan remained a difficult one. Some Kurdish magnates, willy-nilly, cooperated with the Safavids. This was the case with those of Bitlis, for example, which was under Safavid rule from 913/1507-08 till at least 939/1532-33. However, other members of the Bitlis family continued to serve the Safavids such as Sharaf Khan Ruzaki of Bitlis, who was *hakem* of Tonakebun at end of Tahmasp I's reign.[45] Kurdestan proper, ruled by the Ardalan family, came only under loose Safavid control in 930/1524 to 984/1576. In 984-5/1576-7, Safavid control was limited to the Palangan area. 'Abbas I brought Kurdestan firmly under Safavid control, especially after he had taken Baghdad in 1026-27/1617-18.[46] With a minor interruption during Soleiman's reign Kurdestan remained firmly in Safavid hands till the end of the dynasty. It was only in 1093/1682, that for the first time the governor did not belong to the Ardalan family. Between 1113-19/1701-08, once again non-Ardalan and non-Kurdish governors were appointed, one of whom was a Georgian.[47]

Daghestan: The small kingdoms of *Shamkhal* of Kumukhs at Terek and that of *Utsmi* of the Kara Qaytaq on the Caspian littoral were in a vassal relationship to Safavid Persia, while other domains in the mountains were independent. South of the Terek was the small kingdom

[41] Savory, *History*, vol. 1, p. 159, also p. 403.

[42] *Hakem* of Shushtar, Nasiri, *Dastur*, pp. 59, 257; *vali* of Shushtar. Ibid., p. 260.

[43] Sayyed Mobarak Khan Khan *vali* of 'Arabistan, Yusef, pp. 152, 157 gave Arab horses as *pishkesh*, p. 153; DM, p. 40.

[44] Nasiri, *Dastur*, p. 179.

[45] Monshi, vol. 1, p. 141.

[46] *Vali* of Kurdestan, Astarabadi, p. 165; Khan Ahmad Khan Ardalan *emir al-omara-ye* Kurdestan. Yusef, p. 156.

[47] Khosrou b. Moh. b. Manuchehr Ardalan, *Lobb al-Tavarikh - Tarikh-e Ardalan* (Tehran 2536/1977), pp. 12-40.

of Enderi that towards the north formed a kind of buffer state. Its population was usually referred to as Lezgis. The *Shamkhal*, lord of the Brus mountain, who apparently was a Christian in 1585,[48] later became a Moslem. Both he and the *Utsmi* tried to play the Ottomans, Safavids and Russians against one another whenever the occasion arose to do so. However, most of the times the two were subject rulers of the Safavids. From 1046/1636 till 1719, the *Shamkhals* were Safavid vassals and paid tribute. The *Utsmis* were vassals from 1015/1606 till 1719. In 1653, the government of Darband was in the hands of Sorkhay Khan *Shamkhal* and 'Abbasqoli Khan *Utsmi* king of the Kara Qaytaq.[49] The penultimate grand vizier of Shah Soltan Hosein was a member of the *Shamkhal's* family. Both rulers rebelled in 1719.[50]

Shirvan: The *vali* of Shirvan was an ancient enemy of the Safavid family. After having initially accepted the former ruler, Sheikh Shah, as *vali* in 906/1500,[51] the Safavids increased their grip on Shirvan as of 923/1517. "Sheikh Shah the ruler of Shirvan, undertook to pay tribute and taxes and to acknowledge the suzerainty of the shah."[52] The Safavids took over the governing this *velayat* entirely in 945/1538.[53] Thereafter, the governors of Shirvan still continued occasionally to be referred to as *vali*.[54] When the *begler-begi* of Shirvan was entitled *vali* in 1133/1721, this may have been brought about by the desperate need of the Safavid state to bolster the allegiance of its remaining supporters.[55]

Gilan: In Gilan, there were five *valis* (Resht and Fumen [Gilan-e biyapas], Lahejan [Gilan-e biyapish], Gaskar, Kudom, Amol).[56] They became Safavid vassals as of 909/1504 (Resht) and 911/1506 (Lahejan). "The local rulers of the various districts of Gilan undertook to pay

---

[48] Don Juan, pp. 148, 153.

[49] Vahid Qazvini, pp. 160, 271-4.

[50] Barthold, "Daghestan". *El*-1; W.E.D. Allen (ed), *Russian Embassies to the Georgian Kings (1589-1605)*, 2 vols. Hakluyt Society (London 1970 [1972]), vol. 2, pp. 593-5.

[51] Savory, *History*, vol. 1, p. 64.

[52] Savory, *History*, vol. 1, p. 64; *vali* of Shirvan va *hakem-e an velayat*. Valeh Esfahani, p. 109, 283, 598; Astarabadi, pp. 34, 51; Ben Khvandamir, p. 398.

[53] Savory, *History*, vol. 1, pp. 131-2, for the report of Shirvan's subjugation. In general see, B. Dorn, *Geschichte Shirwans unter den Statthaltern und Chanen von 1538-1820* (Beiträge zur Kunde der Kaukasischen Länder und Volker, vol. 2, Mémoires de l'Academie etc. St. Petersbourg 1840, pp. 317-433.

[54] *Hakem-e* Geraili and *vali* of Shirvan. Nasiri, *Dastur*, pp. 81, 96, 117, 177;

[55] Puturidze 1965 doc. 36.

[56] *Vali* of Rasht and Fumen. Valeh Esfahani, p. 154, 168; Kakiya Mirza Ali *vali* of Lahejan. Ibid., p. 155, 270, 273, 402; *vali* of Amol. Ibid., p. 204; *vali* of Kaskar. Ibid., p. 364; *vali* of Gilan-e bipas; also *vali* of Kuhdom. Ibid., p. 626. Pedro Texeira, *The Travels*, p. 208 lists five governments viz. Resht, Kashkar, Lahejan, Lenkoran, and Kuhdom in 1595.

tribute and taxes and to acknowledge the suzerainty of the shah."[57] There were regular revolts, which led to independent rule in 943/1536-37 and between 975/1567-68 till 984/1576 in Resht and 989/1581 and in 1002/1594 for a short while in Lahejan, but these and other events were all put down.[58] The penultimate revolt took place in 1002/1594, when it looked like as if the *vali* of Gilan-e biyapas would make common cause with the Ottomans. 'Abbas I occupied Gilan and declared it to be *khasseh* land to prevent further revolts. 'Abbas I turned the former *vali*doms into governates, which were governed by Qezelbash emirs from the Rumlu and Kurdish clans.[59] To underline that henceforth the quasi-independence of Gilan was a thing of the past, 'Abbas I sent his grand vizier to abolish all local, typically Gilani, taxes. This did not mean that independence sentiments also had been eradicated. For in 1629, after 'Abbas I had died, discontent local chiefs convinced a descendant of the former ruler to lead a rebellion against the Safavids. The rebellion was unsuccessful and was ruthlessly suppressed.[60]

Seistan: Seistan was ruled by a local dynasty that claimed descent from the Sasanids. They styled themselves *malek al-moluk* (king of kings). The Safavids subjugated the local ruler in 916/1510 and put a garrison of 1,000 Qezelbash troops at his disposal. Because of the *malek's* doubtful role during Sam Mirza's rebellion, Tahmasp I, in 943/1537-38, put a Qezelbash emir as *vakil* of the *malek* in part of Seistan (4 out of the 14 districts), while permitting the *malek* to hold sway in the remainder of Seistan. The *malek* did not accept this arrangement and fled, though he returned five years later. As of that time till 985/1577-8 Seistan was ruled by a Safavid prince or Qezelbash governor. In 1006-07/1598-99, 'Abbas I retook Khorasan, and when the *malek* subjected himself to him, the old dynasty was reinstated. Henceforth the rulers of Seistan were referred to either as *hakem, malek* or more commonly as *kalantar.*[61]

Larestan: The *vali* of Lar was ruler of a small kingdom that

---

[57] Savory, *History,* vol. 1, p. 64.

[58] Mirza Kamran ruler of West Gilan promised to remit tribute and taxes annually. Savory, *History,* vol. 1, p. 393.

[59] Fumeni, `Abd al-Fattah. *Tarikh-e Gilan dar vaqaye`-ye salha 923-1038 hejri qamari,* ed. Manuchehr Setudeh (Tehran 1349/1970); Monshi, 451, 541, 1085; Yusef, pp. 16, 17, 85; Rabino, *Gilan,* pp. 445, 455, 457, 463; Vahid Qazvini, p. 308; Don Juan, p. 214. *hakem-*e Gilan, Valeh Esfahani p. 402.

[60] Payandeh, Mahmud. *Qiyam-e Gharib Shah Gilani mashhur beh `Adelshah* (Tehran 1357/1978).

[61] See Bosworth, *The History of the Saffarids* and Hosein Mir Ja`far, "Seistan dar `asr-e Safaviyeh", *BT* 12/4 (2536/1977), pp. 49-67. Malek Jalal al-Din of the Saffari descent is *malek* of Seistan. Yusef, 287; Bahram Beg Gholam was appointed as Emir of Seistan. Ibid., p. 117; *vali* of Seistan in case of Badi` al-Zaman Mirza. Valeh Esfahani, p. 406, 535 (Qezelbash governor); *vali* of Qa'en. Ben Khvandamir, p. 166.

included much of Larestan and the Garmsirat. As of 914/1508-09, the ruler of Lar acknowledged Safavid rule. Membré writes in 1540 that in Lar, "Their King there is King Soprassi, but he is a vassal of the Sophy.... The said King wears the Sophy's cap [= *taj*].[62] Tahmasp I even made emir Ebrahim, the ruler of Lar, his *divan-begi*, one of the most important functions in the state. 'Abbas I as part of his centralizing rule deposed the local dynasty in 1010/1601-02, after its ruler had oppressed the transit trade. Henceforth, Lar would be a governate ruled by a representative of the central government.[63]

Mazandaran: The ruler of Mazandaran had become a Safavid vassal as of 909/1504. Since then the relationship was not always a smooth one. The independent and hereditary ruler of Mazandaran had procrastinated in making payments of tribute and in sending in his tax returns.[64] Despite the fact that Tahmasp I's eldest son, Khodabandeh, was married to a princess from the ruling house of Mazandaran, who was the mother of the later 'Abbas I, this did not prevent part of Mazandaran to rebel from 977/1569-70 till 984/1576. The special relationship that existed with the Safavids is clear from the royal welcome that Khodabandeh gave to Mir 'Ali Khan the *vali* of Mazandaran in 985/1577.[65] The refusal to pay tribute by Begi Malek in 1590[66] led to annexation of Mazandaran as *khasseh* land in 1005/1596.

Emir

Esma'il I granted each tribal and clan chief a land assignment (*olka, teyul, eqta'*), which these chiefs had to govern in the name of the shah. The *teyul*s or land assignments were granted out of the so-called *mamalek* or state lands. The revenues of this land assignment were to be used for its administration as well as for the upkeep of the emir's household and his military forces. The other lands were known as *khasseh* or royal household lands, whose revenues were for the exclusive use of the shah and his household. The only troops that the shah financed out of the proceeds of the *khasseh* lands were his household troops or the *qurchi*s, his *gholam* corps, the arquebuse regiments and his artillery department. *Khasseh* funds also were used to finance emirs without a *teyul* as well as mercenaries, who occasionally were hired.

Depending on the size of the *olka* the tribal clan chief had a large or small military contingent to maintain. For, initially, the Safavid army

---

62 Membré, pp. 48-9.

63 Minorsky, art. Lar, *EI-1*. *vali* of Lar. Valeh Esfahani, p. 540; Ebrahim Khan, *vali* of Lar. Astarabadi, p. 147.

64 Savory, *History*, vol. 1, p. 358.

65 Mar'ashi, Teimur. *Tarikh-e Khandan-e Mar'ashi-ye Mazandaran*, ed. M. Setudeh (Tehran 2536/1977), pp. 213-4.

66 Don Juan, pp. 217-8.

consisted mainly of the Turkoman *ghazis*, i.e. fighters for the faith, who were followers of the Safavid order. These had attached themselves to a clan chief, who had been able to gain some reputation for himself, and grouped themselves into a small or larger tribal group. Apart from religious reasons these, generally poor, soldiers flocked to the Safavid standard in the hope of gore, glory and especially booty. If none of this was to be had religious fervor was not always sufficient to provide staying power. "Their men, who had come to Gilan in hope for action and plunder, began to disperse."[67] The clan chief or *beg* typically did not have sufficient funds himself to pay his retainers. He therefore relied on his supreme leader, the Safavid sheikh, who had become the shah of Iran, to provide him with the necessary resources.[68]

The bestowal of a governorship automatically also meant the promotion to the rank of emir (if the person was not yet one), for the governor was first and foremost the local military commander. In fact, the appointment as emir preceded that of *hakem*, and the governor is also commonly referred to as the emir of [name province].[69] Prior to the military reforms instituted by 'Abbas I after 1590, the emir concerned usually was an emir of a tribal clan. However, also non-Qezelbash individuals, such as Sayyed Mir Mohammad-Yusef, qadi and *sadr* (chief of the religious institution) of Khorasan, could be elevated to the rank of emir with the drum and banner (*tabl va 'alam*).[70] For the Qezelbash emirs were *saheb-e tabl va 'alam ba kheil-e hasham*.[71] For in addition to the drum (*tabl*) and standard (*'alam*) the emir also had cavalry and retainers (*hasham, molazem*). Often only the *tabl va 'alam* are mentioned, while the troops are assumed.[72] The latter, the emir mainly recruited from among his own tribe, but also from among the men of the district that he had been given as fief (*olka, eqta', teyul*).[73] For example, Morshedqoli Khan was also joined by men from the rural districts who had not so far offered their services to Salman Khan.[74]

Emirs, on their appointment, just as the *valis*, were given costly presents (*khela'-ye fakhereh*) which included arms, a horse, and a robe of honor.[75] They sometimes also were given a new name at the occasion

---

[67] Savory, *History*, vol. 1, p. 397.

[68] Aubin, "L'Avènement", pp. 29-35; Sumer, Faruk. *Safevi Devletimin Kurulusu ve Gelismesinde Abadolu Turklerinin Rolu* (Ankara 1976) tr. Ehsan Eshraqi and Mohammad Taqi Emami, *Naqsh-e Torkan-e Anatoli dar Tashkil va Touse'eh-ye Doulat-e Safavi* (Tehran 1371/1992), p. 17f.

[69] See appointment diplomas in Lambton, A.K.S. *Landlord and Peasant in Persia* (London 1953), p. 109; Valeh Esfahani, p. 276.

[70] Khvandamir, vol. 4, p. 576.

[71] Monshi, p. 138.

[72] Qomi, vol. 2, p. 765; al-Qazvini, *Lobb*, p. 420.

[73] Monshi, vol. 1, p. 138.

[74] Savory, *History*, vol. 1, p. 426.

[75] For a detailed discussion of this topic see Floor, *Textile Industry*, chapter 3.

of their investiture. Mohammad Sofrehchi Ostajalu became Chayan Soltan when he was appointed as *vakil* and governor of Tabriz in 920/1514. In 1631, Safiqoli Khan was given the name Shir 'Ali.[76] Durmish Khan became Mansur Khan in 1108/1697 as governor of Qandahar.[77] Mahmud Khan Ghalza'i, the conquerer of Isfahan, received a new name, Hoseinqoli Khan, when he was still a rebel and the shah to placate him granted him new favors in 1719.[78]

In addition to new names, the shah was also in the habit to bestow special honorifics on deserving persons. Mohammad Soltan Turkoman was honored with the title of *mosaheb* (companion), as was Allahverdi Khan, the *emir shekar-bashi* under 'Abbas II, and the Ziyadoghlu governors of Qarabagh.[79] Other emirs were honored by the shah addressing them as *baba* or father. This was the case with 'Abbas I who addressed Ganj 'Ali Khan Zik as *baba*, and he called his son therefore *baba-ye thani* or second father.[80] Some emirs were honored, or adopted, as son (*farzand, pesar*), or brother.[81] Other emirs received the title of *yuldash*,[82] while Soltan Morad Khan was granted the function of *saq dushi* (companion).[83]

Collectively, the emirs were referred to as *omara-ye Iran*, or as *omara-ye sufi*,[84] which terms were of no administrative, political or military importance, other than that it marked them off from emirs belonging to the opposing forces. The importance of the various emirs or military commanders differed, of course. Some had large *olka*s or jurisdictions, others had smaller ones. However, another and more important distinction was that between emirs of the court (*dargah*) and the governors of the marches (*sarhadd*).[85] The latter were the emirs who did not reside at court. When such an emir did not or could not reside at court he automatically was an *emir-e sarhadd*.

---

[76] Qomi, vol. 1, p. 100; Yusef, p. 126. For other and early examples see Shah Tahmasp. pp. 14, 16.

[77] Nasiri, *Dastur*, p. 177.

[78] Floor, *Bar Oftadan*, p. 41; Ibid., *Afghan Occupation*, p. 40; KA 1839, 4/12/1719, f. 288.

[79] Vahid Qazvini, pp. 140, 154; Monshi, pp. 458, 533; Yusef, p. 177; Nasiri, *Dastur*, p. 56.

[80] Monshi, p. 1041; Qomi, vol. 2, p. 695 (*mosaheb*).

[81] Monshi, vol. 1, pp. 290, 462; Shah Tahmasp, p. 35.

[82] Savory, *History*, vol. 1, pp. 339, 381, 422, 486, 112; Esma'ilqoli Beg son of *vali* Khalifeh-ye Shamlu was entitled *yuldash*. Valeh Esfahani, p. 595, 698, 789; 'Aliqoli Khan was called *baradar* and entitled *qardashi*. Ibid., p. 698, 789 (*khan qardashi* as well as the office of *vakil* with the title *khanlarkhani* [chief khan]); Mohammadi Saru Sulagh was entitled *sardashi*. Ibid., p. 698.

[83] Valeh Esfahani, p. 615.

[84] Montazer-Saheb, p. 191, 146.

[85] Savory, *History*, vol. 1, p. 192, 338-9; Montazer-Saheb, p. 246; DM, p. 39; TM, p. 100.

The most important court emirs (*omara-ye dar-e doulat-khaneh* or -*dar-e khaneh*, or -*dargah*)[86] were those who were members of the *janqi* or royal inner council. As with other officials, important emirs accumulated various functions at the same time. Some of the *emir al-omara* were at the same time governor and court official, while in 985/1578, most of 'Eraq-e 'Ajam was distributed among the court emirs.[87] Such an emir could at the same time also be *qurchi-bashi*, *khalifeh al-kholafa*, etc. There was a tendency in the 17th century that certain governorships were attached to specific court functions. The governor of Azerbaijan usually also was *emir al-omara* and *sepahsalar*.

The high-ranking court emirs not only held high office, but also had large sized fiefs or *teyuls*.[88] They deputized a family member or some other person (*vakil*) to manage the affairs of the *teyul* so as not to have to leave court and loose access to power. There is e.g. the case of the *mohrdar* who visited Qom for the first time in 20 years, though he had been its governor during all that time.[89] Governors who could not stay at court kept a *vakil* or representative to take care of their interests. For it was a battle to keep what you had obtained. Competing factions tried to oust a governor by influencing the decision-makers with presents and innuendos. The governors tried to silence their opponents by buying them off and spending large amounts of money on important court officials. Kaempfer states that the further one was posted from Isfahan the more uncertain one's position was.[90] Rivals also tried to organize that a large number of complaints reached court so as to engineer a governor's recall.[91] Therefore, having a *vakil*, one or more relatives, or very influential, a female relative in the harem, was a very effective instrument to maintain one's fortune and one's life. At the same time, this gave the shah access to hostages in case of a wayward governor.[92] Also, when magnates had left the court on expedition or otherwise they could only return after having received permission to do so. Rostam Khan, the *sepahsalar*, e.g., was expressly forbidden to return to court

---

[86] TM, p. 44; Qomi, vol. 1, pp. 307, 346; Emir Mahmud Khvandamir, *Tarikh-e Shah Esma'il va Shah Tahmasp Safavi.* Ed. Mohammad 'Ali Jarrahi (Tehran 1370/1991), pp. 56, 142.

[87] Monshi, vol. 1, p. 227.

[88] Savory, *History*, vol. 1, p. 549.

[89] An *emir shekar-bashi*, who was governor of Kuh-gilu had send a deputy there during 11 years, because he could not leave the shah due to the high favor that he enjoyed. Röhrborn, *Provinzen*, p. 29, n. 196. See e.g. Eskander Monshi, and TM/DM, but these assignments changed over time.

[90] Kaempfer, *Am Hofe*, p. 163.

[91] Chardin vol. 10, p. 49.

[92] Kaempfer, *Am Hofe*, p. 231-2; Chardin, vol. 5, pp. 273-4, vol. 10, p. 126f. In 1668, the *nazer*'s life was saved through the intercession of a female relative. Matthee, *Politics*, p. 66.

when he requested this.[93]

In the 16th century, other, less important court-emirs were without a land assignment (bi olka).[94] If these emirs wished to participate in military campaigns they depended on the shah's largesse to be able to join. 'Abbas I, for example, gave a number of such court emirs a subvention for expenditures (medad-e kharj) so that they could join the campaign in Khorasan in 1589. "New emirs were added to the establishment of every tribe, but since all the provinces had already been allocated in the form of fiefs, they drew their pay from the royal treasury."[95]

The distinction between emirs was also clear from other differences between them. Although each emir received a drum and standard there was nevertheless a difference in the number and quality of drums and standards that they were allowed to display. The valis, like the beglerbegis and other emirs, had a music band, but there the similarity ended. The valis "have the right to the sounding of Twelve Kerona's, which are a sort of long Trumpets like Speaking-Trumpets, in which they bawl aloud, mixing with their confused Cries the Harmony of Hautbois, Drums, and Tymbals, and which they are wont to play upon at Sun-setting, and Two Hours after Mid-night. There's none but the Vali's and Kans that can have so compleat a concert of Musick; for the other more inferior Governours must be content with only Drums, Tymbals, and Hautbois. They carry 'em always with them when they Travel or Hunt."[96] The royal musical instruments were, of course, the most particular. Often made of gold it sometimes happened in times of political unrest that someone, such as Amir Khan Turkoman, made or sounded golden trumpets, which was the prerogative of the royal family.[97]

The pecking-order of the highest officials and emirs remained more or less the same during the entire Safavid period, although with some changes over time. This is clear from a comparison between the description in the DM and the TM and what we know about the situation in the early 16th century, as discussed in this study. The use of the epistolary art (ensha), as demonstrated in surviving manuals, also supports this conclusion, for there is little change in the rules laid down by Tahmasp I in the 1530s.[98]

The governor-emir did not need necessarily be the tribal chief. At a

---

[93] Vahid Qazvini, p. 227 in general and p. 27 in particular; also Ibid., pp. 299-300 a similar case of Allahverdi Khan, and Chardin, vol. 5, p. 226.

[94] Valeh Esfahani, p. 629. May be the term emir-e khordeh also refers to this class of emirs. Qomi, vol. 1, p. 473.

[95] Savory, History, vol. 1, pp. 341, 410.

[96] Sanson, p. 31.

[97] Savory. History, vol. 1, p. 429; Valeh Esfahani, p. 692.

[98] Röhrborn, Provinzen, pp. 21-22.

military review in 1530, the deciding factor of military presence and strength, was being an emir, not being a tribal chief. Sometimes, the tribal chief did not hold a formal government function, but nevertheless exercised much influence. Sometimes the shah also appointed one of the elders (*rish-safid*) of a tribe.[99] But functions were sometimes also split, i.e. both the governor and *rish-safid* held separate functions. The case of Shiraz is instructive, for it had a Dhu'l-Qadr governor and *vakil* at one time. This was not a workable situation, for the Dhu'l-Qadr yeomen (*aqayan*) made the *vakil*, Mehdiqoli, both governor and khan, while they killed 'Ali Khan, the governor appointed by the shah. This act of defiance was not accepted by the pillars of state, of course.[100]

In the early 16th century there seems to be have no major difference in rank between governors who bore the title (*laqab*) khan, *soltan* or *beg*. However, by the end of Esma'il's I reign (930/1524), most governors were either khan or *soltan*. One may therefore question Röhrborn's conclusion that these two title-holders also remained quasi-equivalent in rank till the 1520s. For example, in 924/1518, Ebrahim Soltan did his utmost to obtain a royal decree to change his title from *soltan* into khan.[101] Also, there already was a differentiation between "Sultans of higher rank; ...[and].. Sultans of lesser rank" from the beginning of Tahmasp I's reign.[102] In 1540, it is also reported that Beiram Beg, after having found great favor with Tahmasp I, was given "the title of Khan, with permission to use the kettle-drum and standard,"[103] which implies that as *beg* he did not have this right. The differentiation of the titles was indeed a big deal for the Qezelbash emirs, or those aspiring to become one. This seems to be borne out by the fact that the title of khan was really the ultimate goal for any Qezelbash official to aim for. Mohammad Sharif Khan Chaoslu, a *qurchi-ye tir va kaman*, accepted the governorship of Qazvin with the title of khan from Morshedqoli Khan, the regent (*vakil*), during the shah's absence and fled to Gilan when 'Abbas I took the reins of power.[104] It is therefore not surprising to note that a further differentiation occurred and the titles in order of importance soon were khan, *soltan*, *beg*. This is also clear from the titles used for the function of governor. In early Safavid times usually the title *hakem* was used, while later (around 1550) the designation *begler-begi* and *emir al-omara* was introduced for the more important governors to mark them off from the less important ones.

---

[99] Qomi, vol. 2, p. 765, 772; Monshi, vol. 1, p. 451.
[100] Qomi, vol. 2, pp. 852, 857-8.
[101] Khvandamir, vol. 4, p. 577.
[102] Membré, p. 30.
[103] Jouher, *Private Memoirs of the Moghul Emperor Homayun.* tr. Charles Stewart (Calcutta 1832 [1975]), p. 68
[104] Savory, *History*, vol. 2, p. 594.

Thus, as of the 1540s, the emirs could be appointed as [a] governor-general (*begler-begi*), [b] senior-governor (*hakem*-khan), or [c] junior-governor (*hakem-soltan*) of a province (*eyalat*) or a smaller jurisdiction. The usual term used for that jurisdiction was that of *olka*, meaning not only "administrative region", but also the area which had to pay for the upkeep of the governor's army and administration for which he was responsible. In fact, *olka* was a synonym for the terms *teyul* or *eqta'* which also were used to refer to the governor's administrative jurisdiction.[105] Minorsky was wrong to conclude that the title of *begler-begi* was only introduced under 'Abbas II. The term *begler-begi* was first used in 950/1543-4 referring to the governor of Herat. Soon thereafter, others are mentioned such as the *begler-begi* of Astarabad in 955/1548, and the *begler-begi* of Kerman in 973/1565.[106] This, and the fact that *begler-begis* also were at the same time *emir al-omara* of their jurisdiction, contradicts the view that the term *begler-begi* was simply a Turkish translation of the title *emir al-omara*.[107] In the second half of the 16th century the title was only used for the governors of large jurisdictions. In the 17th century the term was more widely used, also for smaller jurisdictions. Under each *begler-begi* served various khans and *soltan*s.

In the 17th century the emir-*soltan* generally was referred to as the subordinate (*qul-begi* or *tabin*) of the khan, who, in his turn was subject to the *begler-begi* in whose province his *olka* was situated. It is therefore quite usual to read that "*soltan* X was one of the *omara-ye tabin* of khan Y, the *hakem* of Z,[108] or to find mention of the *begler-begi* of a province and his *omara-ye qulbegi*.[109] The term *qul-begi*, which means commander of an army wing, was first used as an administrative title in 1039-40/1630-1.[110] This system of administrative and military hierarchy remained in force till the end of the Safavid dynasty. In 1690 Sanson reports: "Those Kans which are only Governours of Cities and Countrys are called Col Beguis, that is to say, Kans of Support or Strength; because they are obliged to send their Troops to the Kan Begueler-Begu[i]s whenever he shall command them," which is

---

105 Floor, *Fiscal History*, chapter 2.

106 Valeh Esfahani, p. 396; Dhabihi-Setudeh, vol. 6, doc. 10; Neves Aguas ed. *Viagens por terra da India a Portugal* (Lisbon 1991), p. 173. In 931/1525, Durmish Khan Shamlu, was already *emir al-omara* of Khorasan. Qomi, vol. 1, p. 163.

107 For example, Emir Khan Mousellu Turkoman, *hakem* of Tabriz and *emir al-omara* of Azerbaijan. Valeh Esfahani, p. 458. In 1585, Pireh Mohammad Khan accepted to become *begler-begi* and *emir al-omara* of all of Azerbaijan. Qomi, vol. 2, p. 767.

108 Yusef, p. 129.

109 Esfahani, p. 75, 123; see also Shamlu, p. 332; Valeh Esfahani, pp. 617, 623, 658, 690.

110 Esfahani, pp. 75, 129; following Ottoman usage? see Ibid., p. 241 (*qul-aghasi* of Sham and Sivas).

confirmed by the DM and TM.[111]

The *begler-begi*s had total control over their subordinate khans and their troops.[112] The DM states that a *begler-begi* was higher in rank than a khan, and the *soltan*s obeyed the khan.[113] For this reason, and because he also was an emir himself, the *begler-begi* was also referred to as *emir al-omara* of (name of province). We have 11 examples of this from Azerbaijan,[114] Fars,[115] Khorasan,[116] Chokhur-Sa'd,[117] Shirvan,[118] Qarabagh,[119] 'Iraq-e 'Arab (or Baghdad),[120] Erivan,[121] Kurdestan,[122] Lar,[123] and Qandahar.[124] There is also mention made of an *emir al-omara* of half of Khorasan.[125] By the end of 'Abbas I's reign there were 11 *begler-begi*s, of which five were *gholam*s (Fars [Kuhgilu, Lar, Bahrain, Jarun], Qarabagh, 'Iraq-e 'Arab, Astarabad, Shirvan), two were special cases, sort of *vali*s, (Lorestan, Shahrezur), and the remaining four were Qezelbash emirs (Khorasan, Chokhur Sa'd, Azerbaijan, Qandahar).[126] Eskander Monshi does not mention a *begler-begi* of Herat or Kerman, provinces that were among the first areas to be mentioned as having been governed by a *begler-begi*. Not all of these jurisdiction would remain under a *begler-begi* after the 1630s, however. Baghdad was lost to the Safavids as of the peace treaty of 1039/1639. Fars was governed by a vizier between 1632 and 1722. Arvaneq is not heard from in other and later sources and neither is Ghuriyan, which was normally under a *hakem*. Shahr-e Zurpavand also is an exception, because it belonged to Kurdestan. Among the remaining jurisdictions Ardalan, Kurdestan, Lorestan, and Shekar-'Ali had a special position, often being regarded as a kind of *vali*dom. This means that only 13 jurisdictions remained that usually were governed by a *begler-begi*.

The changes probably have to do with political considerations as well as royal favor. This is clear when we observe that later in the 17th

---

111 Sanson, pp. 31-2. DM, p. 39; TM, p. 44.
112 Du Mans, p. 151.
113 DM, p. 39; Richard, vol. 2, pp. 7, 114, 281.
114 Qarakhani, "Buq'ah", doc. 5.
115 Molla Jalal, pp. 95, 97; Horst, Heribert "Ein Immunitätsdiplom Schah Muhammad Khudabandahs vom Jahre 989/1581", *ZDMG* 105 (1955), pp. 290-2; Yusef, p. 146.
116 Molla Jalal, p. 184; Yusef, p. 253.
117 Savory, *History*, vol. 1, pp. 338-9.
118 Savory, *History*, vol. 1, p. 338-9; Yusef, pp. 100, 169.
119 Savory, *History*, vol. 1, p. 338-9; Yusef, pp. 109, 158.
120 Yusef, pp. 126, 156.
121 Yusef, pp. 155, 246.
122 Yusef, p. 156.
123 Yusef, p. 182.
124 Yusef, p. 209.
125 Savory, *History*, vol. 1, pp. 224, 381.
126 Monshi, vol. 2, pp. 1084-6; Savory, *History*, vol. 2, pp. 1314-7.

century the list of *begler-begis* became longer, in fact we number 22 *begler-begis*, to wit: Ardalan,[127] Arvaneq,[128] Astarabad,[129] Azerbaijan,[130] Baghdad,[131] Chokhur-Sa'd,[132] Erivan,[133] Fars,[134] Ghuriyan,[135] Herat,[136] Kerman,[137] Khorasan,[138] Kuhgilu,[139] Kurdestan,[140] Lorestan,[141] Marv,[142] Mashhad,[143] Qarabagh,[144] Shahr-e Zurpavand,[145] Shakki,[146] Shekar-'Ali,[147] and Shirvan.[148] According to Kaempfer, Persia was governed by 25 *begler-begis*, assisted by khans and *soltans*. "Many now are not existing, for the land has been turned into *khasseh* and is managed directly from the capital."[149] This is confirmed by Sanson, who reports

---

[127] Qarakhani "Buq'eh",doc. 5.

[128] Lambton, *Landlord*, p. 119.

[129] This province remained under a *begler-begi* till the end of the Safavid period. Yusef, pp. 24, 234; Dhabihi-Setudeh, vol. 6, docs 21, 20, 23 (in 1077/1066); Ibid., doc. 1 (in 1136/1724).

[130] This also remained under a *begler-begi* till the end of the Safavid period. Yusef, pp. 166, 215; Lambton, *Landlord*, p. 113f; Qarakhani "Buq'ah," docs. 5-7 (in 1116/1704).

[131] Baghdad was lost to the Safavids after the treaty of 1637. Nevertheless in the early 1630s there still was a Safavid *begler-begi* of Baghdad or 'Iraq-e 'Arab. Yusef, pp. 38, 80.

[132] Till the end of the Safavid period. Papaziyan 1959, docs. 21, 28, 29, 30, 35, 39, 40; Yusef, pp. 138, 153.

[133] Till the end of the Safavid period. *2500 sal*, pp. 30 (in 1086/1675) 32, 38 (in 1109/1698); Yusef, p. 153.

[134] Not from 1632, when it was managed by a vizier till 1134/1722, when a *begler-begi* and *sardar* was appointed as a wartime measure. Qa'em-Maqami, Jahangir. *Yaksadupanjah sanad-e tarikhi az Jala'iriyan ta Pahlavi*, Tehran 1348/1969. doc. 40.

[135] Yusef, p. 27.

[136] Yusef, p. 253.

[137] Semsar, Mohammad Hasan. "Du farman va-mohri tazeh az padeshahan-e Safaviyeh va Zandiyeh", *BT* 8 (1352/1973), p. 183.

[138] Yusef, 144; Shamlu, p. 332; Da'udi, doc. 5.

[139] Yusef, p. 215.

[140] Yusef, p. 189.

[141] Yusef, pp. 48, 156, 172.

[142] Yusef, p. 249.

[143] Mashhad was not the same jurisdiction as Khorasan. Yusef, pp. 104, 107, 150.

[144] Till the end of the Safavid period. Musavi, M. T. *Orta asr Azerbaijan tarikhna dair fars dilinda jazylmysh sanadlar*. Baku 1965, doc. 10; Puturidze 1961, doc. 31; Ibid. 1962, doc. 21; Ibid., 1965, doc. 20; Musavi, *Orta asr Azarbaijan tarikhina dair fars-dili sanadlarXVI-XVIII asrlar* (Baku 1977), doc. 10.

[145] Yusef, p. 136.

[146] Musavi 1977, doc. 6; also called *hakem* (in 1061/1650).

[147] Yusef, p. 126.

[148] Till the end of the Safavid period. Puturidze 1961, doc. 21; Musavi, M.T. *Baky tarikhna dair orta asr sandalari*. Baku 1967, doc. 10; Puturidze 1965, doc. 11, 22, 36.

[149] Kaempfer, *Am Hofe*, p. 127; Richard, vol. 2, p. 259.

that there were only 12 *begler-begis*, to wit: Tabriz, Ardabil, Lar, Mashhad, Astarabad, Kermanshah, Hamadan, Shustar, Ganjeh, Shamakhi, Erivan and Kors [Qars].[150] Towards the end of the Safavid dynasty there were 13 high ranking *begler-begis* in Persia according to both the DM and the TM: Qandahar, Shirvan, Herat, Tabriz (or Azerbaijan), Chokhur Sa'd, Qarabagh and Ganjeh, Astarabad, Kuhgilu'i, Kerman, Marv, 'Alishekar and Hamadan, Mashhad and Qazvin.[151] Lower ranking governors were usually referred to as *hakem*, often with the title of khan or *soltan* (see list), of whom there usually five or more under each *begler-begi*.[152]

The following list of provincial emirs and governors (*hakem*) with the title of khan or *soltan*, and their jurisdictions is not complete. It covers a period of about 150 years, and it therefore does not reflect the historical situation at a particular moment in time. Also, it is an incomplete list, because it does not include information from all available sources. However, it seems to bear out Venetian sources that state that Tahmasp I had 50 to 70 khans and *soltans* under him, who governed the country. The main cities, according to the Venetians, were Shamakhi, Sechi, Eres, Servan, Derbent, Caracach, Aradouil, Tauris, Reivan, Genge, Isfahan, Msandran, Gilan, Herat, Cassan, Siras, Starabat, Chilmisnar, Candahar, Iesed, Sapanec, Sultania, Bargo, Cum, Coran, Seva, Casbin and others which have jurisdiction over other towns and villages. Isfahan has 12 *soltans* in its government; Qazvin three *soltans*; Herat also three and 'Abbas Mirza; Candahar three and Rostam Mirza.[153]

Abhar,[154] Abuvard,[155] 'Adeljavaz,[156] Afshar in 1106/1694; Akhasteh or Akhastabad,[157] Aqcheh-Qal'eh,[158] Ardabil,[159] Astara and Talesh (or

---

150 Sanson, p. 31.

151 DM, p. 43-4; TM, p. 44.

152 Richard, vol. 2, p. 260. See for a list of governors referring to the late 1720s in Nasiri, *Alqab*, pp. 71-112, detailing their jurisdiction, revenues and number of their retainers.

153 Minadoi, p. 52. Shamakhi was under one khan who also was in charge of Sechi (Shakki) and other cities. Ibid., p. 64. The 70 *soltans* "are payed in ready money out of the Chamber in Casbin, with a stipend of three thousand, foure thousand, or five thousand Cecchins a piece." Ibid., p. 77. d'Allesandrini has 50 *soltans*. Berchet, p. 181; Gemelli-Careri, vol. 2, pp. 220-22 provides a list of 81 jurisdictions that were under a khan, while another 27 were under a vizier. This list was drawn up for him by a Persian acquaintance and was based on data in the royal chancellery. This matter needs more research and a dated scheduled list needs to be drawn up reflecting annual changes therein.

154 (*soltan, gholam*), Yusef, p. 272.

155 (*gholam, soltan*), Yusef, pp. 22, 199.

156 Fekete, Lajos. *Einführung in die persische Palaeographie. 101 persische Dokumente.* Aus dem Nachlass des Verfassers herausgegeben von G. Hazai, Budapest 1977. doc. 72 (in 960/1553).

157 Yusef, pp. 82, 171.

Kaskar),[160] Astarabad,[161] Bakhtiyari,[162] Baku,[163] Baliyan,[164] Barda',[165] Bestam,[166] Bitlis,[167] Buri,[168] Chokhur-Sa'd,[169] Daghestan and Shirvan,[170] Darabjerd,[171] Darband,[172] Dashtestan,[173] Darun and Chemeshkork?,[174] Douraq,[175] Deilam,[176] Dezful and Shustar,[177] Dinavar, Kolhar, and Sonqor,[178] Erivan,[179] Esfazar,[180] Fakhran,[181] Farah,[182] Faradein, Lenjan and Chahar Mahall,[183] Firuzkuh, Demavand, Khvar and Semnan,[184] Fusanj and Ghuriyan,[185] Garus,[186] Gilan,[187] Hamadan,[188] Hormuz,[189] Jeijektu and Meimand,[190] Jam,[191] Kankarkonan,[192] Kaskar,[193] Khaveh,[194]

---

[158] Puturidze 1962, doc. 34 (in 1111/1699).

[159] Yusef, p. 215.

[160] Yusef, pp. 16, 119; Valeh Esfahani, p. 411.

[161] Prior to the institutionalization of the title of *begler-begi* (in 950/1544) Dhabihi-Setudeh, vol. 6, doc. 3, 6; Valeh Esfahani, p. 408.

[162] Yusef, p. 251.

[163] Busse, *Untersuchungen*, doc. 19.

[164] Molla Jalal, p. 431.

[165] Yusef, p. 245.

[166] In combination with Astarabad and Damghan in 990/1582. Dhahebi-Setudeh, vol. 6, doc. 1.

[167] Valeh Esfahani, p. 161.

[168] (*soltan*), Yusef, p. 240.

[169] Valeh Esfahani, p. 411.

[170] Yusef, p. 192.

[171] Valeh Esfahani, p. 410.

[172] (both *soltan* and khan), Yusef, pp. 1000, 228; Puturidze, 1961, doc. 2; Ibid., 1965, doc. 22.

[173] (khan) Yusef, p. 248.

[174] (*gholam* and *soltan*), Yusef, p. 206.

[175] (khan) Yusef, pp. 117, 215.

[176] Yusef, p. 16, 119.

[177] (khan) Valeh Esfahani, p. 409.

[178] (*soltan*) Yusef, pp. 246, 273.

[179] (khan *va qal'ehdar*), Yusef, p. 169.

[180] (*soltan*) Savory, *History*, vol. 1, p. 376; Valeh Esfahani, p. 601.

[181] (in 1114/1703) Musavi 1965, doc. 12.

[182] (khan and *soltan*) Yusef, p. 192; Valeh Esfahani, pp. 294, 411.

[183] Ra'in, Esma'il. *Iraniyan-e Aramani* (Tehran 1349/1970), doc. 11 (in 1079/1669).

[184] Valeh Esfahani, p. 133.

[185] Savory, *History*, vol. 1, p. 376.

[186] In combination with *begler-begi* of Ardalan, or with *hakem* of Kermanshah and Arumi. Qarakhani, docs. 5 and 6.

[187] (khan) Valeh Esfahani, p. 402.

[188] Valeh Esfahani, pp. 332, 408.

[189] (*soltan*), Yusef, pp. 117, 235.

[190] (*beg*) Yusef, p. 27.

[191] Valeh Esfahani, pp. 410, 606.

[192] (*beg*) Yusef, p. 191.

[193] (*soltan*, khan, *beg*), Yusef, pp. 16, 119, 177, 279.

Khoy,[195] Khvaf,[196] Khvar and Semnan,[197] Kuhgilu,[198] Kusuyeh,[199] Lar,[200] Maneh,[201] Marand,[202] Marv,[203] Maruchaq,[204] Mashad,[205] Moghanat,[206] Nakhjevan,[207] Natanz,[208] Nesavdrun,[209] Nishapur,[210] Panjdeh,[211] Qabanat,[212] Qara Olus,[213] Qazvin,[214] Qebeh,[215] Qezel 'Ajaj,[216] Qom,[217] Resht,[218] Sabzavar,[219] Sajavad,[220] Salmas,[221] Sarakhs,[222] Seistan,[223] Semnan,[224] Shakki,[225] Shiraz,[226] Shamakhi,[227] Shushtar,[228] Somay and Targivar,[229] Tabriz,[230] Tiflis,[231] Tonakebun,[232] Tun,[233] Urmiyeh,[234]

---

[194] Also emir of Lorestan. Valeh Esfahani, p. 411.

[195] Savory, *History*, vol. 1, p. 373.

[196] (*soltan*) Valeh Esfahani, p. 409.

[197] (*gholam* and *beg*), Yusef, p. 240.

[198] (khan), Yusef, p. 117.

[199] (*soltan*), Valeh Esfahani, p. 409.

[200] (*beg* and khan), Yusef, pp. 117, 174, 177, 182.

[201] (*soltan*), Yusef, p. 192.

[202] Puturidze 1961, doc. 4.

[203] (khan) Yusef, p. 28.

[204] (*soltan* and khan), Yusef, pp. 26, 235.

[205] (khan), Yusef, p. 27; Valeh Esfahani, pp. 407, 602.

[206] Valeh Esfahani, p. 86.

[207] Yusef, p. 32; Papaziyan 1959, doc. 20; "2500 sal dar hemayat-e shahanshahi-ye Iran", *Zamimeh-ye majalleh-ye Hur beh monasabat-e 2500 sal-e shahanshahi-ye Iran*. Tabriz 1350/1971, p. 32, 38.

[208] Valeh Esfahani, p. 389.

[209] (*soltan*), Yusef, p. 24.

[210] (*soltan*, khan) Yusef, p. 22; Valeh Esfahani, pp. 294, 606.

[211] (*soltan*), Yusef, p. 166.

[212] (*soltan*, khan), Yusef, p. 43.

[213] Puturidze 1961, doc. 12.

[214] (khan), Valeh Esfahani, p. 613.

[215] (*soltan*) Yusef, p. 192.

[216] (*soltan*), Yusef, p. 192.

[217] (*soltan*) Valeh Esfahani, p. 410.

[218] (*soltan*) Valeh Esfahani, p. 336.

[219] Yusef, pp. 22, 206 (*soltan* and khan).

[220] Valeh Esfahani, p. 412.

[221] Yusef, pp. 147, 157 (khan).

[222] Valeh Esfahani, pp. 279, 409 (*beg, soltan*)

[223] Da'udi, Hosein. "Asnad-e khvandan-i kalantari-ye Seistan", *BT*, 4 (1348/1969), docs. 5, 7; Yusef, p. 132 (khan).

[224] Yusef, p. 240 (*gholam, soltan*).

[225] Musavi 1977, doc. 1; Puturidze 1965, doc. 38.

[226] Valeh Esfahani, p. 410.

[227] Papaziyan 1959, doc. 38.

[228] Valeh Esfahani, p. 409; Yusef, p. 43 (khan, *soltan*).

[229] Lambton, *Landlord*, p. 109f.

[230] Valeh Esfahani, p. 610 (khan).

[231] Valeh Esfahani, p. 409.

[232] (*soltan*) Yusef, p. 22.

[233] Valeh Esfahani, p. 606.

Ushni,[235] Van,[236] and Zakhor.[237]

In the 17th century, the governor's task continued to be the maintenance of law and order and the army. The cost of doing so was borne by the governate's revenues. The governors of frontier areas had to keep a larger number of troops than those in the interior of the country. The governors had to send each year a certain amount of money to the shah and the leading courtiers, which were part of the latter's fees (*rosum*). In addition, they had to send choice goods and produce (*barkhaneh*) from their governate to the royal court. Other means to obtain payment from the governors was to send them a present such as a robe of honor. Although this was a costly affair, the governors tried to turn this financial loss into political gain. For they portrayed this grant as a sign of royal favor and that therefore those who wanted to complain (*shekayatchi*) about their misrule at court had better think twice before doing so.[238]

Kaempfer summed up the duties of a provincial governor as follows: "The governor has to pay for a certain number of troops in his area, to send supplies for the royal kitchen, and to send *pishkesh*. In return he gets a robe of honor of 12 tomans. His annual revenue amounts to 7,000 to 8,000 tomans depending on the size [of the area] and the greed of the khan. Most of them have an agent at court, who takes care of his interests. The khan appoints these himself, with the approval of the grand vizier. In importance these agents are below the *soltan*s.[239]

In the 17th century each governor had the title of khan or *soltan*. The khan's "court is a copy, on a smaller scale, of that of the shah. The ceremonial is similar and when they go out riding they are accompanied by a host of servants and the leading citizens. Daily the *naqqareh-khaneh* strikes up, while he also is the local magistrate. Thus the khan is like a vice-roy whose only fear is to lose the royal favor."[240] From an administrative correspondence (*ensha*) manual for the governate of Astarabad it is clear that the governor's court included a wide range of administrative and other staff, which indeed constituted itself a mini-court.[241] The *soltan*s were in charge of smaller areas. They also behaved like little kings. Most of them were subject to a khan, for they seldom depended directly from the shah. They also had a small military command.[242] What was new about the situation, as compared with the

---

234 Savory, *History*, vol. 1, p. 373; Yusef, p. 138; Puturidze 1965, doc. 23.

235 Savory, *History*, vol. 1, p. 373.

236 Dhahibi-Setudeh vol. 6, doc. 41.

237 Puturidze 1965, doc. 38.

238 Richard, vol. 2, pp. 260, 273.

239 Kaempfer, *Am Hofe*, p. 127-8; Richard, vol. 2, p. 261-2.

240 Kaempfer, *Am Hofe*, p. 127. The governors were all like minor kings. Chardin, vol. 5, p. 255.

241 Dhahibi-Setudeh, vol. 6, pp. 454-78.

242 Kaempfer, *Am Hofe*, p. 130.

16th century, was that the number of governors was smaller. Also, that, probably as of the 1630s, the governors had three watchdogs, appointed by the shah, attached to their administration. Previously, there had only been one, i.e. the vizier. Now, in addition, there was a *janeshin*, or deputy and a *vaqaye'-nevis* or recorder of events. They had to see to it that the governor took good care of the shah's interests.[243]

In the beginning of the Safavid era the governors of large provinces were allowed to appoint their own dependent sub-governors. When shahs were minor then they had no say at all in these matters.[244] Durmish Khan's appointment diploma as governor-general of Khorasan in 930/1524 states that he could appoint and dismiss the sub-governors. The governor-general of Herat also was allowed to appoint his sub-governors at the direction (*esharat*) of the shah.[245] Eskander Beg comments that Emamqoli Khan, *begler-begi* of Fars had full authority over the appointment and dismissal of subordinate governors in the areas under his jurisdiction, which was why he could not discover their names.[246] According to della Valle, all *begler-begis* had this authority, for they had "absolute authority, nominating at pleasure all the officers under him as well civil as military, subject to no orders of the shah in his province than what regard the number of people to be drafted for war, or matters relative to the state." There were nevertheless *soltans* who received their appointment directly from the shah, and, therefore, did not need to recognize the superior authority of a khan.[247] In the 17th century eunuchs and harem inmates also had much to say about appointments.[248] All subordinate emirs could be dismissed and appointed at the *begler-begi*'s request, for "on the latter's report they are appointed and dismissed."[249]

This direct interest and some measure of authority of the governor-generals in the selection of their management team created a situation in which stability was likely to prevail. For a governor was less likely to select somebody with whom he could not get along or whom he considered to be incompetent. Also, the fact that the turnover of governors in a particular jurisdiction was rather low engendered stability as well. A further stable factor was that in the 16th century the assignments of certain governorships were almost automatically tied up with specific Qezelbash tribes. For example, the Ostajalus received governorships in Chokhur Sa'd, Nakhjevan and Khalkhal; the Tekellu in Hamadan and Rey; the Shamlu in Khorasan (Herat); the Dhu'l-Faqr

---

243 Chardin, vol. 5, p. 258.
244 Monshi, p. 381.
245 Röhrborn, *Provinzen*, pp. 24-5.
246 Savory, *History*, vol. 2, p. 1316.
247 della Valle, p. 28.
248 Chardin, vol. 5, p. 278.
249 DM, p. 39; TM, p. 44.

in Fars (Shiraz); the Qajars in Qarabagh; the Afshars in Kuhgilu and Kerman, and the Turkomans in Qom, Kashan, and Saveh.[250] Arbitrary interference in such a process would have caused friction with all the Qezelbash emirs. Don Juan remarked that "The khans could be dismissed by the king at his pleasure, though they hold their land as their own property and consider it hereditary."[251] A similar phenomenon was that certain governorships were reserved for royal princes in the 16th century.[252]

This tradition of appointing prince-governors changed with Esma'il II, who started a new tradition by murdering his kinsmen. 'Abbas I followed his uncle's model, for after 1000/1592 no more royal princes were appointed as governor. He blinded his brothers and killed his own sons. Henceforth all royal sons remained in the harem, and brothers were killed or blinded on accession to the throne. Male children born to the shah's sisters were treated the same way, or were strangled.[253] One of the reasons, apart from royal paranoia, was the fact that during the pre-1590 period many of the Safavid princes had been pawns in the hands of their tutors. 'Abbas I himself had experienced that first hand. Eskander Beg Monshi summed up nicely the potential power of a tutor, whose "ward was like capital in his hands."[254] This constituted a possible source of instability, when power hungry tutors used their wards to advance their own schemes. Usually, a prince not yet of age was assigned a tutor. The usual term for the tutor was *laleh*, while the term *atabeg* (father) was rarely used. The office of *dedeh* (grandfather) also occurred, while in the case of Tahmasp Mirza, who still had to drink mother's milk, the governor's wife became his *dayeh* (wetnurse).[255] Sometimes, it even happened that more than one tutor was assigned. For example, in 932/1526 Hosein Khan Shamlu was governor of Herat and *laleh* of Sam Mirza, and Yar Ahmad Khalifeh was his *dedeh*.[256]

What also changed at that time was that after 998/1590 'Abbas I started to appoint *gholam*s as governor at the expense of the Qezelbash emirs. Eskander Monshi lists 92 powerful emirs of which 21 were *gholam*s in 1037/1627-8. Of the 14 key-provinces 8 were in the hands

[250] Sumer, pp. 172-5; Röhrborn, *Provinzen*, p. 31; the province of Rey was the mine of the Tekellu and Turkoman. Valeh Esfahani, p. 623; the Qajar tribe and the *uymaq* Otuzayeki only inhabited the province of Qarabagh. Ibid., p. 623, see also p. 624 where only Qajars were appointed there as *omara-ye tabin*.

[251] Don Juan, p. 46.

[252] For a complete list see Röhrborn, *Provinzen*, pp. 40-44.

[253] Chardin, vol. 5, pp. 217, 241-3; Sanson, p. 15.

[254] Monshi, vol. 1, pp. 164, 363.

[255] Qomi, vol. 1, p. 397.

[256] Qomi, vol. 1, p. 164. Qurkhoms Soltan Shamlu became *dedeh* of the prince. Qomi, vol. 2, p. 847.

of *gholam*s by the end of 'Abbas I's reign, but only 3 out of 11 under Safi I. A similar percentage as under 'Abbas I was also achieved under 'Abbas II.[257] Some of these *gholam*s even were chiefs of Qezelbash tribes such as of the Bayat and Rumlu. The rationale was that "When a qezelbash emir or a provincial governor died and there was no one in his tribe suitable for promotion to the rank of emir, one of the *gholam*s of the royal household who had distinguished himself by his justice, skill, bravery, initiative, and devotion to his benefactor he was made emir of that tribe, placed in command of those tribal forces, or made governor of that region. As a result of this policy, by the time of the death of Shah 'Abbas, twenty one *gholam*s had been raised to the status of emir with the rank of khan or *soltan*."[258]

As long as the selection of governors was made on the basis of merit and as long as there were objective criteria to judge someone's performance the new system could be as effective as the old one, which also had its drawbacks. However, the new system allowed the greater use of favoritism, because the pool from which the governors were drawn was less uniform and thus they were more antagonistic with one another. We therefore observe that under Soleiman the 'sale' of offices starts. Various contemporary observers remarked on the high turnover of governors and royal viziers. The latter, in particular, bought their posts from the eunuchs, royal favorites, important ministers, and especially the shah's mother. Because the "presents" to these persons were often bought with borrowed money the royal viziers had to pay back their loan as well as to keep their patron happy. All of this and more had to be paid, of course, by the unhappy subjects. Consequently, oppression in the *khasseh* areas was more severe than in areas governed by governors (*hakem*).[259] Whereas in the past the governors only were changed when there were complaints against them during Shah Soltan Hosein's reign the same jurisdiction sometimes had two or more governors in one year. Because the governors also increasingly obtained their post by paying for it they had to recoup their investment as well by making the population pay. Also, justice was more difficult to obtain, in particular against the royal viziers who had their patrons at court.[260] What further facilitated the governor's relative independence was the

---

257 Röhrborn, *Provinzen*, pp. 33-7.
258 Savory, *History*, vol. 2, p. 1315-6.
259 Chardin, vol. 5, pp. 278-9.
260 Brosset, M.F., *Collection d'Historiens Arméniens*. 2 vols. (St. Petersburg 1874-76 [Amsterdam n.d]), [2 vols. in one] vol. 2, p. 204; Chardin, vol. 5, p. 279-82, notes that when there was a vizier the oppression was more severe than when the governor was a khan, and it was rare that they were punished. A late Safavid chronicle criticizes the sale of offices, which often occurred more than once in the same year. *Majma' al-Tavarikh* as quoted by Röhrborn, *Provinzen*, p. 26. see also Floor, *Bar Oftadan*, p. 22; Ibid., *Afghan Occupation*, p. 21; Krusinski, p. 104; Mostoufi, p. 123.

number, variety and sequence of procedures, which were often exploited to delay the performance of promises, whilst the mainly nominal and arbitrary control exercised over the great officers of state in the provinces, meant little interference in their affairs.[261]

Aqa

In addition to the large *teyul*s given to the emirs there were smaller land or revenue assignments, which were given to deserving soldiers. This class of soldiers, which was known as *aqa*, received these entitlements for their upkeep in lieu of which they had to provide two or more armed men in case of war. As Minorsky suspected the *aqayan* mentioned in Persian texts were not always eunuchs, for the TM refers to ushers who are sons of the *aqayan*. He therefore, rightly, suggested that the *aqa*s formed a class of "gentlemen" of a rank inferior to the emirs, *moqarrab*s, *yasavol*s, and *eshik-aqasi*s.[262] According to Don Juan an *aqa* ranked below a khan and a *beg*, for an *aqa* was simply "a rich husbandsman" on whose land many peasants worked.[263] The honorific *aqa* was, for example, not applied to merchants. Tavernier was not called *aqa* in his diploma given to him by 'Abbas II, but simply 'French merchant' despite the fact that in the translation in his book he states *monsieur*. This piece of social climbing was noted by one of his contemporaries, the Carmelite Ange de St. Joseph.[264] However, it would seem that Chardin in a similar case was awarded the honorific *aqa*.[265] As is clear from a small number of decrees the rank of *aqa* was indeed a military function which required that one brought two armed horsemen (*du nafar-e sepahi*) or a well equipped horseman (*savareh-ye mokammal-e yaraq*) to the army when called upon. The *aqa* in this case had received a *teyul* (revenue assignment) with an income of about 11-16 tomans.[266] Another *aqa* only had 8 tomans in the 1690s.[267] In one case the *aqa*s were referred to as *saheb-e soyurghal va cherik* (tax exempt and military obligated).[268] It would also seem that all *aqa*s were members of a Qezelbash tribe. For example, Mehdiqoli Beg Saru Sheikh Dhu'l-Qadr was governor of Shiraz and his substitute was *rish-safid-e aqayan-e Dhu'l-Qadr*. These *aqa*s appointed the substitute as khan and dismissed the governor.[269] In the 1620s and thereafter there is

261 Chardin, vol. 2, pp. 257-64.

262 TM, p. 118, n. 1.

263 Don Juan, p. 180.

264 Bastiaensen, Michel ed. *Souvenirs de la Perse safavide et autres lieux de l'Orient (1664-1678).* (Brussel 1985), p. 196.

265 Chardin, Atlas pl. IV.

266 Puturidze 1962, doc. 17 (1695); Ibid., 1965, doc. 37 (1721).

267 Qa'emmaqami 1348, doc. 2.

268 Nasiri, *Dastur*, p. 65.

269 Qomi, vol 1, p. 552; vol. 2 pp. 627, 557-8, 722-3.

also mention of *qurchiyan va tofangchiyan va aqayan*.[270] In 1106/1694-5, the *sepahsalar* led an army of 12,000 consisting of *qurchis*, *gholams*, *aqas*, *tofangchis* and *tupchis*.[271] There apparently even existed a class (*selk*) of *aqayan*.[272] This is only natural taking into account that that *aqayan* seemed to dominate the palace staff and that their number must have been considerable enough to create a separate department for them, the *sarkar-e aqayan*, which was managed by the *lashkar-nevis*.[273] In Georgian texts the term *malek-agha* is used to refer to a class of landowners, who also had to provide military service, which seems to denote the same group.[274]

The Royal Vizier
Since about 1630, the role and authority of the governor-*teyuldar* decreased while that of the royal vizier increased in importance. This had to do with the further reduction of *mamalek* lands and the bestowal of *teyul-olka*s to emirs, and the consequent growth of *khasseh* lands, combined with the purposeful policy of the central government to increase its control over the military-governors and their lands. This, of course, was the result of the taming of the Qezelbash and the appointment of royal slaves or *gholams* as governors. These changes also had consequences for the relationship between the governor and his vizier.

   Following Timurid practice there was a vizier, or intendent, in each province. In the beginning of the Safavid reign the governor appointed his own vizier and other staff, whom he could dismiss whenever he liked.[275] For example, Emir Khan, governor of Khorasan, appointed his vizier, then dismissed and punished him two years later, but the newly appointed vizier was done away soon thereafter and replaced too.[276] Nevertheless, the emir-governor gave the vizier wide-ranging authority both concerning governance and financial affairs (*molk va mali*). In this respect the relationship between the emir and his vizier was not that much different between that of the shah and his *vakil*, where the latter also was in charge of all matters *molki va mali*. Because the Qezelbash governors did not take a great interest in the mundane affair of managing their governate, for which they also lacked the expertise, the vizier, as manager of fiscal and judicial affairs, had a powerful position. In fact, Budaq Monshi, who became vizier and *vakil* of Mostafa Soltan Varsaq, who was governor of Sabzavar and Turshiz, wrote: "in reality I

---

270 Yusef, pp. 160, 166.
271 Nasiri, *Dastur*, p. 100, also p. 106.
272 Nasrabadi, pp. 17, 24, 31, 98.
273 TM, p. 75-6; Nasiri, *Alqab*, p. 56.
274 Brosset, *Histoire* vol. II 2, p. 89.
275 Röhrborn, *Provinzen*, p. 94; Monshi, vol. 1, p. 165f.
276 Khvandamir, vol. 4, p. 575.

was not his retainer; I was the master, and he the servant."[277] Consequently, the trust between the governor and vizier had to be high, and therefore the viziers are referred to as favorites (*moqarrab*) and deputies (*novvab*) of the governor. The role of these viziers will not be discussed here, because their function is an extension of that of the governor, and, formally, the vizier was but the executor of the latter's will.

However, already early in the Safavid reign the central government started to appoint viziers in provinces that it considered of strategic importance such as Azerbaijan and Khorasan. These viziers received their instructions from the central government, not from the governor. After 1510, the formal powers of these royal viziers (*vozara-ye shahi*), as they were also called, grew. Khvajeh Seif al-Din Mozaffar Betekchi, who was vizier and *saheb-e divan* of Khorasan, became the first of the royal viziers to obtain the right to seal royal decrees (*ahkam-e mota'* and *farmans*) next to the grand vizier.[278] He was probably also singled out for his local knowledge and influence. For Khvajeh Seif al-Din Betekchi Astarabadi's family had been for generations *moqaddam* and *ra'is* of Astarabad.[279] Khvajeh Seif al-Din, who was named *vazir-e koll*, held wide ranging powers, for all matters had to be decided with his approval.[280] His successor, the *sadr* of Khorasan, Ghayath al-Din Mohammad, also had wide ranging powers, but could not get along with Emir Khan, the governor, who had him killed.[281] The governor was recalled and his replacement was henceforth assisted by a *vazir-e koll*.

In Isfahan the central government appointed a royal vizier as early as 914/1508, in Khorasan at least as of 917/1511 and in Azerbaijan at least as of 964/1557, and probably earlier.[282] In Khorasan, Khvajeh Betekchi was appointed as *vazir-e koll-e mahall-e teyul-e khavanin va salatin va 'asaker* in 1511, while at the same time another of Najm-e Thani's partisans, Emir 'Emad al-Din Mahmud-e Nur Kamal was appointed as *vazir-e motlaq* of Khorasan.[283] This new type of royal viziers held the

---

[277] Savory, Roger M. "Some Notes on the Provincial Administration of the Early Safawid Empire", *BSOAS* 27 (1964), p. 120, n. 52 quoting the *Javaher al-Akhbar*.

[278] Valeh Esfahani, p. 186-7.

[279] He was given a robe of honor and a *taj*, when he submitted himself to Esma'il I in 909/1504. Ben Khvandamir, p. 130. Other members of the family also made themselves useful to the Safavids and were honored with titles and functions. Khvajeh Mozaffar Betekchi Astarabadi. Qomi, vol. 1, p. 109, 132, 165, 202; Khvajeh Moh. Saleh Betekchi Astarabadi. Qomi, vol. 1, p. 282, 398; his grandson was made a *saheb-e tabl va 'alam* and promoted to the rank of *soltan*, Astarabadi, p. 68.

[280] Khvandamir, vol. 4, p. 507.

[281] Ibid., vol. 4, p. 576-7, 581-4 588-9.

[282] *Az divan-e a'la mansab-e vazir-e koll-e Khorasan dasht* in 957/1550-1. Qomi, vol. 1, p. 349.

[283] Aubin, "Soufis", p. 119, n. 215; Khvandamir, vol. 4, p. 529.

title of *vazir-e koll* as against the viziers that functioned under them, who were known as *vazir-e jozv*. Because their jurisdiction usually went beyond that of the governor they were attached to and usually encompassed more than one governate. For example, the *vazir-e koll* for Khorasan resided in Herat, but also managed the affairs of Mashhad, which was a separate governate. The history of the *vazir-e koll* of Khorasan is still incomplete and had its ups and downs, but the pattern is clear. The central government wanted to have a royal vizier in place to serve as a controller of the governor.[284] Eskander Beg lists 10 of these royal or provincial viziers, i.e. appointed by the central government, at the end of Tahmasp I's reign in 984/1576 for Azerbaijan, Shirvan, Khorasan, eastern Gilan, Yazd, Isfahan, Kashan, Qazvin, Fars, Ardabil, and parts of Herat.[285] It may be that some of these provinces, or parts thereof, were *khasseh* lands, or that the governors concerned were young or minor, or that the province housed a holy shrine, and that the presence of a provincial vizier was intermittent, but the tendency is clear.[286]

The other major province that was singled out to have a provincial vizier was Azerbaijan. The first *vazir-e koll* there was appointed in 966/1559 with authority over Azerbaijan, Shirvan, Shakki and Georgia. This vizier died shortly before Tahmasp I, and his replacement had not yet left for his post in 1576.[287] No *vazir-e koll* was appointed thereafter, because of the unsettled situation under Khodabandeh, followed by the Ottoman occupation of Azerbaijan. However, under 'Abbas I, a *vazir-e koll* was appointed again in 1016/1607-08 after he had retaken Azerbaijan.[288] Henceforth, a *vazir-e koll* would be operational in Azerbaijan till the end of the Safavid dynasty.[289] It would seem, however, that the vizier of Shirvan was independent from his colleague

---

284 Röhrborn, *Provinzen*, pp. 100-04 for more details on the situation between the years 932/1527-984/1576. There was also, in 1512, a vizier in Herat, Emir 'Emad al-Din Mahmud Esfahani, appointed by the shah as *vazir va saheb-e ekhtiyar-e omur-e molki va mali-ye Khorasan*. Khvandamir, vol. 4, p. 529. Sheikh Majd al-Din Mohammad Kermani was appointed as the *zabet-e amval-e divani-ye mamalek-e Khorasan*. Khvandamir, p. 554, 575 [vizier] (1514).
285 Monshi, vol. 1, p. 165f.; Savory, vol. 1, pp. 259-61.
286 Röhrborn, *Provinzen*, p. 96 with several such examples.
287 Röhrborn, *Provinzen*, p. 104.
288 Monshi, vol. 2, p. 758, 760.
289 Puturidze 1961, doc. 16 (1047/1637); Ibid., doc. 21 (1052/1642); Papaziyan 1959, doc. 35 (1058/1648); Puturidze 1961, doc. 27 (1061/1652); Ibid., 1962, docs. 1, 2 (1072-74/1662-3); Lambton, *Landlord*, p. 113 (1073/1662); Puturidze 1962, doc. 7 (1081/1670); Qarakhani, "Buq'eh," doc. 5 (1106/1694); Puturidze 1965, docs. 4, 6 (1112/1700, 1114/1702); Qarakhani, "Buq'eh," doc. 7 (1117/1705); Musavi 1965, doc. 17 (1120/1798); Puturidze 1965, docs. 23, 33 (1123/1711; 1126/1715).

of Azerbaijan.[290]

Formally, these provincial viziers were appointed to assist the governor in the execution of their task. According to Sanson, "they do the same things as an intendant in France, except that they have no role in the judicial affairs. They are the governor's assistant."[291] That the vizier was the governor (-general)'s assistant is also stated in Persian sources. The vizier of Azerbaijan, for example, is explicitly referred to as *na'eb-e begler-begi* of Tabriz around 1655.[292] According to Chardin, however, the vizier was one of the three officials appointed by the shah to keep an eye on the governor. These were: the vizier, the *janeshin* or deputy and the *vaqaye'-nevis*. All three had to report to the capital on a regular basis any untoward activities undertaken by the governor. In addition there were one or more *darugheh*s in each governate, who also could function as a check on the governor.[293] However, this supervising triumvirate, about whom we know not much beyond the fact that it existed, was a late 17th century development which did not exist in the 16th century, and probably not even in the first half of the 17th century, and was probably only an embellishment of the original vizier's function.[294]

The provincial vizier's[295] duties were as follows: he was "charged with administrative, tax collection, judicial, and record keeping [duties] as well as to maintain good relations and the revenues of the province in such a manner that everybody -*arbab* (landlords), *ahali* (leading citizens) and the entire population- is happy. In addition, he had see to the construction and repairs of buildings, roads and bridges."[296] As such the vizier was not operating independently from the governor, but was both his chief executive officer as well as the eyes and ears for the central government. The vizier was assisted in the execution of his task by a *mostoufi*, who had a shared responsibility with the vizier in fiscal affairs, and a staff of lower ranking accountants and scribes.

Let's have a look at the vizier's functions such as presented by the texts. First administration. The vizier was a focal point for incoming orders and other information. He needed to know who else was appointed to local functions in his jurisdiction. This held for all kind of

---

[290] Monshi, vol. 2, pp. 753, 964, 991; Puturidze 1961, doc. 21 (1052/1642); Ibid., doc. 25 (1059/1649); Musavi 1977, doc. 8 (1077/1667).

[291] Sanson, p. 106.

[292] Vahid Qazvini, p. 190.

[293] Chardin, vol. 5, pp. 258-60.

[294] For the Afshar period the existence of a *kuzaji* [?] *va vaqaye'-nevis* in Merv is reported. Mervi, p. 1085.

[295] (*Vazir-e koll* [name of province: Dar al-Marz, Qazvin, Ray, Khorasan, Mazandaran.]) Molla Jalal, pp. 260, 328, 365.

[296] Afshar, Iraj, "Farmani az Shah Soltan Hosein", *Rahnama-ye ketab* 17 (1353/1974), p. 406f. For similar formulations see TM, p. 78 and Lambton, *Landlord*, p. 119.

functions such as a *sadr*, a *khalifeh*, a qadi, and a *kalantar*. In general he was not only informed about such appointments, but also ordered to assist them, to recognize them in their functions, and above all not to interfere with their tasks.

Tax collection was the flip side of the good administration coin. The vizier also had an important role in this area. Not only did he serve as court of appeal in case of conflict about payment of taxes,[297] but he also was ordered to see to it that orders with regard to *soyurghals*, tax exemption, tax reduction, and illegal excess revenue collection were properly taken care of.[298] Sanson, therefore, writes "There is in every City a Vizier, or Intendant of the Customs, who collects all these Duties, and out of which the Governour has always Ten per Cent. for his part."[299] The vizier played a similar role with regard to the payment of salaries (*hamehsaleh*) and revenue assignments (*teyul*).[300] Similar interventions also occurred with regard to endowment and *molk* property.[301] Together with the provincial *mostoufi*, the vizier was responsible for the management of the provincial revenue administration. In one case, e.g., these two officials were ordered not to make out drafts (*havaleh*s) for the *rasad-e arbab va ra'ayati* (the landlord's and peasants' tax share).[302] The governor had no authority with regard *khasseh* revenues that were collected in his jurisdiction. Any expenditures by the governor which were charged to these *khasseh* revenues could only take place after prior approval by the vizier. For example, when Homayun, the Moghul ruler of India, entered Khorasan, the governor of Herat was instructed by the shah to charge everything to the *khasseh* revenues, but to submit receipts to the *vazir-e koll*.[303] Payment of the cost of visiting royalty, ambassadors, and anyone else whose cost the shah defrayed, were generally all paid out of *khasseh* revenues.[304] In particular, of course, the vizier's task was to see to it that the governors did not oppress the population too much.[305] This is very much implied by Eskander Beg, when he writes "Both viziers were noted for their integrity and concern for the common people, and

---

[297] Dhabihi & Setudeh, vol. 6, doc. 6.

[298] Afshar, Iraj, "Chand farman marbut be Yazd", *FIZ* 11 (1342/1963), doc. 3; Da'udi, "Asnad", doc. 3.

[299] Sanson, p. 71.

[300] Puturidze 1961, doc. 30; Ibid. 1962, doc. 1, 2; Ibid., 1965, doc. 4, 6, 17; Lambton, Landlord, p. 113.

[301] Puturidze, 1961, doc. 30; Qarakhani, "Buq`ah", doc. 5, 7.

[302] Jahanpur, F. "Faramin-e padeshahan-e Safavi dar muzeh-ye Britaniya", *BT* 4 (1348/1969), doc. 13.

[303] Röhrborn, *Provinzen*, p. 109, n. 62. This statement is not included in a published text of this *farman*. Afshar, `Alamara-ye Tahmasp, pp. 408-23.

[304] Monshi, vol. 1, p. 101; Seistani, p. 420 (*mablaghi jehat-e kharj-e rah barat beh vazir Khorasan*). See also the para on the vizier of Isfahan.

[305] *Provinzen*, p. 106, n. 50; Monshi, vol. 2, p. 708.

acquired a great reputation in Khorasan and Azerbaijan. The administrative practices they instituted are still the rule and model in these provinces."[306]

The vizier's judicial role was circumscribed vis à vis that of the qadi.[307] His was the role of both judge and executive arm, although in some cases he was simply ordered to execute a ruling laid down by the court.[308] In case of a conflict about a *vaqf*, the vizier was ordered, together with the *ahali-ye shar'* (leading religious functionaries), to examine the dispute and arrive at a conclusion. The final decision was left to the *begler-begi* and the vizier.[309] Together with other officials, such as the *begler-begi*, the vizier had a role in case of flight of peasants to see to it that these were returned to their land and that a reasonable tax burden was agreed upon as well as any other outstanding conflict was settled.[310] In general, however, no judicial activities could be undertaken without the vizier's orders or without the presence of his representative.[311]

In the final analysis, the vizier had to take proper care of the population so that they were happy. Sheikh Majd al-Din Mohammad Kermani became vizier of Khorasan and *zabet-e amval va tavali-e mamalek* instead of *sadr*. He was credited to have made Khorasan cultivated again and have brought the dispersed peasants together; he was therefore considered to be a *ra'yat-parvar*.[312] This aspect of the vizier's function also included the Christian subjects of the Shah. The vizier of Isfahan, e.g., was reprimanded for his untoward behavior towards Armenian refugees in Jolfa and ordered to help and support them.[313] The vizier of Erivan was ordered to assist Christians whose church had been destroyed and who were rebuilding it and to see to it that they were not taxed.[314]

The vizier of Isfahan held a special place in the country's administration. Like the other viziers he was responsible to the grand vizier, but in the case of Isfahan the grand vizier was breathing down his neck. Also, because Isfahan was the capital as of the 17th century, its vizier was charged with the proper reception and accommodation of foreign visitors and ambassadors. Several decrees are known in which the vizier of Isfahan is ordered to prepare a house with water and a

---

[306] Monshi, vol. 1, p. 167; Savory, *History*, vol. 2, p. 259.
[307] Qa'em-maqami, *Yaksad*, p. 363; see also Horst, Heribert. "Zwei Erlasse Shah Tahmasps I. Von Persien", *ZDMG* 105 (1961), doc. 2.
[308] Qarakhani, "Buq`ah", doc. 5.
[309] Ibid., doc. 7.
[310] Puturidze 1961, doc. 16.
[311] Röhrborn, *Provinzen*, pp. 111-12, n. 78 and 79.
[312] Valeh Esfahani, pp. 248, 284.
[313] Ra'in, p. 115f.
[314] "2500 sal", pp. 30, 33.

garden for a European ambassador or for the Catholic missionaries staying in Isfahan.[315] The *khasseh* lands of Isfahan were administrated by the vizier of Isfahan, who was charged to see to it that they were cultivated and productive.[316] Viziers in other cities performed the same function, when the shah was staying in their town and received foreign visitors and dignitaries. In that case they had to see to it that these were properly fed and housed. If necessary, people were put out their homes to lodge foreign visitors, if the government did not have enough empty homes.[317]

The above information implies that the vizier was not always an uninterested executive, but also one who looked after his own interest. Complaints to the *begler-begi* and/or court could lead to an instruction to the vizier to behave correctly. For example, the vizier of Shirvan, who paid a *gholam* his *hamehsaleh* not in cash, but in kind, for which he charged him an additional fee, was ordered to desist from doing so.[318] In short, it was the task of the vizier (in collaboration with the *begler-begi*, emirs and *hakem*s) to see to it that *abadi, ma'muri va nazm* (prosperity, law and order) reigned in his jurisdiction.[319]

Sometimes the tension between a governor and a vizier led to a serious conflict. Such was the case between Mehrab Khan Qajar govenor of Mashhad and Mirzay-e 'Alamiyan in 1016/1607-8. The latter felt he had to defend himself against the military power of the governor and therefore mobilized the numerous riflemen of the Mashhad area.[320] It could also happen that if a governor was accused of having acted contrary to the state's interest that the governate's vizier was ordered to investigate the matter.[321]

Apart from controlling the governor in fiscal and judicial matters the provincial vizier also had a special function as to the collection and management of revenues from *khasseh* land and *khasseh* properties that were situated within *mamalek* governates. In particular, these revenues concerned the poll-tax for non-Moslem minorities, mint tax (*vajebi*), taxes on natural resources and *khaleseh* properties. Any drafts drawn upon these revenues were at the instruction of the central government and usually made out to personnel belonging to the *khasseh* department.

---

[315] Qa'em-maqami, *Yaksad*, p. 22, doc. 10; Ibid., *Moqaddemeh*, p. 77; Nasrollah Falsafi, *Zendegani-ye Shah 'Abbas-e Avval*, 5 vols. (Tehran 1339-44/1960-65), vol. 3, docs. 1, 3; Mohsen Mofakhkham, "Asnad va mokatebat-e tarikhi", *BT* 2 (1346/1967), p. 158

[316] TM, p. 79; DM, p. 85.

[317] John Chardin, p. 50; Chardin, vol. 7, p. 137. Sometimes there were not enough houses and guests risked to be moved around regularly, reason why della Valle rented a house after a while. della Valle, pp. 96-7; Floor, *Fiscal History*, p. 197.

[318] Puturidze 1961, doc. 25.

[319] Puturidze 1965, doc. 43; Richard, vol. 2, p. 27.

[320] Monshi, vol. 2, p. 760.

[321] Vahid Qazvini, p. 190.

In those *mamalek* governates, which the shah had changed into *khasseh* as well as in traditional *khasseh* governates, such as Isfahan, the shah appointed a vizier instead of a governor. The vizier was in charge of administrative and fiscal affairs, while a *darugheh* (see below) was in charge of judicial and military affairs. Often the vizier also held the function of *darugheh*, which was carried out by a deputy.[322] It would therefore seem that the vizier was the superior of the *darugheh*, also given the fact that viziers had the authority to appoint *darughehs* already from the beginning of Safavid rule. This is also clear from the fact that the provincial vizier had control over the military, i.e. the local levies, in the *khasseh* governates. The conflict between the *vazir-e koll* of Azerbaijan and vizier of Gilan who were fighting about Gaskar and Astara is in this connection instructive. The latter armed farmers to repel the other. Since this was done without the authority of the shah, he ordered that the Gilani troops had to be withdrawn.[323] Normally these local levies were used by the vizier to repel, for example, marauding nomads. In 1049/1639, the vizier of Lar, at Safi I's orders, mobilized the local troops (*qoshun-e Lar va tavabe'*) to take action against marauders.[324] Similar efforts were undertaken by the vizier to repel the attacks of the Cossacks on Gilan in the 1660s.

When the *vozara-ye koll* were the governors of the *khasseh* provinces, they had the same duties as governors in *mamalek* governates, but had to transmit all the revenues to the central government. Their court was much less ostentatious, and there were less servants, who were not in their service, but in that of the royal court.[325] As in the case of *begler-begis* and other governors, the viziers also extracted more from the population than they were supposed to. To prevent having the central government look into their affairs they paid influential courtiers in Isfahan to ignore the complaints that were made about them. This was necessary, for the capital was full of complainants (*shekayatchis*), who wanted attention for their plight.[326]

By the 1680s, according to Sanson, there were only two viziers (of Shiraz [Fars] and Rasht [Gilan]); and only two *soltans* (Soltaniyeh dependent on Tabriz and the other at Ourigerd (Borujerd) under Khorramabad).[327] However, the *Dastur-e Shahriyan*, written in 1700, lists viziers for: Jahrom, Darab, Fars, Qazvin, Komreh, Lar, Yazd and Mazandaran.[328] These provincial viziers, like the khans, had two watchdogs attached to their administration, i.e. a *nazer* and a *vaqaye'-nevis*.

---

322 Vahid Qazvini, p. 216. Chardin, vol. 5, pp. 259, 276; Richard, vol. 2, p. 260.
323 Fumeni, p. 150ff.
324 Yusef, p. 235.
325 Kaempfer, *Am Hofe*, p. 130.
326 Richard, vol. 2, p. 262.
327 Sanson, p. 32.
328 Nasiri, *Dastur*, pp. 81, 96, 206, 273.

Unlike the governor or *hakem* the *vazir-e koll* did not have a *ja-neshin*, according to Chardin.[329] However, a decree of 1131/1718 mentions that the vizier of Fars indeed did have a *na'eb*, so either Chardin was mistaken or this is a later development.[330] The growth of the *khasseh* lands and the appointment of viziers, who had 'bought' their office, led to growing oppression in the *khasseh* provinces. Chardin reports that many Persians believed that this was not in the interest of the country and that its strength was being drained.[331]

The most important *khasseh* governates after 1580 were:[332]

Qazvin and Savokh-Bulagh. Since 996/1588 till the end of the Safavid period, with a short interval between 996/1588 - 997/1598.

Kashan. Since 996/1588 till the end of the Safavid period

Isfahan. Since 996/1588 till the end of the Safavid period.

Kerman. since 998/1590 for two years, then again from 1068-9/1658 till 1106/1694.

Yazd. since 1004-5/1596-7 till the end of the Safavid period

Qom. since 1005/1597 till the end

Mazandaran. since 1008/1599 till the end

Gilan (Rasht, Lahejan, Astara, Gaskar). since 1008/1599 till the end.

Fars since 1042/1633 till 1716

Lar since 1045/1636 till 1120/1708-09

Bakhtiyari since 1054/1644 till 1066/1656

Hamadan since 1064-5/1653-4 till 1105/1694

Ardabil since 1067/1656-7 till ?

Semnan, Damavand and Khvar since 1067/1656-7 till 1072-3/1662-3.

Darugheh or Military Governor

The term *darugheh* is a word of Mongolian origin with the meaning of an official who, as representative of the great khan, had to see to it that his master got his dues. After the Mongol conquest of Iran so-called *darughehchis* were appointed in the conquered territory to administer it. Thus, it was the duty of the *darughehchi* to maintain law and order, collect and forward the revenues, organize corvées, maintain the postal service, compile the population registers, and mobilize and lead the local levies. As of the 14th century, this official was referred to as *darugheh*. Though the *darugheh*'s task remained the same, the function now depended on the provincial governor rather than on the overlord.[333]

In Safavid times the term *darugheh*, apart from referring to

---

[329] Chardin, vol. 5, pp. 275-8.
[330] Parham 1353, doc. 1.
[331] Chardin, vol. 5, pp. 252-3, 277-8.
[332] Röhrborn, *Provinzen*, pp. 118-9.
[333] Manz Forbes, Beatrice. *The rise and rule of Tamerlane* (Cambridge 1991), pp. 121-6, 170; Roemer, p. 166; Lambton, art. "Cities," *E.Ir.* p. 609.

administrative officials in charge of the royal secretariat or the royal household furniture department (respectively *darugheh-ye dafter-e homayun; -ye farrash-khaneh*), was used to denote the military governor or superintendent of an urban or rural administrative district, who [a] was the overseer of law and order, and [b] the collector of taxes, just like his Timurid forerunner. One aspect of the first function concerned in particular the maintenance of law and order in the bazaar, therefore the term *darugheh-ye bazar* also occurs. We will discuss both aspects of this function in what follows.

It has been suggested that the function was gradually transformed into that of a police chief rather than of a military governor.[334] However, this is not the case in the Safavid period, though it is clear that the police function was also part of the *darugheh*'s responsibilities. Olearius, in 1637, states that all lands not governed by a khan were under a *darugheh*, which seems to imply that a *darugheh* was in charge of towns or districts in crownlands.[335] Kaempfer, in 1684, elaborated on this statement and stated that "The governor's (whether khan, vizier, *soltan*) agent in the city is the *darugheh*. He has to maintain law and order. He punishes with money fines and bodily punishment. In Isfahan the *darugheh* since 'Abbas I was a member of the Georgian royal family, who then had to convert to Islam. Sometimes, the *darugheh* is also governor at the same time. In that case, he has a deputy to take care of business if he is not there. He cannot leave the city without having taken care of who deputes for him. Also, small towns sometimes have a *darugheh*."[336]

Based on the little that we know from contemporary Persian chronicles, which never explicitly discuss the function of *darugheh*, Kaempfer's summary statement seems to reflect reality. Khonji, a Persian chronicler writing in 1514, stated that "in the Persian language these *valis* [governors] are called *darughagan*."[337] Under Tahmasp I, Hasan Beg *yuz-bashi*, held the title of *darugheh-ye koll-e mamalek*. This seems to imply that he had some supervisory role over the other *darugheh*s, or may be he was allowed to distribute the various *darugheh* posts. This is not unlikely, because one of his retainers, Maqsud Beg, was appointed as *darugheh* of some localities.[338] Unfortunately we do not learn from other sources about his title or these arrangements. Most of the *darugheh*s had the rank of *beg*,[339] sometimes this is even further

---

334 Lambton, art. "Cities," *E.Ir.* p. 609.

335 Olearius, p. 271.

336 Kaempfer, *Am Hofe*, p. 131.

337 Khonji, Fazlollah b. Ruzbehan, *Ketab-e Soluk al-Moluk*. ed. Mohammad NizamudDin (Hyderabad/Deccan 1386/1966), p. 193; see also Hans Müller, *Die Chronik Khulasat at-tawarikh des Qazi Ahmad Qumi* (Wiesbaden 1964), p. 123a.

338 Natanzi, p. 164.

339 Molla Jalal, pp. 242-5.

specified as the *darugheh* being a *gholam-e khasseh*.[340] In only a few cases the *darugheh* held the rank of *soltan*,[341] and even rarer that of khan,[342] and, in one case, it was a prince of the royal blood, Hamzeh Mirza who became *darugheh* of Isfahan and Kashan, which were his *teyul*.[343]

The latter case seems to underscore the other point that was made above, to wit: that *darugheh*s were only appointed in *khasseh* areas. This is not only clear in the case of Hamzeh Mirza (Isfahan, Kashan), but also from the towns and districts (under *darughehs*) who are mentioned in contemporary texts many of which refer to *khasseh* areas. In a few cases the *khasseh* character of the jurisdiction concerned is explicitly mentioned. "Part of an area was *khasseh* and *darugheh*s were sent there."[344] Also, the fact that *darughehs* were invariably appointed in conquered areas, which by definition were *khasseh* lands, confirms the above mentioned point. The village of Jevim was taken and Qara Bakhtiyar was appointed as its *darugheh*.[345] After the conquest of a village and its fortress a *darugheh* and vizier were appointed[346], and after the defeat of the Ahmadi Arabs a *gholam* was appointed as their *darugheh*.[347] After the ouster of the Uzbegs from Khorasan in 916/1510-11 *darughehs* were appointed.[348] There were also *darughehs* who were appointed to oversee rebellious tribes. Khosrou Soltan Armani, *jadid al-eslam*, was *darugheh* of the Bakhtiyari tribe,[349] while another official was *darugheh* of the Turkomans (near Astarabad).[350] The above is also borne out by the fact that sometimes *darughehs* were appointed as governor to areas that were not *khasseh* lands, such as Tabriz. For these were temporary appointments when the town or area had been retaken from the Ottomans.

Sometimes, the *darugheh* was at the same time *hakem* or governor of the town or district concerned, or of a neighboring jurisdiction. Hasan Khan Qajar, *darugheh* and *hakem* of Shiraz, was welcomed by the guilds (*asnaf*) and notables (*a'yan*) on his arrival. On that occasion festivities were organized and almost 3.000 tomans in cash and goods

---

340 Molla Jalal, pp. 191, 194, 215, 235, 243, 333.

341 Molla Jalal, p. 103.

342 Hosein Khan Qajar, *moqarrab al-hezrah*, was made *darugheh* of Shiraz. Qomi, vol. 2, p. 911.

343 Qomi, vol. 2, pp. 735, 889.

344 Molla Jalal, p. 184; Qomi, vol. 2, p. 889.

345 Molla Jalal, p. 151.

346 Molla Jalal, p. 246.

347 Molla Jalal, p. 268.

348 Jahanara, p. 273; Shirazi,, p. 49.

349 Yusef, p. 272.

350 Qomi, vol. 1, p. 346.

were presented to him.[351] The *darugheh* had an additional, but explicit task, to wit to collect the taxes. The *darugheh-ye Baluch*, for example, was at the same time tax collector (*tahsildar-e vajh-e malujehat-e Baluch*).[352] The previous monarch had not collected the *ahdath* fine, though it was in the tax registers. The *darugheh* imposed and collected it, and it was entered as a separate *ahdath* tax, and people were thus being taxed twice over, 'Abbas I spotted this and put a stop to it.[353]

Some contemporary European sources refer to the *darugheh* as the city's mayor or as a judicial officer, the "lieutenant criminel", and some translate the title as "governor".[354] Fryer, who also referred to him as mayor as well as the captain of the watch, wrote that the *darugheh* was in charge of the guards at the palace gate at night and "thence to make excursions through the city, and to disperse, secure and apprehend idle and vagrant persons."[355] In Isfahan, the *darugheh* was a *moqarreb al-hazreh* and a subordinate of the *divan-begi*. It would seem that in the Safavid capital city the function had acquired mainly the tasks of a police chief, though the aspect of military governor still lingered on. As of the 1620s the function of *darugheh* of Isfahan was usually given to a Georgian prince. The first Georgian *darugheh* was Khosrou Mirza in 1620. He had a Tajik deputy named Mir Qasem Beg.[356] Prior to that time the function seems to have been held by members of the Qezelbash tribes such as in 1028/1618-9 by the *yuzbashi* Takhteh Beg Ostajalu.[357] His task was to guard the town and see to it that no oppression and outrages took place. Also, all *haram* or illicit activities such as prostitution, wine-drinking, gambling were pursued and perpetrators punished by him. Every night he would tour part of the city, while his subordinates or *ahdath* would do the same elsewhere. He was assisted in his task by groups of *qurchi*s, *gholam*s, *aqa*s, *tofangchi*s and *tupchi*s under a *sar-dasteh* or section chief. They kept guard day and night in their area of town and reported any untoward activity to the *darugheh*. Cases involving penalties up to 5 tomans, sometimes up to 12 tomans, were usually judged by the *darugheh* himself. Above that level the *divan-begi* tried the case. The *darugheh* also served as jailer for the *divan-begi*. In case a prisoner died in prison the case was investigated

---

351 Molla Jalal, p. 94 [*beh rasm-e piskesh* and *pa-andaz*], see also Ibid., pp. 97, 438; Natanzi, p. 544; Yusef, pp. 103, 191.

352 Molla Jalal, pp. 375-6; Ibid., pp. 73, 145; Bardsiri 218.

353 Savory, *History*, vol. 2, p. 1112.

354 Don Juan, p. 46; Tavernier, Jean-Baptiste. *Voyages en Perse et description de ce royaume* (Paris 1930), p. 221; della Valle, pp. 18, 41, 65.

355 Fryer, vol. 3, p. 339; also Krusinski, pp. 80-2.

356 Yusef, pp. 202, 268. The *darugheh* of Isfahan in 1701 was 'Abdollah Beg. Valentijn, vol. 5, p. 276.

357 Savory, *History*, vol 2, p. 1169.

and if need be the demise was reported to the shah for a decision.[358]

According to Sanson, the *darugheh* "determines petty differences and executes all Process out of the Kan's Court. This last Office is very profitable at Ispahan, yet it is esteem'd but mean and scandalous, altho' it be executed by a Prince of Georgia. For thereby he not only loses his Precedency at the King's Feasts, but is slighted and avoided by all the great Lords, and reflected upon, as one that executes the Office of a Goaler and Bailiff."[359] Chardin stated that the *darugheh* was one of the higher level judicial officials and he translated the term as governor. He further observed, when discussing the position of khan (governor) and of the provincial vizier, that the shah appointed a *darugheh* or *prévôt* for governors in all the towns and other important localities of the provinces. The shah also appointed a deputy or *na'eb* for the *darugheh*.[360] This was a later development, for, it would seem that initially the right to appoint *darughehs* belonged to the governors, and that already early on the provincial viziers also acquired that authority. However, under Tahmasp I this right became a royal privilege.

"In every town there is Deroga and a Divan Beghi; the Chan puts in the Deroga, and therefore wholly depends on the Chan; but the King appoints all the Divan beghis, and they depend on none but him. The deroga is like the Lieutenant criminal in France; they have recourse to him for all Robberies, quarrels, assaults and fights, or murders, and he does them Justice; it is his care to suppress publick houses of debauchery, and if he catch any man in them, he punishes him by bastinadoes or a fine, but commonly by a fine; and though in the Countrey these men go plain in Cloaths and with Arms, yet it is a great Crime to strike them, or do them the least hurt."[361]

In light of the above it is not unexpected to conclude that the task of the *darugheh* was to manage and govern the area that he was put in charge of, to collect the taxes, and in particular to keep law and order. Molla Jalal reports that Soheil Beg, who was *darugheh* of Yazd, had as task to maintain and safeguard the city (*beh hefz va harasat-e Yazd*).[362] A *darugheh* in Georgia had been appointed to a village in a *khasseh* area and was ordered to investigate matters when required and to collect the *rosum-e darughegi* in accordance with Georgian law (*qanun*) and not to demand more (*ziyadeh*).[363]

The *darugheh* had a staff at his disposal to enforce his authority. 'Aliqoli Beg, *qurchi-ye tarkesh*, had 500 armed men when he was

358 DM, p. 100-01.
359 Sanson, pp. 32-3; Tavernier, p. 223.
360 Chardin, vol. 5, pp. 259-61, 275.
361 Thevenot, J. de. *The Travels of M. de Thevenot into the Levant* (London, 1686 [1971]), vol. 2, p. 103; Richard, vol. 2, pp. 115-16.
362 Molla Jalal, pp. 73, 161, 375, 418.
363 Puturidze 1955, doc. 46.

darugheh of Yazd,[364] Hoseinqoli Soltan was appointed as *darugheh* and governor of Tabriz and also had 500 retainers (*molazem*).[365] However, in the 17th century, probably after the 1630s, the importance of the office was reduced to that of a chief of police. Only in Qazvin the *darugheh* still had the same function by the 1680s as in the 16th century. For Sanson states that only the *darugheh* or governor of Qazvin held the title of khan.[366] This had not always been the case. Sheikh Ahmad Aqa Ostajalu was *darugheh* of Qazvin, and a very harsh man. He had an army of 300 cut throats and his authority went beyond Qazvin. His men, who sported scarlet turbans, soon became a familiar sight. Nobody dared to refuse his orders, even emirs. His punishments were terrible; he had a number of thieves impaled on iron spits and roasted over a fire in the public square. He had became the public executioner. Sheikh Ahmad Aqa was promoted to the function of *ishik aghasi-bashi* of the harem and raised to status of emir, but then he killed a *qurchi*, and was handed over to the *qurchi*'s kinsmen who killed him.[367]

Not only *darughehs* were appointed to towns, but also to rural districts. These officials were technically known as *darugheh-ye jozv* such as in the districts of Kerman: Sirjan, Eqta', Rafsanjan, Bardsir, Khabiz, Ravar and Kubnan, Jiroft, and the *humeh-ye shahr* (peri-urban zone). There was also a *darugheh* of the Zoroastrians in Kerman.[368] In Astarabad there also was a *darugheh* for each district.[369] In Shirvan and Georgia, as reported from the late Safavid period, the governate was managed by a governor (khan, *soltan*) or vice-roy (*vali*), while over the various districts in which the governate was subdivided a *darugheh* held sway. Sometimes a *teyuldar* could be at the same time the *darugheh* of the district that was his *teyul*.[370] Under the *darugheh* a number of *yuzbashi*s were appointed to whom a number of *kadkhoda*s reported, who were in charge of one village. In some districts where Qezelbash clans lived the *yuz-bashi* shared the responsibility for the execution of his function with a *khalifeh* (local leader of the Safavid sufi order). Here also it was the *darugheh*'s task to see to the efficient collection of the taxes, to maintain law and order and that justice was done, when intervention was required.[371]

---

364 Molla Jalal, p. 165.
365 Qomi, vol. 2, p. 778.
366 Sanson, p. 32.
367 Savory, *History*, vol. 2, pp. 877-8. Sheikh Ahmad, the [*divan-begi*'s] "superintendant of police, and all these men dressed in scarlet, from the shoes on their feet to the plume in their caps, this being with us Persians the uniform of the executioners of the king's justice." They killed 10.000 inhabitants of Nohum in Gilan to the sword. Don Juan, p. 215.
368 Barsdsiri, pp. 218-9, 256-8, 331, 344, 531.
369 Dhahebi-Setudeh 1354 a, doc. 20; see also Natanzi, p. 164.
370 Puturidze 1955, doc. 59.
371 "Nachrichten von ... Johann Gustav Gerber" in Müller, F. *Sammlung Russischer*

The *darugheh* of Isfahan had a vizier to manage the administrative part of his duties.[372] It is unknown whether the *darugheh* of other locations than Isfahan likewise had a vizier. Sometimes, a *darugheh*, given his other functions and duties was unable to personally carry out the functions of *darugheh*. In that case he appointed a deputy or *na'eb*, often a kinsman, although Chardin states that this deputy was appointed by the shah.[373] This may be the reason why Chardin reports that the chief of police was called *na'eb*.[374] The *darugheh*'s main concern was to collect his dues that were attached to the function such as *darughehgi*.[375] Chardin observed that in Qazvin the *darugheh* was appointed every two years and drew an annual salary from the central government, while du Mans reported that the *darugheh*, in addition to fees received from litigants, was paid 400 tomans per year.[376] To that end the government appointed a *moshref* to record how much the *darugheh* received in fines. If he received less than 400 tomans the government would pay him the difference. If he received more he would have to hand that surplus over to the state.[377] If a suspect was caught by the *darugheh*'s staff he was clapped in irons and the extortion process started. For the *darugheh*'s retainers chased thieves like a cat chases mice. However, this effort was not so much to make the population sleep easier, but rather to line their pockets, according to du Mans.[378] Despite the fact that the vizier and *darugheh* should work together, the enmity between these two officials in Kerman in the 1098/1687 was such that the latter never met the former, who left at the end of the year after having collected his fees (*vojuh-e darughegi*).[379] The overriding financial aspect of the function is also brought out by the fact that the *darugheh* was not above collecting money illegally.[380] Many people were allegedly punished and mutilated by the *darugheh* of Firuzkuh and others were targeted to be dealt with in the same way. However, the *darugheh* informed the English ambassador who was passing through that for a gratuity he would not punish the miscreants.[381] In case an area was tax exempt it did not have

---

Geschichte, 9 vols (St. Petersburg 1732-64), vol. 4, pp. 100, 109, 111, 116, 118, 122; Puturidze 1955, docs. 46, 59.

[372] *Vezarat-e darugheh-ye Isfahan* in 929/1522-3. Rumlu, p. 231; also Qomi, vol. 1, p. 151.

[373] Yusef, p. 253; Bardsiri, pp. 218, 344, 442; Chardin, vol. 5, p. 259. May be this reflects the weakening of the authority of the central government.

[374] Chardin, vol. 5, p. 263.

[375] Bardsiri, pp. 344, 433, 532.

[376] Chardin, vol. 2, p. 401; vol. 3, pp. 9-10; Du Mans, p. 39.

[377] DM, p. 101.

[378] Richard, vol. 2, pp. 30, 321.

[379] Bardsiri, p. 532.

[380] Bardsiri, p. 439; Savory, *History*, vol. 2, p. 1112.

[381] Herbert, Thomas. *Travels in Persia, 1627-1629*, ed. W. Foster. (New York 1929), p. 149.

to pay *rasm-e darughegi* either and the *darugheh*s were explicitly informed about this.[382]

If there was no *darugheh*, as in most small towns, the function of the *darugheh* was exercised by the *kotval* or castellan. This was the case in, for example, Hormuz, Qandahar, and Lar. In those cases he also was in charge of the night guard. The *kotval* was to be found in fortresses and the like, and was subordinate to a governor (khan).[383] Finally, there was focus on keeping the peace in the economic heart of the cities, the bazaar. Here the *darugheh* played and continued to play an important role, reason why he also was referred to as the *darugheh-ye bazar*.[384] This aspect of the *darugheh*'s task was the same as that of the *'asas* or peacekeepers, who were under his authority.

Conclusion

Safavid Persia was administrated through a variety of institutional instruments. In particular in the border areas the old ruling families were allowed to continue to manage their domain's affairs. In exchange for formal subjugation they were left unhindered in the management of the internal affairs of their jurisdiction. These quasi-independent rulers or *vali*s had to pay a lump sum as tribute to formalize their dependency, as well as have coins struck and the *khutbah* read in the shah's name. The *vali*s also had to provide military support when required. The number of *vali*doms was reduced over time. 'Abbas I did away with most of them and turned them into *khasseh* or crown lands. By the end of the Safavid period there were four validoms left. Governors, who received their jurisdiction as a revenue assignment or *teyul*, administrated the rest of the country. Their jurisdiction's revenue had to be used for the upkeep of the governor's court and his troops, and for the maintenance of law and order. No taxes had to be paid to the royal court beyond annual presents. However, already under Tahmasp I we observe that royal viziers were appointed in the *mamalek* jurisdictions to exercise better control over what happened in these governates. At the same time, the extent of *khasseh* lands was increased to the detriment of the *mamalek* lands and thus of the Qezelbash officials who managed the latter. In the *khasseh* lands royal viziers governed the land. They were directly dependent on the shah and transferred the revenues to the royal court. Like the *begler-begi*s and *hakem*s, the viziers had to see to it that their jurisdiction flourished. To that end the shah had appointed 'watch dogs' in the administration of all governates. However, the need for money caused the governates to be put up for sale, with the result that there was little long-term interest in managing the governates' resources well. This

---

[382] Puturidze 1955, doc. 11.

[383] Kaempfer, *Am Hofe*, p. 131; Richard, vol. 2, p. 115; *ARA*, Collectie Geleijnsen, nr. 100 (unfoliated), *raqam* dated *Shavval* 1050 (*kalantar* of Lar).

[384] Qomi, vol. 2, p. 643; Rumlu, p. 633; Mostoufi, p. 184.

situation was further worsened by the quick rotation of governors, whose only interest was to capitalize their investment as fast as possible. The short-term gain contributed to the long-term deterioration of the country's economy. Whenever land was conquered, the shah used to appoint a *darugheh*, a military governor. This indicated that these lands were *khasseh* property. Towards the end of the 17th century *darughehs* were also appointed in *mamalek* governates where they served as deputy governor. *Darughehs* were appointed wherever there was a need for them, in urban centers and in rural districts. These officials had, apart from a fiscal function, a major role in maintaining law and order and as such the *darughehs* were part of the main judicial executive arm of the Safavid state.[385]

---

[385] For an analysis of the judicial system of Safavid Persia see Floor, Willem. "The Secular Judicial System in Safavid Persia," *Studia Iranica* 29(2000), pp. 9-60.

CHAPTER THREE

The Organization of the Army

Introduction

THE SAFAVID military force consisted of a regular army and auxiliaries. The regular army was usually called *sepah* or *lashkar*. The Safavid auxiliaries were called *hashar*, *kheil* or *hasham*.[1] The army of local rulers, as well as of that of opponents, such as the Uzbegs, also consisted of *hashar* (irregulars) and *lashkar* (regulars).[2] The term *ba kheil va sepah* is also used, sometimes also with an indication of how many cavalry (*savar*) and how many infantry (*piyadeh*). Finally, terms such as *jonud*, *jeish*, and *qoshun* to refer to the army also occur.[3]

Initially, the *sepah* itself consisted of a standing army of only household (*khasseh*) troops, and regular national levies, so-called *yasaq* or *cherik* troops. The household troops were the shah's royal guards, in particular the *qurchis*. They were mainly drawn from the Qezelbash pool, but operated entirely independent from their tribal affiliation, and owed loyalty only to the shah. They were commanded by a chief known as *qurchi-bashi* and were in addition to being the royal guard also the shah's crack troops. The *yasaq* or *cherik* troops were only called upon when needed and were controlled by the tribal chiefs. They were mobilized from allover Persia. As of around 1590, the standing army grew in size. The new household or royal troops consisted of the *gholams*, *tofangchis* and *tupchis*, army groups that were created or strengthened around 1590, in addition to the *qurchis*. Apart from these household or royal troops there also were the provincial forces, which were divided into the levies and the regulars. The levies were those troops that the governors had to train and maintain (the same as the *cherik*), while the regulars were the *qurchis* who could be called upon for service (*safar-kesh*) when needed. Whereas the royal household troops were financed out of the treasury, the provincial troops (levies and *qurchis*) were financed with revenue

---

[1] Valeh Esfahani, pp. 115, 106, 606.
[2] The Seistani army e.g. also consisted of a *lashkar va hashar*. Seistani, p. 271; Adle, Chahryar. *Siyaqi-Nezam – Fotuhate Homayun – "Les Victoires augustes", 1007/1598.* (unpublished thesis Sorbonne – Paris 1976), p. 453.
[3] Rumlu, pp. 63, 80, 115, 256, 275, 544.

assignments on provincial revenues. Part of the royal household troops as well as a part of the *qurchi*s were so-called *hamisheh-keshikan*.[4] These *hamisheh-keshik* troops were always in attendance either at the royal court or in the provincial towns. In 1051/1641, for example, "it was announced that all troops, except for the *hamisheh-keshik* group, had to depart from the capital."[5]

The *cherik* forces, when called upon, had to come with their own weapons and equipment. Each particular territory or tribe had to supply able-bodied men (*cherik-e an vilayat*) as well as supplies (*soyursat*).[6] The term *yasaq* is a synonym of *cherik*. In both cases the term refers to local, especially tribal levies. The *yasaqi*s served as the main elements of the army from the outset of the Safavid state.[7] The term *cherik va yasaq[ha]* is also used to refer to these regular levies. The *yasaq* or *cherik* duty was demanded from both the nomadic and sedentary population. *Yasaqi* service could also mean that one served one of great emirs as a guard at court.[8] The *cherik* should neither be confused with these *yasaqi*s nor with the *yasaqchi*s [see below] who were in charge of "traffic" control of the royal army on the march.

Another term to denote the levies was *mardom jari va cherik* or *cherik va iljari*. In all cases it is clear that both terms could refer to tribal as well as village levies.[9] A related term is that of *jar va yasaq*[10] and *jar va afsar*.[11] A term that came into being in the 16th century was *tofangchi* or riflemen levy, which was synonymous with the term (*piyadeh*) *cherik*.[12] A document written in 1128/1800 informs us, inter alia, about the military organization under Shah Soltan Hosein. The author of this document gives a detailed list of the tribes, who had to supply *cherik* or irregular levies (both mounted and foot), which duty was referred to as *iljari*. The author also adds that the *cherik* troops, referred to as *lashkar-e iljari*, had to bring their own arms and food, but received supplies as soon as the army

---

[4] Afshar, *'Alamara-ye Tahmasp*, p. 107; Esfahani, pp. 159, 222, 293.

[5] Yusef, p. 249; see also Vahid Qazvini, p. 94; Mervi, p. 229.

[6] Monshi, pp. 492, 901; *cherik-e Seistan*, Da'udi, "Asnad", doc. 10; Nasiri, *Dastur*, pp. 68, 85, 153.

[7] Montazer-Saheb, pp. 385, 422, 559.

[8] Membré, p. 19.

[9] Laheji, p. 328; Fragner, B. "Ardabil zwischen Sultan und Schah. Zehn Urkunden Schah Tahmasps II." *Turcica* 6 (1975), docs. 2, 3, p. 222.

[10] Beiburdi, Hosein. *Tarikh-e Arasbaran*. Tehran 1346/1968, p. 160; also Minorsky, V. "A Soyurghal of Qasim b. Jahangir Aq-qoyunlu (903/1498)", *BSOS* 9 (1937-39), p. 959; Savory, *History*, vol. 1, p. 455; Puturidze 1955, doc. 29; ibid., 1961, docs. 12, 26.

[11] Puturidze 1955, doc. 122.

[12] Aubin, Jean. "Note préliminaire sur les archives du Takya du Tchima-Rud" *Archives persanes commentées* 2 (Tehran 1955), p. 17 (1006/1598); we also find mention of an impost on account of the arsenal or *tup-khaneh*, Dehgan, Ebrahim. "Du farman az 'asr-e Safavi", *Rahnama-ye ketab* 11(1347/1968), p. 342f.

purveyors (*sursatchiyan*) arrived.[13] Therefore going on a military campaign was also referred to as *yasaq*, while *yasaqi* meant campaigner.[14] Some communities were not obliged to provide men, but then were called upon to finance part of the military operations. This contribution was referred to as *zar-e cherik* and with the advent of the *tofangchi*s also *zar-e tofangchi*.[15] This contribution was levied from both Moslem and non-Moslem subjects. *Cherik* was also the term by which an impost was known that was exacted from that part of the population that did not have to provide men. Several decrees mention *cherik* as an irregular impost.[16] Also Christians had to pay *zar-e cherik*, because they were exempt from military service.[17] In late Safavid times these revenues were referred to as *vojuh-e mostaradd-e cherik va yasaqi*.[18]

In addition to the regular troops, tribal or otherwise, there was also the local population that was called upon to defend their town or rural district. This was the *hashar* part of the army who generally were badly armed and equipped (*bi sar va pa*).[19] "There were 100,000 souls in Tabriz, they said, of whom at least half were lusty, serviceable lads who would fight for their families and homes. The streets must be barricaded, and the inhabitants must fight on the barricades and prevent the enemy from entering the city"..... the city was divided by wards for this purpose. A local hero was placed in charge of each district, and a qezelbash was allocated to each barricade with a number of reliable men" .. there was some brief resistance before the Ottomans smashed down the barricades with cannon and mortar fire.[20] Sometimes the role of the irregulars was so important that "No action was taken due to the shortage of regular (*lashkar*) and auxiliary (*ansar va a'van*) forces.[21] For example, the Uzbeg governor hoped that, if the local notables and populace would support him, he could hold Mashhad. However, the sayyeds and scholars in

---

[13] Danespazuh, Mohammad Taqi. "Amar-e mali va nezami-ye Iran dar 1128", *FIZ* 20, pp. 397-98, 400.

[14] E.g. Natanzi, p. 177, 450-1; Rumlu, p. 212.

[15] Honarfar, p. 453f.

[16] Bastani-Parizi, Mohammad Ebrahim. *Siyasat va eqtesad-e 'asr-e Safavi* (Tehran 1348/1969), pp. 155, 160; Musavi 1977, doc. 21; Aubin, "Note", p. 15; Semsar, "Du farman", pp. 80-83; TM, pp. 34, 76; Röhrborn, *Provinzen*, p. 51; Bardsiri, pp. 617-8, 662. see in general, Willem Floor, art. "Cherik", *E. Ir.*

[17] Bastani Parizi, *Siyasat*, pp. 155, 160; Bournoutian, George A. *The Khanate of Erevan under Qajar Rule, 1795-1828* (Costa Mesa 1992), pp. 140 n. 164.

[18] DM, p. 112; the auxiliaries, therefore, were also referred to as *mostaradd-e mard- yasaqi*, Puturidze 1961, doc. 26; see also DM, p. 112.

[19] Valeh Esfahani pp. 115, 106, 606.

[20] Savory, *History*, vol. 1, p. 440, 442; also Valeh Esfahani, p. 714 with chiefs in charge of each quarter (*mahalleh*); see also Ibid., p. 744. Similar participation of citizens in Qazvin. Ibid., p. 769. Khalifeh Soltan Shamlu pressed the local population into military service all those who had a horse and arms. Rumlu, p. 344.

[21] Savory, *History*, vol. 1, p. 444.

Mashhad instilled in him a fear of an uprising by the mob; by making him dread the ill-repute.[22] In addition to their combatant role, these irregular local levies generally also provided the work gangs, called *komak* (assistance), doing corvées necessary in military operations.[23] They were pressed to do all kinds of menial tasks such as making trenches and barricades; they were the *bildar*s (diggers) and the *kelengdar*s (pick-axe holders).[24]

These generally non-Turkoman auxiliary elements increased with the use of musketeers (see section on *tofangchi*s). The musketeers had initially a mainly local role, to wit: to defend their *boluk* or rural district. Increasingly, however, they were used to fight the shah's battles outside their home district. Thus, early on, non-tribal elements became a small, but later on an important, and growing part of the Safavid army.[25] It concerned here local levies which supplied musketeers to guard fortresses, defend cities, as well as a central army unit, that of the gunners or *tupchi*s, which were used in sieges of towns and fortresses. Although, the role of the new arms-bearers initially remained limited, they nevertheless played a crucial role at siege work and in regular battles. The *cherik* soldiers were led by their traditional chiefs (*begs*) and later, after the conquest of Persia, by the *begs* who had been appointed emir-governor [see chapter two]. The begs and emirs were assisted by officials referred to as *bozorg, sar-kheil* and *sar-kardeh*.[26] The musketeers were led by their own officers as did those of other army units such as *qurchi*s and *tupchi*s.

When Persian texts use the terms such as *'asaker* or *jonud*, they in fact included all non-combatant personnel as well. This is clear from a description of a review of the Persian army in 1530 which not only lists the tribal military forces but also the administrative officials as well as the workers of the royal workshops. This was not a Safavid innovation because the same phenomenon existed among the Aq-Qoyunlu.[27] This inclusion among the *'asaker* was more than just filling the ranks. In fact, the bulk of the staff of the royal court belonged to the *aqa* class, which constituted a kind a military yeomanry. At many occasions, therefore, the staff of the royal workshops participated in the defense of fortresses as well as in outright battles. For example, in 1576 "the *'azab*s [scribes] of the royal treasury opened fire on the enemy"[28] In 1000/1591-92, "Rostam Mirza's mother, closed the gates of the citadel and set the eunuchs and

---

[22] Savory, *History*, vol. 2, pp. 743-4.

[23] Esfahani, p. 240.

[24] e.g. Rumlu, pp. 230, 576; see also the section below on siege operations.

[25] Aubin, "L'Avènement", p. 94; Brosset, M.F., *Collection d'Histoires Arméniens*. 2 vols in one (St. Pétersbourg 1874-76 [Amsterdam 1979]) vol. 2, p. 66.

[26] Yusef, p. 21.

[27] Minorsky, V. "A Civil and Military Review in Fars in 881/1476," *BSOS* X/1 (1939), pp. 141-78.

[28] Savory, *History*, vol. 1, p. 288; Monshi, vol. 1, p. 195.

workers of the royal workshops to mount guard there."[29] In 1012/1604 "the retainers of the royal household, the personnel of the royal workshops, the contingents of the musketeers from Tabriz and Bafq, and others fought their way up to the rampart."[30] Breastworks had been erected by Maqsud Beg, the *nazer*, and the workmen of the royal workshops participating in the siege of Erivan.[31] Sadeqi Beg, the famous royal painter, also was known for his reckless exploits during battle, in which he participated as part of the *'amaleh* or court staff. As a consequence the staff of the royal workshops were also organized along military lines. They constituted detachments under *yuz-bashi*s.[32] This participation of what normally would technically have been qualified as non-combatants was due to the fact that in Safavid ideology anybody loyal to the shah-*pir* was a *ghazi*, a fighter for the faith and good cause. Therefore, all supporters and adherents of the shah were expected to physically show their allegiance. For example, both under the Aq-Qoyunlu as well as during the first 85 years of Safavid reign, religious leaders such as the *sadr* can be found participating in military reviews and campaigns, including actual battles.[33]

The Army Under Esma'il I

The Safavid army initially was composed of Turkoman tribal elements (nomadic, semi-sedentary and sedentary Turkic speaking groups) and some Iranic speaking groups, many of whose members were adherents of the Safavid sufi order since the days of its founder.[34] In fact, there were two main groups: (a) an Azerbaijani group from Khalkhal, Talesh and Moghan and (b) an Anatolian group from Chokhur Sa'd and Mingol. This distribution also was reflected in the manner in which the battle formation of the Safavid army was organized. The Azerbaijani group was led by the Shamlus and the Anatolian group by the Ostajalus.[35] Also noteworthy was the fact that among the Turkoman troops the sufis of Qarajehdagh stood out, for they were especially mentioned among the 7,000 troops of Esma'il I next to the Ostajalu, Rumlu and other major Qezelbash tribal groups.[36] The term Qezelbash (litt. red heads) was a pejorative name given by their enemies to the red hat wearing Safavid supporters.[37] The

---

[29] Savory, *History*, vol. 2, p. 660.

[30] Savory, *History*, vol. 2, p. 845; Monshi, vol. 2, p. 645.

[31] Savory, *History*, vol. 2, p. 843; see also Seistani, pp. 169-70.

[32] Vahid Qazvini, p. 68 mentions e.g. a *yuz-bashi* of the *qushchi*s (falconers).

[33] Minorsky, Military Review, p. 161; Sayyed Beg Kamuna was in the center of Hamza Mirza's troops in 1585. Monshi, vol. 1, p. 335.

[34] TM, p. 189; Sumer, Naqsh; Mazzaoui, Michel M. *The Origins of the Safawids* (Wiesbaden 1972), p. 71; Valeh Esfahani, p. 189.

[35] Haneda, pp. 48-60.

[36] Valeh Esfahani, p. 95; Rumlu, p. 61.

[37] On the *taj* or *taj-e Heidari* see Floor, *Textile Industry*.

Qezelbash were also referred to as *kolah-e sorkh*, *qezel bórk*, and *qezel qalpaq*,[38] and *sorkh-saran*, which terms all mean red hats, except for the last one, which means red heads.[39]

It is doubtful whether, as is the accepted wisdom, that the red hats of the Safavid sufis were indeed introduced under Soltan Heidar (1459-1488). First, the *taj* itself was not a new Safavid invention. For the red *taj* was also worn by other darvish groups prior to its alleged creation by Soltan Heidar. Second, the twelve folds of the *taj* were not peculiar to the Safavid order either and already existed prior to that period among the Bektashis, for example. Also, other groups wore a *taj* with e.g. 24 folds. These folds did not have anything to do with the 12 emams, but rather with the 12 acts to be strived after by darvishes such as the Ne'matollahis and others. Wearing the *taj-e tark* was a sign of abandonment of this mundane life and the adoption of the darvish way of life. It has been suggested that the red hat was only introduced by Esma'il I after his victory over Elvand Mirza.[40] In fact, Don Juan states that Esma'il I instituted the *taj*.[41] Indeed, it would seem that the term is not used prior to Esma'il I. Khonji e.g. uses the term regularly in his *Mehmannameh*, but not in his earlier *Tarikh-e Amini*. Also, the *taj-e Heidari* is not mentioned by Barbaro, the Venetian ambassador to Uzun Hasan. Other Venetians accounts that mention the *taj* all date from a period after 1500. Wearing a red head dress as a sign of total commitment to die or win already occur in the days of the prophet.[42] But whatever the truth of the matter the red *taj* was a distinctive feature of the Safavid troops.

The Qezelbash tribes, as mentioned in the various contemporary texts, numbered (a) eight large tribal confederations: Rumlu, Ostajalu, Tekellu, Shamlu, Dhu'l-Qadr, Qajar, Afshar, Turkoman, and (b) 12 smaller groups: Varsaq, Chepni, 'Arabgirlu, Turghudlu, Buzjelu, Ajrlu, Khanislu, Chemishkazaklu, Sa'dlu, Alpavat [or Alpaut], Bayat, Qaramanlu, Bayburtlu, Baharlu, Aspirlu.[43] According to the *Tarikh-e Qezelbashan* (written about 1010/1601) the number of Qezelbash tribes was 33. The difference is mainly in the number of smaller tribes, and the fact that the *Tarikh-e Qezelbashan* also lists the Aq-Qoyunlu, the Qara-Qoyunlu, the

---

[38] Khonji, Fazlollah b. Ruzbahan, *Mehmannameh-ye Bokhara*. ed. Manuchehr Setudeh (Tehran 1341/1962), pp. 57, 104-07.

[39] von Mende, Rana, *Mustafa 'Ali's Fursat-name. Edition und Bearbeitung einer Quelle zur Geschichte des persischen Feldzugs unter Sinan Pasa 1580-1581* (Berlin 1989), p. 71.

[40] Hinz, Walther. *Irans Aufstieg zum Nationalstaat im fünfzehnten Jahrhundert* (Berlin - Leipzig 1936), p. 93.

[41] Don Juan, pp. 49, 110.

[42] Mansuri, Firuz, "Pazuheshi darbareh-ye Qezelbash", *BT* 10/4, pp. 145-62.

[43] For a discussion of all Qezelbash tribes, both small and big, as well as their clans, and their participation in military or administrative operations between 1500 and 1620 see Sumer, *Tashkil*.

Kurds and the Lors as Qezelbash tribes.[44] There is no difference as far as the names and number of the larger tribes is concerned, however. It would seem that the number of Qezelbash tribes in the 1570s was 22, for it is reported that Esma'il II gave orders that "44 *qurchi*s, two from each tribe had to kill Hasan Mirza."[45] The fact that Shah Tahmasp I decided that Sam Mirza be given a guard of 30 *qurchi*s originating from all [Qezelbash] clans (*uymuqat*)[46] does not invalidate this report. For this does not necessarily mean that there were 30 or 15 tribes, if two *qurchi*s per tribe were selected. However, according to Don Juan, the Qezelbash were indeed composed of 32 tribes around 1600.[47] This is confirmed by della Valle, who reports that the Qezelbash were composed of 32 tribes; 16 of which were of the right hand and 16 of the left hand in the battle formation. "They are free, independent, and serve as long as they are paid, being at liberty to change their masters when they please, from one khan to another, or to the King, or from the King to a khan, as seems best to them. Not all the kizilbashi are soldiers, but as almost all the lands are in the hands of the Shah, or his governors or khans, for subsistence they are obliged either to make choice of the profession of arms, or exercise some kind of trade, handicraft or husbandry; in consequence, the number of these soldiers is very considerable. Moreover, their different tribes are not equal in point of number, some consisting of from ten to twelve thousand men, and some of not more than five hundred. Of some of them all are soldiers, of others but few."[48] The number 32 most likely has a politico-religious meaning, for it is also found among other Safavid institutions such as the royal household departments (*boyutat*) and among sufi orders.

Non-Turkoman Army Elements Important
Although rightly much has been made of the role of the Turkoman tribes in supplying the bulk of the military force to make the creation of the Safavid state possible, it would seem that non-Turkoman elements played an equally important role. Already from the very beginning of Esma'il I's grab for power the Qezelbash were in a substantial way supported by non-Turkoman elements, mainly Georgian troops. According to various independent Venetian reports Christian cavalry supported Esma'il I already in 905/1499. In that year, Esma'il I sent messengers to Iberia (Georgia) to ask the Georgian kings "for assistance, promising wealth to all who joined him, and agreeing, in case he took Tauris, to free them [the Georgian kings] from the tribute they paid to the King of Persia. Each of these Christian chiefs sent three thousand horse, being nine thousand in all. These Iberians are famous horsemen, and valiant in war; on their

---

[44] Mohaddeth, Mir Hashem ed. *Tarikh-e Qezelbashan* (Tehran 1361/1982).

[45] Savory, *History*, vol. 1, p. 314.

[46] Qomi, vol. 1, p. 550.

[47] Don Juan, p. 45.

[48] della Valle, pp. 79-80.

arrival in Sumacchia [Shamakhi], Ismael bestowed rich presents on them."[49] A Venetian merchant, Morati Augurioto, who returned from Tabriz in 1503, reported that "the major part of those [Safavid troops] are Curgi [*Gorji* or Georgians], a ferocious and warlike people and well-armed inhabitants of a region at a distance of little more than two months by road."[50] The Georgian element of 9.000 troops was indeed quite substantial, if we take into account that the Qezelbash troops, according to Persian sources, only numbered 7.000 men. The Georgians seem to have fought as a separate unit of the Safavid army, as is clear from a Venetian account of the battle against Morad Mirza.[51] Although, the Georgian presence seems to have been somewhat diminished in subsequent years, the retreating victorious Ottoman troops, after the battle of Chaldiran in 1514, were continuously harassed by Georgian light cavalry far into Ottoman territory.[52]

The recruiting of non-Turkomans got a substantial boost after the defeat against the Uzbegs at Ghac-davan in November 1512 and against the Ottomans at Chaldiran in 1514, which battles had decimated the Qezelbash forces.[53] Immediately after the Chaldiran defeat Esma'il I sent, amongst others, ambassadors to the Georgian kings, who "agreed to assist Ismael with the largest force they could raise every time he went against Selim."[54] In 1517-19, Esma'il I is again reported to have received support from Georgians and Tartar green hat (*Yeshelbash*) cavalry troops.[55] Here, as is clear from the context, the term green hats referred to troops supplied by the Shirvanshah. Otherwise, the term referred to opposing Uzbeg forces, or to captive Uzbeg troops who had taken service with the Safavids in exchange for their lives. The Safavids also received support from Iranic speaking tribes, foremost among them those from the Talesh area. In the first decade of the 1500s, the Persian army consisted of elements from Fars, Kerman, 'Iraq, Azerbaijan, Aran, Kurdestan and Lorestan when destroying the Dhu'l-Qadrs of Diyarbekr.[56] Although the

---

[49] *Travels to Tana*, part 2, pp. 189-90, 192-3, 50, 63, 121. Esma'il I was following Aq-Qoyunlu practice. Ibid., pp. 24, 27, 86.

[50] Amoretti, Biancamaria Scarcia. *Shah Isma'il I nei <<Diarei>> di Marin Sanudo* (Roma 1979), p. 61.

[51] *Travels to Tana*, part 2, p. 193.

[52] *Travels to Tana*, part 2, pp. 50, 63, 121.

[53] Aubin, "L'Avènement", pp. 30-6; Bacqué-Grammont, *Les Ottomans*, p. 57, n. 102.

[54] *Travels to Tana*, part 2, p. 122; in general see Bacqué-Grammont, *Les Ottomans*, p. 52, n. 102.

[55] Amoretti, pp. 124, 398, 399, 407-09, 469-70; Bacque-Grammont, *Les Ottomans*, pp. 57 n. 102, 162, n. 632, p. 165, n. 648, pp. 185, 233, 256, 295 and p. 315 n. 1083 re the term *pranqah* or forced laborers, pressed soldiers in this case. For green hats also see Membré, p. 36 here referring to Khvarezm and Uzbeg forces. On this term see Bacqué-Grammont, *Les Ottomans*, p. 42 n. 71

[56] Valeh Esfahani, p. 159.

Kurds generally opposed Esma'il I they nevertheless also supported the Safavid cause when given not much choice in the matter.[57]

The Army in Numbers

Aubin has discussed, in detail, the strength of the Safavid army during the first three decades of the 16th century. He convincingly argued that the Safavid forces were small and that the large inflated numbers, that are often quoted, cannot be true. In the first place, the men could not be away for too long a period, because their herds demanded attention, and furthermore, there often was not enough food and fodder to allow long campaigns and/or to sustain large armies. It was for this reason that at the end of each campaign the army was demobilized. The Safavid government was facing a serious problem in financing and feeding its troops. In 1502, a Venetian document reports that Esma'il I "does not keep anything for himself, but gives [his troops] all the money, when he has it."[58] They all received pay from Esma'il I, including, the part of the booty that belonged to the *divan* he distributed among his troops.[59] Also, various documents witness the difficulty of several emirs to provide the obligatory number of cavalry, based on the capacity of their *teyul* (revenue assignment), because of the adverse agricultural situation in their area. This may also explain why the number of troops attached to a particular emir fluctuated over time. In fact, in 1513-4, a governor asked the shah to reduce the number of troops assigned to him, because his revenues were diminishing, to enable him to join the colors as required in strength. The situation was sometimes so bad that some 40% of the troops were not properly armed, as was the case in 1516 and Esma'il I had to dismiss 20% of the *qurchi*s, while in another case the troops had to sell their arms and horse to stay alive.[60] Although less well armed and less experienced than the Ottomans or Mamluks the Qezelbash were considered fierce fighters.[61]

A provincial army, i.e. commanded by one or more emirs, engaged in a limited local campaign usually varied in strength between 1,000 to 3,000 men. An important battle usually involved some 10-12,000 troops, such as on the important campaign to Transoxiania in 1512, although the high figure of 45,000 is also reported. Even at the battle of Chaldiran only some 10,000 troops participated on the Persian side.[62] In 935/1528, the

---

[57] *Travels to Tana*, part 2, pp. 151-2, 157; Bacqué-Gramont, *Les Ottomans*, pp. 111-3, 222-4.

[58] Amoretti, p. 14.

[59] Amoretti, p. 23; *Travels to Tana*, part 2, pp. 49, 52, 104; Qomi, vol. 1, pp. 57, 67.

[60] Aubin, L'Avènement, pp. 30-1, 36.

[61] Amoretti, p. 141.

[62] Aubin, "L'Avenement", pp. 28-36. Esma'il I had three kind of paid soldiers: [i] foot, who were his body guard, [ii] armed men on big horses, well-ordered, whose arms had been supplied by those of Uzun Hasan, and [iii] light cavalry. Amoretti, p.

Qezelbash army against the Uzbek numbered 28.000-30.000 men.[63] The sometimes very high and inflated numbers for Esma'il's army was induced by a number of factors. First, it arose from a natural sense of exaggeration among the reporters. For example, in 1508, a spy found that Esma'il I only had 10,000 armed men and horse, another report said 30,000 mail-clad horse and men, whilst a third document reported an army of 200,000 amongst whom 15,000 Christians.[64] Second, the inflated number may have been occasioned by the large number of horses that were part of any mounted force, the large number of non-combatant irregulars or *hashar*, and the camp followers, consisting of the *ordu-bazar* (see below). In 1502, for example, it is reported that Esma'il I had 12,000 horses, three for each well-armed man.[65] It is also noteworthy that Safavid historians at times report a small Safavid army facing a very large army to underline the uneven odds and the divine nature of the Safavid cause. For example, in 907/1501-02, an army of 7,000 Qezelbash marched to Shirvan to fight the overwhelming force of the Shirvan-shah.[66]

Beginning of Reforms Under Shah Tahmasp I

The shah had no military power-base himself, beyond the small *qurchi* corps, and had to rely on his authority as shah and leader of the Safavid order to make the military obey him. At times of weak royal authority powerful Qezelbash emirs tried to get hold of the reins of government. The tribesmen, as a matter of course, supported their own tribal candidate. This led to conflicts between the various tribal groups, who aligned themselves along tribal affiliation. The inter-tribal rivalry even led to altercations in the shah's presence. This situation led twice (1524-32 and 1576-84) to civil war on a limited scale and made the shah a play-ball of the various powerful emirs.

Shah Tahmasp I, who had been the object and victim of such inter-tribal conflict during the early years of his reign, therefore sought to create ways and means to reduce the power of the Qezelbash emirs. First, he used the growing importance of his own *qurchi* corps as a check on too powerful emirs, by giving its command to those who would be beholden to him rather than to a tribal chief (see below section *qurchi*s). Second, he laid the foundation of the creation of an independent army of slaves (*gholam* or *qol*). Gholams, though in small numbers, existed already under

---

23.

[63] Savory, *History*, vol. 1, p. 89; Savory, "Principal Offices under Tahmasp", p. 68, n. 10 mentions 30,000 men.

[64] Amoretti, p. 124; also 120.000 men both foot and horse, Ibid. p. 17; 80,000 men and higher see also Ibid., pp. 34, 61, 141, 272, 429, 451, 533.

[65] Amoretti, pp. 11-14.

[66] Valeh Esfahani, p. 95, also p. 103 with no mention of the Georgian troops. For other examples see Ibid., pp. 117, 127.

Esma'il I and prior to the Safavids.[67] Together with the *qurchi*s, the *gholam*s were the shah's household troops (*molazem-e shah*).[68] They also participated, on a small scale, in some military expeditions.[69] Third, he continued to expand the role of Georgian and other non-Turkoman troops in his military strategy,[70] a measure initiated by his father as we have seen. According to d'Allessandri, the Georgians were tributary to the Safavids and were to support them with 10.000 "Georgian horse, all robust and valiant men."[71] In 933/1526-7, Badenjan Soltan Rumlu marched with 4,000 Rumlu, Chagani (Kurdish), and Tavalesh troops.[72] Also in 938/1531-2, the governor of Damghan asked the Gerayli, a tribe from Astarabad, to assist him against the Uzbegs.[73] In Eastern Persia, Badi' al-Zaman Mirza had an army consisting of Qezelbash and Tajik troops.[74] As is clear from an army review in 1530, some 20% of the troops mustered were non-Turkoman, a sign that he had a good basis to build upon. Fourth, he reinforced the trend, started by his father, to entrust the management of financial affairs of the country to non-Qezelbash officials. Finally, Tahmasp I tried to disband or disperse the unruly tribes, in which he was not very successful, because he could not impose himself on the major tribes.

By 936/1530 the size of the Safavid army was about 100,000 as is clear from a military review in that year.[75] Of this number the strength of the Afshar and Dhu'l-Qadrs, and Turkoman emirs seems to be underestimated, because no number of troops is listed for some of these emirs. Also, Qomi states that the total number of troops was 120,000 men. All these troops were cavalry, expect for the sayyeds [non-combatants], Betekchi [bowmen], Mazandaran [both cavalry and foot], Turshiz [bowmen], *tabara'iyan* [cavalry with equipment], viziers etc, [horsed]. The presence of Iranic speaking troops from Mazandaran and Astarabad is striking, who represented about 20% of the total force. Also, that Kurdish troops participated (Zik, Chagani) as did Georgian and Tcherkes troops.

---

67 Tehrani, Abu Bakr. *Ketab-e Diyarbekriyeh*, ed. Faruk Sumer and Nejati Lughal, 2 vols. in one (Tehran, 2nd. 1356/1977), vol. 1, p. 63 mentions a corps of 7.000 *gholam*s.

68 Montazer-Saheb, p. 682; Afshar, *'Alamara-ye Tahmasp*. p. 627; Savory, *History*, vol. 1, p. 470.

69 Mohammad Hosein Beg who led, amongst others, the *gholam*s of the governor of Khorasan in battle. Shamlu, p. 334.

70 Qomi, vol. 1, p. 601; Shah Tahmasp, *Tadhkereh*. ed. 'Abdol-Shokur (Berlin 1343/1925), pp. 12 (Gilaki troops) 64, 68, 70, 72 (Georgians).

71 *Travels to Tana*, part 2, p. 228.

72 Savory, *History*, vol. 1, p. 80.

73 Savory, *History*, vol. 1, p. 97.

74 Seistani, p. 168, also p. 170.

75 Qomi, vol. 1, pp. 198-204.

Table 3.1 List of participants of the army review in 1530

Elqas Mirza	4,000	Bahram Mirza	3,000
Tekellu emirs	15,000	Ostajalu emirs	16,000
Afshar emirs	6,000	Shamlu emirs	9,150
Dhu'l-Qadr	8,000	Qajar emirs	6,000
Turkoman, Mouselli	1,000	Zik, Chagani etc .	15,550
Sayyeds, naqibs,	4,000	Khvajeh Betekchi	1,000
Mazandaran emirs	2,000	Khvajehha-ye Tursiz	1,000
Tabarra'iyan	400	Viziers, *'amaleh*	1,700
Boyutat	3,800	Qurchis, *yuz-bashis*	5,000

The army review was either held by having troops pass the shah while marching, or they put themselves in a large circle, grouped per unit under their chief. The muster officers would pass and note each officer and his unit and would check these with their rolls. This review formation was referred to as *yasal*.[76] Whether, as is noted in the DM and TM, the names of each individual soldiers and their arms were checked is a moot question. Under 'Abbas II the army review also took the form of both a by-pass review as well as of a *yasal*, where the soldiers stood lined up on both sides of the path the army reviewers would pass through.[77] In 961/1553-4, Tahmasp I again reviewed his troops. About forty thousand cavalry, men who received regular salaries, passed in review before him, mounted on Arabian horses and fully equipped; they were followed by the rest of the men who were in the royal camp on a comparable basis.[78] This number seems to tally with, what Eskander Monshi called, the largest Qezelbash army ever mobilized (80,000), which took place in 990/1582.[79] According to Venetian reports the Safavids could muster more than 100,000 men, but given logistical (food, fodder) and political problems the normal size of a large army was likely to be only around 60,000 men.

Table 3.2 Geographical distribution of the Safavid cavalry in the 1570s

Isfahan and territories	8000
Bargo (?)	2000
Cassan (Kashan)	4000
Seva (Saveh)	1000

---

[76] Natanzi, p. 594; Afshar, *'Alamara-ye Tahmasp*, pp.97, 347, 381. For a detailed description of an army review or *yasal* under Uzun Hasan see *Travels to Tana*, vol. 1, p. 65-6.

[77] Vahid Qazvini, p. 108.

[78] Savory, *History*, vol. 1, p. 129. Shah Tahmasp, p. 53 himself provides a much lower number, viz. 15.850 men.

[79] Savory, *History*, vol. 1, p. 411.

Table 3.2 (continued)

Sultania (Soltaniyeh)	1000
Ardaouil (Ardabil)	1000
Shiraz	8000
Tauris (Tabriz)	4000
Cum and Crchiuc-Tauris (Qom and ?)	2000
Genge & rest of Georgia (Ganjeh; Georgia)	4000

"In addition they can hire soldiers, while there are also always volunteers, both in rather large numbers. So that the largest number that they can raise is not more than 60,000 horse, assuming that these cities send the soldiers assigned on their lands. However, if all the captains would unite, many of whom are now rebellious and obstinate, the Shah could muster an army of about 140,000." Here Minadoi refers to the forces of Rostam Mirza of Qandahar (25,000 horse) and Ahmad Khan, lord of Gilan (20,000 horse); also the Mir-Miran, lord of Yezd, who refused to send his 4,000 horse; Ebrahim Khan lord of Lar, and finally 'Abbas Mirza (18,000 horse). In Khuzestan, the Arabs were in league with the Turks.[80] A 1586-7 report stated that there were 30.000 Qezelbash troops paid in lands, except those of Khorasan and Shiraz, who constituted another 30,000 men.[81] The Venetian figures seem to be borne out by Persian sources. For example, according to the *Ahsan al-Tavarikh* the army's strength was said to have been 70,000 men. The *Tarikh-e Heidari* states that in 984/1576 the shah had 114,000 *'alafkhvor* (literally grass eaters; paid troops) on the lists.[82] Qomi states that the shah had 200,000 Qezelbash *mavajeb-khvor* (wage earners),[83] which did not necessarily mean that these would all be called to arms or were all paid. Another Venetian report exceeds the above figures, and, moreover, points out that the 100,000 strong Qezelbash cavalry was paid in *teyul*s or land assignments, while the 200,000 strong irregular foot and the less than 100,000 musketeers were mostly paid, when mobilized, directly out of the shah's treasury.[84] A great number of these troops were irregulars (*bi esm va rasm*), who swelled the number of the army, but not necessarily of the combatants. For example, Eskander Monshi observes that "Some two-thirds of the troops, and all those who had no regular military affiliation and were subject to no particular discipline, retired to their homes in 1576.[85]

By the time Shah Tahmasp I died (1576) neither corps (*qurchi* and *gholam*) was strong enough to prevent or contain the second period of

---

[80] Minadoi, pp. 70-72.

[81] Berchet, p. 290.

[82] Röhrborn, *Provinzen*, p. 48, n. 288.

[83] Qomi, vol. 1, p. 600.

[84] Berchet, p. 288.

[85] Savory, *History*, vol. 1, p. 289; Monshi, vol. 1, p. 196.

tribal civil war; the *qurchi*s, moreover, were not entirely able to deny their tribal affiliation and remain neutral. Also, the short and bloody reign by Esma'il II (r. 1576-7) proved to be an unsettling rather than a consolidating element. His successor, Mohammad Khodabandeh (r. 1577-87), was too weak an individual to lead and use the two corpses to impose his will. However, his son, 'Abbas I, was a different person altogether, and was able to build upon the foundations laid by his grandfather, Tahmasp I.

Reforms Under Shah 'Abbas I

When 'Abbas I (r. 1587-1629) had taken the reins of power, he created forthwith the *qollar* corps, reinforced the *tofangchi*s and *tupchi*s and established discipline among the Qezelbash. Eskander Monshi, Shah 'Abbas I's historian, explains these changes as follows: "Because of the rivalries of the Qezelbash tribes had led them to all sort of enormities, and because their devotion to the Safavid royal house had been weakened by dissension, Shah 'Abbas decided to admit into the armed forces groups other than the Qezelbash. He enrolled in the armed forces large numbers of Georgian, Circassian, and other *gholam*s, and created the office of *qollar-aghasi*, which had previously not existed under the Safavid regime. Several thousand men were drafted into regiments of musketeers from the Chaghatay tribe, and from various Arab and Persian tribes in Khorasan, Azerbaijan and Tabarestan. Into the regiments of musketeers were drafted all the riff-raff from every province - sturdy, serviceable men who were unemployed and preyed on the lower classes of society. By this means the lower classes were given relief from their lawless activities, and the recruits made amends for their past sins by performing useful service in the army. All these men were placed on the *gholam* muster rolls. Without question, they were an essential element in 'Abbas's conquests, and their employment had many advantages."[86]

The Qurchis

The *qurchi*s, under the Safavids, were the royal life guards. The Mongol term *qurchi*, (meaning quiver bearer), already referred to a royal guard in the times of Jenghiz Khan.[87] Although the term was also used in that sense by the Timurids[88] it was apparently not used by the Qara- or Aq-Qoyunlu, who used terms such as *'enaq* and *buy-nokar* to refer to the royal guards.[89] During early Safavid times the term *buy-nokar* is still

---

[86] Savory, History, vol. 1, p. 527; Monshi, vol. 2, p. 1106. see also Don Juan, pp. 52, 209 and Röhrborn, Provinzen, p. 32.

[87] Doerfer, vol. 1, p. 429.

[88] Tehrani, *Ketab*, vol. 2, p. 302; Khurshah b. Qobad al-Hoseini. *Tarikh-e Qotbi*. ed. Sayyed Mojahed Zeidi (New Delhi 1965), pp. 400; Khvandamir, vol. 4, p. 92.

[89] Haneda, Masashi. *Le Chah et les Qizilbash. Le système militaire safavide* (Berlin 1987), pp. 144-5; see also Woods, p. 8.

sometimes used but then in the meaning of *yasaqi* or military campaigner.[90] Haneda submits that the creation of the *qurchi*s or Safavid life-guards dates from 1500, when they are mentioned for the first time in Safavid sources, when the Turkoman tribal Safavid followers assembled at Arzenjan.[91] Sumer also submits that the *qurchi*s did not exist under the Aq-Qoyunlu; he therefore suggests that the corps may have been formed following a Chaghatay-Timurid model.[92] However, Sumer fails to explain how that would have been possible, because by 1500 the incipient Safavid state entirely relied on Aq-Qoyunlu personnel and institutions only.

It would seem, therefore, that the *qurchi*s either already existed in Aq-Qoyunlu Persia, or only came into being around 1507, the known date of the first *qurchi-bashi*. The anonymous *Tarikh-e Shah Esma'il* mentions that Rustam Shah Aq-Qoyunlu sent a *qurchi* with a letter to Karkiya Mirza 'Ali, the ruler of Gilan, who was hiding the young Esma'il.[93] He later even sent 300 Turkoman *qurchi*s to Gilan to seek and take Esma'il prisoner.[94] The use of the term *qurchi* probably is an anachronism because the chronicle referred to was written around 1670. However, prior to 1500 a large number of *qurchi*s were said to live around Ardabil who were fierce adherents to the Safavid cause. These *qurchi*s were descendants of the 2,000 prisoners who were released by Timur at the request of Khvajeh 'Ali, the leader of the Safavid order, who were then settled around Ardabil.[95] The captives, sufis of the Safavid order, either returned to Anatolia or were settled around Ardabil, near the Ganjeh-ba-kul cemetery where they became known as Rumlu. This also seems to be borne out by the fact that *qurchi*s are mentioned when the Safavid tribal troops were mustered for the first time at Arzenjan.

Composition of the Qurchi Corps
Whatever the year in which the *qurchi*s were created, they constituted four categories: [a] the *qurchi-bashi* or the head of the *qurchi* corps; [b] the *qurchiyan-e molazem* or *qurchi*s-in-waiting; [c] the *qurchiyan-e yaraq* or *qurchi*s responsible for the shah's arms and accoutrements; and [d] the *qurchiyan-e 'ezam* or the rank and file.

The Qurchi-bashi
The head of the *qurchi* corps had the honorific of *'alijah* and the rank of *moqarrab al-khaqan* and bore the title of *qurchi-bashi*. He always was

---

90 Shirazi, pp. 98, 108; Qomi, vol. 1, p. 328. Also, Shah Esma'il's I response to Soltan Selim prior to the battle of Chaldiran was send by his envoy Shah Qoli Aqa-ye Buyi Nukar. Thabetiyan, Dh. *Asnad va Namehha-ye Tarikhi-ye Doureh-ye Safaviyeh* (Tehran 1343/1964), pp. 86-7.

91 Qomi, vol. 1, p. 71, vol. 2, p. 202.

92 Sumer, *Naqsheh*, p. 102.

93 Ross, "Shah Isma'il", p. 292; Montazer-Saheb, pp. 36-7.

94 Ross, "Shah Isma'il", p. 295.

95 Chardin, vol. 10, p. 188 (commentary by Langlès); Mazzaoui, p. 54.

selected from the corps itself, for the rule was that their general is a *qurchi*, "and the King cannot put one over them who is not of their Body."[96] This did not mean that *qurchi*s could not serve under non-*qurchi* commanders during military operations. In the 16th century *qurchi*s were regularly commanded in the field by other officials than *qurchi*s, including by royal *gholam*s such as Mokhles Beg Gorji (the Georgian).[97] It was the oldest state function created by the Safavids as the DM and TM rightly remark. The *qurchi-bashi* was to the *qurchi*s what the emir was to the Qezelbash *uymaq*, *tayefeh* or *il* (tribal unit, clan). This is clear, amongst other things, from the fact that conspiring emirs in 996/1587 agreed that "the *qurchi-bashi* needed to have a voice in matters else he would loose respect with the *qurchi*s."[98] Röhrborn is wrong to state that the *qurchi*s were subordinate to their tribal *rish-safid*, although the appointment diploma for Emir Mohammadi Beg Mousilli, which is the basis for his argument, indeed implies such as conclusion.[99]

The *qurchi-bashi*s until 1587, allegedly, never received the rank of khan, although some had the rank of *beg*. This seems to indicate, according to Haneda,[100] that despite the importance of the function it was considered not a function of the first-order. To prove his point Haneda cites a case of a *qurchi* who abandoned his hereditary function as *qurchi* because of the allure of the rank of khan that had been promised to him by the then regent of Persia.[101] Moreover, when *qurchiyan-e yaraq* were made khan this received special attention in the chronicles.[102] Haneda further argues his point by submitting that Persian sources do not pay attention to the nomination of the *qurchi-bashi* as they do in case of the *emir al-omara*, *vakil* or *sadr*. In short, the *qurchi*s and their *qurchi-bashi* played second-fiddle to that of the leading Qezelbash emirs.

However, as is clear from Persian sources, the *qurchi-bashi* was a very important central government official, although he was neither the Minister of War nor did he usually bear the title of *emir al-omara* as Minorsky has it.[103] The first *qurchi-bashi*s were all close to Shah Esma'il I and members of the inner circle that governed the state. The first *qurchi-*

---

[96] Thevenot, vol. 1, p. 101; Chardin, vol. 5, p. 302; Richard, vol. 2, p. 116.

[97] Qomi, vol. 2, p. 694; Qarachqay Beg, who was a *gholam*, also commanded a group of *qurchi*s, Astarabadi, pp. 173, 187; for other examples see Ibid. pp. 103, 105, 150, 173; Valeh Esfahani, p. 354.

[98] Savory, *History*, vol. 2, p. 553; Monshi, vol. 1, p. 383.

[99] Rohrborn, *Provinzen*, p., 49, n. 301; Ibid., *Regierung*, pp. 36-7; Qomi, vol. 2, p. 1040.

[100] Haneda, pp. 182-4.

[101] Monshi, vol. 1, p. 418.

[102] Moh. Sharif Beg, *qurchi-ye tir va kaman* was appointed khan. Savory, *History*, vol 2, p. 576; Qara Hasan *qurchi-ye tir va kaman* was made khan, Savory, *History*, vol. 2, p. 578.

[103] TM, pp. 116-7. On the title *emir al-omara* see chapter one.

bashi was chosen from among the sufis of Lahejan (Abdal 'Ali Beg Dedeh) and so was the third *qurchi-bashi* (Saru Pireh Ostajalu).[104] Haneda[105] himself points out that during periods of weak royal authority the function was immediately taken by members of the leading Qezelbash tribes such as the Ostajalu, Tekellu or Shamlu (see Table 3.3). During the hey-day of Qezelbash power, the leading military commander, or *emir al-omara*, at the same time also claimed the function of *qurchi-bashi* for his tribe. Why would he do that if the function was of secondary importance? Qadi Ahmad Qomi, a contemporary source, stated that Duraq Beg Tekellu *qurchi-bashi* (1529-30), held precedence over most of the emirs and the pillars of state during divan sessions.[106] According to a late Safavid source the *qurchi-bashi* was even the deputy of the *vakil*.[107] Like other important officials the *qurchi-bashi* had a deputy, who probably took care of routine business, in his absence.[108] Also, the *qurchi-bashi* was not the only important official whose nomination or dismissal was not recorded in a regular fashion. The same fate struck leading state officials such as the *vakil*, the *emir al-omara* and the *khalifeh al-kholafa*.

Table 3.3 List of *qurchi-bashi*s[109]

911/1506-07	Abdal Beg Dedeh[110]
915/1509/10	Yakan Beg Tekellu[111]
918/1512	Saru Pireh Ostajalu[112]
919/1513	Montasha Soltan Ostajalu[113]
920/1514	Yarash Beg Ostajalu[114]
924/1518	'Ali Soltan Chichkelu[115]
930/1524	Nadhr Beg[116]
933/1526-27	Bakr Beg Ostajalu[117]

---

[104] Valeh Esfahani, p. 155; Montazer-Saheb, p. 170.

[105] Haneda, pp. 179-80.

[106] Qomi, vol. 1, p. 203.

[107] Nasiri, *Alqab*, p. 13.

[108] 'Ali Beg Soklan Dhu'l-Faqr was *na'eb* of Amir Khan *qurchi-bashi*, Yusef, p. 228.

[109] For details see Haneda, pp. 170-2, 194-7; also Ibid., "The evolution of the Safavid royal guard", *IS* 22 (1989), pp. 77-8.

[110] Rumlu, p. 118; Valeh Esfahani, p. 155.

[111] Bidlisi, vol. 1, pp. 124, 411; Aubin, "Soufis", p. 12.

[112] Montazer-Saheb, pp. 170, 480-1, 490, 492, 523; Valeh Esfahani, pp. 236, 238, 242; Qomi, vol. 1, pp. 130-1.

[113] Rumlu, p. 183.

[114] Aubin, "Soufis", p. 12.

[115] His actual name was 'Ezz al-Din; he was *qurchi-bashi* only for some time. Qomi, vol. 1, p. 146; Ben Khvandamir, p. 212.

[116] Shah Tahmasp, p. 11.

[117] Haneda, p. 170, n. 35.

Table 3.3 (continued)

935/1528-29	Tatar-oghli Tekellu[118]
936/1529-30	Duraq Beg Tekellu[119]
937/1531	Dura Beg - or Dedeh Beg[120]
937/1531	Parvaneh Beg Tekellu[121]
940/1533-34	Khalifeh Mohammad Shamlu[122]
940/1534	Ughlan Khalifeh Shamlu[123]
940/1534	Shir Hasan (Dhu'l-Qadr?)[124]
940-969/1534-62	Sevenduk Beg Afshar[125]
?	
982/1574	Ahmad Beg Afshar[126]
984/1576-77	Yusefqoli Soltan Afshar[127]
984/1576-77	Qoli Beg Afshar[128]
985/1577	Eskander Beg Afshar[129]
985/1577	Qoli Beg Afshar[130]
985/1577	Tahmaspqoli Soltan Afshar[131]
985/1577	Kachal Mostafa Afshar[132]
993/1584	Esma'ilqoli Khan[133]
996/1587-88	Yusef Khan b. Qoli Beg Afshar[134]
996/1587-88	Badr Beg Afshar[135]

---

[118] Haneda, p. 171, n. 36.

[119] Qomi, vol. 2, p. 204.

[120] Rumlu, p. 310; Qomi, vol. 1, p. 214.

[121] Shah Tahmasp, p. 18.

[122] Shah Tahmasp, p. 25; Qomi, vol. 1, p. 228; Astarabadi, p. 63.

[123] Shah Tahmasp, p. 25. He may be is the same as Khalifeh Mohammad Shamlu.

[124] Shah Tahmasp, p. 39; Haneda, p. 171, n. 42.

[125] Qomi, vol. 1, pp. 236, 278, 316, 332, 343, 348, 360, 435 (death); Ghaffari Qazvini, p. 236.

[126] Qomi, vol, 1, p. 587; Haneda, p. 172, n. 44.

[127] Haneda, p. 172, n. 45.

[128] Qomi, vol. 2, pp. 622, 656; Haneda, p. 172, n. 47. Allahqoli Beg Afshar is most likely the same as Qoli Beg. Haneda, p. 172, n. 46.

[129] Qomi, vol. 2, p. 696. He stayed in office during the "regency" of Khodabandeh's wife, and then was replaced again by predecessor.

[130] Qomi, vol. 2, pp. 622, 656; Haneda, p. 172, n. 47. Allahqoli Beg Afshar is most likely the same as Qoli Beg. Haneda, p. 172, n. 46. He defected to the Ottomans.

[131] He was the son of Emir Aslan Khan Arshlu Afshar. Valeh Esfahani, p. 742; Natanzi, pp. 64, 85, esp. 177.

[132] According to Savory, *History*, vol. 1, pp. 459, 478 and Valeh Esfahani, p. 754, this person succeeded Qoli Beg not Tahmaspqoli Soltan.

[133] Valeh Esfahani, p. 789; though Monshi also mentions his elevation, he does not mention his appointment as *qurchi-bashi*. Monshi, p. 301; Savory, *History*, vol. 2, p. 433.

[134] Qomi, vol. 2, p. 872; Haneda, p. 194, n. 99; Monshi, vol. 1, p. 381. Son of the previous and defected *qurchi-bashi*.

Table 3.3 (continued)

997/1588-89	Vali Khan Afshar[136]
1000-21/1591-1612	Allahqoli Beg Qapameh-oghli Qajar[137]
1021-40/1612-31	'Isa Khan b. Sayyed Beg Safavi[138]
1040/1631-32	Cheragh Khan Pirzadeh[139]
1040-6/1632-38	Emir Khan Soklan Dhu'l-Qadr[140]
1046-55/1638-45	Jani Khan Shamlu[141]
1055-58/1645-48	Mortezaqoli Khan Begdeli Shamlu[142]
1058-74/1648-63	Mortezaqoli Khan Qajar[143]
1077-79/1666-8	Hoseinqoli Khan Lur-e Kuchek[144]
1079-93/1668-82	Kalb 'Ali Khan[145]
1093-1103/1682-91	Saru Khan Sahandlu[146]
1103-10/1691-99	Shahqoli Khan Zanganeh[147]
1110/1698-99	Mortezaqoli Khan Bijerlu[148]
-1119/-1707	Shahqoli Khan Zanganeh[149]

---

[135] Monshi, vol. 1, pp. 140, 384; Savory, *History*, vol. 2, p. 554.

[136] Monshi, vol. 1, pp.384, 402; Savory, *History*, vol. 2, p. 579.

[137] Monshi, vol 1, pp. 439, 858-9; Savory, *History*, vol. 2, p. 613; Natanzi, p. 474. According to one source (Astarabadi, p. 196) Barkhordar Beg, a *gholam*, was *qurchi-bashi* in 1017/1608-09, but since he was *tupchi-bashi* at that time this must be a scribe's error.

[138] Monshi, vol. 2, p. 859; Savory, *History*, vol. 2, p. 1068-9; Yusef, pp. 71, 93, 257-8; Astarabadi, p. 235 till the end of 1629, when he and his children were killed p. 243. In 1039/1630, a certain Hasan Beg is also mentioned as *qurchi-bashi*. Mostoufi, p. 107.

[139] Yusef, pp. 92, 98, 258.

[140] Yusef, pp. 99, 259.

[141] Yusef, p. 259; Vahid Qazvini, pp. 64-9.

[142] He became *qurchi-bashi* on November 1, 1645 (*ARA*, KA 1057, f. 246) as a reward for his role in the execution of Jani Khan and his followers. For more details see Floor, Mirza Taqi", p. 265; Vahid Qazvini, p. 138; Savory, "Sipahsalar", p. 610.

[143] Nasrabadi, p. 23; Shamlu, p. 514; Vahid Qazvini, pp. 68, 138, 180, 331; Savory, "Sipahsalar", pp. 609-10.

[144] Nasrabadi, pp. 24, 31; Chardin, vol. 9, p. 566.

[145] Bardsiri, pp. 402, 413, 429; *ARA*, VOC 1307 (12/12/1675) f. 639 vs; Chardin, vol. 9, p. 331.

[146] *Qurchi-bashi* since 1672-91; *ARA*, VOC 1373 (19/4/1683), f. 83 vs; Khatunabadi, Sayyed 'Abdol-Hosein al-Hoseini. *Vaqaye' al-senin va a'lam* (Tehran 1352/1973), p. 537; Kroell, p. 35f; Bardsiri, p. 395; Sanson, pp. 87-96. He was executed on August 14, 1701. Valentijn, vol. 5, p. 251. He was also governor of Semnan, Hamadan and Kazerun. He was the son of Mortezaqoli Khan. Brosset, II/1, p. 560.

[147] Kroell, pp. 36, 70; Hedges, William. *The Diary of William Hedges Esq. during his Agency in Bengal; as well as on his Voyage out and Return Overland.* ed. R. Barlow & H. Yule. (London 1887-89), vol. 1, p. 216; Khatunabadi, p. 548; Bardsiri, p. 626.

[148] Nasiri, *Dastur*, p. 272. He may be was Shahqoli Khan's son. Ibid., pp. 129, 133.

Table 3.3 (continued)

171?	Ja'farqoli Khan Hatemi[150]
1123/1711	Mohammad Zaman Khan Shamlu[151]
1127/1715	Safiqoli Khan[152]
1128-33/1716-20	Mohammadqoli Khan Shamlu[153]
1133/1720-21	'Aliqoli Khan Zanganeh[154]
1133/1721	Sheikh 'Ali Khan Zanganeh[155]
1133/1721	Mostafaqoli Khan Sa'dlu[156]
	Farajollah Khan 'Abdollu
	Mohammad Khan 'Abdollu[157]
1138-42/1726-30	Tahmaspqoli Khan Afshar[158]
1142-46/1730-33	Mohammad Reza Khan 'Abdollu[159]
1146-49/1733-36	Qasem Beg Qajar[160]

When Tahmasp I had restored royal control in 1534, he appointed again a sufi from Lahejan, Sevenduk Beg Afshar, from a minor Qezelbash tribe, as *qurchi-bashi*.[161] After the latter's death the shah continued to appoint members of the Afshar tribe as *qurchi-bashi* (see Table 3.3). But even though the *qurchi-bashi* was selected from among the minor Afshar tribe this had no diminishing influence on the importance of the function. This underlined the importance of the function rather than its lack thereof.

---

[149] Nasiri, *Dastur*, p. 129 [1107/1695-6]; *ARA*, VOC 1763, f. 75, 135.

[150] DM, p. 9.

[151] Lockhart, p. 91; Floor, *Bar Oftadan*, p. 233; Ibid., *Afghan Occupation*, p. 176; Mostoufi, p. 117. He was also *sepahsalar* and brother to the grand vizier, Mohammad Mo'men Khan.

[152] *ARA*, KA 1778 (11/3/1716), f. 2. At the end of July 1715 he was send to Qandahar as *sardar*.

[153] Floor, *Commercial*, p. 20, (July 1715).

[154] Lockhart, *Fall*, p. 156.

[155] Lockhart, *Fall*, p. 156; Floor, *Bar Oftadan*, pp. 26, 39, 193; Ibid., *Afghan Occupation*, pp. 36, 184; Mostoufi, pp. 125, 128 He served as of December 1720 and was dismissed on 18/7/1721. In October 1722, he continued to serve under the Afghans in the same function replacing Mostafa Khan, Ibid., p. 232.

[156] Lockhart, *Fall*, p. 164; Mostoufi, pp. 131-2; Floor, *Bar Oftadan*, p. 193; Ibid., *Afghan Occupation*, p. 148, 184. He was the brother of Rostam Mohammad Khan Sa'dlu, governor of Kerman, and was appointed on 18/7/1721.

[157] Nasiri, *Alqab*, pp. 8-9. This source does not provide a date for their appointments. However, since is was written in 1728 they must have served before 1726, because we have dates for the later *qurchi-bashis*.

[158] Mervi, vol. 1, pp. 66-7; Mostoufi, pp. 147, 183 refers to him by his old name Naderqoli Beg; Nasiri, *Alqab*, p. 9. He was the later Nader Shah.

[159] Mervi, p. 51; Sha'bani, Reza. *Hadith-e Nader Shahi* (Tehran 2536/1977), p. 11; *ARA*, VOC 2254 (9/6/1732), f. 884.

[160] Mervi, p. 404.

[161] Qomi, vol. 1, p. 244.

Tahmasp I just wanted to make sure that none of the leading tribes could hold this pivotal function again.

Membré, in 1539-40, mentions the *qurchi-bashi* always among the group of the highest state officials, whom he refers to as the Great Lords, who accompanied Tahmasp I.[162] In fact, the *qurchi-bashi* had a *tabarra'i* or public curser crying out in front of him, just like other leading magnates.[163] During emperor Homayun's visit to Persia, it is stated that "the Kurjy Bashy, and a number of inferior people ... came ... the object of their being introduced was, to prove that all the Persians, whether of high or low rank, were all on a footing with our King."[164] Sevenduk Beg Afshar, the *qurchi-bashi*, was indeed among the party that welcomed Homayun.[165] Rumlu named the *qurchi-bashi* as one of the famous emirs (*omara-ye namdar*) in 960/1552-3.[166] When Qoli Soltan Afshar became *qurchi-bashi* in 1576, he also became a *rokn al-saltaneh*, or pillar of the state.[167] Other instances also underline the leading role of the *qurchi-bashi* as one of the great emirs.[168] Esma'ilqoli Khan received the honorific of companion or *yuldash* and the office of *qurchi-bashi* with the right to seal the inside (*zemn*) of the royal decrees (*ahkam-e mota'*) parallel (*barabar*) to the *vakil*'s seal.[169] Yusefqoli Khan, who became *qurchi-bashi* during Esma'il's II reign, was one of the principal officers of state.[170] Qoli Beg *qurchi-bashi*, was also one of the most powerful of the principal officers of state.[171] In 1597, the *qurchi-bashi* was honored with the title of *sahrvan*.[172] Eskander Beg Monshi referred to the office as "the greatest of the offices of the supreme divan,[173] which is echoed one century later in the DM and TM.

Qurchiyan-e Molazem or Qurchis-in-Waiting

[b] Second, there were the *qurchiyan-e molazem*, of which the *qurchi-ye rekab* was the most important. He was a *moqarrab al-khaqan* who attended the shah and with one hand held the stirrup of the shah's horse

---

162 Membré, pp. 21, 24, 31.

163 Membré, p. 21.

164 Jouher, p. 64.

165 Savory, *History*, vol. 1, p. 163

166 Rumlu, p. 479.

167 Qomi, vol. 2, pp. 665, 681, 699, 733, 744, 768 - he was a leader and *rish-safid* of the one-thousand Afshars, Ibid. vol. 2, p. 1031.

168 Qomi, vol. 2, p. 740; Valeh Esfahani, p. 566, also pp. 580, 586, 621, 679, 721.

169 Valeh Esfahani, p. 789.

170 Savory, *History*, vol. 1, p. 225. Qoli Beg Afshar *qurchi-bashi*, one of the leading officers of state known to all as a man of integrity, wisdom and experience. Ibid., vol. 1, p. 368. The quarrel between the emirs and Mirza Salman was patched up by the *qurchi-bashi* and the *mohrdar*. Ibid., vol. 1, pp. 375, 383.

171 Savory, *History*, vol. 1, pp. 423, 454.

172 Qomi, vol. 2, pp. 699-700.

173 Monshi, pp. 402, 439; Savory, *History*, vol. 2, pp. 579, 613.

and with the other helped the shah mount.[174] Also, the *davatdar-e mohr-e bozorg* and the *davatdar-e mohr-e athar* belonged to the group of the *qurchiyan-e molazem* as did the Ajrlu *qurchi*s, the investigators of murder cases and executors of death sentences.[175] Membré mentioned a *qurchi-mosaheb*, who probably also belonged to this category.[176]

Qurchiyan-e Yaraq

[c] Third, there were the *qurchiyan-e yaraq*. These were divided into two groups. Those who were *moqarrab al-hazrat* and those who were not and were lower in rank. The first group was composed of: the *qurchi*s having the responsibility for respectively the shah's *shamshir* (sword), *sadaq* (quiver bearer), *tir va kaman* (bow and arrow), *sheshpar* (hexagonal headed mace), *khanjar* (dagger), *zereh* (coat of mail), *separ* (shield), *tofang* (musket), *mazdaq* (?), *najaq* (staff). The second group had the responsibility for the shah's *kafsh* (shoes), *neizeh* (spear), *chatr* (parasol), *qalyan* (water-pipe), *sandali* (chair), *choghan* (polo stick), and *jarid* (javelin).[177] Bedik mentioned a number of other *qurchiyan-e yaraq* who are referred to by Turkish terms for the tasks mentioned in the official list, but he also mentioned a few additional functions such as those *qurchi*s holding the shah's *mandil* (turban), *qelich* (sword), *qalqan* (shield), *giyim* (coat of mail), *bahleh* (gloves), *chakmeh* (top boots), *bashmaq* (shoes), *jam* (cup), *hazier* (?) (trappings), and *jelou* (reins).[178] In another, unpublished, manuscript of the TM other additional functions of *qurchi*s are mentioned, to wit: those responsible for the royal *dahaneh* (bit of the bridle), *yaraq* (trappings), *dastkesh* (gloves), and *dastar* (head-dress).[179]

---

[174] DM, pp. 83-4; Under Safi I mention is made of the *qurchi-ye rekab*, which function was held by *gholam*s (Ghayath Beg and Da'ud Beg). They were *mehtar-e rekabkhaneh*. Esfahani, pp. 78, 142.

[175] DM, pp. 102-03; Sumer pp. 66, 129, 209, and 213 in particular; also Nasiri, *Dastur*, p. 29 who mentions that the *davatdar* represented the *qurchi* corps. See also Floor, "Secular Judicial".

[176] Membré, p. 21.

[177] DM, pp. 106-07. Some of these functions are also mentioned in Manuchehr Setudeh, "Raqamha-ye divani-ye begler-begi-ye Astarabad", *FIZ* 26 (1365/1986), pp. 391-2. Savory, *History*, vol. 2, p. 612 (*qurchi-ye chatr*); Yusef, pp. 239, 247, 280 (*qurchi-ye tarkesh*; *qurchi-ye separ*); Yusef, p. 281 (*qurchi-ye tarkesh*); Vahid Qazvini, p. 68 (*qurchi-ye tofang*). Dabir-Siyaqi, pp. 16, 27, 37; Gemelli-Careri, vol. 2, p. 379.

[178] TM, p. 117; Tavernier, p. 220; Gemelli-Careri, vol. 2, p. 379.

[179] Atabay, Badri. *Fehrest-e Ketabkhaneh-ye Saltanati, fehrest-e tarikh, safar-nameh, siyahatnameh*, etc. (Tehran 2537/1977), pp. 45-6. This source also confirms some of the functions mentioned by Bedik such as for the *mandil* (here *dastar*), and *jam* (cup). He also lists most of the other attributes mentioned by the DM (*kafsh, khanjar, shamshir, kaman, neizeh, tarkesh, separ, chatr* and *tofang*); Vahid Qazvini, p. 216 (*zereh*); *ukyay-qurchisi* bow and arrow), *eligu qurchisi* (sword), Richard, vol. 2, pp. 17, 276.

The term *hazier* may be a wrong rendering of the term *yaraq* or, as Minorsky has suggested, of *ozangu*, meaning "stirrup", which function is mentioned by Du Mans and Tavernier as the *zengou-qurchisi*.[180] This official is also mentioned by Chardin who placed this *qurchi* under the *emir akhor-bashi*, adding that he always rode close behind the king and had a staff of ten stirrup-holders or *ozangu-qurchis*.[181] Terms such as *qurchi-ye houzkhaneh* and *qurchi-ye haram*[182] do not refer to special functions, but rather to the location of the guard duties, which were often taken care of by *qurchis*,[183] and are similar to, but more specific than, the term *qurchi-ye keshik* or guard-*qurchi*.[184] Other terms that occur are *qurchi-ye chemesh kereki, qurchi-ye dash, qurchi-ye evji*, and *qurchi-bashi-ye padar*, but it is not known what these terms mean or whom they refer to.[185] It is also not clear what, if any, the relationship is between the *qurchi-ye mandil* (turban holder) and the *saruqchi* (royal turban holder).[186] The term *qurchi-ye jadidi* most likely just refers to its literal meaning, a new(ly appointed) *qurchi*.[187]

These *qurchiyan-e yaraq* were not just simple guards, but rather high-ranking officers of the royal life guards and important members of the shah's court. They held high functions of trust. According to an unpublished manuscript of the TM only the leading members of the Qezelbash tribes qualified for these functions.[188] For example, a special position was held by "the *qurchi-ye mosaheb*, Hosein Beg, who is one of the *mosaheb*, or beloved and closest to Shah Tahmasp I."[189] 'Abbas I made Hosein Beg Shamlu *qurchi-ye shamshir* and gave him his own

---

[180] Du Mans, p. 24; Richard, vol. 2, p. 17; he had a salary of 40 tomans per year; Tavernier, p. 220.

[181] Chardin, vol. 5, p. 366; vol. 6, p. 120. See also appointment decrees for some *qurchiyan-e yaraq* such as the *qurchi-ye tarkesh* and the *qurchi-ye zereh*. Setudeh, "Raqamha-ye divani", p. 396. Da'ud Beg *uzangu qurchi-ye homayun*. Shamlu, p. 283.

[182] Savory, *History*, vol. 1, pp. 291, 336, 472.

[183] Aqa Jan beg Afshar with the *qurchiyan-e hameh-keshik-e haram-e harim* was ordered to guard the *doulat-khaneh*. Valeh Esfahani, p. 776.

[184] Natanzi, p. 21.

[185] Ghaffari Qazvini, p. 290; Rumlu, p. 371; Bardsiri, p. 373. Savory, *History*, vol. 1, p. 133, n. 132 suggests that the term *padar* may refer to a clan name, for Olearius mentions the *Padar* as a robber tribe, while near Shamakhi a Turkoman clan named Padar can be found. The term *qurchi-ye evji* may refer to one of sons of the noble class, who were palace trained and had taken service as *qurchi* (see below section on *gholams*).

[186] Mohammad Beg Saruqchi son of Aslamas Beg the *saruqchi-bashi* (head keeper of the royal turban), Savory, *History*, vol. 2, p. 577-8; *saruqchi-* [*bashi*], Astarabadi, p. 144; *darugheh* of Isfahan, Mohammad Beg Saruqchi. Shamlu, p. 134.

[187] Dabir-Siyaqi, p. 37.

[188] Atabay, p. 45.

[189] Membré, pp. 21, 19.

sword.[190] Also, they were leading men at court (one of the *moraqqaban*) and of their tribe, not just simple soldiers.[191] Heidar Soltan Turkoman died at 90 and had held the function of *qurchi-ye tir va kaman* for 70 years.[192] *Qurchiyan-e yaraq* also were sent as ambassadors to Russia and India.[193] In all of these cases the *qurchi* was always identified by name. The function of *qurchi-ye yaraq* tended to become hereditary, which was in line with the practice of all official functions in Safavid Persia, whether military, civil or religious. The specialized *qurchi* function such as that of holders of the shah's weapons, in particular, became a hereditary patrimonial function, and was indeed mentioned as such (*mansab-e moruthi*).[194]

Under Safi I many of these functions were carried out by *qurchi*s who were eunuchs, not Qezelbash but *gholams*.[195] By the 1670s, it would seem that all of the functions traditionally carried out by the *qurchiyan-e yaraq* were seemingly taken over by eunuchs.[196] Under both Soleiman and Soltan Hosein, down to the end of the latter's reign, the *qurchiyan-e yaraq* continued to perform their function.[197] Bell reported that in 1717, the shah went nowhere without, inter alia, *qurchi*s, who bore his sword, quiver, bow, musket, dart, and target.[198]

Neither the DM nor the TM mentions the function of the *salehdar-bashi*. In Ottoman usage, the *silihdar*s were the sword or weapons bearers, who operated on the left of the Soltan, and were part of the Janissary cavalry.[199] The very few Persian sources that mention the existence of the function do not describe his duties. A late Safavid source reports that the chief of the royal arsenal or *jabbehdar-bashi*, when he was not a eunuch, was called *salehdar-bashi*.[200] He was a member of the Qezelbash tribes, as is clear from the *nesbah*s that are mentioned. For example, Qanbar 'Ali Beg Ostajalu, the *salehdar-bashi*, was placed in charge of the construction of the fort at Khoy.[201]

---

190 Qomi, vol. 2, p. 1047. He had Natanz as governate, Ibid., vol. 2, p. 1069; later Qom, Ibid., vol. 2, p. 1083.

191 Valeh Esfahani, pp. 382, 659; Qomi, vol. 1, pp. 406, 415; vol. 2, p. 727, 893, 983.

192 Qomi, vol. 2, p. 710.

193 Savory, *History*, vol. 2, p. 681; Yusef, p. 200.

194 Savory, *History*, vol. 1, pp. 418, 885; Ibid., vol. 2, p. 594; Sanson, p. 30.

195 For example, Da'ud Beg was a former *qurchi-ye terkesh*, who was a *gholam-e khasseh* and *rish-safid-e harem*. Yusef, p. 281, 295; Vahid Qazvini, p. 317, see also Qazvini, pp. 331, 68.

196 Kaempfer, *Am Hofe*, pp. 183-4, 204.

197 Nasiri, *Dastur*, pp. 20, 33, 108, 167.

198 Bell, p. 215.

199 Gibb and Bowen, vol. 1, p. 70 and its index.

200 Nasiri, *Alqab*, p. 2.

201 Savory, *History*, vol. 2, p. 876; Monshi, pp. 539, 710. Qanbar Beg Qozuboyuklu, the *salehdar-bashi* in 1014/1605-6. Ibid., p. 888. At the end of the

Qurchiyan-e 'Ezam or the Rank and File

[d] Fourth, there was the rank and file, mostly referred to as *qurchiyan-e 'ezam*,[202] which like other similar terms, such as *qurchi-ye 'ezam-e shahi*, *qurchi-ye shahi*, and *qurchi-ye homayun*, referred to the royal life guards *in strictu sensu*, to wit, those permanently stationed at the royal palace to guard the shah's person.[203]

In addition to the royal guards present at court there were *qurchi*s who were stationed in the provinces, as is clear when they are identified by the name of the city they served in. For example, mention is made of the *qurchi*-ye Qazvin, Tehran, Mashhad, Nakhjevan, Shakki and Darband.[204] Each group in a particular city (although this has only been reported for Mashhad and Najaf) was commanded by an officer who was also called *qurchi-bashi*, but who nevertheless was subordinate to the corps commander, the supreme *qurchi-bashi*. This is clear when Qadi Ahmad Qomi mentions that Hosein Beg, son of Sevenduk Beg Afshar *qurchi-bashi*, was *qurchi-bashi* of Mashhad, and in command of 1500 *qurchi*s.[205] Also, under 'Abbas I and Safi I there was a *qurchi-bashi* of the *qurchi*s garrisoned in Najaf,[206] while under Soleiman mention is made of Emir Aslan Beg, *qurchi-bashi* of Talesh.[207] Qurchis were still stationed in Mashhad in 1107/1695-96, as were *tofangchi*s, *qushchi*s (falconers) and *tushmal*s (chamberlains) who were attached to the shrine.[208]

Qurchis Assigned to Princes

In addition to *qurchi*s who guarded the shah's life, there were also *qurchi*s assigned to various royal princes. In the case of Sam Mirza, Shah Tahmasp I decided that 30 *qurchi*s from all *uymaqat* would be his retainers or *molazem*.[209] Being a princely *qurchi* had its advantages. The *qurchi*s serving Soltan Soleiman Mirza were his *mosaheb*.[210] Doulatyar Siyah-Mansur, was a *qurchi* in the service of Hamzeh Mirza, whom he had made emir of the Kurdish Siyah-Mansur tribe.[211] The commander of such a princely corps of *qurchi*s was also called *qurchi-bashi*.[212]

Safavid dynasty the function of *salehdar-bashi* still existed. Asaf, p. 100.

[202] Astarabadi, pp. 57, 59, 64, 72-3, 77, 80, etc.; Monshi, vol. 1, p. 49.

[203] Ibid., vol. 1, p. 47-8; one of the *qurchiyan-e shahi*, Qomi, vol. 1, p. 185; *qurchi-ye khasseh*. Natanzi, p. 26; Dabir-Siyaqi, p. 7.

[204] Qomi, vol. 1, pp. 328, 355, 651; Ibid., vol. 2, pp. 355-6; Rumlu, pp. 433, 463, 465; Musavi 1977, doc. 15. Vahid Qazvini, p. 44 *qurchi*s present in provinces.

[205] Qomi, vol. 2, pp. 651, 673; Valeh Esfahani, p. 524. For another similar case see Qomi, vol. 2, p. 724.

[206] Safiqoli Khan Gorji [*gholam*] Monshi, vol. 2, pp. 1012, 1014, 1088.

[207] Bardsiri, p. 426 (in 1085/1674-5).

[208] Nasiri, *Dastur*, p. 119.

[209] Qomi, vol. 1, p. 253, 550.

[210] Qomi, vol. 2, p. 622.

[211] Savory, *History*, vol., 1, p. 471.

[212] Haneda, p. 176, n. 57; Monshi, vol. 1, p. 319; Valeh Esfahani, p. 740; Qomi,

Qurchis also in Service of Magnates

Local rulers and magnates also had *qurchi*s among their court entourage, although their number undoubtedly must have been limited. The *vali* of Georgia had a *qurchi* corps to serve him complete with a *qurchi-bashi* and the specialized *qurchi*s for his accoutrements (*kafsh, tarkesh, zereh, shamshir,* etc.)[213] Malek Latif became the *qurchi-ye shamshir* and Malek Mostafa the *qurchi-ye tarkesh va tir va kaman* of the *malek al-moluk* Ghayath al-Din of Seistan.[214] Khvajeh Hosam al-Din Gilani's brother was the *qurchi-bashi* of Ahmad Khan, the ruler of Gilan.[215] Also, Membré, in the early 1540s, mentions that each *soltan* was preceded by an *ukyay-qurchisi*, or a bow and arrow carrying guard. From this practice one may infer that *qurchi*s, maybe even prior to 1500, were a standard feature of a magnate's entourage. Durmish Khan Shamlu reported that during his attack on Herat in 930/1524 his own *qurchi-bashi* (Mohammad Beg known as Qara Ishek) led one of the forays.[216] From an administrative manual for the *begler-begi* of Astarabad it is clear that the governor of this area also had in his service a full array of administrative staff as well as *qurchiyan-e tir va kaman, -tarkesh, -tofang, -zereh, -separ, -shamhir,* and *-neizeh*.[217] As late as 1139/1726, a *qurchi-bashi* of Marv is reported.[218] It would seem that the institution also existed among the Ottomans (for Qomi mentions the *qurchi-bashi-ye khondekar*) and the Uzbegs, but these were cases of accidental misnomers or, more likely, extrapolations of Persian concepts to a foreign situation.[219]

Recruitment of Qurchis

Unlike previous dynasties, where the shah was a tribal leader at the same time, the Safavid family was not part of a tribe. The Safavid leader therefore needed a warband that was loyal to him rather than to a tribal leader to provide him with the necessary force to counter balance that of the tribal leaders supporting him.[220] *Qurchi*s were either recruited from among the Qezelbash tribes initially, or from other sources. Mention is made of the tribal affiliation of various *qurchi*s such as: *qurchi*-ye

---

vol. 2, p. 724; Shamlu, vol. 1, p. 71.

[213] Puturidze 1955, docs. 23, 78, 91, 172.

[214] Seistani, p. 205.

[215] Savory, *History*, vol. 2, pp. 942-3; Monshi, vol. 2, pp. 750-1.

[216] Ben Khvandamir, p. 231; in the 1530s the governor of Herat also continued to have a *qurchi-bashi*. Qomi, vol. 1, p. 304 ('Ali Soltan).

[217] Dhahebi-Setudeh, vol. 6, pp. 468-72; Setudeh, "Raqamha-ye divani", pp. 391-2.

[218] Mohammad Emin Beg, Mervi, pp. 66, 69.

[219] Qomi, vol. 1, p. 244; Mukminova, R.G. *Ocherki po istorii remesla v Samarkande i Bukhare v XVI veke* (Tashkent 1976), pp. 118, 150. The Uzbeg term for *qurchi* was *chuz-aghasi*. Monshi, vol. 2, pp. 962, 978.

[220] See Haneda, pp. 178-9.

Ostajalu, Dhu'l-Qadr, Turkoman, Afshar, Rumlu, Qajar, Bayat, Shamlu, Tekellu, Varsaq, Buzjelu, and Kurd.[221] From the fact that Shah Tahmasp I decided that Sam Mirza be given a guard of 30 qurchis originating from all Qezelbash uymuqat, one may infer that all Qezelbash tribes supplied qurchis.[222] The Qezelbash remained the recruiting grounds for the qurchis, also in late Safavid times. In 1065/1654-5, there were qurchiyan-e Shahseven, while in 1083/1673 mention is made of Eslam qurchi-ye Ostajalu.[223] Sometimes an entire group, in the known case 18 persons, joined the corps such as in 1079/1688 when an unnamed group or jama'eh joined the qurchiyan-e Darband.[224] Apart from Turkoman Qezelbash, qurchis also were recruited from Kurdish and Lor tribes, who had been incorporated into the Qezelbash movement.[225]

Also, in a limited way, persons other than Qezelbash Turkomans entered into the ranks of the qurchis, who were referred as ghariblu or gharibler (foreigner, stranger), which group also existed among the Ottoman forces.[226] These outsiders were recruited in various ways, such as:

[a] from among the troops of disgraced governors (the remainder were left for his successor),[227] or rebels who asked for pardon.[228] Shah 'Ali Chapni, a Kurdish chief who had subjected himself to Tahmasp I, received the governorship of Khoy, and his son Dede Beg was made one of his qurchis.[229]

[b] soldiers who had proved their mettle in battle. A person would be singled out because of his good military service and proven value.[230] After the campaign in 'Iraq-e 'Arab, 'Abbas I enrolled those whose service had been outstanding into the ranks of the qurchis or the court retainers.[231] This also explains that some gholams could join the ranks of the qurchis. Mention is made, e.g., of a yuz-bashi-ye gholam who had been qurchi-ye

---

[221] Qomi vol. 1, pp. 162, 214, 243, 601; vol. 2, pp. 657, 769; Rumlu, p. 196; Shamlu, vol. 1, pp. 42-3; Hajji Aqa Lur, yuz-bashi and khalifeh-ye qurchiyan-e Kurd. Sam Mirza, p. 354; Haneda, p. 169.

[222] Qomi, vol. 1, p. 550; see also Savory, History, vol. 1, p. 314; Rumlu, p. 643 and the use of the term uyqamat-e qurchi. Shamlu, vol. 1, p. 423.

[223] Vahid Qazvini, p. 203; Bardsiri, p. 400.

[224] Musavi 1977, doc. 15.

[225] Savory, History, vol., 1, p. 471; Ibid. vol 2, pp. 832, 996; Rumlu, p. 409.

[226] Sumer, p. 101-2; Valeh Esfahani, p. 364; Rumlu, pp. 578-9; Savory, History, vol. 1, p. 187; De Chinon, p. 43.

[227] Monshi, pp. 806-07; Savory, History, vol. 1, p. 438.

[228] Monshi, p. 820. Dhu'l-Faqr Khan was killed, those of his retainers belonging to the Qaramanlu tribe were enrolled into the ranks of the qurchis. Savory, History, vol. 2, p. 1009.

[229] Membré, pp. 35, 20.

[230] Monshi, p. 1057; Puturidze 1962, nr. 14.

[231] Savory, History, vol. 2, p. 1281.

tarkesh.[232] Finally, mention is even made of a Georgian *qurchi* (*qurchi-ye Gorji*),[233] which was a normal development given the fact that two *qurchi-bashis* were *gholams* during the first two decades of the 17th century. This seems to indicate that the Qezelbash exclusivity of the corps had come to and end,[234] though it had not as we will see later.

Whenever a person was appointed as a *qurchi* he became a subordinate (*tabin*) of an officer, called *yuz-bashi*. These officers of 100 (*yuz*) men also originated from the same tribal groups from which the *qurchis* were recruited. It is therefore normal to see also reference made to the same tribal origins of the *yuz-bashis* as it is for the *qurchis*.[235] The *yuz-bashi* also had a *na'eb* or deputy, who was in charge of the unit of nominally 100 men during his absence.[236] However, a *yuz-bashi* often commanded groups that exceeded the number of 100 persons.

It would seem that the slogan 'once a *qurchi*, always a *qurchi*' did not hold. For instance, mention is made in 919/1513-4 of Montasha Soltan Ostajalu "at the time that he had been a *qurchi*,"[237] which means that he was not any more. Also Mohammadi Beg Mousellu had been a *qurchi* for a while.[238] This implies that some *qurchis* were active for an unspecified period only. This may also explain why they could not marry without the shah's permission. This probably meant that the *qurchis* were supposed to be totally devoted to the shah-*pir*, having no other ties. This may explain Rumlu's commiserative remark about the *mehnat-e qurchigari*, or about the "trials" of being a *qurchi*.[239] An event reported by Membré sheds light on this. The *soltan* or governor of Qazvin had died in April 1540 (Dhu'l-Hijja 946). "And the Shah set one of his *qurchis* in his place, a *qurchi* who never in his life thought that the Shah would make him a Sultan. ... And in all the land that day they took this for miracle. For one thing is clear, *qurchis* were no *soltans* and sat in the assembly behind the *soltans* of the lowest rank."[240] However, in 1516, Esma'il I, according to an Ottoman report, had promoted "to the rank of khan and *beg* Khalil Beg, 'Omar Beg, Bekr Beg, and Tekeltu Khan, who are *qurchis* and are at his side."[241] Also, *qurchi* Emamqoli Beg Qajar was appointed as governor of Qarabagh, and elevated to the rank of *soltan*.[242] However, this must have meant that they

---

232 Yusef, p. 281; Vali Beg Ev-oghlu was a *qurchi*. Savory, *History*, vol. 2, p. 793; *qurchi* Shah-geldi Ev-oghlu. Ibid., vol. 2, p. 1154.
233 Natanzi, p. 19.
234 Röhrborn, *Regierung*, p. 39.
235 Haneda, p. 169.
236 Qa'emmaqami, *Yaksad*, doc. 2, 28-29; Puturidze 1962, doc. 14, 35.
237 Rumlu, p. 183.
238 Qomi, vol. 2, p. 765.
239 Rumlu, p. 382.
240 Membré, p. 19.
241 Bacqué-Grammont, *Les Ottomans*, p. 165.
242 Qomi, vol 2, p. 645.

lost their function as *qurchi*. For d'Allesandri clearly states that "the Curzibassa, chief of the king's guard, although he may not be a Sultan."[243] Another similar event underscores this. Mohammad Sharif Khan Chaoslu, a *qurchi-ye tir va kaman*, accepted the governorship of Qazvin with the title of khan from Morshedqoli Khan during the shah's absence and fled to Gilan when 'Abbas I took the reins of power.[244]

Qurchis Different from Qezelbash

As Haneda has pointed out, although recruited mainly from among the Qezelbash tribes the *qurchi* corps was independent and distinct from the Qezelbash army units. The *qurchi*s were mentioned as a group of 5,000 men separate from the Qezelbash troops during a military review of troops in 1530.[245] Shah Tahmasp I mentioned in his *Tadhkereh*, when describing his campaign in Van, that "among the 5,400 soldiers, 1,600 were *qurchi*s, the remainder were under the command of [Qezelbash] emirs."[246] The special position of the *qurchi*s is also clear from the fact that those who died, often, at the shah's orders, were buried at Ardabil.[247] When the Tekellu tribe was purged because of their chiefs' defection to the Ottomans under Tahmasp I, the Tekellu *qurchi*s were allowed to resume their duties on the same basis as before.[248] Also, *qurchi*s could only marry with the permission of the shah.[249] The feeling that despite coming from the same source *qurchi*s were different and separate from the Qezelbash troops was evident to the latter. When *qurchi*s had been send to execute a rebel, Mirza Khan of Mazandaran, whom the Qezelbash troops had captured after having given their word to spare his life, the Qezelbash troops told the *qurchi*s who demanded that they surrender him: "We Qezelbash will bring the khan's person in the presence of Her Majesty."[250]

Administration and Payment of Qurchis

Unlike the Qezelbash troops, who were paid by the emirs, the *qurchi*s were paid by the shah through the *qurchi-bashi*. The latter had the privilege to appoint, dismiss, and muster the *qurchi*s as well as determine the salaries and the manner of their payment. Consequently, there was a separate financial administration for the *qurchi* corps, with its own budget and financial staff, managed by a *mostoufi* and vizier, who were accountable to the *qurchi-bashi*. These two officials were in charge of the *sarkar* or the *daftar-e qurchi* (the department of *qurchi*s). The first such

---

243 *Travels to Tana*, vol. 2, p. 221.
244 Savory, *History*, vol. 2, p. 594.
245 Qomi, vol. 1, pp. 198-204.
246 Shah Tahmasp, p. 53.
247 Membré, p. 40.
248 Savory, *History*, vol. 2, p. 707.
249 Membré, p. 43.
250 Monshi, p. 242; Savory, *History*, vol. 1, p. 361.

official, a *vazir-e qurchiyan*, is mentioned in 1511-2.[251]

These administrative functions also tended to be hereditary. For example, 'Aliqoli Beg of the 'Arabgirlu clan of the Shamlu tribe held the office *vazir-e qurchi*yan, which office had been vested in his family since early Safavid times.[252] It was the vizier's duty to write the employment certificates for the *qurchi*s, *yuz-bashi*s and *yasavolan-e qur*. He kept files with their employment history, and their behavior (were they absent, service record, etc.). He further was responsible, together with the *mostoufi* for the financial management of the *qurchi* department. The *mostoufi* kept records on the pay of the *qurchi* department staff, their attendance, whether they were *hamisheh-keshik* (in garrison at court) or *rekabi* (in attendance when the shah traveled), etc. He also kept the muster roll which was checked during the annual review. Each year therefore he prepared an up-to-date list of the state of the corps (death, dismissal, mission, etc.) which served as an input for the *divan*'s budgeting purposes.[253]

There was not one single pay rate for the *qurchi*s, because there were several kinds or ranks of *qurchi*s as we have seen above. The middle and lower ranks of the *qurchi*s received annual salaries (*mavajeb-e saliyaneh*) from the treasury as well as the necessary arms from the arsenal or *qurkhaneh*.[254] The *qurchi*s-*bashi*, as one of the leading emirs of the country, of course received various sources of income, the most important of which was a *teyul* or assignment on a source of revenue. Although towards the end of the 17th century the *qurchi-bashi* got Kazerun as a *teyul*,[255] this type of land assignment varied per office holder. For example, Qoli Khan Soltan *qurchi-bashi*-ye Afshar, was assigned Aberquh and Banavat as *teyul*,[256] while Emir Khan, Jani Khan and Mortezaqoli Khan were governors of Kerman.[257] The *qurchi-bashi*'s income was reported by du Mans to be 1,000 - 1,500 tomans per year in 1660.[258] The leading *yaraq qurchi*s, apart from holding a function at court, usually also held other administrative functions to provide them with an

---

[251] Haneda, p. 178, n. 63; Khvajeh Shahqoli, *vazir-e qurchiyan*, one of the old *gholam*s in 939/1532. Qomi, vol. 1, p. 225; and in 949/1542-3 a *mostoufi-ye qurchi*. Ibid., vol. 2, p. 707; a *vazir-e qurch-bashi*, Ibid., vol. 1, p. 436, see also Ibid. vol. 2, pp. 743, 746, 826, 987; see also Astarabadi, pp. 62 [in 939/1532-3], 203.

[252] Savory, *History*, vol. 1, p. 258.

[253] DM, pp. 88, 94-5.

[254] Shirazi, p. 98.

[255] TM, p. 86; in 1105/1694, the *qurchi-bashi* had a share in Kazerun. Nasiri, *Dastur*, p. 20.

[256] Qomi, vol. 2, p. 656.

[257] Yusef, p. 133, 259; Nasrabadi, p. 23; Bardsiri, pp. 207, 653. Another had Hamadan as *teyul* and asked this to be changed to Kerman. Bardsiri, p. 522.

[258] Richard, vol. 2, p. 18; 150 or 6-10 times less tomans around 1650. Tavernier, p. 226.

income and the means to participate in military campaigns. Morshedqoli Soltan, *qurchi-ye shamshir-e khasseh* was also governor of Natanz who had 50 retainers (*molazem*).[259] It would seem that the *qurchi-ye shamshir* usually held the governorship of Qom,[260] and the *qurchi-ye tir* that of Yazd,[261] but more data are needed to confirm this. The bow and arrow carrying *qurchi* had an annual salary of 30 tomans in 1660.[262]

The rank and file *qurchi*s were paid partly in cash, partly in entitlement grants such as a *hameh-saleh*, and less frequently a *teyul* (land assignment) or *soyurghal* (tax exempt revenue grant). They were 4,000 in number by 1576. In 1540, according to Membré, the shah paid "his *qurchi*s high wages, so that there are those of them that have 30 tumans a year; some have 10 and some 4 or five."[263] However, at the end of Tahmasp's I reign the *qurchi*s as the rest of the army had not been paid for 10 years. "Instead of salaries [Tahmasp I] gives them clothing and horses, putting these at such prices as suits him."[264] This lack of pay led to exactions from the population, as well as participation of *qurchi*s in criminal activities, reason why Tahmasp I's successor, Shah Khodabandeh paid their arrears in one lump sum payment and henceforth paid them regularly.[265] "The two thousand Curchi, that remaine to be paide for their attendance, (who have no landes assigned to them for their pay, as the foure thousand abovenamed have) doe also receive their ordinary wages out of the kinges Chamber, from a hundred & threescore, to two hundred Cecchins [ducats] a man."[266]

In the 17th century, according to European travelers, a *qurchi* received 300 *Reichsthaler*, or 12,5 tomans, per year, while he also was allowed to keep his horse.[267] "Their pay is from 10-15 tomans a year; but for the first three years they receive nothing."[268] According to du Mans the *qurchi*s were paid 7 to 12 tomans per year in 1660.[269] By the 1690s, the amount of pay still was the same. "These are Troops which are never reform'd or broken. Every Kortchi has an hundred Crowns paid him a Year out of the Exchequer. The Sons succeed the Fathers, if the General will consent."[270]

---

259 Qomi, vol. 2, p. 852.
260 Qomi, vol. 2, p. 878, 889, 894; Savory, *History*, vol. 2, p. 614; Yusef, p. 253.
261 Savory, *History*, vol. 2, p. 580.
262 Richard, vol. 2, p. 17.
263 Membré, p. 35.
264 Carmelites, vol. 1, p. 53.
265 Monshi, p. 228, 142; Rumlu, p. 623; *Travels to Tana*, part 2, p. 46; Carmelites, vol. 1, p. 46. They had not been not paid for 10 years, see Savory, *History*, vol 1, p. 341.
266 Minadoi, p. 77; Berchet, p. 287.
267 Olearius, p. 668.
268 Thevenot, vol. 1, p. 101; 6 tomans per year without charges (= food and fodder allowance). Fryer, vol. 3, p. 62.
269 Richard, vol. 2, p. 18.
270 Sanson, pp. 20-1.

An armed royal guard got 9-10 tomans; an *on-bashi* 15, a *yuz-bashi* 30, a *min-bashi* 70 and the commander 150 tomans. The *gholam* got a little less, and the foot soldiers even less.[271] However, the few surviving documents that are payment orders for *qurchis* inform us that the annual wages of a *qurchi* could be a salary (*mavajeb*) of 8 tomans,[272] a *soyurghal* of 4,5 tomans in 1057/1647,[273] a *mavajeb* of 4 tomans in 1079/1688,[274] or a *mavajeb* of 5 tomans in 1099/1688.[275] Payments were either in cash or in kind.[276] Payment orders were first verified with the commanding *yuz-bashi*. When the *qurchis* were on military campaign they did not receive their normal salary (*mavajeb* and/or *hameh-saleh*) for its duration, for whenever a payment order was issued it was stated that the *qurchi's yuz-bashi* confirms that he is not currently serving on a military campaign.[277] In addition to their normal wages, the shah organized every three years a review and gave the *qurchis*, on average, one-third more than they normally would have received. I.e. some would receive more, other less, according to their merit and skill in handling their arms or royal favor.[278]

Dress and Equipment of Qurchis

Qurchis were not only well paid, they were also well equipped, for in 1540 even "the most wretched of them has four or more camels and three or four mules and horses" which they received from the shah.[279] Moreover, these were good horses, arms "and they are edged weapons. They do not wear anything but cuirassines and coats of mail."[280] The royal *qurchis*, fully armed with their helmets and chain mail over their quilted vests, were stationed with the *qurchis* in the center.[281] Also, when on campaign or travelling the *qurchis* each had a tent where they tethered their horses. They further had servants (*nokaran-e qurchiyan*) who were untried youths (*javanan-e nusakhteh*).[282] They wore "swords with scabbards of massy gold - that is those *qurchis* who have done some deed

---

271 Kaempfer, *Am Hofe*, pp. 74-5; Tavernier, p. 226. A *qurchi* received 6 tomans without charges, while a *jaza'eri* received 5 tomans while all charges were defrayed. Fryer, vol. 3, p. 62.
272 Qa'emmaqami, *Yaksad*, doc. 2.
273 Papaziyan, A.D. *Persidskie dokumenty Matenadarana* (Erivan 1956) doc. 33.
274 Musavi 1977, doc. 15.
275 Puturidze 1962, doc. 14.
276 Puturize 1962, doc. 35; Qa'emmaqami, *Yaksad*, doc. 28-9. See also DM, p. 48 and TM, p. 46, according to whom they received *mavajeb-e barati*, *teyul* substitutes and *hameh-saleh*s.
277 Puturidze 1962, doc. 35; Qa'emamaqi, *Yaksad*, doc. 28-29.
278 Tavernier, pp. 227, 218-9.
279 Membré, pp. 24, 28;
280 Membré p. 35.
281 Savory, *History*, vol. 1, p. 89-90.
282 Montazer-Saheb, p. 145.

of bravery - and the dagger, which they call *khanjar*, of massy gold with turquoises, and also all the Lords. And they wear a belt of massy gold with turquoises and rubies. They go well-dressed in velvet and brocade, which is made in the city of Yazd; and of these I have seen many. They also wear on their heads, upon their turbans, a strip of gold with turquoise and ruby stones. And there are those of them who wear three or four gold strips; and they wear plumes, and at the foot of the said plumes there is massy gold with precious stones. And when the King makes any festival they all dress like this."[283] *Qurchi*s wore the *taj*, the red cap instituted by Esma'il I. By the time of 'Abbas I it had become usual for *qurchi*s to wear a helmet with mail protectors down their cheeks instead of the *taj* during military campaigns.[284] They also wore a long moustache, a trademark for Safavid sufis. In addition to a sword, bow, lance and dagger the *qurchi*s also used modern arms. As defensive arms they wore a shield on their back; they also wore helmet. Some regiments were armed with muskets and served on foot.[285]

Functions of the Qurchis

The *qurchi*s performed all kinds of functions. Their most important function, of course, was to guard the shah's person and the palace. The *qurchi*s therefore were the shah's household troops as well as his crack fighting troops.[286] *Qurchi*s were also charged to go on official mission in the various parts of the kingdom to execute the shah's orders or to make them known.

Guard duty: In Tabriz, in 1540, the first door the palace, "as one enters, on the right hand side is the guard-station of the Qurchibashi."[287] It was here that "The king keepeth also for the gard of his Palace-gate certaine orders of souldiours; wherof the most noble and greatest in nomber are those that the Persians call Curchi, which are as it were the Kinges gentlemen, being six thousand, all of them divided under several captaines; which Captaines also doo yeeld obedience to their generall called Curchi Bassa, a person alwaies of great authority."[288]

Various Persian sources also confirm that *qurchi*s performed guard duty, when they also were referred to as *qurchiyan-e keshik*.[289] These *qurchi*s, together with the other royal palace staff (*molazem-e khasseh*)

---

[283] Membré, p. 27.

[284] Chardin, vol. 5, p. 300.

[285] Chardin, vol. 5, p. 302; Rumlu, p. 580. for a picture of *qurchi* see Dhoka, p. 188 from Chardin's atlas.

[286] Savory, *History*, vol. 2, p. 906.

[287] Membré, p. 29; Qomi, vol. 1, p. 583, the *qurchi* guard-house was next to the pond in Qazvin.

[288] Minadoi, pp. 68-9. The other palace guards were the *yasavols*; see also Berchet, p. 287 in a report by Teodoro Balbi.

[289] Ghaffari Qazvini, p. 280.

which constituted the group on permanent active duty (*hamisheh-keshik*), were at their posts in the *doulat-khaneh* (Government House).[290] The *qurchi*s also guarded the shah's person during battle. "And besides all this multitude [of army personnel], the King was guarded with his ordinary Guarde of Curchis and Esahul [*yasavol*]."[291] In the 16th century it was still quite common to identify the *qurchi*s by their tribal affiliation and always *qurchi*s of more than one tribal group were on guard duty.[292] Although the *qurchi*s guarded the shah's life, in the palace, they were usually not stationed close to the shah, but at a location below that of higher placed persons.[293] When 'Abbas I, to avoid bad luck, had a substitute installed on the throne for three days the *qurchi*s also mounted guard around the pseudo-king.[294] The *qurchi*s also guarded the harem in the field during military campaigns.[295]

Military tasks: "The valor and bravery of the *qurchi*s was so renowned that one hundred men of the household troops were a match for a thousand men drawn from other categories of soldiers."[296] Being the shah's crack troops the *qurchi*s were used for all kinds of military operations. As such they were not singled out for special functions, but performed all kinds of military duties just like other military units, who were less well armed and trained.[297] *Qurchi*s also were used for manual labor such as the filling of a moat with rocks,[298] as messengers to get military help, to do reconnaissance work, defend towns and attack the enemy in the field.[299]

Executors of the shah's will: *Qurchi*s were used to relay royal orders,[300] to act as tax collector (*tahsildar*),[301] to mobilize auxiliary troops,[302] to execute high placed persons,[303] and lead troops in battle.[304] "When the King would put any great man to death, he commits the Execution

---

[290] Valeh Esfahani, pp. 755, 799. The other staff included the *yasavol*s and the *gholam*s. Montazer-Saheb, p. 682; Afshar, *'Alamara-ye Tahmasp*, p. 627; Savory, *History*, vol. 1, p. 470.

[291] Minadoi, p. 388.

[292] Qomi, vol. 1, p. 214, 601; Ghaffari Qazvini, p. 285; Monshi, vol. 1, p. 47. For guard duty at the palace in general see Valeh Esfahani, pp. 491, 493, 510, 760, 768; Natanzi, pp. 19, 21; Rumlu, p. 602.

[293] Membré, pp. 19, 30.

[294] Savory, *History*, vol. 2, p. 649.

[295] Astarabadi, p. 128.

[296] Savory, vol. 1, p. 228.

[297] Qomi, vol. 1, p. 235; Shah Tahmasp, pp. 52, 54, 56, 58.

[298] Qomi, vol. 1, p. 66.

[299] Qomi, vol. 1, pp. 136, 243; Montazer-Saheb, p. 64; Rumlu, p. 194.

[300] Bacqué-Grammont, *Les Ottomans*, p. 216.

[301] Qomi, vol. 2, p. 696.

[302] Bardsiri, pp. 373-4; Savory, *History*, vol, 1. pp. 95, 409; vol. 2, p. 861; Fragner, "Zehn Urkunden Schah Tahmasps II.", doc. 2.

[303] Seistani, p. 190.

[304] Seistani, pp. 267-8.

commonly to a Corchi."[305] These may have been the same as the *qur-yasavols*, or the *qurchi-ye* Ajrlu, who according to Chardin formed a small group of 100 men, that functioned as a kind of gendarmerie.[306] There is indeed evidence that this group was used to carry out executions. Emir Khan Soklan Dhu'l-Qadr, *qurchi-bashi*, was ordered by Safi I to kill his predecessor with some of the *qurchiyan-e* Ajrlu.[307] The Ajrlus seem to have been a small tribe, from which these *qurchis* were drawn. For mention is made of Saru Khan Beg Ajrlu, *yuz-bashi* (hundredman) and *hakem-e il-e* Ajrlu (tribal chief).[308] It fact, it would appear that they were a sub-group of the Shahseven confederacy, though in the *Tarikh-e Qezelbash* they are mentioned as one of the 32 tribes.[309] They also had the exclusive right to investigate murders.

Qurchis and the Shah-loyalty and Self-importance

Qurchis were supposedly fiercely loyal to the shah. *Qurchis* were told in 929/1522-3 by the *rekabdar*, Shahqoli 'Arabgirlu, that it was the shah's order to cut Mirza Shah Hosein to pieces, which, believing that it was true, they did.[310] As executors of the shah's orders the *qurchis* expected to be obeyed by everybody, including the emirs, without questioning. In their own words, "The most important people at court were the members of the royal bodyguard. We are involved in every aspect of state affairs, and other people have no option but to obey us."[311] Not all emirs were agreeable to this high and mighty behavior. Qaitamiz Beg, for example, did not like the attitude of a *qurchi* who insisted that he immediately obeyed his orders, "whom did he think he was" the emir asked.[312]

The *qurchis* themselves did not obey the shah's orders always either. At one occasion, in 1540, some of the *qurchis* were not ready to ride out for a military campaign. Bahram Mirza complained to his brother the shah, who ordered that those *qurchis* who had "remained behind should ride backwards on a donkey, with bells everyone, and come into the city and come riding thus into the presence of the shah." After having heard and judged them they left.[313] Two *qurchis* were suborned by promises of governorship and monetary rewards to abduct Tahmasp Mirza, thus

---

305 Thevenot, vol. 1, p. 101.

306 Chardin, vol. 7, p. 421.

307 Yusef, p. 99; see also Vahid Qazvini, p. 48. Chardin, vol. 7, p. 421 mentions the palace of the *yuz-bashi* in charge of a group of Agellou, i.e. mountaineers, to indicate that they are fierce and intrepid. The term, as suggested by Minorsky, probably means "wage (*ajr*) takers". TM, p. 51, n. 1.

308 Yusef, p. 227.

309 Beiburdi, Hosein. "Panj farman-e tarikhi", *BT* 4 (1348/1969), p. 69.

310 Qomi, vol. 1, pp. 150-1.

311 Savory, *History*, vol. 1, pp. 462-3.

312 Montazer-Saheb, p. 194.

313 Membré, p. 35.

betraying the royal trust.[314] *Qurchis* killed the Tartar chief 'Adel Geray Khan against the wishes of the shah, and were only prevented by circumstances to kill the shah's wife as well.[315] This attitude may have been caused by the fact that Tahmasp I, an avaricious man, did not "even pay [them] in money, but gives them uniforms and horses, putting on them whatever value he thinks fit in advance for their salaries."[316] Also, that these events occurred when there was strife among the various Qezelbash tribes and royal authority was weak.

The *qurchis* were royal retainers (*molazem-e khasseh*) par excellence, but despite the loyalty to the shah at times the loyalty to the clan or tribe was stronger. "We say, said the *qurchis*, a plague on both your factions. We are concerned only to guard the palace, and to protect the harem and the honor of the Shah." However, they did not let Heidar Mirza, the heir-apparent out of the palace. He rightly feared for his life as did his followers, and the *qurchis* did not protect him.[317]   For example, when central authority had broken down in 994/1585 and the Turkoman emirs, who were joined by those of the Dhu'l-Qadr, wanted to usurp the hold of the Ostajalu and Shamlu emirs over Shah Khodabandeh the *qurchis* and other retainers joined the usurpers when the senior Turkoman emir, Adham Khan, joined them.[318]

The Number of Qurchis

During the 16th century the *qurchi* corps never became bigger than 6,000 men. The total number of *qurchis* grew from about 1,000-3,000 men under Shah Esma'il I to some 6,000 men under Esma'il II.[319] When Shabik Khan Sheibani was killed in 1510 the *qurchis* numbered 3,000-4,000 men.[320] In 1516, according to an Ottoman intelligence report there were only 1,000 *qurchis*, while there had been 3,000 at the battle of Chaldiran in 1514.[321] In 1512, Mirza Mohammad Talesh left with 2,000 *qurchis* to help Hosein Beg in Lorestan.[322] An Italian report from 1503

---

314 Savory, *History*, vol. 1, p. 465.

315 Qomi, vol. 2, p. 696-7.

316 *Travels to Tana*, part 2, p. 226.

317 Savory, *History*, vol. 1, pp. 285-6. For similar sentiments where the *qurchis*, who were guarding the palace gates, stated that they were drawn into the conflict through the split of the Qezelbash because of the death of Tahmasp I. Valeh Esfahani, p. 491; for a similar situation in 937/1530-31 see Ghaffari Qazvini, p. 285.

318 Qomi, vol. 1, pp. 778-80; see also Valeh Esfahani, pp. 694-5. Also, the case of the *qurchi-bashi* who disobeyed the Shah. Monshi, p. 418.

319 Aubin, "L'Avènement", pp. 35-6; Bacqué-Grammont, *Les Ottomans*, p. 152, n. 590, and p. 180.

320 Valeh Esfahani, p. 193.

321 Bacqué-Grammont, *Les Ottomans*, pp. 206-07.

322 Montazer-Saheb, p. 175.

mentions a much larger number of *qurchi*s, who at one particular battle allegedly numbered 10,000, which cannot be true.[323] Duraq Beg Tekellu *qurchi-bashi* [1529-30], had 5,000 *qurchi*s.[324] Sevenduk Beg *qurchi-bashi* Afshar had at least 2,500 *qurchi*s.[325] When Tahmasp I held a review of troops in 936/1530 among the 100,000 odd troops the *qurchi*s and their *yuz-bashi*s commanded by their *qurchi-bashi* numbered 5,000 horsemen.[326] By the 1570s their number had grown to six thousand. Because of internal troubles among the Qezelbash the *qurchi*s numbered less than 3,000 under Mohammad Khodabandeh.[327]

"At the time of the death of Shah Tahmasp, the total number of *yuz-bashi*s of senior rank, office holders, *qurchi*s, and *yasavol*s was six thousand. Of this number, four thousand five hundred were *qurchi*s of the royal bodyguard, and one thousand five hundred other officials - namely, *qurchiyan-e dash*, *yasavol*s, *bokavol*s, and so on. Among this group were *yasavol*s, trusted *qurchi*s, *eshik-aghasi*s, *yasavol-bashi*s of the arsenal and of the central administration, *mir shekar* and *tupchi bashi*s. In each category and lot there were many who deserved to be emirs, and though they were not honored with the rank of emir, yet in esteem they did not yield to the emirs. Each officer had an appropriate number of efficient servants subordinate to him; this number varied from five to fifty, so that some six thousand of these servants were on the staff of the royal household. But if an accurate account were to be made of these servants and attendants, their number would probably be twenty thousand, if not more."[328]

Military Reforms Change Status of Qurchis

The military reforms introduced by 'Abbas I, which reduced the role of the Qezelbash emirs by giving prominence to a countervailing power, i.e. that of the *gholam*s or *qollar*, did not diminish the role of the *qurchi*s, who continued to be a group separate from the other old and new army elements. Molla Jalal at two occasions lists the troops engaged in the siege of respectively Erivan in 1012/1603-04 and Shamakhi in 1015/1607-08. He mentions the *qurchiyan-e 'ezam* as a separate unit from the *gholam*s, Qezelbash troops and local levies.[329] Qezelbash commanders present at the siege were not *qurchi*s at the time, and their adoption in its ranks only

---

323 Amoretti, p. 62.

324 Qomi, vol. 1, p. 203.

325 Qomi, vol. 1, p. 332.

326 Qomi, vol. 1, p. 204; Natanzi, p. 185 mentions a force of a least 4.000 *qurchi*s, without mentioning its total size.

327 Valeh Esfahani, p. 768.

328 Savory, *History*, vol. 1, p. 228; these numbers 4.500 + 1.500 are confirmed by Valeh Esfahani, p. 412, Minadoi, p. 77 and Balbi in Berchet, p. 287; Carmelites, vol. 1, p. 53. see also Savory, *History*, vol. 1, p. 187.

329 Molla Jalal, pp. 305, 308; Haneda, p. 163.

occurred later.[330] Towards the end of 'Abbas I's reign, the Qezelbash troops had ceased to be separate force, and were all under the *qurchi-bashi*. The Qezelbash were not mentioned anymore as a separate group, but the *qurchi*s were. For mention was made of the presence of *qurchi*s, *gholam*s and *tofangchi*s.[331] This is also clear from Della Valle's statement when he reported that many were serving provincial governors, while 12,000 were *qurchi*s.[332] The number of the Qezelbash troops also grew less, in consonance with their reduced importance.

This seemingly fading away of the Qezelbash in fact did not really happen. When discussing the provincial regular troops Chardin makes it clear that, though he refers to them as *qurchi*s, he actually meant Qezelbash. Elsewhere he talks about the "race of *qurchi*s" again referring to the Qezelbash.[333] Chardin was not confused, for the *qurchi-bashi* was as of the early 17th century the *rish-safid* of all Qezelbash clans. Though the *qurchi*s as the royal household troops continued to exist, the Qezelbash levies were henceforth reorganized along territorial, not tribal lines. This meant that their emirs were not *emir-e sufi* anymore, but an emir attached to a certain jurisdiction. This also explains why the estimated number of *qurchi*s is so much higher in the 17th than in the 16th century.

In the 17th century the number of *qurchi*s would grow to 10,000 and even 20,000 men.[334] Purchas reported that among the guards of the king's palace, the most noble and the greatest in number were the *qurchi*s, "being eight thousand in number." He added that the *qurchi-bashi* is "a man alwaies of great authoritie."[335] The *qurchi*s continued to be mainly recruited from amongst the Qezelbash tribes. Della Valle states that the *qurchi*s, or the king's guards, "were the most noble [of the four army groups], chosen from among the kizilbashi, and entirely and immediately in the pay of the Shah himself."[336] The *qurchi-bashi* is the head of a 12.000 men corps created by Esma'il I, who live freely in the provinces, and have to come when there is a war and they are summoned, according to Olearius.[337] Estimates by other European travelers are in the same range. Whereas Chardin still estimates them at 30,000, Kaempfer reports that there were only 20.000 at most.[338] At present, the Qezelbash are

---

330 Monshi, vol. 2, p. 806 (Dhu'l-Faqr Khan). See also Savory, *History*, vol. 2, pp. 1010, 1025.
331 Yusef, pp. 80-1.
332 Della Valle, p. 80; see also Chardin, vol. 5, p. 299.
333 Chardin, vol. 5, pp. 225, 302.
334 Haneda, pp. 191, 154-62.
335 Purchas, vol. 8, p. 511, which statement is copied from Minadoi.
336 della Valle, p. 80.
337 Olearius, p. 670.
338 Chardin, vol. 5, p. 302; Kaempfer, *Am Hofe*, p. 72; Gouvea, A. *Relation des grandes guerres* etc. (Rouen 1646), p. 116 (6.000); Gabriel de Chinon, *Relations nouvelles du Levant* (Lyons 1671), p. 43-4 (12,000); Thevenot, vol. 1, p. 191

weakened, writes Chardin, but there were still thousands of them. They served under the *qurchi-bashi* who always must be one of their own, because they refuse to serve under someone else. He adds that the *qurchis* are the real Qezelbash.[339]

When on military duty Qezelbash troops were also commanded by non-Qezelbash emirs, when they were stationed in a province that was governed by e.g. a *gholam*. This was the case in Astarabad which between 1012/1604 till 1075/1664 was invariably governed by a *gholam begler-begi*.[340] These developments led to a situation where the Qezelbash troops, as a distinct category, faded away, so that the term was being used to refer to Persian troops in general. In 1039/1629-30, mention is made of the *sepah*-e Qezelbash (Qezelbash army), which included all services.[341] The Qezelbash troops did not figure anymore as a group with a separate identity after the 1640s, for, when marching to Qandahar in 1648, the troops were described as "*laskar-e zafar-athar az omara va qurchiyan va gholaman va aqayan.*"[342] In 1106/1694, the *sepahsalar* led an army consisting of *qurchiyan*, *gholam*s, *aqayan*, *tofangchi*s and *tupchi*s.[343]

Role of Qurchi-bashi Grows in Importance

Both Minorsky and Savory were wrong to conclude that the role of the *qurchi*s and their chief had diminished.[344] They were misled by an observation made by Chardin, who reports that after 'Abbas I had the *qurchi-bashi* (he meant Allahqoli Beg Qajar) beheaded he broke up the *qurchi* corps by splitting them up in small groups that were distributed throughout the provinces.[345] 'Abbas I broke up the Qezelbash, but he continued to rely on his *qurchi*s as much as on his *gholam*s, and he had great trust in the former. For example, those that remained with him in Mashhad were later promoted. Also, 'Aliqoli Beg, his *ishik aghasi-bashi* was a *qurchi-ye terkesh*. 'Abbas I's most trusted collaborators were Qara Hosein Chavuslu, *qurchi-ye tir va kaman*, 'Ali Beg Shamlu *qurchi-ye terkesh* and Allahverdi Beg, a *gholam*.[346] Only five people knew the plans about the attack on Bahrain, one of whom was Allahqoli Qajar, the former *qurchi-bashi*. Thus, what the *qurchi*s lost vis à vis the *gholam*s they gained vis à vis the Qezelbash emirs.[347]

(25,000).

339 Chardin, vol. 5, pp. 299-302.

340 Monshi, vol. 2, p. 1088; Röhrborn, *Provinzen*, p. 34 (Herat); Nasrabadi, p. 22.

341 Esfahani, p. 89; for earlier instances see Monshi, pp. 500, 460, 471, 681, 888.

342 Vahid Qazvini, pp. 97, 114-5.

343 Nasiri, *Dastur*, pp. 100, 106.

344 Savory, art. "Kurchi", *EI-2*.

345 Chardin, vol. 5, p. 301f.

346 Monshi, p. 400.

347 Monshi, p. 305; Haneda, pp. 188-9, 418. Savory thinks that Mehdiqoli Beg must be a mistake for Allahqoli Beg (Savory, *History*, vol. 2, p. 828), which seems to be right. Monshi, p. 858; Savory, *History*, vol. 2, p. 1069.

Persian and European sources reflect the enhanced importance of the function of *qurchi-bashi* and are careful to record his appointment just as in the case of other major government officials. Also, as of 1587, all *qurchi-bashi*s were khans, while the chronicles gave them more prominence than before, noting their appointment and demise.[348] European sources mention the *qurchi-bashi* regularly as one of the leading government officials. For example, all Dutch ambassadors (1651, 1666, 1691, and 1702) make a point of it to visit the *qurchi-bashi* and bring him appropriate presents.[349] Also, the Portuguese ambassador in 1696 did not forget the *qurchi-bashi*.[350] In addition to the growing number of *gholams* as governors to the detriment of the old tribal leaders, we also observe that *qurchi*s continue to occupy important state functions such as governor, *divan-begi* and *ishik aghasi-bashi*.[351]

The *qurchi-bashi* had indeed become the most important state official by the 1630s, after the grand vizier. Chardin reports that in the days of 'Abbas I, the *qurchi-bashi* "passed for a Lord more stayd, and freer to speak his Mind [to the shah] than the rest [of the grandees]."[352] In the 1630s, the *qurchi-bashi* was the most important of the *arkan-e douleh* or the pillars of the state after the grand vizier.[353] 'Isa Khan, son of Ma'sum Beg Sheikhavand, was the first *qurchi-bashi* of Safi I, who, at the same time, also was *vakil al-saltaneh* or the shah's deputy.[354] In 1046/1637, the *qurchi-bashi* was considered to be the most important of the pillars of state.[355] Mortezaqoli Khan Begdeli Shamlu, *qurchi-bashi* in 1055/1645, was referred to as *navab*, a honorific normally only used for the grand vizier and the *sadr*.[356] His successor, Mortezaqoli Khan Qajar, was *sepahsalar* at the same time.[357]

European observers, however, do not always rank the *qurchi-bashi* as the highest Pillar of the State. Chardin's reference to the *divan-begi* as the second in dignity does not refer to the civil administration only, as Minorsky has it, for he clearly lists the *qurchi-bashi* as second to the *divan-begi*.[358] Likewise, Fryer stated that the *qurchi-bashi* is second to the

---

348 Haneda, p. 197.

349 Hotz, p. 160; Valentijn, vol. 5, p. 280. See also for presents given to the *qurchi-bashi*, *ishik aghasi bashi*, *nazer*, *vaqaye'-nevis* and *mehmandar-bashi*, ARA, VOC 1476, f. 397 (3.9.1690).

350 Aubin, Jean. *L'Ambassade de Gregorio Pereira Fidalgo à la cour de Châh Soltân-Hosseyn* (Lisbon 1971), p. 59.

351 Haneda pp. 200-01.

352 John Chardin, p. 146.

353 Yusef, p. 199.

354 Yusef, pp. 257-8.

355 Yusef, p. 199.

356 Shamlu, vol. 1, p. 472.

357 Shamlu, vol. 1, p. 514.

358 Chardin, vol. 5, p. 341.

qollar-aghasi.[359] These observations reflect the vagaries of fickle royal favor. For, in general the *qurchi-bashi* was the most important official after the grand vizier.[360] This is also borne out by Kaempfer, who stated that the *qurchi-bashi*, or the head of the royal household troops, was the first ranking military commander.[361] Sanson, reporting on the situation in the 1680s, wrote that the "Kortchi Bashi, who is now no more than the Second Person of the realm, was heretofore the First: He had as great Authority as the ancient Constables of France. He was born General of all the Armies; but now the King disposes of that Great Trust at his Pleasure. Nevertheless, he is still Captain-General of the Cavalry, call'd Kortchis, which are always commanded to cover the Frontiers. ..... The King commonly conferred one of the Principal Governments of the Kingdom upon this Person. But he seldom leaves the Court, till he has the Command of some Army; which very seldom happens; For the King knowing he is oblig'd to provide him a Court suitable to so great a Charge, is commonly very backward to put him at the Head of his Troops, when he can reserve to himself both the Honour and Profit."[362]

The Carmelites[363] refer to the *qurchi-bashi* in 1694 as the general of the old militia, but this did not mean an eclipse of the function as Minorsky[364] has it, but rather a reference to the almost one century old transformation of the composition of the armed forces. According to the DM "he is the most important of the emirs who are the pillars of the brilliant state" and is the *rish-safid* or senior officer of all tribes of the kingdom. As such he was in charge of all *yasaqi*s, *yasavolan-e qur*, *mehmandar-bashi*s, *yasavol-bashi*s and *nasaqchi-bashi*s. The *qurchi-bashi* had a voice in the appointment and level of pay of the *qurchi*s. He also examined and judged disputes among them. Fiscal issues were referred to the grand vizier, while *shar'i* issues were refered to *shar'i* judges. He was also *motavalli* of the Qom royal tombs. He further was responsible for maintaining the off-limits zone (*qoroq*) around the harem when the shah was travelling as well as for guard-duty of the shah's person during the night. As the most important emir, he was permitted to present the shah with a present on his birthday, which was given to the poor as alms. In return the *qurchi-bashi* received the clothes that the shah had worn that day as well as the right to ask for three favors such as the release of emirs.[365] The *qurchi-bashi*, according to the TM, had the privilege to submit the candidature of such high officials as *vali*s. However, as Minorsky has already suggested, this privilege was only

---

[359] Fryer, vol. 3, p. 56.
[360] Hotz, p. 160.
[361] Kaempfer, *Am Hofe*, pp. 71-2.
[362] Sanson, pp. 20-1.
[363] Carmelites, vol. 1, p. 468.
[364] TM, p. 117.
[365] DM, p. 47-49.

valid if the candidate was a *qurchi*, as is clear from the DM.[366]

The Demise of the Qurchi Corps

The importance of the function of *qurchi-bashi* persisted till the end of the Safavid dynasty as attested by the appointment of the later Nader Shah to that function by Tahmasp II. The *qurchi-bashis*, such as Mohammad Reza Khan 'Abdollu and Qasem Beg Qajar, continued to function until the end of the dynasty, while the fighting role of the *qurchis* also is mentioned.[367] The function of *qurchi-bashi* lost its importance under Nader Shah, who even abolished it in 1736.[368] However, *qurchis* continued to participate as a separate recognizable group also under Nader Shah. They participated in battle[369] as well as in ceremonial activities such as forming the honor guard for the Indian grandees who came to submit their surrender after the battle of Karnal.[370] *Qurchis* also continued to be part of Ahmad Shah Durrani's military, who even had a *qurchi-bashi*, who still bore the honorific of *'alijah* and still was a *moqarrab al-khaqan*.[371] Under the Zands the *qurchis* probably continued to exist and were under a *qurchi-bashi*, although we know nothing about their actual doings.[372] The Qajars appointed a *qurchi-bashi*, but the function had lost its function and importance, while the *qurchi* corps also had ceased to exist and with it the Qezelbash identity.

In Shustar there were still remnants of the Qezelbash identity alive and well towards the end of the 18th century, in particular among the Chaghatay group.[373] The same source even mentions the presence of a grand vizier in Jahanabad in India, who was one of the leading men of the Khorasan Qezelbash, whose forebears presumably had been one of troops that had been left behind by Nader Shah.[374] In Machli, the port of the Dekkan, Qezelbash merchants were living and doing business, although in this case the term may just refer to Persians.[375] Also Qezelbash groups were living in the Iraqi shrine cities, presumably Persian pilgrims.[376] That these were not just Persians is clear from the fact that Shushtari later

---

366 DM, p. 48; TM, pp. 46, 117.

367 Mervi, vol. 1, pp. 51, 85, 87, 388, 404.

368 Mervi, vol. 2, p. 457.

369 Mervi, vol. 2, pp. 479, 730, 600; vol. 3, p. 891.

370 Mervi, vol. 2, pp. 732, 794.

371 al-Monsh, Mahmud al-Hoseini, *Tarikh-e Ahmad Shahi*, ed. Dustmorad Seyyed Muradof vol. 1, f. 177b, 213b, 215b, 248b.

372 Gulestaneh, Abu'l-Hasan b. Mohammad Amin. *Majmal al-Tavarikh*. ed. Razavi, Modarres (Tehran 2536 [3rd. ed.]), p. 46.

373 Shushtari, Mir 'Abd ol-Latif Khan. *Tohfat al-'Alam*, ed. Samad Muhed. (Tehran, 1363/1984), pp. 84, 88.

374 Shushtari, p. 120.

375 Shushtari, p. 237.

376 Shushtari, pp. 135-6.

mentions both 'Ajam (Persian) and Qezelbash within the same context, clearly marking one group off against the other.[377] However, these were the last vestiges of a once proud and mighty group, whose role and importance had come to an end.

The Qollar or Gholams

The institution of a *gholam* corps was no innovation and has a long tradition in Persian history.[378] For, although the *gholam* corps would become important under 'Abbas I, he was not its creator, although della Valle states: "Both the slaves (*gholams*) and fuzileers (*tofangchis*) are of modern date and owe their origin to this king."[379] As with most new institutions that 'Abbas I further developed and relied on, these were created by his grandfather Tahmasp I or already existed in nascent form. For example, in 994/1586 Hamza Mirza had his own *qollar-aghasi*.[380] 'Abbas I, who 'inherited' Yulqoli Beg as *qollar-aghasi* from his deceased brother in 995/1587, increased the number of *gholams* substantially, however, significantly transforming the relatively small group of royal retainers into a major fighting force. From the very beginning of his reign, 'Abbas I relied on his *qurchis* and his *gholams* to extend his power over the state.[381] Rebellious governors, who did not want to mend their ways, were done away with by his *gholams*. For example, Yusef Khan, the Dhu'l-Qadr governor of Shiraz, was cut to pieces by Shah 'Abbas I's *gholams* in 999/1590-1.[382] Where a difficult situation existed that required resolute action 'Abbas I send his *gholams*.[383] Also, in areas where a potential conflict with resentful Qezelbash tribes festered, because they had been divested of the control over a province or district, which their tribe had held for years, 'Abbas I send in his *gholams*. Allahverdi Khan installed members of the *gholams* as local governors throughout the province of Kuhgilu in 1005/1596-7 after having ousted the traditional Dhu'l-Qadr governors.[384] Yusef Soltan, a *gholam*, was made an emir with the rank of *soltan*, and was appointed governor of Gaskar and chief of the Chaghni tribe, replacing a Qezelbash emir.[385] In reaction to this trend rebellious Qezelbash governors were quick to try and neutralize those

---

377 Shushtari, p. 138.

378 See article "Barda" in *E.Ir*, and "Gholam" in *EI*-2.

379 della Valle, p. 79.

380 The same point is made by Savory, "Sipahsalar", p. 598.

381 Röhrborn, *Provinzen*, p. 32 has shown convincingly that the *qollar* corps was created in 995/1587, the year of 'Abbas I's accession to the throne. Mirza Beg Hasan b. Hosni Janabadi, *Rouzat al-Safaviyeh*. ed. GholamReza Majd Tabataba'i (Tehran 1379/1999), p. 716.

382 Savory, *History*, vol. 2, p. 610.

383 Savory, *History*, vol. 2, p. 627.

384 Savory, *History*, vol. 2, p. 701.

385 Savory, *History*, vol. 2, p. 1307.

local units that were loyal to the shah. In 998/1590, Yusef Khan Afshar, governor of Kerman rebelled and sent the *qurchis* and court retainers (*molazem-e dargah*) charged with *divan* affairs out of the city.[386] Also, there was opposition when governors other than from a particular tribe were appointed to an area which that tribe considered as being "its own" lands. In 996/1588, when 'Abbas I appointed Budaq Khan Chaghani as governor of Mashhad the Ostajalus were upset; how could the shah appoint a non-Ostajalu in Ostajalu lands? Were not there any good Ostajalu candidates that could serve as governor? Feelings ran so high, and 'Abbas I was still uncertain about his position, just having rid himself of his Ostajalu regent (*vakil*), that he gave in and appointed an Ostajalu governor.[387]

Initially, the large number of Georgian, Armenian, and Circassian children and young men captured during the wars did not constitute the main recruiting grounds for the *gholam* corps as della Valle has it. According to Eskander Monshi they, at first, consisted also of Chaghatay, Arab and Persian tribes from Khorasan, Azerbaijan, and Tabaristan as well as riff-raff from the main urban centers.[388] Thus, early in the history of the *gholam* corps Moslem recruits, voluntarily, joined the ranks of the *gholams*, although their number remained limited in later years. For example, sons of Emir Hamzeh were treated kindly by Shah 'Abbas I and enrolled in the ranks of the *gholam* corps in 1590-1.[389] However, 50 and more years later "The king's slaves, were originally all Christians, either bought or furnished by the various nations. At present, they are mostly Georgians and Mussulmen, either from their having been brought up in that faith, or having apostatized."[390] There were, however, also groups of Turkoman *gholams* such as 'Aliqoli Beg one of the *gholaman-e* Keyubeg.[391] Finally, there was even a former *qurchi* who had become a *yuz-bashi-ye gholam*.[392]

In Safavid Persia there were two kinds of *gholams*. Those that were eunuchs (*khvajeh*) and those that were not (*sadeh*). The Safavid shahs obtained slaves through warfare (prisoners of war), purchase, and gifts. As to the prisoners of war these usually were ransomed or employed in the crafts that they knew. Purchased slaves were either acquired because of their skills or their beauty. Such slaves were bought, for example, to work in the royal workshops, the palace at large or in the royal harem. Qanbar Aqa-ye Laleh, for example, was a *gholam-e zar-kharid* of Soltan Heidar

386 Monshi, vol. 1, p. 433.
387 Qomi, vol. 2, p. 885-6.
388 Monshi, vol. 2, p. 1106.
389 Savory, *History*, vol.2, p. 616.
390 della Valle, p. 79; Chardin, vol. 5, pp. 226, 306-9; Kaempfer, *Am Hofe*, p. 72.
391 Yusef, p. 100.
392 Yusef, p. 281.

and a valued members of Shah Esma'il I's household.[393] The main areas from which slaves were procured were the Caucasus (Georgians, Armenians, Cherkes), Russia, Central Asia (Qalmaqs), India and even China. Eunuchs (*khvajehsarayan*) from India and Georgia are sometimes explicitly mentioned. Usually children were bought, preferably virgins.[394] From the Caucasus the Georgian kings as well as the Shirvan emirs regularly send male boy (*gholam*) and female girl (*kaniz*) slaves to the shahs.[395]

The *sadeh* or non-eunuch *gholam*s were trained for royal service in the army, the administration, and the royal workshops. Chardin states that there were 1.000-1.200 young men which the honorific *gholam-e shah*.[396] In the mid-17th century, the young *gholam*s were housed in the *khaneh-ye gav*, while around 1717 in the Goldasteh palace.[397] This was a location different from the *anbar-e gholaman* where the *gholam*-soldiers received their food.[398] Kaempfer does not make this distinction, for he states that the *anbarak-gholaman* or the slaves-house served to train young slaves, mostly Georgians, in the art of reading and writing, so that they later could serve the shah, either at court or in the workshops.[399] Du Mans also reports that the shah assigned some 400 to 500 young children to this training institution, where they were fed and learnt to read and write. After their training they were apportioned among the heads of the workshops to learn the various trades.[400] According to a late Safavid source the so-called *gholaman-e anbar* were those royal slaves who still were unbearded or youths, who indeed received training to serve the shah at court. These youths all had their hair done up in ringlets, until the reign of Shah Soleiman, who banned that fashion. He ordered them to shave the ringlets and banned them from court service as soon as they got a beard. They then were turned over to the *yuz-bashi*s for other services. [401] The training of both *sadeh* and non-*sadeh gholam*s were the responsibility of the same official, a tutor known as the *laleh-ye gholaman-e khasseh va gholaman-e anbari*, who had the high rank of a *moqarrab al-khaqan*. This position was first held by one person, but in the last decades of the Safavid reign two persons fulfilled these functions.[402] As is clear from the rank of

---

393 Montazer-Saheb, p. 67.
394 Montazer-Saheb, pp. 86, 149, 214, 394. Twelve virgin boy and girl Georgian slaves and 10 *khvajehha-ye Hindi*. E. Delmar Morgan & C.H. Coote eds. *Early Voyages and Travels to Russia and Persia by Anthony Jenkisnon and other Englishmen*. 2 vols. (London 1886), vol. 1, p. 89.
395 Molla Jalal, pp. 368, 429.
396 Chardin, vol. 5, p. 308.
397 Chardin, vol. 8, p. 38; Bell, p. 309.
398 Chardin, vol. 7, p. 388; Nasiri, *Alqab*, p. 3.
399 Kaempfer, *Am Hofe*, p. 124; Ibid., *Amoenitatum*, p. 132; Nasiri, *Alqab*, p. 3.
400 Richard, vol. 2, p. 276; Tavernier, p. 222.
401 Nasiri, *Alqab*, p. 3.
402 DM, p. 71.

moqarrab al-khaqan, the tutor of the *gholam*s was an important official. For example, Mohebb 'Ali Khan, the *laleh-ye gholaman-e sarkar-e khasseh*, advised 'Abbas I on diverting the waters of the Zayandeh-rud in 1029/1620. He also was in charge of the administration of the royal palaces.[403] The tutor of the *gholam*s was a eunuch. The teachers of the harem population, both princes and women, also were eunuchs, of course.[404]

The *gholam*s must not be confused with the young noblemen who received a similar palace education. These were referred to as *ev-oghli*, *evchi-zadeh* or *khanzad*, sons of the house, usually referring to future aides-de-camp (*yasavol-e sohbat*) in training.[405] The *ev-oghlu*, who in one instance are also referred to as *jama'at va il-e ev-oghlu*, were tax exempt.[406] These young palace trained sons of the military and landed elite were under a so-called *evji-bashi*.[407] Sharaf Khan Bidlisi, who was a young page in the inner royal palace from 1551-1554, relates how the young pages were trained. Here they received "instruction in the Qur'an and in the principles of the faith, and were taught to avoid the vile and to associate with the virtuous. Then came the manly arts - archery, polo, racing, swordmanship, and the precepts of chivalry (*ensaniyat va adamgiri*). Beyond this the shah used to tell us: 'Also stick to painting whenever you can - it is your good guide to taste.'"[408]

'Abbas I was very fond of his *gholam* corps which he called his "mounted janissaries."[409] When peace reigned the recruiting of *gholam*s took other forms than using slaves and captives. Olearius mentions that the *gholam*s sold themselves into the royal service.[410] It also happened that the sons of *gholam*s were enrolled into the ranks of the *gholam* corps,[411] or that some volunteered to become a *gholam*.[412] What is clear from many documents is that the function of *gholam-e khasseh* tended to be hereditary, for several times appointment documents state that the newly appointed *gholam* concerned inherited the same payment as that of his

---

[403] Savory, *History*, vol. 2, p. 1170; under Soleiman, Aqa Latif, was the *laleh-ye gholaman-e sarkar-e khasseh*. Busse, *Untersuchungen*, p. 197, doc. 15; TM, p. 128; Nasiri, *Alqab*, p. 3.

[404] Kaempfer, *Am Hofe*, p. 184.

[405] For example, Savory, *History*, vol. 2, pp. 975, 977.

[406] Vahid Qazvini, p. 55.

[407] Mahmud Agha *evji-bashi* in 940/1533-34. Rumlu, p. 328; *vaji-bashi*, Ghaffari Qazvini, p. 289; *evji-bashi*, Qomi, vol. 1, pp. 235, 223; Esfandiyar Beg *evchi-bashi* 'Arabgirlu in 1018-9/1609-11. This function was the hereditary post of the 'Arabgirlu clan. Savory, *History*, vol. 2, p. 1018; Yusef, p. 262.

[408] Bidlisi, vol. 1, pp. 449-50; Dickson & Welch, vol. 1, p. 242.

[409] Chardin, vol. 5, p. 307.

[410] Olearius, p. 670.

[411] Savory, *History*, vol. 2, p. 1307.

[412] Nasrabadi, p. 147; Carmelites, vol. 1, p. 144.

father or brother.[413] Thevenot also remarked that the *gholam*s were either slaves or the sons of slaves. In fact, he adds that "The sons of soldiers receive pay so soon as they are seven years old, and is augmented proportionely as they grow in age."[414] Kaempfer therefore is mistaken when he writes that "They are enslaved when young, castrated and then trained for military life." He was confused by the fact that the harem eunuchs also were called *gholam*s, but they formed a different and much smaller group. Nevertheless, the corps continued to draw mainly on manpower from non-Moslems, and in particular from the Caucasus. This was still true in the 1670s, when Kaempfer remarks that "The shah relies most on them for security because they are the least likely to disobey. Rivalry with the *qurchi*s is encouraged to restrain them."[415]

According to della Valle the total number of *gholam*s numbered about 30,000 in 1618, of whom some 15,000 served as soldiers.[416] Later authors give varying estimates of the number of *gholam*s. According to Olearius there were about 8.000 of them.[417] Thevenot writes that there were 14,000,[418] while Chardin states that there were 10.000 *gholam*s, and notes that a *qol* was no less free than a non-*qol*.[419] Finally, Kaempfer writes that they were 15,000-18,000 men strong, and so do Tavernier and du Mans.[420]

"These [*gholam*s] fight on horseback, and make use of different arms, such as pikes, arrows, guns [as the fuzieleers], iron loaded sticks, scymitars, and daggers. There are none but carry a kind of light hatchet, the iron of which is rounded at one end, and on the other a little curved and pointed. The bow and arrow, considered by the King as useless, are by degrees laid aside, and replaced by fire-arms, as well as among the rest of the soldiery. The King's slaves are allowed on certain occasions to wear the tag [*taj*]."[421] The shah armed the *gholam*s with weapons made in his arsenal. However, they did not get uniforms and dressed as they liked.[422] They were, nevertheless, distinguishable from other military groups by their dress, for Fryer remarks "these are the King's own regiments walking with feathers in their high hats, armed with muskets and axes."[423] Du Mans states that they only had sword, bow and arrow, that they wore

---

[413] Puturidze 1961, doc. 17; Ibid., 1962, doc. 24; Ibid., 1965, doc. 25. Musavi 1977, doc. 16.

[414] Thevenot, vol. 1, p. 101.

[415] Kaempfer, *Am Hofe*, p. 72; Chardin, vol. 5, p. 228 observed the same rivalry as did Nasiri, *Alqab*, p. 16.

[416] della Valle, vol. 7, p. 79.

[417] Olearius, pp. 670-1.

[418] Thevenot, vol. 1, p. 101.

[419] Chardin, vol. 5, p. 306.

[420] Kaempfer, *Am Hofe*, p. 72; Richard, vol. 2, p. 264; Tavernier, p. 227.

[421] della Valle, p. 79; see also Chardin, vol. 5, pp. 306-9; Tavernier, p. 227; Thevenot, vol. 2, p. 101; Kaempfer, *Am Hofe*, p. 72.

[422] Chardin, vol. 5, p. 312.

[423] Fryer, vol. 3, p. 63.

some mail, but not helmet and that many wore some distinguishing items. However, none of them wore the uniforms such as of the European soldiers.[424]

The *gholam* corps had a special section that consisted of musketeers and artillery men. The *min-bashi* of the *jazayeri-andaz gholams*, a subordinate of the *qollar-aghasi*, had to be always in attendance of the shah's person. They also took turns in guarding the shah at night.[425] In 1652, guards carrying heavy arquebuses were observed in Isfahan, who may have been the *jazayeri-andaz gholams*, who were under their own *yuz-bashis*.[426] According to Nasiri this special section numbered 700 and wore golden stitched (*chakin*) and velvet clothes, a *quroqi* hat with fringes, and a broad silver belt. [427] Part of the *gholam* corps, as were regiments of other army corpses, were *hamisheh-keshik*,[428] and like the *qurchis*, the *tofangchis* lived dispersed over the country, where they were allowed to work their fields.[429]

The *gholams* acquired a dominant role in the Persian state. They held leading military, administrative and political functions. The very successful *gholams*, who became *begler-begi* or occupied some other leading function, became of course very rich. Allahverdi Khan, *begler-begi* of Fars was one of the richest men in Iran. He was succeeded in his functions by his son Emamqoli Khan, who likewise was both rich and very influential. But *gholams* also held functions at a much lower levels of the royal bureaucracy such as in the royal workshops, the royal secretariat and in the administration of small towns.[430] The Persians hated the Georgian slaves and called them *qara-oghlu* or "sons of blacks."[431] However, for those who were *gholam-e shah* it was the title "they of the highest Dignity price themselves on."[432] According to Chardin the title of that of *gholam-e shah* was equal to that of marquess in France.[433] Andersen also remarks that royal servants were inordinately respected.[434]

---

[424] Richard, vol. 2, p. 264.

[425] DM, pp. 103-04.

[426] Hotz, pp. 147-8; Nasiri, pp. 59, 61, 196.

[427] Nasiri, *Alqab*, p. 16.

[428] Nasiri, *Dastur*, pp. 67, 205; Mostoufi, pp. 126-7, 168.

[429] Olearius, pp. 670-1; Chardin, vol. 5, p. 305.

[430] Chardin, vol. 5, pp. 306-9. Zaman Beg, the later *nazer* and *tofangchi-aghasi*, was a *gholam-e shah*. Yusef, p. 269.

[431] Chardin, vol. 5, p. 228. On the pejorative meaning of "black" see Southgate, Minoo. "The negative images of blacks in some medieval Iranian writings" *IS* 17 (1984), pp. 3-36.

[432] Fryer, vol. 3, p. 56; see also Hotz, p. 150.

[433] Chardin, vol. 5, p. 308.

[434] Andersen, *Orientalische Reisbeschreibungen*, p. 150.

Organization of Gholams

The *gholams* "have one particular general and several captains."[435] The chief of the *gholams* was the *qollar-aghasi*, who already soon after the creation of the *gholam* corps had become one of the most important officials in Safavid Persia. This is also reflected in the choice of some of the *qollar-aghasi*s. 'Abbas I's most famous general, Emamverdi Khan, was a *gholam* and *begler-begi* of Fars, one of the most powerful men in Persia at that time. The latter's son succeeded his father as *begler-begi* of Fars. It is as yet unknown who succeeded Allahverdi Khan as *qollar-aghasi*. According to Falsafi it was Qarchaqay Khan, another *gholam*, but he offers no textual evidence for his statement, apart from the fact that he appears to have fulfilled the same functions as Allahverdi Khan. However, after his death in 1034/1624-5 no successor seems to have been appointed by 'Abbas I.[436] Safi's I first *qollar-aghasi* was Khosrou Mirza (later renamed Rostam Khan) who was also *vali* of Georgia.[437] His successor was a simple *gholam*, Siyavosh Beg.[438] The function, which was later also filled by non-*gholam*s, existed till the end of the Safavid dynasty when in 1736 Nader Shah abolished the function.[439]

Table 3.4 List of *qollar-aghasi*s

998/1590	Yulqoli Beg[440]
999/1591	Allahverdi [Beg] Khan[441]
1026-34/1617-24	Qarchaqay Khan[442]
1038-42/1629-32	Khosrou Mirza (Rostam Khan)[443]
1042-66/1632-55	Siyavosh Beg[444]
1066-1073/1655-63	Allahverdi Khan[445]
1074/1663-37	Jamshid Khan[446]

---

[435] Della Valle, vol. 7, p. 79; see also Chardin, vol. 5, pp. 306-9; Kaempfer, *Am Hofe*, p. 72.

[436] Falsafi, *Zendegani*, vol. 2, p. 402. For Qarchaqay Khan's career see Savory, "Sipahsalar", p. 605-06.

[437] Yusef, pp. 140, 136, 268; Shamlu, p. 210.

[438] Yusef, pp. 171, 176, 190, 205, 208.

[439] Mervi, p. 457.

[440] Röhrborn, *Provinzen*, p. 32; Janabadi, pp. 649, 716.

[441] Röhrborn, *Provinzen*, p. 32; Savory, "Sipahsalar", pp. 603-5; Janabadi, p. 716, 778.

[442] Savory, "Sipahsalar", p. 606.

[443] Khosrou Khan was renamed Rostam Khan [in 1038/1628-9], Shamlu, p. 210; Yusef, p. 114, 136, 140, 268; Rahmat Khan *qollar-aghasi* (heir of the Kartli throne), Yusef, p. 117; Esfahani, p. 47.

[444] Vahid Qazvini, p. 68; Olearius, p. 670-1; Yusef, pp. 171, 176, 190, 205, 208, 269; Shamlu, pp. 215, 471.

[445] He died in 1663. Vahid Qazvini, pp. 180, 216, 322-3.

[446] Vahid Qazvini, p. 328; Chardin, vol. 10, p. 32, 38, 45.

Table 3.4 (continued)

?

prior to 1104/1693	Keikhosrou Khan[447]
prior to 1104/1693	Mansur Khan[448]
1104/1693	'Isa Beg[449]
1105-06/1693-95	Aslamas Khan (Beg)[450]
1113/1701	Musa [Beg] Khan[451]
111?-27/170?-1715	Fath 'Ali Khan Daghestani[452]
1127-30/1715-17	Safiqoli Khan[453]
1130-35/1717-22	Rostam Khan (Hoseinqoli Khan)[454]
1135/1722	Ahmad Agha[455]
1135/1722	Bakar Mirza, king of Kartli[456]
1137/1724	Mohammad 'Ali Khan[457]
1143-45/1730-32	Mohammad Mo'men Beg[458]
1146/1733	Rezaqoli Khan[459]
1147-48/1734-36	Mohammad 'Ali[460]

By the 1680s, "The Third Pillar of the Empire, is the Quwer-Koule Agasi, who is Captain of the Band of Slaves. This is a Body of Men composed of many Persons of Quality, who call Themselves the King's Slaves: They are much less in number than the former [qurchis], but they have altogether as great Pay. They that have a mind to arrive to great Employments, should pass thro' this Militia, whose General is always provided of a great and wealthy Government, and consequently able to

---

447 Mostoufi, p. 114.

448 Nasiri, *Dastur*, p. 30; Bardsiri, p 638.

449 Bardsiri, p. 664.

450 He was also *amir akhor-bashi*, Nasiri, *Dastur*, pp. 33, 58; Nasiri, *Alqab*, p. 15. He is probably the same as Aslan Khan, father of Mohammad 'Ali Khan, the *qollar-aghasi* in 1724; see also Tehrani, Mohammad Shafi'. *Tarikh-e Nader Shah*. ed. Sha'bani, Reza. Tehran 1349/1970, pp. 6, 81.

451 Valentijn, vol. 5, p. 282; Nasiri, *Alqab*, p. 15.

452 Floor, *Commercial*, p. 16 (April 1714); Nasiri, *Alqab*, p. 15.

453 Floor, *Commercial*, p. 21 (July 1715); Ibid, *Bar Oftadan*, pp. 27, 29; Ibid., *Afghan Occupation*, pp. 29-30; he was also *begler-begi* of Fars. He was dismissed on 21/1/1717.

454 *ARA*, KA 1789 (8/3/1717), f. 133; Ibid (22/1/1717), f. 272, he also was *sepahsalar*; Brosset, vol. II 2, p. 33, 36; Mostoufi, p. 128. His Moslem name was Hoseinqoli Khan. He died in the battle of Golnabad of March 1722.

455 Lockhart, *Fall*, p. 147; he was only the deputy *qollar-aghasi*. Floor, *Bar Oftadan*, p. 113; Ibid., *Afghan Occupation*, p. 92.

456 Brosset, vol. II 2, p. 36.

457 Mervi, pp. 63-5, 78, 88f., 1304; Tehrani, *Tarikh*, p. 6; Mostoufi, p. 147.

458 Mervi, pp. 282, 284f.

459 Sha'bani, *Hadith*, p. 11. He died that year near Baghdad.

460 Tehrani, *Tarikh*, pp. 81, 126; RiazulIslam, *Calender*, vol. 2, pp. 43-45, 56, 58, 74.

prefer 'em.'"[461] Kaempfer states he was the second highest ranking, but he referred to the military only.[462] Fryer wrote that the *qollar-aghasi* was the most important military official, followed by the *qurchi-bashi* and the *min-bashi* and *yuz-bashi*. Below this rank of *yuz-bashi* no noblemen would accept a function, unless that of *gholam-e shah*.[463] The *qollar-aghasi* was paid 1.000 tomans in assignments, which in reality had a quadruple value.[464]

By the end of the Safavid dynasty he was the most important military official after the *qurchi-bashi*. The *qollar-aghasi* also was a *rokn al-douleh* and a council emir. He was in charge of all *min-bashi*s, *yuz-bashi*s, *qur*s armed with muskets (*jazayer*) and all *gholam*s. These were appointed and paid with his approval. He also tried all common law ('*orfi*) cases in which his subordinates were involved. All religious law (*shar'i*) cases were referred to the *shar'i* judges and fiscal cases to the grand vizier.[465]

The *gholam*s were organized along the same lines as the other army units. There were *yuz-bashi*s, an *ishik aghasi-bashi*, and a *jarchi-bashi*, for example.[466] Once their beard began to grow the young *gholam*s were organized into units of 100 and 10 (*yuzdeh*) and became subordinates of the *qollar-aghasi*.[467] The rank-and-file served under *yuz-bashi*s or hundred-men who were assisted by *dah-* or *on-bashi*s.

The *gholam* department had its own administrative and accounting chiefs, to wit a vizier and a *mostoufi*, who were supported by a bureaucratic staff. As an indication of the changed situation a casual remark of Eskander Monshi may serve. He reports that in 1018-9/1609-11, "Mir Feizollah, who was *vazir-e qurchiyan*, was appointed as *majles-nevis*, which office he continued to hold when he also was appointed *vazir-e gholaman, which is an important position nowadays*."[468] The vizier was also referred to as "koulam vasiri, Pay master to the Band of Slaves."[469] The vizier and the *mostoufi* of the *gholam*s performed the same functions as their colleagues of the other military departments.[470] Sometimes, the vizier held more than one function, such as the *vazir-e nazer-e boyutat*, at the same time.[471]

---

461 Sanson, p. 21.
462 Kaempfer, *Am Hofe*, p. 72.
463 Fryer, vol. p. 3, 56.
464 Chardin, vol. 5, p. 322; Richard, vol. 2, p. 18. The *qollar-aghasi* was at the same time governor of Kuh-gilu in 1645. Vahid Qazvini, p. 68.
465 DM, p. 50; Nasiri, *Alqab*, p. 16.
466 Astarabadi, p. 178; Yusef, pp. 240, 272.
467 DM, p. 71; Nasiri, *Alqab*, p. 3.
468 Savory, *History*, vol. 2, p. 1035.
469 Sanson, p. 26.
470 DM, pp. 88-9; Nasiri, *Alqab*, pp. 56-7.
471 Yusef, p. 274.

Table 3.5 Variation in pay scale for *gholam*s

1051/1641	11 tomans hs	Puturidze 1961, doc. 18
1058/1648	29 tomans hs	Puturidze 1961, doc. 24
1059/1649	11 tomans	Puturidze 1961, doc. 25
1069/1658	9 tomans	Dhabehi-Setudeh, vol. 6, doc. 18
1070/1660	32 tomans	Puturidze 1961, doc. 31
1074/1663	15 tomans t	Puturidze 1962, doc. 2
1075/1664	39 tomans	Puturidze 1961, doc. 34
1095/1684	180 tomans m	Musavi 1977, doc. 16
1098/1687	50 tomans m	Puturidze 1962, doc. 13
1107/1696	12 tomans m	Puturidze 1962, doc. 24
1109/1698	11 tomans m	Puturidze 1962, doc. 32
1116/1705	30 tomans m	Puturidze 1965, doc. 8
1120/1708	20 tomans	Puturidze 1965, doc. 16
1125/1713	6 tomans	Puturidze 1965, doc. 25

hs = *hameh-saleh*; t = *teyul*; m = *mavajeb*

The treasury did not finance all *gholam*s, only some, the remainder was stationed in the provinces, and at their charge. About 8.000 of them, and like the *qurchi*s, lived dispersed over the country. They received pay from the royal coffers, but were not exempt from royal service.[472] According to du Mans a *min-bashi* in the *gholam* corps earned 50-70 tomans per year, a *yuz-bashi* 30 tomans, an *on-bashi* 15 tomans and the rank-and-file 8-10 tomans per year.[473] This pay scale is reflected in Table 3.4 which shows that the remuneration or *dunluq* of the *gholam*s differed considerably and depended very much on their position, which, unfortunately, the documents concerned do not reveal. There does not seem to have been a general rule as to the kind of remuneration, for payment in *hameh-saleh*, *mavajeb* and *teyul* all occur. Although some of the wages were in cash, mostly they were [partly] in kind.[474] "The pay is not paid in cash but in drafts on the finance department. They indicate exactly the location, resulting in sale of drafts to get 50% of value."[475] Generally speaking, one may say that the starting salary of a regular *gholam* was 6-9 tomans or thereabouts, in addition to food and clothing. According to du Mans, the wages of the *gholam*s were doubled every three years and in addition they would receive a present equivalent to their annual salary. Salaries higher than about 30 tomans were for the crême of the *gholam*s.[476] "All these

---

472 Olearius, pp. 670-1.

473 Richard, vol. 2, p. 263; Tavernier, p. 227.

474 Puturidze 1961, doc. 24; Richard, vol. 2, p. 116; Gilanetz, *The Chronicle of Petros di Sarkis Gilanetz*. ed. Caro Owen Minasian (Lisbon 1959), pp. 21, 41.

475 Kaempfer, *Am Hofe*, pp. 74-5.

476 Chardin, vol. 5, p. 312; Thevenot vol. 1, p. 101; Kaempfer, *Am Hofe*, p. 74-5; Fryer, vol. 3, p. 62; Richard, vol. 2, pp. 116, 263.

[*gholams*] receive the pay out of the king's treasury or from set rents."[477] They usually spend more money than they were paid, reason why they financed their deficit spending through all kinds of odd jobs, including robbery.[478]

Tofangchis

Introduction of arms: Guns and cannon had been introduced around 1470 into Persia and had been used prior to the establishment of the Safavid dynasty.[479] In fact, 'Abdor-Razzaq Donboli wrote that, it was during the reign of Soltan-Hosein Mirza Beiqara (873/1469 - 911/1506) that Molla Hosein Sabzevari introduced the arquebus (*tofak*) which was used in Europe.[480] Qomi, therefore, is wrong when he wrote that in the year 907/1501-2 the sound of a gun was heard for the first time in Persia[481] as is the myth that "the prevailing Persian hath learned Sherlian arts of war, [who] before knew not the use of ordnance."[482] From the very beginning of the creation of the Safavid army modern arms (arquebus and cannon) constituted an integral, albeit small part of its armament. Already in 1502 a message from one of its agents in the Levant reached Venice in November 1502 reporting that the "Sofi (Esma'il I) wanted to secure artillery from the Christians."[483] It would seem that Venice promised to provide aid and artillery.[484] In fact, Zeno reports that, Mr. Giosafat Barbaro was elected as ambassador to Persia by Venice in 1473, "and send with him several gifts to the king [Uzun Hasan], which were six immense siege guns, arquebuses, and field-pieces in great number, powder, and other munitions of war; six bombardiers, one hundred arquebusiers, and other men skilled in artillery."[485] The same issue was raised during the embassy of 1508, when Esma'il I again asked for cannon and technical assistance in the form of trainers.[486]

Nevertheless it is a fact that the majority of the Persian army continued to be equipped and to fight in the traditional way with lance, sword, bow, mace and dagger throughout the Safavid period. In the 1670's Fryer observed that "they fight with bow, sword and spear, though they are long

---

[477] Fryer, vol. 3, p. 63.

[478] Richard, vol. 2, p. 116.

[479] See Floor, article "Barut", *E. Ir.*; Tehrani, *Ketab*, vol. 1, p. 63, vol. 2, pp. 569, 580.

[480] Donboli, 'Abdol-Razzaq Maftun, *Ma'ather Soltaniyeh.* ed. Gholam Hosein Sadri Afshar (Tehran 1351/1972), p. 132.

[481] Qomi, vol. 1, p. 72.

[482] Purchas, p. 31.

[483] Amoretti, pp. 9-10.

[484] Fischer, Sydney N. *Foreign Relations of Turkey: 1481-1512* (Urbana, Ill. 1948), p. 92; *Travels to Tana*, part 2, pp. 180, 182.

[485] *Travels to Tana*, part 2, p. 15. According to Zeno the artillery indeed arrived, Ibid., p. 78.

[486] Bacqué-Grammont, *Les Ottomans*, p. 168.

skill'd in Weapons of another nature, as Guns and Pistols."[487] However, when for example, Elvand Mirza attacked Tabriz in 907/1501-02, the population barricaded the streets (*kucheh bandi kardand*), while the young Tabrizis and the Halvachi-oghlu (a Qezelbash clan), who had been left behind by Esma'il I to defend the city, installed themselves on the roofs with arrows and arquebus (*tir va tofang*).[488] They also made holes in walls of streets so that they became like beehives (*khaneh-ye zanbur*) and shot with arrows and arquebus at the enemy which led to a general massacre.[489] Similarly on the Eastern front, Persian forces used guns against the Uzbegs. In Sabzevar, in 916/1510-11, people were on the roofs and defended themselves against Uzbegs with *tir va tofang* (bow and gun).[490] Nevertheless, the use of modern arms was still relatively limited, in the beginning. Even Elvand Mirza, who had modern arms, but not enough, sought rifled help from the Ottomans.[491]

Use of arms by Safavid opponents: The use of modern arms, however limited, was only a normal development, given the fact that the Safavids' main contenders for power, the Ottomans and the Uzbegs, also used them from the beginning of their strife.[492] The Qezelbash and the Uzbegs shot at another with bows and arquebuses (*tir va tofang*) when Najm-e Thani attacked as well as in later operations.[493] There is also mention of the Uzbeg having *tofangchiyan-e naftbaz* or pyrotechnic handling fusiliers.[494] The Uzbegs continued to use arquebuses throughout the 16th century in their battles with the Safavids, e.g. in 965/1557-8 and in 998/1589-90.[495]

As to internal rebellious forces guns were used by all non-Qezelbash tribal groups. For example, in 1007/1598-99, the Siyahpush in Astarabad were ordered "to raze your castles, hand over to your local governor your weapons and equipment, to be stored at Mobarakabad in case of need ....they razed their forts and took several thousand arquebus, pieces of chain mail, quivers, and bows to the castle of Mobarakabad."[496] In 988/1580-1, the Lors ambushed Khalil Khan in a mountain valley, and they hurled large rocks down from the tops of the hills, and fired arrows

---

[487] Fryer, vol. 3, p. 57.

[488] Montazer-Saheb, p. 64.

[489] Valeh Esfahani, p. 230.

[490] Montazer-Saheb, p. 345; for the use of cannon (*zarbzan*) and guns in Gilan, at the siege of the fortress Usta in 909/1503-04. Rumlu, p. 107, for another event in 918/1512-13, Ibid., p. 171.

[491] Montazer-Saheb, p. 73.

[492] Montazer-Saheb, p. 523.

[493] Montazer-Saheb, p. 420; Afshar, *'Alamara-ye Tahmasp*, p. 64; see also Seistani, p. 383 (*tofangchi-ye Uzbeg*); Rumlu, p. 516; Khvondamir, vol. 4, pp. 479, 527, 547, 560.

[494] Adle, p. 550.

[495] Savory, *History*, vol. 1. p. 180, vol. 2, p. 539.

[496] Savory, *History*, vol. 2, pp. 770-1.

and arquebus.[497] In 1018/1609-10 "the Baradust [Kurdish] tribesmen surrendered all clad in chain mail and carrying their arquebus and full equipment."[498] Furthermore, as we will see, the rural population was well armed with arquebuses and formed a reservoir for *cherik* troops for the Safavid shahs. This situation did not change in the 17th century. Tavernier states that the mountain people between Ninevé and Isfahan would not sell anything but for gunpowder and bullets.[499] The Za'farlu Kurds however considered the use of guns unmanly, but they were the exception.[500] The use of guns was observed in the Heidari-Ne'mati battles in Shamakhi.[501] The Baluch and Afghans who invaded Persia did so with the use of arms, both arquebus and cannon.[502] Contemporary observers also reported that the invading Afghan force used 609 *zanburak*s, or camel mounted swivel-guns, to good effect in the battle of Golnabad in 1722.[503]

Formation of the tofangchi corps under Esma'il I: It does, therefore, not come as a surprise that already in 922/1516, Esma'il I gave orders to constitute a corps of *tofangchi*s or musketeers under the regent (*vakil*) Mirza Shah Hosein, who was also entitled *tofangchi-bashi*. The shah had 2.000 arquebuses produced as well as 50 pieces of cannon.[504] This was undoubtedly due to the fact that the Qezelbash had been defeated in the battle of Chaldiran in 920/1514, because of the monopoly of firearms by the Ottomans in that battle. In 1515-16, the Portuguese ambassador Fernam Gomes de Lemos, noted among the welcoming party at Kashan "forty musketeers bearing muskets of metal."[505] In 1516, the Qezelbash captured 70 pieces of artillery and 200 arquebuses, which they needed, and "which the cavalry first shunned, but now use."[506] In 923/1517, Esma'il I allegedly already had 8,000 musketeers.[507] Their number would fluctuate over the years; the highest number mentioned, amongst whom many Portuguese, is 15,000 to 20,000 in 929/1521.[508] Esma'il I had obtained the guns from the Portuguese in Calicut in exchange for Hormuz, according to the Venetians.[509] Portuguese military, deserters or officially

---

[497] Savory, *History*, vol. 1, p. 403.

[498] Savory, *History*, vol. 2, p 1013; Ibid., vol. 2, p. 989; Kurds fired with artillery and arquebus at the Qezelbash. Ibid., vol. 2, p. 993.

[499] Tavernier, vol. 1, p. 180 (1676 ed).

[500] *FIZ* 20, p. 410.

[501] "Mémoire de la Province du Sirvan" in *Nouveaux mémoires des Missions de la Compagnie de Jesus dans le Levant*, vol. 4, (Paris 1780), p. 44.

[502] Floor, *Bar Oftadan*, pp. 64, 73-81; Ibid., *Afghan Occupation*, pp. 31, 46, 58.

[503] Gilanetz, Petros di Sarkis, p. 7. *Soqut-e Esfahan*. tr. Mehryar, Mohammad (Isfahan 1344/1965), p. 39; Lockhart, *Fall*, p. 139.

[504] Aubin, L'Avènement, p. 118, n. 486; Bacqué-Grammont, *Les Ottomans*, p. 165.

[505] Smith, p. 44.

[506] Amoretti, p. 340.

[507] Amoretti, p. 377.

[508] Amoretti, pp. 405-06; see also p. 533.

[509] Amoretti, p. 398.

designated, trained Persian musketeers in the use of arms.[510] The number of musketeers was also reinforced by the occasional Portuguese who stayed on, but equally important by Ottoman janissaries who deserted to the Safavids. In 924/1518, for example, 700 janissaries and in 925/1519 some 1500 janissaries were reported to have deserted to the Safavids.[511] Like later shahs, Esma'il I liked to show off the prowess and skills of his musketeers.[512]

There was also under Tahmasp I widespread use of guns, and in some cases thousands of musketeers participated in battle or in the defense of fortresses,[513] for *tofangchis* were usually garrisoned in fortresses with the task to defend it against any comers.[514] "Sometimes, the air was dark with the smoke of guns and powder, while the area was quite unsafe because the hail of bullets", is a recurring description of the defense of a fortress in the 16th century.[515] We learn, however, relatively little of the use of arquebuses in outright battle during most of the 16th century. In one interesting case, Mostafa Pasha drew a small gun (*tofang-e kuchek-e khazaneh'i*) and shot at Shah Esma'il I, but the ball got stuck in his *taj*, and the shah skewered the pasha with his spear.[516] Also the use of a *tapancheh* or handgun is mentioned in 929/1522-23.[517] Kepek Soltan Ostajalu was killed by a gun at the battle of Arpa Chai in 1527.[518] In 1555, 300 musketeers on foot participated against the Uzbegs.[519] The use of guns increased considerably during the century. In 1585, we read that the Tekellu musketeers were so close that bullets were raining all around Hamzeh Mirza.[520] Similarly, the fire from the musketeers of the royal household *gholams* was so effective that the Gilan emirs abandoned their struggle in 1010/1592-3.[521]

Late 16th century European reports are somewhat ambivalent as to the use of modern arms by the Persian army. Under Tahmasp I the Safavid troops were already very well trained in the use of modern arms. D'Allessandri, around 979/1571, remarked that "there is not a soldier who does not use [the arquebuse]; they have brought their skill in it to such a

---

[510] Amoretti, pp. 451, 469-70.
[511] Amoretti pp. 398, 478; Bacqué-Grammont, *Les Ottomans*, p. 165.
[512] Amoretti, p. 546; Bacqué-Grammont, *Les Ottomans*, p. 166.
[513] Afshar, *'Alamara-ye Tahmasp*, pp. 64, 78, 123, 157, 181, 193, 204-5, 272, 280, 297, 314, 329, 332, 335, 341, 357, 369, 376-7; Rumlu, p. 473.
[514] Montazer-Saheb, pp. 115, 178; Afshar, *'Alamara-ye Tahmasp*, p. 369; Yusef, pp. 24, 32, 42, 54; Molla Jalal, pp. 388, 408; Shamlu p. 108.
[515] Montazer-Saheb, pp. 282, 524; Natanzi, pp. 80-1; Shirazi, p. 64.
[516] Montazer-Saheb, p. 79.
[517] Rumlu, p. 310.
[518] Bidlisi, vol. II/1, p. 551.
[519] Afshar, *'Alamara-ye Tahmasp*. pp. 357, 377.
[520] Savory, *History*, vol.1, p. 475.
[521] Savory, *History*, vol. 2, p. 624.

perfection that it surpasses [what is seen] anywhere else. The barrels of these arquebuses are 7 palms [one Roman palm = 25 cm] in length. The soldiers carries less than 3 ounces of shot, disposing of it so cleverly so that it does not hinder him from drawing his bow, or wielding his sword, while the shield is held to the saddle-bow. When there is no need to use it the arquebuse is slung behind the back with such facility that one thing does not get in the way of the other."[522] In 994/1586-7, another Venetian reported that, the cavalry fought with sword, lance and bow. He categorically added "they have no arquebuses, neither do they have artillery."[523] But later he qualified his statement that "although there want not among them some that can handle the Arcebuse also, the exercise of whereof hath of late yeares grown more familiar and usuall, then it was in the time of Ishmael, and in the first years of the raigne of king Tamas." Sherley's interpreter stated that 'Abbas I could mobilize 50,000 arquebusiers, who were also armed with scimitars. Further, 100.000 horse armed with bows, arrows and scimitars. "At one time he did not use arquebusiers, but now he delights in them. Quite recently they have acquired some arquebuses."[524] Though admitting the use of modern arms Herbert opined that "The use of muskets they have had only since the Portuguese assisted King Tahamas with some Christian auxiliaries against the Turk."[525]

Not only were Europeans thus shedding doubt about Persians using arms, but also were implying that they did not or could not make these themselves, but had to import them. It is true that 'Abbas I tried to get modern arms from European states. He sent e.g. an embassy to Moscow to buy inter alia arms.[526] In 991/1583, 'Abbas I asked the Duke of Tuscany and the Pope, through Italian envoys, for artillery instructors. The latter only offered cannon.[527] 'Abbas I also asked the EIC for guns and is said to have received 1,500 arquebuses as a result.[528] European powers also were aware of the shah's interest in European arms and therefore considered offering them to him provided Persia continued to wage war against the Ottomans. For example, pope Gregory XIII in 1590, considered sending "up to a limit of 2,000 arquebuses, and up to 5,000 or 6,000 hand-

522 Carmelites, vol. 1, p. 53.
523 Berchet, p. 290.
524 Sherley, pp. 163, 29, 31.
525 Herbert, p. 235.
526 Bushev, P.P. *Istoria posol'stv i diplomaticheskikh otnoshenii russkogo i iranskogo gosudarstvo v 1588-1612 gg* (Moscow 1976), pp. 226-7 and subsequent missions invariably returned with arms. Ibid, pp. 347, 360; Bellan, L.L. *Chah Abbas Ier, sa vie, son histoire* (Paris 1932), pp. 36, 69, 73.
527 Ugo Tucci ed. "Une relazione di Giovan Battista Vechietti sulla Persia e sul regno di Hormuz", *Oriente Moderno* 35 (1955), p. 156; Palombini, Barbara von. *Bündniswerben abendländischer Mächte um Persien* (Wiesbaden 1968), pp. 106, 108, 111.
528 Carmelites, vol. 1, p. 255; Calendar of State Papers, p. 152.

arquebuses, and up to 15 or 20 pieces of field artillery, provided he indicate the route by which they can be sent."[529] However, by the time that 'Abbas I allegedly was begging for arms, he was fielding a large number of musketeers in his military campaigns. In 1011/1603, 'Abbas I was accompanied by 300 cannon (*tup-e zarbzan*) and 10,000 *tofangchi*s on the Balkh campaign.[530] In 1590, there were 70,000 *tofangchi*s gathered to welcome shah in Isfahan.[531] To impress the visiting Uzbeg khan a salute was given by 480 cannon and 40,000 arquebuses were fired.[532]

Europeans therefore had to admit that "They are very expert in their pieces or muskets; for although there are some which have written now of late that they had not the use of pieces until our coming into country, this much must I write to their praise, that I did never see better barrels of muskets than I did see there."[533] Such a high opinion of the skills of the Persian gunners was also reported by Eskander Beg. "The gunners, who, without the slightest exaggeration, were capable of hitting the eye of an ant if it presented itself as a target."[534] This opinion apparently also was held by others for it is reported that "the Qezelbash have a body of musketeers who are incomparable marksmen, said the Uzbegs."[535] Europeans also had to admit as much, "so as now they are become very good shots."[536] The use of large numbers of musketeers in battles with the Ottomans in the late 16th and early 17th century is a regular feature.[537] In fact, the battles about Baghdad in 1620-30s was mainly between the *tofangchi*s on both sides.[538] Although, the use of modern arms became less normal after the 1650s they were still used, even on a local scale to fight Baluch marauders towards the end of the 17th century. The Baluch, who were adopting a tactic of shooting with the bow from afar, were defeated by musket fire laid down by the pursuing *tofangchi*s in 1106/1694-5.[539]

The *tofangchi*s were basically local levies, from allover Persia. They both had a role to play in the defense of their own district or province. The

[529] Carmelites, vol. 1, p. 24; other popes and the Spanish king offered artillery and engineers, Ibid. pp. 53, 105, 127, 163.
[530] Monshi, pp. 619-20, 622.
[531] Seistani, p. 518.
[532] Molla Jalal p. 442.
[533] Sherley, p. 222.
[534] Savory, *History*, vol. 2, p. 1121; see also C.R. Boxer ed. *Commentaries of Ruy Freyre de Andrade* (London 1930), p. 67, the Persians, "who are so dextrous in shooting them [muskets] that they fire at the smallest object without missing their mark."
[535] Savory, *History*, vol. 2, p. 639.
[536] Herbert, p. 235.
[537] Rumlu, p. 496; Natanzi, p. 85; Afshar, *'Alamara-ye Tahmasp*, pp. 64, 78.
[538] Yusef, pp. 65, 57, 59, 105, 136, 139, 150, 166, 177, 190.
[539] Nasiri, *Dastur*, p. 70; other military operations also involved bowmen and musketeers. Ibid., p. 149.

Uzbegs, for example, were pursued by contingents of local musketeers from Bafq and Behabad on several occasions.[540] They could also be called upon for military campaigns outside their immediate area such as Khorasani *tofangchi*s who participated in the siege of Erivan or Baluch *tofangchi*s at Baghdad.[541] To participate in the main military campaigns against the Ottomans the shah gave orders that ten thousand musketeers be mustered from all parts of the Safavid dominions.[542] We find therefore mention of *tofangchi*s from Bafq, Baluchestan, Barangar, Isfahan, Khavaf, Khorasan, Mazandaran, Rostamdar, and Tabriz, which included also musketeers from Qezelbash tribes such as the Ajrlu, Chaghni, 'Enanlu, and Rumlu as well as from non-Qezelbash tribes such as the Chaghatay, Lakhi, and Mamasani.[543] In Seistan, the local magnates also assisted the Safavids with a regiment of *tofangchi*s as well as to defend the local borders and fortresses.[544]

Despite their large scale participation in military campaigns on Persia's borders the musketeers very much remained a local defense force, living mostly dispersed in the countryside.[545] When Sten'ka Razin attached the Caspian provinces the local defense was organized by *min-bashi*s and *tofangchi*s from Nur, Kujur, Larejan and Hazar-Jarib and the royal troops garrisoned in Mazandaran.[546] Similar cases are reported in the Shirvan area in the 1720s,[547] and in the Kerman area in the 1680s. The *tofangchi*s from Na'in and other areas were mostly untrained levies who could not stand up against the desperate Baluch raiders in an outright battle in 1106/1694-5.[548] In peace time the *tofangchi*s worked their land, until called to arms.[549] The *tofangchi*s were mainly raised in villages and chiefly renegado Armenians, according to Thevenot, which is clearly wrong, for they were mostly Tajiks.[550]

Already in 926/1520 the Venetians reported that the *tofangchi*s were mounted,[551] but at that time there were also 10,000 musketeers on foot.[552]

---

[540] Savory, *History*, vol. 2, p. 702; Montazer-Saheb, p. 328.

[541] Yusef, pp. 132, 165, 189.

[542] Savory, *History*, vol. 2, p, 728.

[543] Yusef, pp. 57, 102, 104, 132, 165, 171, 189, 215; Savory, *History*, vol. 2, pp. 805, 924, 996, 1092; Monshi, vol. 2, p. 1106; Afshar, 'Alamara Tahmasp, p. 78; Astarabadi, p. 196; Seistani, p. 347. These also included *bunduqchiyan-e* Khorasani. Adle, p. 653; Savory, *History*, vol. 1, pp. 489-90.

[544] Seistani, pp. 241, 259, 283, 300, 304, 334, 372, 385, 463.

[545] E.g., Dhahebi-Setudeh, vol. 6, p. 26; document with wage allocations for *tofangchi*s and their chiefs known as *tofangchi-bashi*s.

[546] Vahid Qazvini, p. 308.

[547] Muller, *Sammlung*, vol. 4, pp. 131f.

[548] Nasiri, *Dastur*, pp. 83-4; see also pp. 70, 149 for more sucessful interventions.

[549] Chardin, vol. 5, pp. 304-6; Richard, vol. 2, p. 264.

[550] Thevenot, vol. 2, p. 101.

[551] Amoretti, p. 545.

[552] Amoretti, p. 545.

For, the *tofangchis* usually fought on foot, and they were therefore also referred to as *piyadegan-e tofang*.[553] Della Valle also confirms this. "In the beginning, these fuzileers fought on foot, however now they are mounted, and fight on horseback, with guns somewhat smaller that our muskets, with matchlocks, which have a fork fastened by a cord to the stock, by which when they dismount, they have a rest for taking aim."[554] Also, later in the 17th century, Chardin stated that the *tofangchis* served on foot, but that en route they were on horse-back. They were peasants and armed with a sabre, a dagger, and a musquet with a bandoleer at their belt.[555]

Despite their long service in the military the infantry was held in poor esteem by the Qezelbash military around 1600.[556] Nevertheless, they were highly esteemed by 'Abbas I.[557] Despite the royal esteem, "The fuzileers were the last in rank." The reason for this low esteem was that "These troops consists of peasants and artisans.... This order is composed of the native inhabitants of the country, and is similar to a militia. .... The Qezelbash did not join this order, but only the *ra'yat*, "vasals or *tat*, composed of the refuse of the nation" reported della Valle in 1618.[558] However, "The bow and arrow, considered by the King as useless, are by degrees laid aside, and replaced by fire-arms, as well as among these [musketeers] as the rest of the soldiery."[559] 'Abbas I considered the use of musketeers more effective in the defense of fortresses and siege operations than that of cavalry. He scoffed at the use of arrows. "What can they do with their arrows, which go *ter, ter*" he remarked discussing an imminent attack of Tatar troops.[560] Nevertheless, in the 1670s, when the military arts of the musketeers were less made use of, the cavalry still looked down on the infantry and called them "sable fodder."[561]

According to della Valle, "they number 20,000 but do not wear the *taj*, only the turban."[562] Chardin estimated their number at 12,000[563], while Koci Bey, a contemporary Turkish author, mentions that there were 12,000 *tofangchis*.[564] This number also is mentioned by a contemporary Persian historian.[565] According to Kaempfer, "They are not less than

553 Rumlu, p. 563; Seistani, p. 259.
554 della Valle, vol. 7, p. 79.
555 Chardin, vol. 5, pp. 304-06; Thevenot, vol. 2, p. 101; Richard, vol. 2, pp. 264-5.
556 Sherley, p. 163.
557 della Valle, p. 79.
558 della Valle, p. 79; Chardin, vol. 5, pp. 304-06; Tavernier, p. 228.
559 della Valle, p. 79.
560 della Valle, pp. 31, 66.
561 Kaempfer, *Am Hofe*, p. 73; Richard, vol. 2, pp. 117, 265, 285.
562 della Valle, p. 79.
563 Chardin, vol. 5, pp. 297, 304-06.
564 *ZDMG* 15 (1861).
565 Yusef, pp. 78, 117.

50,000 men," which seems too high a number.[566] May be Tavernier and
Thevenot had it right when they write that the *tofangchi*s were about
8,000 men strong.[567] The royal fuseliers were the most colorful part of the
Safavid army; they wore velvet clothes, broad silver belts, felt hats
embellished with feathers, and carried many colored flags on their back.[568]

Organization of the musketeers: The *tofangchi*s were organized like
other army units. There was one corps commander, the *tofangchi-bashi* or
tofangchi-aghasi, who was assisted by various officers such as *min-bashi*s, *yuz-bashi*s, *panjah-bashi*s, *dah-bashi*s and an administrative staff.
Molla Jalal also mentions a *piyadeh-bashi*, who may or not have been an
officer in charge of infantry.[569] Formally the *tofangchi*s were all listed in
the muster rolls of the *gholam*s (*daftar-e gholaman*) according to
Eskander Monshi.[570] Chardin confirms this. The slaves, *qollar*, were the
musketeers; their general was the *tofangchi-aghasi* or *qollar-aghasi*, who
earned some 1,000 tomans per year in 1660.[571] According to Don Juan the
*tofangchi*s were the royal guard, i.e. *gholam*s, which indeed included
2,000 musketeers.[572]

The *tofangchi-aghasi* was a *rokn al-douleh*. All *min-bashi*s, *yuz-bashi*s, *jarchi-bashi*s, *tofangchi*s, *rika*s and *tabardar*s were his
subordinates. He approved their appointments and payments. The
tofangchi-aghasi was assisted by a vizier and *mostoufi*, who kept the
muster rolls.[573] The fact that infantry and musketeers were considered to
be the lowest but one on the military totem-pole is also reflected in the
rank that its commander had in the military hierarchy as well as the fact
that the appointment or the person of the *tofangchi-bashi* is not often
mentioned. "The Fourth Pillar is the Tefanktchi Agasi; that is, General of
the Infantry."[574] This lack of weight was also reflected in the fact that the
tofangchi-aghasi, despite being a *rokn al-douleh*, was not a member of the
inner royal council or the *janqi*. Nevertheless, scions of 'noble' families
held function of *tofangchi-aghasi*.[575]

---

[566] Kaempfer, *Am Hofe*, p. 73.

[567] Tavernier, p. 228; Thevenot, vol. 2, p. 101; Nasiri, *Alqab*, p. 19 (10,000 under
'Abbas I and 7,390 men under Safi I).

[568] Nasiri, *Alqab*, p. 20.

[569] Molla Jalal, p. 100; a similar officer, *piyadeh-bashi-ye jelou* is mentioned by
Montazer-Saheb, p. 151; Richard, vol. 2, p. 265.

[570] Monshi, vol. 2, p. 1106; Savory, *History*, vol. 1, p. 527.

[571] Chardin, vol. 5, p. 304-06; Richard, vol. 2, p. 18.

[572] Don Juan, p. 52.

[573] DM, pp. 53-4; Nasiri, *Alqab*, pp. 19-20; *rika*s were a kind of armed guards, like
the *yavasol*s, and at the back and call of their chief. Mervi, pp. 28, 229, 762.

[574] Sanson, p. 20-1. The third military commander is the *tofangchi-aghasi*.
Kaempfer, *Am Hofe*, p. 73.

[575] Nasrabadi, pp. 52, 144.

Table 3.6 List of *tofangchi-aghasi*s

922/1516	Mirza Shah Hosein[576]
936/1529	Kur Hasan[577]
?	
984/1576	Mir Saheb-e Qoshun[578]
?	
1023/1614-15	Esma'il Beg[579]
?	
1039/1629	Zaman Beg[580]
1040/1630	Rostam Beg[581]
1044-45/1634-35	Mir Fattah Qumesheh'i[582]
1045-53/1635-43	Aqa Taher[583]
1053-71/1643-61	Qalander Soltan Chuleh[584]
1071-79/1661-68	Budaq Soltan[585]
1079-80/1668-69	Sheikh 'Ali Zanganeh[586]
1080/1669-70	'Abbas Beg Zanganeh[587]
1080-85/1670-74	Keikhosrou Khan[588]
1085-1101/1674-91	Hajji 'Ali Khan Zanganeh[589]
?	Eshaq Khan[590]
1123-8/1711-15	Musa Khan[591]

---

[576] Bracqué-Grammont, *Les Ottomans*, p. 165.

[577] Qomi, vol. 1, p. 190.

[578] Qomi, vol. 2, p. 622.

[579] Savory, *History*, vol. 2, p. 1088.

[580] He was *nazer* and *tofangchi-aghasi*. Yusef, p. 20.

[581] Esfahani, p. 116.

[582] Yusef, p. 270.

[583] He was his predecessor's brother and was called Mir Fattah-e Thani. Yusef, pp. 227, 270.

[584] He was *tofangchi-aghasi* and *tupchi-bashi* in 1071/1660-61. Vahid Qazvini, pp. 58, 60, 66, 69, 86, 290; Shamlu, pp. 283-4, 335; he received Aberquh as a *teyul*, which, since then, always has been bestowed on the *tofangchi-bashi*. Röhrborn, *Provinzen*, p. 29.

[585] Chardin vol. 10, p. 126.

[586] Chardin vol. 10, p. 126; Bardsiri, p. 355. He remained in this function till June 1669.

[587] Chardin, vol. 2, p. 202, who only reports that the son of Sheikh 'Ali Khan was appointed. 'Abbas Beg was his eldest son, who became later *emir shekar-bashi*. Bardsiri, p. 485.

[588] Nasrabadi, p. 17; Chardin, vol. 2, p. 202; Ibid., vol. 8, p. 452; Nasiri, *Dastur*, p. 273; Bardsiri, p. 381, 388, 413, 423. He was *hamshirzadeh* of Rostam Khan, the *sepahsalar*, and died in 1085/1674.

[589] Kaempfer, *Am Hofe*, p. 68; Kroell, p. 29.

[590] Floor, *Bar Oftadan*, p. 233; Ibid., *Afghan Occupation*, p. 176.

[591] Floor, *Commercial*, p. 11 (September 1712); he was dismissed on 26 September 1715. *ARA*, KA 1778 (29/9/1715), f. 230.

Table 3.6 (continued)

1131-20/1717-20	Hosein 'Ali Khan[592]
1133-4/1720-22	Mohammad 'Ali Khan Mokri[593]
1136/1723	Ahmad Khan[594]
1137/1724	Shahverdi Khan Cheshmkazik[595]

The commander of a provincial regiment was a *min-bashi*, who earned some 300 to 400 tomans per year in 1660.[596] For example, "A detachment of 300 crack Isfahani musketeers, under the command of Mir Fattah, the *min-bashi*, of the Isfahan regiment of musketeers, was stationed in the citadel.[597] Other provincial *min-bashis* included Mohammad Pirzadeh, *min-bashi-ye tofangchiyan*-e Khorasan and Baba Khalil, *min-bashi-ye* Mamasani.[598] These *min-bashis*, who had the title of *moqarrab al-hazreh*, seem to have been local hereditary leaders such as in the case of Bafq.[599] The *min-bashi*, therefore, often was at the same time appointed as governor such as of Bafq, Behabad and peri-urban areas.[600] In the 1720s, it was the *min-bashi* of Yazd who defended the city against the Afghans.[601] In addition, there were the *min-bashiyan-e tofangchi-ye qelij-e jelou*, who also bore the title of *moqarrab al-hazreh*. They had to be always in attendance of the shah, and were subordinates of the *tofangchi-bashi*.[602] These *min-bashis* were in charge of the *tofangchiyan-e rekab-e aqdas*,[603] who probably were the same as the *tofangchis* of the royal household (*khasseh*) or the *tofangchiyan-e jelou*.[604] Qomi mentions already *tofangchiyan-e khasseh* under Tahmasp I. There was also a *min-bashi-ye tofangchi*-ye Isfahan. He had always to be in Isfahan, especially when the shah travelled.[605] He was in charge of the musketeers on permanent guard duty (*tofangchiha-ye hamisheh-keshik*), whose existence is also attested

---

[592] He was appointed on 27 September 1715. *ARA*, KA 1778 (29/9/1715), f. 230; KA 1789 (8/3/1717), f. 133; Floor, *Bar Oftadan*, p. 29; Ibid., *Afghan Occupation*, pp. 29-30, he was disgraced in the alleged conspiracy of 1720.

[593] Nasiri, *Alqab*, p. 8; Mostoufi, pp. 125, 128, 140; Floor, *Afghan Occupation*, p. 37.

[594] Mostoufi, p. 144.

[595] Mostoufi, p. 147, on p. 151 he is referred to as Shahverdi Khan Kivanlu..

[596] Richard, vol. 2, p. 18.

[597] Savory, *History*, vol. 2, p. 627; Yusef, p. 157.

[598] Yusef, pp. 165, 171; 'Abbasqoli Beg Min-bashi Lakhi. Ibid., p. 189.

[599] Bafqi, Mohammad Mofid Mostoufi-ye. *Jame'-ye Mofidi*. 3 vols. ed. Iraj Afshar (Tehran 1340/1961), vol. 3/1, pp. 278-9; Nasiri, *Dastur*, p. 204.

[600] Bafqi, vol. 3, p. 279.

[601] Floor, *Bar Takhtegah*, pp. 93-4; Ibid., *Afghan Occupation*, p. 227.

[602] DM, p. 104.

[603] Yusef, p. 102, also p. 132.

[604] Yusef, pp. 28, 238, 227.

[605] DM, p. 104.

by an appointment diploma of 1096/1684-5.[606] The *Dastur-e Shahriyan* mentions a *mir-e vafadar* and a *mir-e tashrif* among the *tofangchi* organization, but it is unknown what these functions entailed.[607]

Under the *min-bashi* served a number of *yuz-bashis*, or officers of units that nominally had 100 men. Each *yuz-bashi* earned 200 tomans per year in 1660.[608] Usually the *tofangchis* operated in a group of 100.[609] However, "Mirza Fetta has in his brigade fifty sub-Bashaws of note, each of them commanding three hundred."[610] Although local levies, who usually served under their local commanders, it also happened that "a contingent of one thousand foot musketeers, who had arrived from Isfahan, was placed at his disposal under the command of Alpan Beg Qajar, an aide-de camp."[611] Under the *yuz-bashis* served lower-ranking officials. Their titles have not been reported, but probably were similar to those in other army units, to wit: *panjah-bashi* and *dah-bashi*. However, it would seem that these lower ranking officers were also referred to as *tofangchi-bashi*.[612] Amongst the *tofangchi-aghasi*'s subordinates the DM and TM mentions the *rika*, a staff bearer armed with pole axes, who guarded the king's person and sometimes acted as executioners.[613] The *tofangchi-aghasi* was further assisted by a vizier and *mostoufi*, who kept the muster rolls. The *vazir-e tofangchi* was often at the same time *vazir-e tupchi*. His duties were the same as those of the vizier and the *mostoufi* of the *qurchi* and other military departments.[614]

Payment of tofangchis: *Tofangchis* seem to have been recruited from *khasseh* lands, because they were paid by the royal treasury. "In Persia, however, the individuals of this order [of musketeers] receive pay quarterly from the King, and are bound to appear at his summons."[615] They received 4 to 5 tomans, without rations, while an ax-holder (*tabardar*) would receive 4 tomans plus rations.[616] According to Olearius a *tofangchi* received 200 *Reichsthaler*, which seems much too high compared with other estimates, even allowing for the payment of rations.[617] According to du Mans a *tofangchi* received 5 to 7 tomans per

[606] Sazman-e Asnad-e melli-ye Iran, *Fehrest-e Rahnama-ye Asnad*, p. 14.

[607] Nasiri, *Dastur*, p. 83.

[608] Yusef, pp. 38, 215; Richard, vol. 2, p. 18.

[609] Seistani, pp. 244-6.

[610] Herbert, p. 242.

[611] Savory, *History*, vol. 2, p. 667.

[612] Yusef, p. 27.

[613] Richard, vol. 2, p. 23; Du Mans, p. 32.

[614] DM, pp. 88-9; Yusef, p. 253.

[615] della Valle, vol. 7, p. 79. All these receive the pay out of the king's treasury or from set rents. Fryer, vol 3, p. 63.

[616] Fryer, vol 3, p. 63; Chardin, vol. 5, p. 312; Tavernier, p. 228.

[617] Olearius, p. 668.

year in 1665.[618] The sons of soldiers received pay so soon as they were seven years old, which was increased proportionely as they grew in age.[619]

The Tupchis
From the early beginnings of the formation of the Safavid army, cannon constituted a regular, but insignificant, part of the army's capability. Prior to the introduction of cannon, around 1470, the Persian army had used various pyrotechnic devices.[620] Initially, the Safavid army had very few cannon, and a limited capability to cast or use cannon well.[621]

Although the Persian military never were very comfortable with artillery they had no choice but to use it. Their major enemies, the Ottomans and Uzbegs, also used artillery, the former power holding the superior position. In fact, due to its superiority in the use of modern arms the Ottomans had been able to deal a crushing defeat to the Safavid army in 1514 at Chaldiran. The Uzbegs also had guns and cannon,[622] as did smaller opposing forces. The ruler of Mazandaran, Bangi Malek, had several pieces of small ordnance to repel the attack by Safavid forces.[623] The Uzbegs also had artillery, for in 995/1587 two *digs*, launching rock projectiles, were installed. The chief cannon-foundry-man (*mir rikhtegar*) started to cast seven others in the courtyard of the Gouharshad Mosque at Mashhad as soon as the required quantities of copper and *khuleh* [tin?] had arrived. They could throw balls weighing three *mann-e* Bokhara.[624] Qazi Ahmad states that these *digs* even threw balls of 20 *mann* and more. Molla Jalal and Eskander Beg state that the mouth of the *digs* was so large that a man could easily fit in them and its power was strong enough to throw their balls into the city of Herat.[625]

Safavid artillery capability was first obtained through the capture of Soltan Morad Aq-Qoyunlu's cannon (*tup-khaneh*) with its equipment (*yaraq*) and personnel, which meant that Esma'il I now also had a *tup-khaneh*.[626] During the siege of Van in 1507, the fort of Zidibec, a Kurdish chief, the Safavids used two moderate-sized cannons to batter the castle. "But they were able to do no harm, as the walls were too strong and the

---

618 Richard, vol. 2, p. 265.

619 Thevenot, vol. 2, p. 101.

620 Tehrani, *Ketab*, vol. 1, p. 63; vol. 2, p. 569, 580. In the 1440s there were e.g. the *takhsh-andaz* (rocket thrower) and the *ra'd-andaz* (projectile launcher). Taj al-Din Hasan b. Shehab Yazdi, *Jame' al-Tavarikh-e Hasani*. Iraj Afhar and Hosein Modarresi Tabata'i eds. (Karachi 1987), pp. 27, 42, 156 and a *tir-andaz-e Khorasani*, p. 160.

621 Floor, article "Barut", *Ency Iran*.

622 Seistani, p. 347.

623 Don Juan, p. 218.

624 Adle, p. 550.

625 Monshi, p. 387; Molla Jalal, p. 154.

626 Montazar-Saheb, pp. 70-1, 74-5.

gunners too little skilled."[627] Sometimes, however, the army totally lacked artillery, as in the case of the siege of Darband around 1503. However, the Safavid army made two mines which led to the fort's surrender.[628] Albeit the skills were limited, it is clear that the Safavid army during its first years of existence had both the capacity to use artillery and to cast cannon. This capability predated that of the Safavids and had been developed by the Aq-Qoyunlus, whom they had replaced. During the siege of the Hisn Keif, the stronghold of Soltan Khalil, a Kurdish chieftain, the Safavid army employed "a mortar of bronze, of four spans, which they brought from Mirdin, where it used always to stand before the door of the fort of that city, was useless. This mortar was cast in that country at the time of Jacob Soltan [r. 1478-90], and by his orders. And while I was at Asanchif I went several times to see the fighting and the firing of this same mortar; and Custagialu also had another larger one cast by a young Armenian, who cast it in the Turkish manner-all in one piece. The breech was half the length of the whole piece, and the mortar was five spans in bore at the muzzle. They had only these two pieces to bombard the castles, in which there was no artillery, except three or four muskets of the shape of Azemi ['Ajami or Persian], with a small barrel, which, with a contrivance locked on to the stock about the size of a good arquebuse, carry very far."[629] We continue to find references to the use of artillery in the early Safavid period. Najm-e Thani, for example, attacked the fortress of Qarshi with amongst other things *zarb-e tup* (cannon blasts) and *zakhm-e tofang* (musket-shot).[630] In 914/1508, Esma'il I also had artillery, which were pulled by 60 pairs of oxen.[631] However, the artillery capacity was limited, for in 917/1511 it was reported that when Esma'il I wanted to take a fortress he could not do so, because he did not have artillery.[632] Esma'il I certainly did not have artillery at the battle of Chaldiran (1514), but in 922/1516, the Qezelbash captured 70 pieces of artillery, which they needed.[633] In that same year, according to Ottoman reports, Esma'il I had 50 cannons with their carts made.[634] In 923/1517, Esma'il I allegedly already had more than 100 pieces of artillery on carriages. This artillery he allegedly had obtained from the Portuguese in Calicut in exchange for Hormuz, which is contradicted by other sources.[635] Sometimes, the number of cannon used was significant such as in 919/1513-4, when allegedly 700 large cannon (*tup-e badlij*) were aimed at the fortress and

---

[627] *Travels to Tana*, part 2, p. 163.
[628] *Travels to Tana*, part 2, pp. 203-04.
[629] *Travels to Tana*, part 2, p. 153.
[630] Valeh Esfahani, p. 216; see also Khvandamir, vol. 4, p. 479.
[631] Amoretti, p. 125.
[632] Amoretti, p. 184.
[633] Amoretti, p. 340.
[634] Bacqué-Grammont, *Les Ottomans*, p. 166.
[635] Amoretti, p. 398.

the wall was breached defense from roofs with guns.[636]

The use of cannon, especially at siege operations, continued to be a standard feature for the rest of the century.[637] For artillery was mainly used as a defensive weapon, in particular mounted on the walls of the citadels of the major towns and of strategic fortresses. In Bandar 'Abbas, the two fortresses had "fourscore pieces of brass ordnance, part of the spoils of ransacked Ormus; two hundred others great and small were sent to Lar, Shiraz, Isfahan, and other places."[638] Olearius comments that "they also have cannon, but they mostly use in forts and not during siege and battle."[639] Herbert, who gives much information on these matters relates that "in the castle at Lar, which has battlements and platforms, "whereon are mounted twelve brass cannon-pedros [i.e. swivel-guns] and two basilisks (the spoils of Ormus). Within the fort are many small houses or huts which lodge the soldiers, who have sometimes there an armoury sufficient to furnish with lance, bow, and gun three thousand men."[640] However, these cannons were more for parade than for real use.[641]

The Safavid army used artillery seldom in a tactical manner to press its advantage in the field. A rare instance occurred in 1529, when Tahmasp I used Ottoman style field artillery on chariots, such as used by Selim I at Chaldiran, to defeat the Uzbegs. In front of the army wagons were placed on which were mounted Frankish light cannon; these guns were under the command of Ostad Sheikhi Beg, the *tupchi-bashi*.[642] One of the reasons why cannon were seldom used was logistics. Don Juan mentions that "no field artillery was then commonly in use" as well as that "the Persians make no use of no waggons, coaches nor litters of any kind or sort."[643] Although very much aware of the advantage of having artillery, "they detest the trouble of cannon and such pieces as require carriage," Herbert

---

[636] Montazer-Saheb, p. 536.

[637] Afshar, *'Alamara-ye Tashmasp*, pp. 133, 241, 264; the fortress of Arjish was bombarded by the Persians in 959/1552. Rumlu, p. 474; other bombardments, Ibid., p. 491. Emir Khan Torkman used muskets and cannon to fire into town, a few even at the royal palace [992/1584]. Savory, *History*, vol. 1, p. 432.

[638] Herbert, p. 46, see also p. 235.

[639] Olearius, p. 666.

[640] Herbert, p, 57; others also mention these captured cannon. Chardin , vol. 7, 338, 484-5; vol. 8, p. 482 (Lar); Tavernier, p. 443 (Isfahan). Olearius, p. 478 mentions 20 cannon at Soltaniyeh; Portuguese cannon at the 'Ali Qapu gate. Kaempfer, *Am Hofe*, p. 164-5. The cannon captured from the Portuguese in 1622 served as ornaments. Some were used as part of the urban defenses such as in Bandar 'Abbas and Hormuz. The cannon sent by Holstein in 1637 adorned the entry to the royal garden. Ibid., p, 73.

[641] Bell, pp. 307 (Isfahan), 311 (Rasht).

[642] Savory, *History*, vol. 1, pp. 89-90. battle of Jam against the Uzbeks in 1529; Rumlu, p. 281.

[643] Don Juan, pp. 50, 218.

wrote in 1629.[644] Due to the lack of carrosable roads and wheeled transport this is an understandable sentiment. Kaempfer remarks that transportable cannons were not available.[645] Also, Persian military strategy was built on speed and mobility, which would only be constrained when heavy cannon had to be hauled over long distances. Cannon were therefore mainly used for long sieges, reason why the cannon were also referred to as *qal'eh-kub* or the castle-smasher.

Another reason was the fact that the cavalry deemed it an unmanly weapon. Minadoi comments that Persian do not use artillery, "more on account of their obstinate belief that it is a shame to use such cruel engines against men than because of their inability to fabricate them or their deficiency in material to cast them." Similar sentiments are aired by Cartwright discussing the siege of Tabriz in 1603. "In which siege he for battery used the helpe of the Cannon, an engine of long time by the Persian scorned, as not beseeming valiant men, until that by their owne harmes taught; they are content to use it."[646]

European sources sometimes mention that Persian troops were afraid of artillery. However, Persian sources mention, for example, that the Qezelbash, undismayed by the hail of cannon and musket fire, launched an attack.[647] Minadoi, qualified his opinion by adding, that sometimes they have not been afraid and have attacked the enemy's trenches and camp, but "yet have not hitherto received the use" [of cannon] although they know the practical advantage of it.[648] However, in their decades long wars with the Ottomans, the Persian army invariably faced an army that was well provided with modern arms with lots of fire power. The Ottomans themselves remarked that "the hail of bullets and cannon does not bother the Sheikhoghlu [= Qezelbash]."[649] Despite their alleged fear the Persian troops were able to overcome the Ottomans, whose standard battle formation forced the Persian troops to face especially cannon. "The Ottomans, as was their usual practice, constructed a barricade of gun carriages and chains in front and behind their forces. Janissaries armed with muskets were stationed under cover of the gun carriages.[650] Therefore, the Europeans must have been influenced in their thinking by the fact that the way the Persian gunners fired their cannon seemed to be fearful. "The gunners here were not very expert; for, when they had occasion to give fire, I could perceive them to stand on one side of the

---

[644] Herbert, p. 243.

[645] Kaempfer, *Am Hofe*, p. 73.

[646] Purchas, vol. 8, p. 503; see also the excellent use made of cannon by the Persians at the siege of Hormuz in 1621. Boxer, p. 67.

[647] Savory, *History*, vol. 2, p. 1278.

[648] Minadoi p. 74; Carmelites, vol. 1, p. 287.

[649] Montazer-Saheb, p. 513.

[650] Savory, *History*, 1, p. 68; the Ottomans were ranged as usual with their *tup*, *tofang* and *'arabeh*. Yusef, p. 139.

piece and in a fearful manner (though with a linstock as long as a half-pike, which had a lighted match) to touch the powder - which was a bad way to take aim by."[651]

This may also explain why early European reports are quite dismissive about the use of cannon by the Persian army. Mestre Afonso, in 1565, maintained that the Persian army did not use cannon,[652] which as we have seen is not borne out by the facts. Pincon, Sherley's secretary, stated that "They have no artillery at all, nor corselets nor cuirasses."[653] This feeling was further reinforced by the fact that European travellers were not impressed with the state of readiness of the Persian artillery in the various fortresses that they observed. Olearius sarcastically commented that if you did not stand right in front of the firing mouth of the cannon you were quite safe.[654] In 1649, Andersen only took three cannons from the Hormuz fortress when he was send there to get cannon for the Qandahar campaign. He found that some of the cannon was of French origin and that their fuse holes had been burnt through due to frequent use.[655] These cannon served more to adorn a fortress and make it look martial. Often, if the cannon still worked, they were used for ceremonial purposes to greet arriving or departing important visitors. The governor of Shamakhi had "an arsenal in his palace, provided with some cannon; two of which are at the entrance and are discharged upon publick rejoicings."[656] Valentijn also mentions the firing of cannon to greet the arrival or departure of VIPs.[657] However, other cannon apparently still were in a state of readiness. Schillinger reports that in 1702 at night guards were on duty at loaded cannon in Erivan.[658]

Even though the Safavids had the capability to cast cannon they also continued to obtain cannon by capturing them from the Aq-Qoyunlu and Ottoman forces. Whenever the Ottomans fled cannon was taken as booty.[659] Therefore, when cannon was needed, and it was not cast on the spot, it was captured from the enemy, when "the janissaries fled out of fear of the swords of the Qezelbash and left their guns and cannon."[660] In

---

[651] Herbert, p. 46. There were, of course, people who (rightly) were afraid of firearms, of which Persian soldiers took advantage. Seistani, p. 334.

[652] Neves Aguas, pp. 168, 170, 181.

[653] Sherley, p. 163. A Venetian also reports that "they have no arcebusi, neither do they have artillery." Berchet, p. 290.

[654] Olearius, p. 555; see also p. 478; Kaempfer, *Am Hofe*, p. 73; Chardin, vol. 7, p. 338, 484-5; Ibid., vol. 8, p. 482; Tavernier, p. 443.

[655] Andersen, p. 153.

[656] Le Bruyn, vol. 1, p. 149.

[657] Valentijn, vol. 5, p. 267.

[658] Schillinger, F.C. *Persianische und Ost-Indianische Reis* (Nürnberg 1707), p. 110.

[659] Montazer-Saheb, p. 536; both small and big cannon used, again some were captured. Ibid., p. 541-2;

[660] Afshar, *'Alamara-ye Tahmasp*, p. 193.

1578, Hamzeh Mirza defeated Mostafa Pasha and captured "two hundred peeces of Artillerie, that were left in the Fort by Mustapha, and presently sent them to Casbin to his father."[661] Barkhvordar Beg *tupchi-bashi* and 100 pieces of artillery were captured.[662] This implies that native capacity to produce modern arms was still limited. This was also clear to the Ottomans, who in 1514 "carried away with him three thousand families, the best Artificers in that Citie [Tabriz], especially such as were skilfull in making of Armour and weapons."[663] Bacqué-Grammont disputes the Venetian report that after the Chaldiran defeat Selim I took arms craftsmen from Tabriz, because no Ottoman source mentions this.[664] When Bayazid, the Ottoman prince, sought refuge at the Persian court in 966/1559 he brought 30 pieces of artillery with him according to d'Alessandri.[665] This explains why della Valle reported that the Persian chiefly use ordinance captured from their enemies, which indeed they continued to do.[666] Nevertheless, the Venetian Angelo Corrai stated that "there is no lack of masters to manufacture new ones, these masters have turned against the Turk and have come to serve the King of Persia."[667]

Persians not only had problems in casting cannon, but also in its use and the production of its munitions. Europeans therefore were regularly asked to provide lead, powder and gunners. Consequently, European gunners are mentioned in Persian and European texts as those manning the Persian cannon. Esma'il I, in 914/1508, had requested Venice to supply him with cannon and instructors to train his gunners, as well as to conclude an offensive treaty with him against the Ottomans. The Venetians kindly turned down the request.[668] Albuquerque, the Portuguese vice-roy, gave a Safavid officer, who visited Hormuz in mid-1515, a tour of the entire artillery complex on the island and told him that this was only a sample, of which there was much more in Portugal that could be used against common enemies. To that end Albuquerque had written at various occasions to king Manual recommending him to obtain permission from the pope to send him master gun-founders, because cannon was what

---

[661] Purchas, vol. 8, p. 501.

[662] Savory, *History*, vol 2, p. 897.

[663] Purchas, vol. 8, p. 503.

[664] Bacqué-Grammont, *Les Ottomans*, p. 168.

[665] *Travels to Tana*, part 2, p. 227; See however, Rumlu, p. 526, according to whom only *tofangs* were brought; Qomi, vol. 1, p. 407; he brought *tabr, shamshir* and *tofang*. Afshar, *'Alamara-ye Tahmasp*, p. 157; according to another manuscript of d'Allessandri, Bayazid "left 17 pieces of small artillery, one of 50 and a 'terrier' of 120, together with a large number of arquebuses." Carmelites, vol. 1, p. 60.

[666] Large cannon and siege guns captured at Hormuz. Savory, *History*, vol. 2, p. 1204; guns, balls and supplies captured during the Bahrein conquest, Molla Jalal, p. 215.

[667] Sherley, p. 29.

[668] Berchet, pp. 25-6.

Esma'il I lacked to destroy his enemies. He also sent cannon and arquebuses with Fernao Gomez to Esma'il I in 1515. However, Esma'il I refused the Portuguese military aid and technical assistance offered by Gomez.[669] Venetian reports continued to attest the presence of a well-equipped artillery capability of the Safavids in the years thereafter. Also, that Safavid troops were being trained in their use by deserted Janissaries and Portuguesè renegades or official Portuguese military advisors. To show their proficiency in handling the artillery occasionally a demonstration was given. Esma'il I's army also had many bombarders.[670] In 927/1521, the artillery corps was trained by a master gunner named Jachoino, who had many Portuguese with him. They wore large black and red caps.[671] Local magnates also used external technical assistance such as the *vali* of Gilan who used a *tupchi*-ye Rumi [during the days of Esma'il I].[672] Vechietto noted that the bombardment of the Tabriz citadel only improved after the Persians used an Indian gunner. Vechietto concluded that the Persians did not have enough expertise to use artillery and were outclassed in this respect by the Ottomans.[673] 'Abbas I, despite his efforts to create a local capacity to handle the artillery also had to continue to rely on foreign military assistance. Cartwright discussing the siege of Tabriz in 1603 observes the presence of skilfull Cannoniers, furnished by the Portugals from Ormuz."[674] This also mentioned by Figueroa, who stated that Europeans, in particular Portuguese gunners, manned the Persian cannon,[675] and so does Herbert when he observed that "skilfull Cannoniers, [were] furnished by the Portugals from Ormuz."[676] Under Safi I also foreign gunners were hired.[677] He formally asked the English, for example, for a *tofang-saz* and a *tupchi-ye atesh-baz*.[678] Prior and during

---

[669] de Albuquerque, Afonso. *The Commentaries of the Great Afonso de Albuquerque, second viceroy of India*. tr. Walter de Gray Birch. 4 vols (London 1875-85/Haklyut), vol. 4, p. 183; Bacqué-Grammont, *Les Ottomans*, p. 170.

[670] Amoretti, pp. 405-06, 451, 469-70, 481, 546, 533-4.

[671] Amoretti, p. 534; see also Bacqué-Grammont, *Les Ottomans*, pp. 295-6 for a French translation of this Venetian report and Ibid. pp. 168-70, on the role of Janisarie deserters as a source technical assistance. There is little information available on the role of the Portuguese military training activities in Safavid Persia, but most likely it will have been similar to the activities deployed in India. On the role of the Portuguese renegades in India see Maria Augusta Lima Cruz, "Exiles and Renegades in early 16th century Portuguese India", *The Indian Economic and Social History Review*, XXIII/3 (1986), p. 257-60. For the presence of Italian cannon-founders in Cochin in 1503. Jean Aubin, "L'apprentissage de l'Inde. Cochin 1503-04", *Moyen-Orient & Océan Indien* IV (1987), p. 38-9.

[672] Laheji, p. 88.

[673] Tucci, pp. 154, 156.

[674] Purchas, vol. 8, p. 503.

[675] Figueroa, p. 263.

[676] Purchas, vol. 8, p. 503.

[677] Andersen, p. 147.

[678] Fekete, doc. 96.

the Qandahar siege 'Abbas II also asked for gunners.[679] 'Abbas II's master-gunner, Mohammmad Beg, was also observed, in 1649, to be supported by a group of European gunners.[680] Andersen, who himself served as a hired cannoneer during the Qandahar campaign, observed that the Persians liked to employ Europeans who know how to handle cannon. Because of the presence of the Moghul embassy he was ordered to wear clothes such as Europeans were wont to be dressed in, so that the embassy would know that the best expert help was available to the shah. His salary was 30 tomans or 480 thalers per year, the same as for a diamond worker and watchmaker.[681] During actions against the Baluch the commanding Persian *sardar* had one piece (*luleh*) of heavy cannon (*badlij*) and muskets with him in 1106/1694-95. However, he was constrained in their use because of a lack of lead and powder, for which he had to send regularly to Kerman.[682] In 1702, the discussions between Persia and the bishop of d'Ancyra dealt inter alia with the desire of the shah to receive "some engineers, artillerymen and artificers experts in the methods of making mines, fortifications, cannons, bombs and other implements of war."[683] When some Dutch sailors deserted their ship in Bandar 'Abbas and became Moslem to avoid being send back to their ship they were at first employed as artillery instructors by the *tupchi-bashi*. They shortly thereafter returned to their ship.[684] Even at the battle of Golnabad against the Afghans in 1721, the Persian guns were actually directed by a French gunner, Philippe Colombe, rather than by Ahmad Khan, the *tupchi-bashi*.[685]

Organization of the tupchis: Given the fact that artillery was regularly used by the Safavids it comes as no surprise to learn that there was some kind or organization to operate and manage it since early Safavid times. In 1507, a Venetian merchant mentioned a certain Camusabec [Hamza Beg] of Trebizonde, who was chief of the bombarders.[686] Later, we learn about a certain Mahmud Beg Tupchi, who was one of Esma'il I's leading

---

679 Riazul Islam, *A Calender of documents on Indo-Persian relations (1500-1750)*, 2 vols. (Karachi 1979), vol. 1, p. 328; also two Dutch gunners for a brief period. VOC 1170, f. 739r and VOC 1168, f. 687. The English also provided gunners W. Foster, *English Factories in India* (1646-1650) (Oxford 1913), pp. 211, 217.

680 Shamlu, p. 352.

681 Andersen, pp. 149-50. Qandahar was one of the strongest fortresses in the Moslem world and 'Abbas II went well prepared. Vahid Qazvini, p. 127; Shamlu, p. 361 for a description of the fortress; also Andersen, p. 160. The cannon did its job. Vahid Qazvini, pp. 115-7; Shamlu, p. 352; Andersen, p. 159.

682 Nasiri, *Dastur*, p. 73.

683 Carmelites, vol. 1, p. 496.

684 *ARA*, KA 1726 (23/4/1714) f. 2630.

685 Lockhart, *Fall*, pp. 134, 142.

686 *Travels to Tana*, part 2, p. 163 and Rumlu, p. 75.

military staff, who also held the post of governor.[687] The *tupchi*s were organized like the other army units. The corps was headed by a *tupchi-bashi*, who was assisted by an administrative staff, and by various lower-ranking officers. The *tup-khaneh* was under the *tupchi-bashi* who also was responsible for all the required accessories for the cannons.[688] The artillery batteries were under a number of *yuz-bashi*s, who were assisted by *na'eb*s or deputies.[689] The *dafter-e tupchiyan* was managed by a vizier and a *mostoufi*, who kept the muster rolls and who were assisted by a number of clerks. They kept the registers of new and current *tupchi*s, cleared *tupchi*s from the register who had died, processed payments, and organized the regular musters. The *mostoufi* of the *gholam*s was also the one for the *tup-khaneh*.[690] By the end of the Safavid reign, the *tupchi-bashi* was an *'alijah* and in charge of all *min-bashi*s, *yuz-bashi*s, *tupchi*s, and *jarchi*s. Their appointment and pay was approved by the *tupchi-bashi*. The *tupchi-bashi* earned 2,000 tomans per year in 1660.[691] Du Mans also reports that the *tupchi-bashi* was in charge of cannon founders, carpenters, pioneers and musketeers.[692]

Table 3.7 List of *tupchi-bashi*s

913/1507	Hamza Beg[693]
922/1516	Mahmud Beg *tupchi*[694]
935/1528-29	Ostad Sheikhi Beg[695]
945/1538-39	Sheikh 'Ali *tupchi-bashi*[696]
959/1551-52	Darvish Beg *tupchi*[697]
964/1556-57	Soleiman Beg[698]
988/1580-81	Morad Khan[699]
1014/1605-06	Qoreiqchi Khan[700]

---

[687] Ben Khvandamir, p. 188.

[688] Kaempfer, *Am Hofe*, p. 120; *Ibid.*,Amoenitatum, pp. 126-7.

[689] Puturidze 1962, doc. 28.

[690] DM, pp. 88-9.

[691] DM, p. 59; Richard, vol. 2, p. 18. Formally he was the equal to the *tofangchi aghasi*. Nasiri, *Alqab*, p. 24.

[692] Richard, vol. 2, p. 273.

[693] *Travels to Tana*, part 2, p. 163 and Rumlu, p. 75.

[694] Ben Khvandamir, p. 188.

[695] Savory, *History*, vol. 1, pp. 89-90; Ostad Sheikhi Tupchi in 935/1528-29 with a regiment of *tofangchiyan*. Rumlu, p. 277; with *tofangchiyan-e* Rumlu, Afshar, *'Alamara-ye Tahmasp*, p. 78; Dickinson and Welch, vol. 1, p. 54 mention a picture of Taj al-Din, a relative of Ostad Sheikhi *rikhtehgar* in the Bahram Mirza album.

[696] Shirazi, p. 88; Rumlu, pp. 277, 379, 474.

[697] Rumlu, p. 474.

[698] Qomi, vol. 1, p. 288; Rumlu, p. 379.

[699] Shamlu, pp. 335-6, 344; Savory, *History*, vol. 1, p. 390.

[700] He was a *gholam*, who started his career in the *qeichigari* (tailor workshop), then became *mir-tup[khaneh]*, *sardar*, khan, and finally *sepahsalar*. Savory, *History*, vol. 2, p. 1260.

Table 3.7 (continued)

1019/1610	Barkhordar Beg[701]
1047/1637-38	Mortezaqoli Beg[702]
1051/1642	Morad Beg[703]
1059/1649	Mohammmad Beg[704]
1066/1655	Hoseinqoli Khan[705]
1071/1660-61	Qalandar Soltan Chuleh Chaghatay[706]

[taken care of by the *jabbehdar-bashi* till 1661; thereafter vacancy?]

1080-95/1669-79	Najafqoli Beg[707]
1095-/1679-	Mohammad Hosein Beg[708]
1104/1692	Musa Beg[709]
1105-06/1693-95	'Abd ol-Razzaq Beg *tupchi-bashi-ye jelou*[710]
1109/1697-98	'Abdi Aqa[711]
1128-34/1716-21	Mohebb 'Ali Khan[712]
1134/1721	Ahmad Khan[713]
1134/1722	Mohammad 'Ali Khan[714]
1134/1722	His son[715]
1141/1728-29	Emin Khan[716]
1143/1730-31	Taher Beg[717]
1144/1731-32	Mohammadqoli Khan[718]
1145/1732	Yar Beg Khan[719]
1146/1733	Mehdi Khan[720]

---

[701] Molla Jalal, pp. 388, 408; Savory, *History*, vol. 1, pp. 452; vol. 2, p. 997; Esfahani, p. 259.

[702] Esfahani, p. 259. He was the son of Barkhordar Beg.

[703] Shamlu, p. 258; Vahid Qazvini, p. 164 (however, Qalandar Soltan Chuleh kept command over total artillery and its logistics at Qandahar Ibid., pp. 106, 115, 229 (his death).

[704] Shamlu, p. 352.

[705] Chardin, vol. 5, p. 312.

[706] Vahid Qazvini, pp. 290, 297, 300, 309.

[707] Bardsiri, p. 359, 410. He was also *rekabdar*.

[708] Bardsiri, pp. 472, 491, 507

[709] Bardsiri, pp. 626, 629.

[710] Nasiri, *Dastur*, p. 30.

[711] Nasiri, *Dastur*, p. 257.

[712] Floor, *Bar Oftadan*, p. 27; Ibid., *Afghan Occupation*, p. 29; Mostoufi, pp. 128-9. He died at the battle of Golnabad in March 1722.

[713] Lockhart, *Fall*, pp. 135, 142.

[714] Appointed on 10/3/1722. He was the son of Aslan Khan. Floor, *Bar Oftadan*, p. 106; Ibid., *Afghan Occupation*, pp. 90, 99.

[715] Mohammad 'Ali was dismissed on 14/6/1722 and succeeded by his seven year old son. Floor, *Bar Oftadan*, p. 176; Ibid., *Afghan Occupation*, p. 138.

[716] Mervi, pp. 115, 153, 155.

[717] Mervi, pp. 153, 155.

[718] *ARA*, VOC 2255 (30/4/1732), f. 1983.

[719] Mervi, pp. 260, 266f.

In 1654, 'Abbas II reorganized the artillery corps and separated it from the rest of the army. He created a new artillery regiment which employed light iron cannon (*tupha-ye yashmari*), that, as usual, were put on carts which were linked together with chains so as to constitute at the same time a line of defense.[721] However, the following year, according to Chardin, 'Abbas II abolished the artillery corps, which under 'Abbas I still had been 12,000 men strong. It had been reduced in importance since the loss of Baghdad in 1637. When Hoseinqoli Khan, the old *tupchi-bashi* died in 1655, Shah 'Abbas II, did not appoint a new one.[722] What Chardin meant was that no new person was given the function of *tupchi-bashi*, who had died without male issue. For the Persian army could not do without artillery given its conflict with the Moghul army over Qandahar. For the function of *tupchi-bashi* was temporarily taken over by the *jabbehdar-bashi*.[723] Chardin's statement is not borne out by Persian sources. In fact, the abolition of the function of *tupchi-bashi* indeed seems to have been only a temporary measure, for later we observe the continued existence of this office. It was not unusual for the Safavids to temporarily not fill a function so as to save money.[724] In 1659, an army group moved to Daghestan with 2,000 *tofangchi*s and *tupchi*s with their *tup-khaneh* under the command of 'Aliqoli Beg, the *tupchi-bashi-ye jelou*.[725] The term *tupchi-bashi* [*ye-jelou*] was also used for commanders of the local artillery battery (*tup-khaneh*). For example, a *tupchi* in Tiflis was appointed *vakil* or representative of the *tupchi-bashi* of Tiflis castle in 1112/1701.[726] For some time we do not hear anything about the *tupchi-bashi* and the function was taken care of by the *tofangchi-bashi*, probably till 1661. Tavernier mentioned the existence of the function of *tupchi-bashi* in 1666.[727] Kaempfer in 1672, observed that his office was neither demanding nor very important. He just mentioned it for completeness' sake.[728] In that year the *tofangchi-aghasi* was no longer

---

[720] Mervi, pp. 336-7, 379.

[721] Vahid Qazvini, pp. 186, 273, 277; these may be the same as the "*Feldschlangen*" or cannon mentioned by Olearius, p. 478.

[722] Chardin, vol. 5, pp. 312-3. In 1665, du Mans mentions that the last *tupchi-bashi*, Barkhordar Khan, had been appointed 8 years ago, which shows that the situation of the command of the artillery corps still was unclear. Richard, vol. 2, pp. 273-4; see also Chardin, vol. 2, p. 409. The corps usually numbered about 9,000 men, but its was reduced in size after Safi I and only numbered 4,990 men under Soleiman. Nasiri, *Alqab*, p. 24.

[723] Chardin, vol. 5, p. 376.

[724] Kaempfer, *Am Hofe*, p. 50.

[725] Vahid Qazvini, p. 273. See also Puturidze 1962, nr. 16 and Puturidze 1965, nr. 2.

[726] Puturidze 1965, nr. 2.

[727] Tavernier, p. 154.

[728] Kaempfer, *Am Hofe*, pp. 73, 53. This opinion is shared by Tavernier, p. 229.

responsible for the artillery.[729]

In the 1680s, Sanson wrote that "The Fifth Pillar is the Toptchi Bachi, who is Great Master of the Artillery; He has under him Troops, which answer to our Musquetiers, and Gard du Corps in France. There is but Four thousand of 'em, who are Commanded more immediately by Four Colonels, and are always about the King on any Days of Ceremoney."[730] The function is also mentioned in both DM and TM, although the level of his income, as compared with his colleagues, and his lower place in the pecking order, clearly shows that he was a less important emir.[731] In battle, the *tupchi-bashi* was obliged to wear a felt hat and *gorgabis* (a kind of sandal) on his feet and direct the cannons.[732]

The Navy

According to Kaempfer, "The *tupchi-bashi* also commands the naval forces, and thus also is an admiral. However, the shah has no navy, but for some armed merchantmen on the Gulf and the Caspian sea."[733] Don Juan also mentioned that Persia did not have a navy, "only a kind of light boat is in common use."[734] Whenever, the Persians needed a naval force in the Gulf this was provided by other forces such as the English (1622) or the Dutch (1697), and at various occasions both were asked to provide naval assistance. The sole exception being the conquests of Bahrein (1614) and Qeshm (1618) where the Persian invading force made use of the light Gulf boats.[735] The Persians could not do anything about pirates in the Gulf or on the Caspian sea, even when they infested the littoral itself. Rasht, for example, was plundered by not more than 1,200 Cossacks in 1072/1661-2, who could do what they liked, because of lack of a defensive Persian force. Thereafter warning posts were erected.[736] As a result, Chardin reports, a start was made to equip barques to deal with the attacks of the Cossacks, but these deserved neither the name of a fleet nor of an escadre. The barques on the Caspian were strong, made of wood and iron, but they also were heavy and badly made, due to lack of good carpenters and

---

[729] Chardin, vol. 9, p. 480-1; Vahid Qazvini, p. 58.

[730] Sanson, p. 21.

[731] DM, p. 59; TM, pp. 51, 86; Nasiri, *Alqab*, p. 24.

[732] Nasiri, *Alqab*, p. 24.

[733] Kaempfer, *Am Hofe*, p. 73; Tavernier, p. 229; see also Sanson, p. 76.

[734] Don Juan, p. 50; for contemporary miniatures depicting ships see Gray, p. 131; Welch, S.C. *A King's Book of Kings. The Shah-nameh of Shah Tahmasp.* New York 1972 [1976]p. 84 (fig. 18); Ibid., Persian Paitning, p. 19 (fig. B)

[735] Floor, Willem. "The Iranian Navy in the Gulf during the Eighteenth Century," *IS* 20 (1987), pp. 31-53. ; Ibid., "First Contacts between the Netherlands and Masqat or A Report on the Discovery of the Coast of 'Oman in 1666", *ZDMG* 132 (1982), pp. 289-307.

[736] Vahid Qazvini, p. 308; Chardin, vol. 5, p. 324; Tavernier, p. 274.

maritime know-how.[737]

Despite these belated measures the Persians still could do very little against Sten'ka Razin who in 1669 attacked Astrakhan abandoning Gilan, Mazandaran and Daghestan which he had infested in 1668, despite Persian defensive efforts. The Persian defense had been hindered by high-level bureaucratic and astrological interference. The shah had commanded that the Persian 'fleet' consisting of small barques had to be ready on such and such a date, on an exact hour, because the heavenly constellations promised victory. The sailors had linked the small boats, on which 10,000 soldiers armed with arquebuses had been embarked, with chains, so as to prevent that the wild sea would separate them from one another. In this way the Persian 'fleet' formed one chain. This should have caused the small Cossack boats to become separated from one another so that they could be caught as if they were in a net. At the exact and auspicious hour the Cossacks aimed their artillery and other infernal war machines at the first Persian boat. This boat, suffering from many wounded and lacking fenders such as used by Europeans, sank due to a massive influx of water, and drew the next boat chained to it to the same misfortune. The latter tugged the next one and so on. Thus, the small boats with their soldiers and arms all went down. It was true that the hour was auspicious, for the Cossacks, but not for the Persians.[738] Although offers of technical assistance to build ships were made by the Swedes nothing came of it. It was only in 1734 that a new effort to build a fleet in the Persian Gulf and the Caspian was made, which had no lasting influence due to the death of Nader Shah, its instigator.[739]

The Development of the Army (1590-1722)

In addition to the creation of the *gholam* corps 'Abbas I also increased the participation of Iranic speaking tribal levies. This had become such a common and normal event by the early 1600s that the *Tarikh-e Qezelbash* classified some of them as Qezelbash tribes. Lors and Afshars, for example, were involved in the battle for the governorship of the Kuhgilu in 999/1590-1.[740] Ostajalus, Kurds (e.g. Kalhors), and others held the fortress of Esfara'in against the Uzbegs in 999/1590-1.[741] Near Sarakhs, in 1001/1592-3, 'Abbas I had mobilized about a thousand men, regular

---

[737] Chardin, vol. 5, pp. 327-32. There were also manned boats on lake Van, who were subordinate to the governor of Urmiyeh and the *kutval* (castellan) of Tiflis. Puturidze 1965, doc. 23.

[738] Richard, vol. 2, p. 359.

[739] Kaempfer, *Am Hofe*, p. 45, 49, 59; Chardin, vol. 5, p. 252; vol. 10p, p. 114-5 however; pp. 133-9. Rabino, H.L. *Mazandaran and Astarabad* (London 1928), pp. 49, 160. For pictures of Persian ships see Gray, p. 131, which show small boats used for pleasure or at best to transport soldiers. See also Floor, "Navy".

[740] Savory, *History*, vol. 2, p. 608.

[741] Savory, *History*, vol. 2, p. 618.

troops and militia.[742]

Apart from breaking the Turkoman hold on the state, 'Abbas I also appointed *gholams*, in the place of the seditious Qezelbash, "to the highest offices, and to the emirate, promising officers who owed their rise to himself alone. Gradually, the former class faded into oblivion, he managed to reduce the dissension among the Qezelbash, and thus the king's demands were once more obeyed by the army."[743] A beginning was made with the Dhu'l-Qadrs, who had supplied governors of Fars from 1503 to 1592, when they were penalized for not having send troops to participate in the Khorasan campaign. After a brief Qaramanlu interlude, a *gholam*, Allahverdi Khan, became *begler-begi* of Fars; later he was succeeded by his son Emamqoli Khan.[744] This was the first time a *gholam* was appointed as *begler-begi*.[745] Also, henceforth it was normal accepted practice that a *gholam* was in charge of an army that contained Qezelbash troops. This was a pattern that continued to prevail, i.e. the troops garrisoned in the provinces rather than being commanded by their own tribal emirs, were commanded by others such as *gholams*. For until the 1590s the army consisted of Qezelbash, *qurchis* and non-Qezelbash *cherik*, who were mainly commanded by Qezelbash emirs. After that date the army consisted of Turkomans, *qurchis*, *gholams*, musketeers, and gunners commanded by increasing numbers of non-Qezelbash emirs. Gradually the Turkoman-*qurchis* blended into one group, which was referred to as Qezelbash. The *qurchis* did not belong to the household troops anymore, but to the regular provincial forces as did the tribal Turkoman levies.[746] This led to a loss of identity of the Qezelbash, the *qurchis* in fact being the only group of the original Safavid supporters that kept its identity. Future governors, even if from the tribe in the province over which he governed, did not derive their power from the strength of their tribe, but from the support given by the shah. We even notice cases where the shah appointed a Tajik as chief of a Turkoman tribe.[747] Thus, there was a gain in importance for the *qurchis* and the *gholams*, but an eclipse of power for the Qezelbash. For example, there was no longer an

---

[742] Savory, *History*, vol. 2, p. 630; Kurdish tribesmen in 1002/1593-4. Ibid., vol. 2, p. 653; in 998/1589-80 an army of 5,000 Qezelbash, 3.000 Seistanis and 2.000 others, or some 10.000 men. Seistani, p. 283. Also infantry (*piyadeh*) levies (*komaki*). Ibid., pp. 236, 341;

[743] Savory, *History*, vol. 1, p. 518.

[744] Eskander Beg, vol. 1, pp. 458, 500, 515; Savory, *History*, vol. 2, p. 631. Qomi, vol. 1, pp. 87-8.

[745] *History*, vol. 2, p. 690; Monshi, vol. 1, p. 515. Yoli Beg, another *gholam*, had been appointed as governor of Isfahan in 998/1589. Savory, *History*, vol. 2, p. 602; Monshi, p. 426.

[746] Haneda, p. 208.

[747] Haneda, p. 206.

assembly of all tribes such as under Khodabandeh,[748] for henceforth it was the *qurchi-bashi* that represented the *qurchi*s as well as the Qezelbash Turkoman tribes. He was "the senior officer (*rish-safid*) of all tribes and clans (*uymaqat*) of the kingdom."[749] This is also clear from the fact that all European travellers after della Valle equated the *qurchi*s with the Qezelbash troops.[750] The fact that non-Qezelbash emirs were leading provincial Qezelbash troops also confirms that the exclusive character of the Turkoman levies had been discontinued.

According to della Valle, Shah 'Abbas I detested the Qezelbash, though not openly. In many ways he tried undermine their influence, and to unsettle them, by frequently punishing their chiefs, and keeping them in fear of him rather than seeking their affections.[751] He further twice appointed a *gholam* as *qurchi-bashi*, which function was the personification of Qezelbash identity. The fact that the Qezelbash did not react is a sign how cowed they were. 'Abbas I also instituted a strict control over the readiness to the call at arms by the Qezelbash. In 1590, "the grand vizier (Hatem Beg), the *qurchi-bashi*, and various other officers were ordered to look into the affairs of the army, and to see that they received their pay, allowances, and fodder allowance. They were also ordered to scrutinize the rolls of the Qezelbash tribes and other tribes liable for military service, and if they found any soldier drawing pay, in possession of a horse, and capable of bearing arms who had not reported for duty in Khorasan, he was to be charged with failing to report for duty. This time, delinquents were to be fined, and the money distributed as bounty to those retainers of the court and *qurchi*s who had been the first to answer the call to arms and had endured the hardships of the campaign. This was both to be a punishment and a warning to the guilty parties. In future, anyone failing to answer a mobilization call would be subject to a variety of penalties. The result of these measures was that, whenever a levy was made, the Qezelbash and other tribesmen, for fear of being punished by the shah, would set off to court without even waiting for their own mobilization orders, each contingent trying to outstrip the other."[752] It is a sign that things had changed considerably compared with the 1570s that 20 years later Hatem Beg, the grand vizier, was in charge of a Qezelbash army to besiege the castle of Domdom.[753] Two decades earlier the fact that the then grand vizier, Mirza Salman, had taken command of the army, had led to his murder by the Qezelbash.[754]

---

748 Monshi, vol. 1, p. 223.
749 DM, p. 47; TM, p. 46.
750 See section of *qurchi*s.
751 della Valle, vol. 7, pp. 79-80.
752 Savory, *History*, vol. 2, p. 628;
753 Savory, *History*, vol 2, p. 994.
754 Savory, vol. 1, p. 375 fight about who should be commander-in-chief, and blaming Mirza Salman who was. Ibid., "The Significance of the Political Murder of

By about 1600, the Persian army consisted of five groups: the musketeers, the gunners, the king's slaves or *gholams*, and the *qurchi*s in addition to the Qezelbash and other tribal levies. The organization of the three non-tribal military corpses was all similar and based on the model of the *qurchi* corps. They were headed by a chief, who generally speaking, was usually was selected from their own ranks. I.e. a *qurchi-bashi* would normally be from a Qezelbash tribe, while the *qollar-aghasi* would be a *gholam*. The relative importance or the pecking-order of these military commanders changed over time. However, generally speaking the *qurchi-bashi* was the most important one.[755]

Also, under the corps commanders served so-called *min-bashi*s, officers in charge of 1,000 men. These regiments were subdivided into units of 100 men and commanded by *yuz-bashi*s. Each *yuz-bashi* in charge unit of 100 men was assisted by a deputy or *na'eb*, a *yasavol* or adjutant and 10 subalterns, known as *on-bashi*s or *dah-bashi*s, who were in charge of units of 10 men.[756] Towards the end of the Safavid period the existence of *panjah-bashi*s, subaltern officers in charge of 50 men are also mentioned.[757] Each individual corpsman, of whatever rank, was a *tabin* or subordinate of his direct superior.

Another innovation was the fact that the corpsmen were not dependent on a tribal chief or emir, but directly on the shah via their commander just like the *qurchi*s. This meant that for each corps a separate administration was established under the direction of the corps commander. The day-to-day work was done by a vizier and a *mostoufi* for each corps, who kept files on each active corps member, as well as on their absence, death, etc. They further monitored the revenue basis out of which the *qurchi*s, *tofangchi*s, *gholam*s and *tupchi*s were to be paid. The vizier and *mostoufi* of the four military departments all performed the same functions. Sometimes, two corpses shared the same vizier and/or *mostoufi*. The viziers of the four corpses were jointly referred to as the *vozara-ye kharj*.[758]

Paying the army remained a problem throughout the Safavid reign. Even 'Abbas I, who did the most to put the financing of his army and bureaucracy on a sound basis, had to have recourse to irregular forms of payment. Prior to 'Abbas, the cost of the army was not borne by the royal treasury. The shah assigned land and other sources of income to the tribal leaders to enable them to come armed when the muster was called.

Mirza Salman", *Islamic Studies* 2 (1963), pp. 181-91.

755 "After the *divan-begi* comes the *qurchi-bashi*, then the *tofangchi-bashi*, then the *qollar-aghasi*." Chardin, vol. 5, p. 342; Richard, vol. 2, p. 263. See DM and TM for the official pecking-order.

756 Chardin, vol. 5, 314; Olearius, p. 667; Du Mans, p. 124.

757 Daneshpazhuh, "Amar", p. 399.

758 Yusef, pp. 283-4; the army administration was occasionally also referred to as *dafater-e jonud*. Shamlu, p. 104; DM, pp. 88-9.

However, the *khasseh* troops, such as the *qurchi*s, the *tofangchi*s, as well as the emirs who did not receive a land assignment received their pay from the royal treasury. In addition, when campaigning, the troops were supposed to receive additional payment from the treasury. By 983/1575 the troops had not been paid for 14 years, because "they loved shah so much."[759] In reality, Tahmasp I had become an avaricious person, who did not care how and where his troops obtained their pay, even through criminal means. As a consequence, under his successor, Esma'il II, the grand vizier, Mirza Salman, immediately paid the troops 3 years of pay.[760] This fast hand-out emptied the treasury and undermined the fiscal soundness of the state. In 994/1586, Hamzeh Mirza, Khodabandeh's son, for example, had to break up "all the gold and silver vessels belonging to his establishment and distributed them among the Qezelbash"[761] Before putting 'Abbas I on the throne, his self-styled protector, Mortezaqoli Khan in 989/1581-2 "announced that his troops would receive a handout of gold, intending to raise the money from the rich citizens of Mashad... he even laid hands of the shrine treasury."[762]

When around 1590 'Abbas I wanted to take revenge for Uzbeg invasion he was in dire straits and short of funds. "Verily gold is the nerve and the true motive power of war: he who has money will always find soldiers." The shah therefore ordered that all his service of plate be melted down; his administrators stalled, telling him that it had cost 90,000 ducats to make, and all that would be wasted. But the plate was melted and the army of 80,000 marched.[763] Allahverdi Khan, before he joined 'Abbas I's army, sent out messengers to mobilize his troops in Fars; he also had to pay to his *gholam*s and retainers.[764] While en route he distributed considerable amounts of red and white gold from Qasr-e Zard in Yazd to his troops.[765] However difficult it was, 'Abbas I always made sure that his troops were paid and gave his staff strict orders to that effect.[766] Whenever necessary large sums of money were drawn for the royal treasury to pay the troops.[767]

Although 'Abbas I tried to put his kingdom and army on a sound fiscal footing he was not able to achieve either objective. During the siege of Baghdad in the 1620s, 'Abbas I had no money to pay his troops. He

---

[759] Shamlu, pp. 94-5.

[760] Shamlu, p. 107.

[761] Savory, *History*, vol. 1, p. 468.

[762] Savory, *History*, vol. 1, p. 407.

[763] Don Juan, pp. 221-2; 'Abbas I distributed quantities of gold, jewellery, dinars, derhams, and arms among his horse and foot in 1591 during the Khorasan campaign. Adle, p. 434.

[764] Adle, p. 441.

[765] Adle, p. 442.

[766] Savory, *History*, vol. 2, p. 1015, 1059; Monshi, vol. 2, p. 811, 849.

[767] Savory, *History*, vol. 2, p. 1265.

therefore gave the soldiers round pieces of leather, marked with his name and that of the town of Baghdad. He promised to pay them later in coinage exchanging the leather pieces for copper money on return to Isfahan, which promise he kept.[768] At another occasion, 'Abbas I intended to pay his soldiers with cloth that he had traded with the EIC in 1624. Some 35,000 of them would get 2 covids which represented 2,000 cloths yearly according to the EIC agent.[769]

'Abbas I was very strict where discipline was concerned, in particular as to the army's behavior towards the population. Pacifique de Provins was astounded that the peasants instead of hiding their produce and possessions, like in France, offered them voluntarily for sale. This was due to the fact that 'Abbas I punished severely any soldier who extorted money or goods from the population or an official who was not diligent in seeing to it that supplies were available on time and at the location ordered. He also prohibited anybody to lend money to his soldiers, on pain of forfeiting the money. The shah's argument was that he paid his army well to feed and clothe themselves. If they borrowed money it would mean that they were up to something bad which would led them astray from concentrating on their service to him. Also, foreigners would think that he did not care for his men, because they had to borrow money to get by.[770]

Regularly reviews were held by the shah or one of his generals. Each soldier had to present himself with his arms and horse for inspection. Also, his personal conduct and the kind of company he kept was also looked into. If fault was found on any of these points the soldier was excused. According to Pacifique de Provins, 'Abbas I personally observed such proceedings and witnessed that soldiers were send away because they had no relatives who could vouch for them. If everything was found in order this was noted in the muster lists. If the army held a review in town, in the presence of the shah, each soldier had to present himself in person to the shah, who gave them a red head-dress. This cap, the *taj* was meant, was made of thick material so that it stopped a sword blow. Pacifique de Provins personally assisted at such a *taj* presentation review in Kashan.[771] A similar practice also existed under Safi I.[772] In 1041/1631-32, Hasan Beg *yasavol-sohbat* had been ordered to take review of the troops taking with him the rolls (*noskheh*) that Rostam Khan the

---

[768] Kutelia, Tinatin. *Catalogue of the Iranian Copper Coins in the State Museum of Georgia* (Tiflis 1990), p. 46.

[769] Ferrier, R.W. *British-Persian Relations in the 17th century,* unpublished dissertation Cambridge University 1970, p. 330. Tavernier mentions that all the cut-offs that were left from the royal tailor workshop were used to make clothes for the soldiers who received these in lieu of part of their pay. Tavernier, p. 222.

[770] Pacifique de Provins, p. 258.

[771] Pacifique de Provins, p. 257.

[772] Yusef, pp. 138, 248.

sepahsalar had prepared.[773]

The size of the army varied of course with military needs and the losses suffered during previous battles. Also, the shahs did not like paying for troops that they did not need. Therefore, the army of combatants was about 70-80.000 as Minorsky has already argued, of whom may be 40-50.000 were actually used on campaign. Nevertheless, it has also been reported that an army consisted of as many as 120,000 in 1020/1611-12 when marching to Balkh.[774] "But the King of Persia's judgement agreeth with that of the best experienced captains: that multitudes are confusers of ofers and devourers of time, and of those means which nourish the wars, and are good for no other use but to make a war soon break off, and to consume the world."[775] 'Abbas I therefore, at several occasions, sent back home half-trained or ill-equipped troops, because he considered these more of a nuisance than an advantage.[776]

Thus, as of 1587, there was a significantly increased number of royal household troops, who were paid out of the royal treasury, and a reduced number of provincial troops, who were paid out of the *mamalek* revenues. The provincial troops were subdivided into regular levies and regular troops. The levies constituted of the troops which the provincial governors were obliged to maintain. The regular troops were the *qurchi*s. These comprised the old *qurchi* corps. The estimated strength of this corps was both higher than that of the *qurchi* corps and lower than the usual Qezelbash force in the 16th century. May be some of the tribal levies were counted among the *qurchi*s, who henceforth were the Qezelbash troops par excellence, just as their chief or *qurchi-bashi* was considered to be the chief of all Qezelbash. Both militias, i.e. levies and troops, were stationed in the rural areas where they lived of the lands assigned to them. This land entitlement could be inherited by the soldiers' children, if they undertook to bear arms, and would appear at 12 hours' notice under the colors, if needed.[777] The royal household troops consisted of the *gholam, tofangchi* and *tupchi* corpses. They were paid out of the royal treasury.[778] Both the household troops and the *qurchi*s were divided into *hamisheh-keshik* (permanent duty) and *safar-kesh* (reserve) forces.

The military, when not on active duty, were quartered in the rural areas, where they were engaged in husbandry and other related activities. Here, the lower ranks, were at the back-and-call of their *yuz-bashi*s, who, together with other officials (*darugheh, khalifeh*) also exercised administrative functions. It is, as yet, unclear whether this type of organization was limited to areas where Qezelbash groups were located.

---

[773] Esfahani, p. 153.
[774] Natanzi, p. 469.
[775] Sherley, p. 323.
[776] Allen, *Russian Embassies*, vol. 2, p. 419, n. 2; Adle, p. 480.
[777] Chardin, vol. 5, pp. 298-304.
[778] Chardin, vol. 5, pp. 304-07.

However, the fact that similar configurations also seem to have existed outside Qezelbash areas, such as Georgia, Armenia, and Isfahan, suggest that this was a general national pattern.[779]

As to the size of the army, della Valle gave a total of 100,000 (including 30,000 at the frontiers) to which should be added the retainers of the governors, so that the grand total could reach 200,000 men, which is much too high. Herbert's estimate of 300,000 horse and 70,000 foot or musquetons is too high as well. He realized that this was too high, for he added "such force [the shah] can readily advance, but seldom exceeds 50,000", which is more realistic. According to Herbert "Upon muster the Persian King can march (as appears by roll and pension) three hundred thousand horse and seventy thousand foot, or musketeers: such force he can readily advance, but seldom exceeds fifty thousand - enough to find forage and proviand in such barren countries."[780] In 1665, according to du Mans, the shah had about 60,000 provincial troops in addition to the force of the four regular army corpses. These provincial troops were mostly concentrated in the frontier provinces. The important governors had 15,000 to 20,000 men on their pay-roll, while the less important khans had 1,500 to 2,000 men. In total, therefore, the shah could field 80,000 to 100,000 men.[781] According to Chardin, at the end of 'Abbas I's reign, the Safavid army was 120.000 men strong. The three royal corpses together numbered 50.000 and the provincial troops 60.000, while the royal guards numbered 10.000. He further estimated that battle-experienced and trained troops only numbered some 30,000 soldiers, who were mostly located on the Ottoman border.[782]

Kermanshah	6.000	Armenia	5.000
Georgia	5.000	Khorasan	8.000
Qandahar	8.000		

The cavalry amounted to 60,000 horsemen, many of whom were double-horsed, but out of these 6,000 horsemen "are upon constant Duty every day."[783] These permanent troops or the *hamisheh-keshik* forces, the household troops and *qurchis*, were always in attendance on the shah. The other troops were dispersed over the country, where they lived off their revenue assignments (*teyul* or *hameh-saleh*).[784] The soldiers served also as messengers and tax collectors. "These Troopers are maintined out of the King's Demesn [*khasseh*] Lands. He gives a county to a Colonel, and such

---

779 See on this issue Willem Floor, "The Khalifeh al-kholafa of the Safavid sufi order," (forthcoming).

780 Herbert, p. 242 with some details on the strength of the forces of the various khans.

781 Richard, vol. 2, pp. 260, 262, 265, 285, 295.

782 Chardin, vol. 5, pp. 315, 323.

783 Fryer, vol. 3, p. 57.

784 Vahid Qazvini, p. 94; Mostoufi, p. 127.

a number of villages to a Captain, on condition they raise their Soldiers Pay out of 'em. A Trooper's pay is a Hundred Crowns a Year. The Generals are also provided of Governments to defray their Charges, and those Princes that retire into Persia."[785] This is also clear from various Persian documents which mention that the various categories of soldiers received their pay as an entitlement on the output and/or tax burden of villages.[786] This also held for tribal groups who had been stationed in frontier areas to protect the border, who e.g. the Arqutlu received the *jezya* or poll-tax of 10 villages as their *teyul* or revenue assignment. From this document it is also clear that this policy was initiated by 'Abbas I.[787] A decree of 1113/1702 required that a *soyurghal* holder provided "seven men all ready (*safar-keshi*) to the shah's call and service (*beh jar va yasaq-e shahi*),"[788] while another had to bring eight armed horsemen.[789] The same system continued to exist throughout the Safavid period, and was also adopted by Nader Shah and his successors in Eastern Persia under Shah Ahmad Dorrani.[790]

Already under Safi I the situation of the army began to deteriorate. After 1039/1639, peace reigned with the Ottomans. The lack of a serious external threat and the existence of internal security, made the need for keeping the army on its toes less of a priority. The tendency to neglect was not kept into bounds anymore. After the death of 'Abbas II's grand vizier, Saru Taqi, in 1645 the situation of the military further deteriorated. This was partly due to factionalism, partly to his having starved the military of funds. To alleviate that situation 'Abbas II, in 1645, distributed 100,000 tomans among them.[791] However, this was a one-time occurrence and no structural changes were made. This was clear from the campaign for the control over Qandahar where the Persian soldiers were famished for want of food, because of lack of pay and supplies, which resulted in their defeat.[792] The Dutch observed in 1651-2 that 6,000 Persian soldiers defected and that those that remained demanded their wages. The Persian cavalry had only received one toman for one horseman, one servant and two horses.[793] In 1665, merchants were therefore forced by the shah to each pay for the upkeep of one to three soldiers.[794] There were apparently

785 Sanson, p. 71.
786 Puturidze 1955, doc. 141; Ibid., 1965, doc. 19; Vahid Qazvini, p. 94.
787 Puturidze 1965, doc. 18.
788 Minorsky, "A *soyurghal*", p. 959.
789 Petruchevshi, I.P. *Ocherki po istorii feodal'nikh otnoshenij v Azerbaidzhane i Armenii v XVI-nachale XIX vv.* (Leningrad 1949), doc. 3.
790 Mervi, vol. 1, pp. 86, 137, 229, 253; al-Monshi, *Tarikh-e Ahmad Shahi*, vol. 2, f. 486a, 487b.
791 *ARA*, VOC 1152, Daghregister Winninx, Oct. 12, 1645; see Floor, "Mirza Taqi", p. 261.
792 Foster, *The English Factories 1645-50*, pp. 267, 270.
793 Hotz, pp. 211-2, 249, 286.
794 *ARA*, VOC 1215 (11/12/1655), f. 810.

not enough well-trained Persian soldiers, for 'Abbas II, in addition to European gunners, also hired 400 Turkish mercenaries to fight in the Qandahar campaign.[795] The Dutch further noted that soldiers from the North were the only good ones, from the south only peasants could be recruited.[796]

The review of fuzeleers, according to Tavernier, was organized by the provincial governors every three months and also served to assess the soldiers' ability to handle their arms. The governor had them ride past him in groups of ten. He further had 10 half-pikes planted in the ground on top of which an apple had been placed. The ten soldiers had to shoot at the apple on the half-pike in front of them with an arrow. They shot at a distance of 100 paces and those that hit the apple received a bonus. A similar procedure existed for the cavalry, whose members had to hit a target while galloping past the shah. The horsemen also saluted the shah on that occasion by pressing a hand on the stomach and then on their forehead[797]

However, other observers concluded that as of the 1650s, political and bureaucratic control had weakened and corruption increased. The muster rolls that were made for the annual reviews did not respond to reality. Control by various officials was rendered useless due to bribery. These reviews which normally had been held twice during three days per year now only were held once per year or even only once per three years.[798] The soldiers had to come armed and horsed to the review. But there was neither military order nor discipline. Though real maneuvers were never held the general reviews were the closest to this kind of operation.[799] In 1654, 'Abbas II examined complaints by soldiers and as a result he fired the *sepahsalar* 'Aliqoli Khan on the spot.[800] During a review held in 1666 'Abbas II discovered that the same arms, horses and men passed before him 10-12 times. Although 'Abbas II took the necessary measures to correct this its impact proved to be only of a temporary nature.[801] The reviews of garrisons did not limit themselves to the soldiers and their arms, but also included that of the arsenal.[802] Under 'Abbas II's successors reviews were still held but it was a pageant rather than an army review

---

[795] Andersen, p. 156.

[796] *ARA*, VOC 1242 (20/6/1664), f. 1092.

[797] Tavernier, pp. 228, 218.

[798] Kaempfer, *Am Hofe*, p. 74; Manucci, Niccolao. *Storia do Mogor or Mogul India 1653-1708*. Tr. William Irvine, 4 vols (London 1907), vol. 1. p. 30; Chardin, vol. 5, pp. 304, 317.

[799] Chardin, vol. 5, pp. 316-7.

[800] Vahid Qazvini, p. 174.

[801] Chardin, vol. 5, p. 315; Richard, vol. 2, pp. 261, 285. Vahid Qazvini, p. 332 mentions a review of the *hamisheh-keshik* troops (*qurchis, gholams*, etc.) with the qualification "excellent".

[802] Nasiri, *Dastur*, p. 251.

showing the troops' readiness. One army inspector told Chardin: "We have a good army for army reviews, but a bad one for wars."[803] This nevertheless had the desired effect. For the martial looking and splendidly dossed out cavalry made such an impression on the visiting Ottoman ambassador, Esma'il Aqa, in March 1657, that he remarked: "God has singled out the Osmanlis by his grace by not permitting the Persians to know their might, force and glory, for otherwise they would conquer and destroy almost all of the Turkish state which is inferior to them, whether in order, wealth, generosity and military might."[804] However, European observers were much less impressed. The EIC Agent wrote in November 1668 that the country "was never in a poorer condition to defend itselfe having neither men nor moneys."[805]

Because there was no war, some thought it was a good idea to enroll and receive an income for doing nothing. By greasing the hands of the army inspectors even those unfit to enlist, such as children, were enrolled. They started with a pay rate of 0.5 tomans per year, which amount was raised every year. "If one wants to serve one presents oneself to the general, who assigns you a vacancy. But if there is none, he asks the shah to create a post and you and your descendents receive your pay for eternity. The luxury is what sappens the Persian soldiers; they receive 400 pounds and spend more than double that on clothes alone."[806] But the soldiers felt that their pay was not remunerative anymore, they lost interest in keeping their skills honed. Also they did not train their children in the military arts, who sought employment in other occupations. Therefore, instead of showing up for reviews or training many reported sick, or left the military. The court, in stead of being perturbed, thought it a good development because it saved money.[807] And money was something that the court always seemed to be short of. In 1669, recruitment of troops to oppose the Uzbeks went very slow due to lack of funds.[808] The neglect of the army under Soleiman (r. 1666-94) led to an effective reduction of soldiers' pay by 25% due to administrative 'fees' and rising cost of living and arms.[809] Also, Kaempfer noted that Soleiman refused to pay a large part of the troops from the treasury, who therefore were paid with money orders (barats), i.e. in kind, not cash.[810] In 1681, the soldiers' pay had been

---

803 Chardin, vol. 5, p. 323.
804 Richard, vol. 2, p. 266.
805 Matthee, *Politics*, p. 161. The Dutch agreed with this conclusion. *ARA, VOC* 1266, f. 930 (28 Febr. 1669).
806 Chardin, vol. 5, p. 315-6.
807 Chardin, vol. 5, p. 325-6; Kaempfer, *Am Hofe*, p. 75. A Dutch report notes that the majority of experienced soldiers had died, while poverty had weakened those remaining. *ARA, VOC* 1343 (2/6/1680), f. 608 r.
808 *ARA, VOC* 1266, f. 930.
809 Chardin vol. 5, pp. 325-6.
810 Kaempfer, *Am Hofe*, pp. 106; 97.

in arrears for 5 years.[811] Consequently, there was a lack of troops, which Sanson believed, was the reason why Soleiman in 1691 did not want to go to war with the Ottomans and the Baluch, because he lacked troops in the Darband and SW area.[812]

It was difficult to maintain the army's readiness and efficiency. There was a short-lived attempt under Soleiman to improve military readiness. Kaempfer estimated the army at a strength of 90,000. They were maintained by the land on which live. The governors commanded and maintained them. Out of greed they kept less men than required which the shah in vain tried to contain by regular reviews. The review staff was corrupt, however, thus invalidating the regular reviews. Moreover, the soldiers were forgetting their trade and considered their pay a gratuity. The waning of the sufi ideology, in spite of the continued existence of the network of *khalifeh*s, also meant that there was little commitment to the shah anymore among the rank and file.[813]

According to Sanson, the shah by 1690 had 150,000 troops excluding some garrisons in the interior of the country. These were all financed out of the *khasseh* revenues and those of confiscated estates. There was hardly any infantry, because it was too arduous for them given the kind of terrain. For the same reason they used little or no artillery, "for they have no need of it to defend their Towns, which have neither Walls nor Fortifications, and therefore must trust wholy to their Bodies."[814]

---

811 *ARA,* VOC 1355 (5/3/1681), f. 3398 v.
812 Anne Kroell, *Nouvelles d'Ispahan 1665-1695* (Paris 1979), pp. 48-9. See, however, Matthee, "Iran's Ottoman Policy Under Shah Sulayman 1666-1694", in: Kambiz Eslami ed. *Iran and Iranian Studies. Essays in Honor of Iraj Afshar.* (Princeton 1998), pp. 148-77.
813 Kaempfer, *Am Hofe*, p. 74.
814 Sanson, pp. 74-5.

Table 3.8 Number of soldiers and their location around 1690

Name of province	Number of soldiers
Qandahar	12,000
Khorasan	20,000
Mazandaran and Gilan	15,000
Darband and Shirvan	12,000
Georgia	large number
Kurdestan	20,000
Erivan	12,000
Lorestan	12,000
Shushtar	15,000
Kerman and Isfahan	12,000
Royal guards	14,000
Total	150,000
Excluding the garrisons in the cities of the interior.	

By 1696, the state apparatus had become so unwieldy and ineffective that it took at least six months to mobilize 12,000 troops.[815] There was also a lack of food, fodder and military supplies in dealing with incursions which left the punitive actions against, for example, marauding Baluch, weak and ineffective,[816] and was a warning on the wall of the disastrous events to come under Shah Soltan Hosein. Sometimes, after a job considered well done, as in 1107/1695-96, members of the five corpses were awarded with a grant from the treasury. Their representatives had to present themselves with a list of names and had to see to it that each got his fair share in exchange for a receipt.[817] According to Le Bruyn "The pay of these troops is very considerable, and particularly the pay of the officers. Every private trooper has yearly five or six hundred florins each, and they augment their pay in proportion, as they deserve it by extraordinary services in times of action. The sons of these cavaliers are paid also as such; tho' indeed they are obliged to furnish a man at their own expense, in times of war, when they happen to be under age. At this review there were children on horseback that were not above eight or ten years old, with a servant at the side of them."[818]

Despite all the difficulties the royal court was still able to mount sufficient number of troops to deal with local incursions. In 1106/1694-5, a *sardar* led an army consisting of members of his own tribe, *qurchi*s, *gholam*s, *tofangchi*s, *tupchi*s and *jazayer*s.[819] Also, the Persian troops accompanying a Moghul prince in 1107/1695-96, who were referred to as Qezelbash, had to submit to a review and were checked with the muster rolls when they arrived at the frontier,[820] but this undoubtedly was done more for financial than for military reasons. Several campaigns in Khorasan and Qandahar in the early 18th century showed that the military capability was still there. But slowly and surely, things got from bad to worse thereafter. In 1714, Masqat Arabs attacked Kong. A totally stupefied Safavid court wrung its hands, but did nothing. Baluch incursions, which sometimes came close to the capital, were not dealt with anymore by beating the marauders, but either by buying them off or hoping that they went away.[821] Mir Weis the leader of the Ghalza'i Afghans of Qandahar, having seen first hand, the weakness and unpreparedness of Safavid government during his stay in Isfahan in 1712, rebelled and in 1715 defeated the Safavid troops that were send against

815 Nasiri, *Dastur*, p. 104. On how troops were mobilized see Ibid., pp. 72, 108. See also Floor, *Bar Oftadan*, pp. 29, 35, 40; Ibid., *Afghan Occupation*, pp. 34, 36-7.
816 Nasiri, *Dastur*, pp. 73, 83.
817 Nasiri, *Dastur*, pp. 106-07.
818 Le Bruyn, vol. 1, p. 160.
819 Nasiri, *Dastur*, p. 67.
820 Nasiri, *Dastur*, p. 121.
821 Floor, *Bar Oftadan*, pp. 23-40 Ibid., *Afghan Occupation*, pp. 23-40.

him.[822] This set a rebellion in motion as series of events which finally would result in the appearance of an Afghan-Seistani army before Isfahan to challenge the Safavid state in 1721. By that time the regular militia had been reduced to some 60,000 men, which were referred to as *molazem* and not as Qezelbash anymore. The data given in Table 3.9[823] is incomplete, not only are some areas not quantified, but Isfahan is missing.

Table 3.9 Number of soldiers and their Location according to the TM

Tabriz	11,439
Chokhur-e Sa'd	4,287
Qarabagh	6,084
Shirvan	5,865
Herat	5,462
Mashad	5,440
Qandahar	1,785
Merv	2,352
Seistan	1,000
Astarabad	2,453
Gilan	2,525
Kerman	?
Hamadan	2,947
Kurdestan, Lorestan	1,811
Fars	6,055
'Arabestan	?
Total	59,496

It is also interesting to compare this table with a late Safavid estimate of the state's military strength. This report was allegedly drawn up in 1128/1715-6 by Mohammad Hosein, *mostoufi al-mamalek*. The estimated nominal strength of the army at that time was a total of 180,000 men, of which on horse 120,000; on foot 50,000; the artillery (*'amaleh-ye tup-khaneh*) 10,000; tribal levies and *cherik* made up 110,000 of this total. The *cherik* consisted of 57,000 horse and 53,000 men on foot, and were mostly Tajiks at that time. This army was not a standing army, but operated under

---

822 On the fall of the Safavid dynasty see Lockhart, *Fall*; Floor, *Bar Oftadan*, chapter one, and Ibid., *Afghan Occupation*, chapter one. "In the days of the *molla-bashi* and the *hakim-bashi* money was not spend on the army; sometimes the troops only received pay for 10 months, then for 8, 6, 4 and sometimes they did not anything during one year. Gradually the army was dispersed. When Mir Weis was at court, he saw the emirs without authority and irresolute, and the molla-bashi and the hakim-bashi in charge. The army was dispersed, and the little army that was still there was less than 30,000 men." M.T. Daneshpazhuh, "Amar-e mali va nezami-ye Iran dar 1128", *FIZ* 20, pp. 396-300.
823 TM, p. 161.

their chiefs (*il-begi*s), and was called upon in case of war. They had to bring their own arms and horse; the *cherik* their guns and other arms. Food and fodder had to be supplied as purveyance (*sursat*) by the shah till the end of the war. The non-*cherik* part consisted of 70,000 standing army (*laskar-e hazer al-rekab*): 40,000 horse; musketeers (*jazayerchi*s) 10,000; swivel-gunners (*zanburak-e shotor*) 3,000; artillerists (*tupchi*s and *qomparehchi*s) 3,000; 12,000 arquebusiers (*tofangchi*s), or in total 70,000 men. Each horsemen received 500 rupis per year; *tupchi*s and *zanburakchi*s (may be a mistake for *qomparehchi*s) 400 rupis; *tofangchi*s 200 rupis, and *zanburakchi*s 300 rupis. These troops on active duty served under *dah-bashi*s, *panjah-bashi*s, *yuz-bashi*s, *beg*s, and *soltan*s. They earned from 600 to 3,000 rupis, while khans as well as the *ilbegi*s had *jaigir*s (*teyul*s). The estimated cost to the treasury was 4 *korur* of rupis per year.[824]

The figures from the TM seem reasonable, especially if we compare them with the little we know from other sources on Safavid military strength in the Caucasus. The population of towns such as Darband and Baku consisted mostly of military men.[825] Schiller in 1702, therefore, noticed more soldiers there than anywhere else in Persia.[826] However, these numbers and strength were rather inflated. The Russians, after their capture of Darband in 1723, noted that the city only held 1,000 cavalry and 2,000 foot. These received their pay from the state, but also were engaged in agriculture.[827] Moreover, these troops were badly armed, trained and equipped. When the Russians took Baku in 1723, they found that the Persian troops only had 80 metal and iron cannon, and two howitzers, which were without carriage so that these could not be directed. Also, the store of ammunition, bullets and balls, and gun-powder was low, in particular balls for the howitzers.[828] The Persian troops that faced the Russian invasion force in Gilan in 1723, consisted of local levies of *tofangchi*s who were likewise badly armed. They had sabers and some were armed with flint-lock guns which had no locks and had to be started with a fuse. However, they did not have many flints, while their bullets were wrapped in grass.[829] How ready these frontier troops really were may also be clear from a review held by the khan of Shamakhi of his cavalry in

---

[824] Daneshpazhuh, "Amar", pp. 296-300. The report must have been written in the late Zand or early Qajar period. How much of its contents reflected reality is difficult to assess. The numbers are certainly inflated, though the relative strengths of the various units may be correct, as is the organization of the troops.

[825] Müller, *Sammlung*, vol. 4, pp. 98, 130.

[826] Schiller, p. 110. Bell, 15 years later, echoes this observation. Darband is "provided plentifully with cannon and ammunition, and a strong garrison." Bell, p. 286.

[827] Müller, *Sammlung*, vol. 4, p. 98.

[828] Müller, *Sammlung*, vol. 7, p. 327.

[829] Müller, vol. 7, p. 284.

1703. They were completely armed for the field. "Some had lances, bows and arrows, others had firearms, and some had bows and arrows only; indeed these last had canes with a button at the end [jerid], which they use with great dexterity. Under their vests they had coats of mail and brassets, and little morions in form of caps upon their heads, with visors; and were perfectly well dressed after the Persian manner, and especially the officers, who had vests of gold and silver brocade. There were some of the gentlemen who had six or seven led horses; and private men that had one, besides another the servant that led him rode upon, and other servant on foot."[830] It was a similar well caparisoned, but badly led, armed and trained Safavid army that was defeated by a numerically inferior Afghan force in 1721. What was lacking in the Safavid army was not the men or the equipment, but the will to win due to the lack of leadership. In 1720, a Persian army had defeated Mahmud Khan Ghalza'i near Kerman, but lack of independence for the commanding generals, lack of funds, and lack of political leadership led to the defeat of the Safavid army and the fall of the dynasty.[831]

Military Dress, Arms and Equipment

Dress: "The color of the clothing (of the soldiers) is different for everyone, they have no uniform" according to Kaempfer.[832] Although Kaempfer is right that most Persian troops did not have a uniform dress, they nevertheless wore military garb, thus distinguishing them from civilians. For example, Eskander Beg mentions that a group of defeated Qezelbash, changed their military dress for civilian clothes, and pressed on, riding at night and hiding by day.[833] The well-armed military units wore jerkin and armor. They used for personnel protection a coat of mail. Also, the various military groups such as *gholam*s, *jazayer*, etc. wore a dress that made them distinct from other military groups. This in particular held for regional groups of military. For example, Gilani local troops wore the black clothes of the Gilaki infantry (*lebas-e piyadegan-e gilak-e siyah-push*).[834]

According to Schiller, in 1702, the common soldiers had a tall cap on their head, almost like a German animal-skin hat, or a Hussar hat, which at the bottom had a wide rim. On top, it was rather pointed. The subaltern officers, however, wore an tin-iron helmet (*pickel-hauben*), on top of which a small vane was stuck, which could turn into all directions just like

---

830 Le Bruyn, vol. 1, p. 159.
831 Floor, *Bar Oftadan*, and Ibid., *Afghan Occupation*, chapters 1-3. Persia wants "neither men nor money; but their soldiers were undisciplined, and, above all, they had no officers of sufficient abilities to command them." Bell, p. 304.
832 Kaempfer, *Am Hofe*, pp. 75-6; see also Chardin, vol. 5, p. 312 and Richard, vol. 2, p. 287.
833 Savory, *History*, vol. 2, p. 1056.
834 Natanzi, p. 543.

the weathervanes on the roofs in Europe. The officers had a tanned tiger, panther or lion head skin stretched around their iron helmet, so that they might appear even more formidable to their enemies.[835] "On top of the helmet they have a number of feathers embellished with silver, gold and precious stones or other jewelry. All soldiers in general, officers and musketeers, wear a short coat, fastened in front or on the side, which does not reach the calf. Over this they wear a sabre, quiver and bow or bandoleer and powder flask, so that they are not hindered by their clothes. All cavalry and officers who are permitted to have a horse wear boots, mostly from red leather; the other soldiers have shoes without heels. The officers have a round shield on their left arm which should stop a bullet. The shah's life-guards are armed with axes. The musketeers [are armed] with muskets like European [soldiers]. Further, all soldiers wear rather heavy swords and have no knowledge about a long thrust sabre. The king's pages, cavaliers, khans or court-Turks wear special turbans. From [this turban] protrudes in front a silver or golden small tube with a silver or golden button. This button, which is often costly embellished with pearls and jewelry, is flanked by other tubes on both sides in which fluttering feathers have been stuck."[836]

Armor: The armor of the regular army consisted of a helmet, coat of mail, body, arm and leg protectors. Under the coat of mail a thick padded jerkin or garment was worn, which was thick enough to resist a sword cut. Armor was also worn by horses.[837] A contemporary description summarizes how a leading Persian officer was equipped. "A well set-up Moor armed with chain-mail which reached down to his knees, girdled with a sash of blue and gold; on his head he had an octagonal morion of blue and gold which could be clearly seen despite the turban that was twined around it; he carried a shield inlaid with golden flowered-work, and a scymetar garnished with overgilded silver in a scabbard of green velvet."[838] As far as I know, there does not, as yet, exist a careful description or an analysis of the body armor and arms in the various musea that hold such items. Therefore, this description is solely based on literary sources.

---

[835] Andersen observed a Qezelbash horseman in his body-armor and with a tiger skin on his back. Andersen, p. 160. See for picture of soldier, with tiger head ornament and military dress, Welch, *A King's Book of Kings.* The Shah-nameh of Shah Tahmasp (New York 1972 [1976]), pp. 144 (fig. 110), 146 [detail], 148 (fig. 120), 161 (fig. 294).

[836] Schillinger, pp. 194-6 (drawing on p. 194 and 196). Welch, *A King's Book,* also has a picture of a soldier, fig 110, p. 146.

[837] For pictures of helmets and cuirasses [*chahar a'ineh*] see Yahya Dhoka, *Artesh-e Shahenshahi-ye Iran az Kurosh ta Pahlavi* (Tehran 1350/1971), p. 189ff.; and Rumanowski Dubencha, "Tarikhcheh-ye asleheh-ye sard dar Iran", *BT* 2/3-4, pp. 263-280; *BT* 2/5-6, pp. 77-100, 89-112.

[838] C.R. Boxer, p. 74; see also p.135.

Helmet: The *kolah-e khod* or iron helmet, also called *tas,* was of thin steel plate,[839] or of brass[840] and was strong.[841] The Venetians commented that the Persians had helmets like those of the Mamluks.[842] The helmet was of two kinds. One which offered no protection of the neck and the other that did by means of a chain-mail curtain. There were many soldiers who wore a helmet, but not all of them.[843] Many soldiers either wore the *taj* or sufi head-dress under their helmet or had another head-cover under it, made of felt or raw silk in 7 layers. Those who wore the 12 folded *taj* believed that when they died this would send them to heaven directly; others wore a chainmail protected helmet as did the cavalry.[844] The helmets were embellished with embossed gold or copper on which a prayer or some other text was written. On top of the helmet was a spear-like point. Here the soldiers fastened a small piece of cloth so that foe and friend could recognize one another. On both sides of the helmet there were two small tubes in which colorful feathers were put.[845] Qezelbash soldiers also wore crane feathers at the back of their helmet. In front of the helmet there was a nose-face protector to withstand sword cuts, while the entire neck and face was protected by a mail curtain,[846] or on both sides broad brass ear protectors were worn.[847]

Mail-shirt or Zereh: The early Safavid tribal troops were badly armed and equipped. The opposing force, Elvand Mirza's army, was metal-clad or *pulad-push,* while that of Esma'il I was without armor or *bi-jabbeh.*[848] The other enemy, the Ottomans were armor-clad or *jabbeh-push.*[849] However, that soon changed. Soon part of Esma'il's I army also consisted of "armed men on big horses, well-ordered and all those arms have been supplied by those of Uzun Hasan."[850] This situation continued, for the Venetian reports continue to confirm that Esma'il's army, both the horse and its rider wore mail.[851] Tenreiro, in 1523, saw Esma'il I's troops with a

---

839 Don Juan, pp. 50-51.
840 Andersen, p. 160.
841 Minadoi, p. 73; "they also have helmets or head-pieces of great weight of metal." *Travels to Tana,* part 2, p. 115.
842 *Travels to Tana,* part 2, p. 207.
843 Carmelites, vol. 1, p. 53.
844 Berchet, p. 288 (1578-1582 period). For a picture of a *taj* worn by the shah and the nobles see Welch, *A King's Book,* p. 154 (fig. 225).
845 Andersen, p. 160; the king of Hormuz wore a helmet "encircled with a crown of smelted gold, studded with many precious stones." Boxer, p. 135.
846 Dhoka, p. 191.
847 Andersen, p. 160. For pictures of helmeted soldiers see Welch, *A King's Book,* pp. 136, 137, 147.
848 Rumlu, p. 82.
849 Rumlu, p. 200; *jushan-push* (mailed) *va khanjar godhar* (dagger carrying). Rumlu, p. 89.
850 Amoretti, p. 23.
851 Amoretti, pp. 34, 74, 105, 124.

coat of mail, made of very fine steel, which fell transversely upon the thigh when riding.[852] Under Tahmasp I the soldiers "do not wear anything but cuirassines and coats of mail."[853] For defense they wore shirts of mail, some of them cuirasses after our style, the Carmelites reported.[854]

The coat of mail or *zereh* consisted of a network of metal or small iron rings. "Their harness is very strong, bound with cotton; sometimes it is of the fine steel of Siras, and sometimes of copper, but not like ours, but all in pieces like that of Soria."[855] To reduce irritation of the skin the coat of mail was worn over by a piece of quilted cloth made of raw silk which was known as *kazhaghand*, which usually referred to a kind of thick quilted jerkin worn in battle instead of armor. Zeno observed that "some [are] covered with strong, thick hides, able to save the wearer from any heavy blow. Others were clothed in fine silk with doublets quilted so thickly that they could not be pierced by arrows."[856] The coat of mail reached from the shoulders till the knees. Sometimes it was like a half-dress (*nim-taneh*) on which iron studs were fastened in front and short sleeves. One other piece of dress was the so-called *baktar* and *khoftan*, which was a generic term, which referred to body armor in general, whether of the *zereh* or the other thick quilted types.[857] More in particular, it may have referred to fish-scale armor.[858] The best coats of mail were known as Da'udi.[859] Therefore, Da'udi coats of chain mail, and muskets decorated with jewels, were among presents given to emperor Homayun by Tahmasp I.[860] Safavid soldiers wore good corselets, "many of them able to keepe out an Arcebusse shot, much more to daunt the force of a Darte."[861] According to Pincon, Sherley's secretary, "Many of the coats of mail which they wear are brought to them from Moscovy."[862] Pincon's other statement that "They have no corselets nor cuirasses"[863] clearly is also wrong.

Breast-plates or Chahar a'ineh: To protect themselves from being

852 Smith, R.B. *The First Age* (Bethesda 1970), p. 75.
853 Membré, p. 35. Hamzah Mirza wore a jerkin and armor. Savory, *History* vol. 1, p. 450.
854 Carmelites, vol. 1, p. 53. For a description of the armor worn under Uzun Hasan, *Travels to Tana*, part 1, p. 66.
855 *Travels to Tana*, part 2, p. 207.
856 *Travels to Tana*, part 2, p. 16. The short cuirasses worn by the Persian soldiers "stop arrows and arquebuse shots." Carmelites, vol. 1, p. 287.
857 Rumlu, p. 209; Valeh Esfahani, p. 777; Afshar, *'Alamara-ye Tahmasp*, pp. 137, 143; Montazer-Saheb, p. 153.
858 'Allami, vol. 1, p. 118, plate xii, no. 44.
859 Dhoka, pp. 191-3.
860 Savory, *History*, vol. 1, p. 164.
861 Minadoi, p. 73.
862 Sherley, p. 163.
863 Sherley, p. 163; see also Don Juan, p. 50.

pierced by a lance the soldiers also protected their body with four (in the 17th century with five) square plates of thick Damascened steel, made to fit back, breast and sides. These were held in place with leather straps and metal buckles and were known as *chahar a'ineh*. Like the helmet, the body protectors also were gold and silver embossed, inlaid and embellished with prayers, poems, etc.[864] Some of the fine suits of armor, made at Shiraz, were "quite master-pieces, like mirrors, with gilt borders wonderfully polished and a marvel to behold."[865] In a recent publication these breast-plates and other pieces of body armor are described as follows. "They are of damascened steel (sometimes called 'watered' steel) with a design carried out in 'false damascening' (*kuftgari* or *talakubi*) a process by which the design is either built up from fine gold wire hammered on to a hatched surface, or inlaid."[866]

Vambrace or Bazu-band: To protect their arms from sword cuts and other damage soldiers wore vambraces or arm protectors which were known as *bazu-band* or *zand-band*. These reached from the elbow to the wrist, while the hands were protected by chain-mail. The arm protectors were fastened with leather straps and buckles, and were also embossed and embellished as the helmet and body protectors.[867] They wore armor on the right arm, as did the light cavalry for safety, when employing the sword.[868]

Belt or Kamar-band: Over the coat of mail a thick leather belt was worn with gold embossed metal rings. Sometimes these were adorned with small boxes in which small Qorans in *ghobar* (minute) script were kept. Knives and other military equipment hang from this belt over which sometimes the shawl shash was knotted in which they kept their dagger.[869] Soldiers also carried a *taqvim* or almanac on their breast which they consulted at all occasions to know the conjunction of the planets.[870]

Greaves or Zanu-band: To protect their knees and legs soldiers wore metal greaves referred to as *zanu-band* or *saq-band*. They protected the front of the leg and were fastened at the back with leather straps.

---

[864] Dhoka, p. 193; Montazer-Saheb, p. 153. " Their armour consists of cuirasses of gilt plates made of the finest steel of Syras." *Travels to Tana*, part 2, p. 115, also pp. 16-7, 207; Mervi, pp. 97, 394, 489f.; Boxer, p. 135; for a picture see *Persian Art*. An illustrated souvenir of the exhibition of Persian art at Burlington House (London 1931), p. 26.

[865] *Travels to Tana*, part 2, p. 91.

[866] Elwell-Sutton, L.P., "Persian armour inscriptions", in Robert Elgood ed. *Islamic Arms and Armour* (London 1979), pp. 5-19; Zdzislaw Zygulski Jr. "Islamic weapons in Polish collections and their provenance", in Elgood, pp. 213-38 which has various pictures of Persian armor, including that of Shah Soleiman.

[867] Dhoka, p. 193; Elwell-Sutton, pp. 5-19; Welch, *A King's Book*, p. 167 has a miniature with combattants with a *bazuband*.

[868] Carmelites, vol. 1, p. 53.

[869] Dhoka, p. 193.

[870] della Valle, p. 30.

Sometimes the *saq-band*s were gold embossed.[871]

Horse Mail or Bar gostvan: Many of the cavalry horses wore also armor (*bar gostvan*). Zeno observed that "their horses [are] armed after the manner in Italy," while Angiolello writes that "their horse-armour is of copper: not like ours, but in pieces like those of Soria [Syria]."[872] Horses were protected with plates which covered their body, head, breast and neck.[873] The horses also were covered "with good silk covers such that an arrow cannot go through them."[874] However, d'Allessandri states that "The horses have armour, but of plates so thin that arrows pierce them, and with it their head, breast and crupper are covered: there are 10 percent of them like these."[875] In 1650, Andersen observes that a Qezelbash's horse was protected by a leather deck covered with square metal pieces.[876] Normally, riders wore a bag at the back of their saddle with food, and a second bag, one ell long, to keep the horse's fodder. Also, a noose with a nail to tether the horse when dismounted.[877] The horses' fodder consisted of barley only, because there were no oats, which was sometimes mixed with cut-straw.[878]

European observers considered Persian horses to be very good and agile. Cartwright states that "They are wonderfull swift in course, fierce in battell, long breathed and very docile."[879] The Persian horses had great staying power. "They can go thirty hours without a feed of corn, and in skirmishing raids they will travel for a whole day and a night..... the cavalry ride with the short stirrup."[880] A horse's value was about 1,000-1,300 ducats.[881] Horses cost 1,000-2,000 ducats around 1580.[882] "I have seen them sold for a thousand, and sometimes a thousand and six-

---

[871] See picture of total armor, Dhoka, p. 194.

[872] *Travels to Tana*, part 2, pp. 16, 115.

[873] Berchet, p. 288; Montazar-Saheb, p. 550.

[874] Membré, p. 14. For a picture see Dickson and Welch, vol. 1, p. 105, plate 12.

[875] Carmelites, vol. 1, p. 53, n. 2.

[876] Andersen, p. 160. For a picture of mailed horses see Welch, *Kings Book*, p. 136 (fig. 102), 165 (fig. 341); Ibid. , *Persian Painting. Five Royal Safavid Manuscripts of the Sixteenth Century* (New York 1976), pp. 60 (fig. 40), 108 (fig. 39). Basil Gray, *La Peinture Persane* (Geneve 1961 [1977]) [tr. from English], p. 128 has a battle scene with chain-mailed horses and soldiers, see also pp. 134-5, incl. music and banners on p. 135.

[877] Andersen, p. 149.

[878] Andersen, p. 161. Horses were given straw softened by a sledge used to tread out corn, which was good fodder. "There is no hay in Persia; and the best horses are kept in condition for any service by this food, and a small quantity of dried barley, twice a-day". Bell, pp. 307-08.

[879] Purchas, vol. 8, pp. 514-5.

[880] Don Juan, p. 50; see also Andersen, p. 161 on the quality and thus the price of Persian horses as compared with the Indian horses. For the saddle see Zygulski, pp. 213-38.

[881] Amoretti, pp. 34, 74, 105, 124, 141, 283, 405-6; Minadoi, p. 73; Smith, p. 75.

[882] Berchet, p. 288.

hundred Duckets a piece."[883] Consequently, foreigners, whether Indians, Portuguese, Dutch or English tried to export Persian horses, especially to India. The Dutch and English tried likewise to continue this trade, which was carried out under royal privilege. However, neither the Dutch nor the English were able to obtain the right to the unchecked export of horses. They only were allowed to export some 10 horses per year as a special grant, and there was no change in this situation during the entire Safavid period.

Arms

As to the main body of cavalry, "They generally fight on horseback, with spear and shield, bows, arrows, scimitars, coats of mail, and maces; and ride with short stirrups, and with their horses caparisoned. In warfare they are formidable, and very dogged therein."[884] Thus, Safavid soldiers were mostly armed with scimitar, lance, and javelin, but especially the scimitar in the 16th century.[885] Persian sources report the same type of armament. The army was armed with the *kaman* (bow), the *takhsh-andaz* (cross-bow), *gorz* (mace), spear (*senan*), sword (*shamshir*), dagger (*khanjar*) and the *tofang* (arquebus).[886] By the 1670s, they still fought with sword, dagger, lance and ax, but were also skilled in the use of pistol and guns.[887] They fought on horseback, and wore a shield, helmet, and mail dress. Some regiments had a musket, and served on foot; but en route they were on horse back.[888] We start with a description of the arms used for fighting at closer quarter (sword, shield, mace, ax, dagger, and spear) followed by those for fighting at a distance (bow, arquebus, pistol, and artillery).

Sword: Persian swords (*shamshir*) were very sharp. "Swords have only one edge, the guard is simply a cross, the blade is usually damasked. The sheaths are shagreen of either black or red colour, the extremity like the hilt damasked after the Persian manner; the belt, narrow and very handsome, is of the natural colour of the doe-skin of which it is made."[889] Their swords afford them no small delight, the blades being exceeding good and the hilts no less valuable, for with the better sort usually they are

---

883 Purchas. vol. 8, pp. 514-5.
884 Texeira, *The Travels*, p. 251. For miniatures with battle scenes and accoutre-ments of the soldiers and horse see Welch, *A King's Book*, p. 136 (fig. 102); Ibid, *Persian Painting*, p. 60 (fig. 40); Gray, p. 128; R. Hillenbrand, *Imperial Images in Persian Painting* (Edinburgh 1977), p. 66 (fig. 147).
885 Minadoi, p. 73; Berchet, p. 288.
886 Rumlu, p. 468; Natanzi, pp. 294, 363, 401, 504; Herbert, p. 243; Berchet, p. 288; Olearius, p. 666.
887 Fryer, vol. 3, p. 57.
888 Chardin, vol. 5, pp. 299-302.
889 Della Valle, p. 42. For a picture and description see Valadimir Loukonine & Anatoli Ivanov, *Lost Treasures of Persia – Persian Art in the Hermitage Museum* (Washington DC 1996), nr. 201, 216.

of gold, according to Herbert.[890]

Persian swords were much more curved than the Ottoman ones.[891] "Their swords (shamsheers they call them) are not straight as ours be, but more hooked and bending than our falchions; of pure metal, broad and sharp as any razor; nor do they value them, unless, if the arm be good, at one blow they can cut in two an asinego."[892] According to Molla Jalal an European ambassador praised European swords; however, when a test was done by beheading sheep, Persian swords proved to be better.[893] Chardin also found Persian swords better. "Cimiters are very well Damask'd, and exceed all that the Europeans can do, because I suppose our Steel is not so full of Veins as the Indian Steel, which they use most commonly."[894] In fact, Chardin states that "The Gunsmiths make very good Weapons, especially Bows and Swords.[895] Nevertheless, the EIC gave six sword blades to Khalilollah Khan.[896]

In 1565, Mestre Afonso mentioned the fame of swords made in Qom.[897] Nevertheless, foreign swords, or swords modeled after foreign imports, were considered to be better. The *qurchi*s had Egyptian swords, for example.[898] Swords also were imported from Afghanistan and India.[899] Even in the beginning of the 19th century swords were made in Shiraz using Indian steel, "purchased in cakes at Hydrabad.'[900] Swords made from India steel were known as *mohendeh* and may also have been known as *akbari* steel.[901] These swords were above all appreciated because of their 'water'. For example, swords made of *akbari* steel had water that could be traced on the blade, "like a skein of silk, down the entire length of the blade. Had this water been interrupted by a curve or cross, the sword would have been comparatively valueless." The type of 'water' also made a difference. The type known as *begumi* had lines that did not run straight down, but waved like a watered silk fabric. A so-called black Khorasani sword was of the water known as *bidr*. This had neither straight nor

---

[890] Herbert, pp. 60-1.

[891] Della Valle, vol. 7, p. 42.

[892] Herbert, p. 234.

[893] Molla Jalal, p. 234.

[894] John Chardin, pp. 270-1. For the process see Richard, vol. 2, pp. 120-1. These damascened arquebuses were known as *tofang-e jouhardar*. Monshi, p. 99.

[895] John Chardin, p. 270-1.

[896] Foster, 1651-54, p. 173.

[897] Neves Aguas, p. 158.

[898] Savory, *History*, vol. 1, p. 91. Khvandamir, vol. 4, p. 505 already mentions *shamshirha-ye modhahhab-e mesri*.

[899] Dhoka, p. 196; Richard, vol. 2, p. 120 mentions the import of Indian steel to make swords.

[900] Waring, p. 47.

[901] Nasiri, *Dastur*, p. 341; Alexander Burnes, *Cabool, a Personal Narrative of a Journey To, And Residence In That City in the Years 1836,7, and 8* (London 1841 [Karachi 1986]), p. 111.

waving lines, but was mottled with dark spots. "One test of the genuiness of a sword is that it can be written upon with gold; others, more certain, are its cutting through a large bone, and severing a silk handkerchief when thrown into the air."[902]

The sword handles were made of bone, jasper, or antler.[903] The head of the handle or *kolahak*, also had a guard or *qolchaq* made of iron or embossed metal. On the blade usually the name of the maker or suitable poems or prayers were written.[904] "The hilts were without wards, being of gold, silver, horn, ivory, ebony, steel, or wood; sometimes of the ribzuba, or morse's teeth, usually taken at Pochora [Petchora] in Russia."[905]

Scabbards were made of metal or wood with a leather covering of black of green *sagheri* with gold bosses. It was worn with a warband on the right hand side.[906] Under Esma'il I, soldiers girded themselves "with some folded sword belts of slender leather, worked in iron, in which they wear their sword with a sharp edge, four spans in length."[907] Under 'Abbas I, "Their scabbards are of camel's hide, on solemn days covered with velvet embroidered with gold and stones of price."[908]

Shield: There were two kinds of shields: [a] small shields to parry sword cuts and [b] large shields to provide protection against sword, lance, and mace. Especially the latter was used. The shield or *separ*, was usually made of buffalo or rhinoceros skin, and sometimes of steel. Its was round in shape and embellished with nails, which also served to strengthen it. The armor was made in one piece and therefore the same embossed and embellished patterns were used on all parts. The shield was held with a leather strap on the forearm, and when not used was hung on the back.[909]

Mace: The Persian soldiers were armed with amongst other things a mace (*gorz*).[910] The mace is famous throughout Persian history. It came in many forms: conical, with spikes, and protruded into a hephtagonal (*hasht*

---

[902] Burnes, p. 111.

[903] Dhoka, p. 197.

[904] Dhoka, p. 197 with pictures of swords hilts. For various pictures of Persian swords and inscriptions see Zygulski, pp. 213-38; Yuri A. Miller, "Iranian swords of the seventeenth century with Russian inscriptions in the collection of the State Hermitage Museum", in Elgood, pp. 136-48.

[905] Herbert, p. 234 (*riba-zub* is Russian for fish-tooth).

[906] Dhoka, p. 197.

[907] Smith, p. 75.

[908] Herbert, p. 235.

[909] Dhoka, p. 200; *Travels to Tana*, part 2, p. 17; for pictures of shields see Zygulski, pp. 213-38; Welch, *A King's Book*, p. 136 (fig. 102); *Persian Art.* An illustrated souvenir of the exhibition of Persian art at Burlington House (London 1931), p. 27; The king of Hormuz allegedly had a steel shield. Boxer, p. 135. For a picture and description see Valadimir Loukonine & Anatoli Ivanov, *Lost Treasures of Persia – Persian Art in the Hermitage Museum* (Washington DC 1996), nr. 200.

[910] Rumlu, p. 468; *Travels to Tana*, part 2, p.

par) globe or sphere at the end. A leather strap permitted the user not to loose it while braining, bruising or battering someone.[911] The mace was also refered to by the term *tupuz*.[912] The mace was still in use in the 1007/1598 Khorasan campaign against the Uzbegs.[913] Andersen in 1649 observed a Persian soldier with a regiment's staff in his hand, which have been a mace.[914]

Battle-ax: The battle-ax or *tabar-zin* was also used, mostly by the royal body-guard, in particular the sufi-guards and royal *rikas* down to the end of the Safavid period.[915] Whether the same or similar weapons, but battle-axes known as *najaq*[916] and *tupuz*[917] also were used.

Daggers: Every self-respecting Safavid male wore a knife outside the house and soldiers also had daggers or *khanjar*. These short arms were indeed used in battle.[918] There were two kinds of daggers, to wit: Kurdish and Indian. The Kurdish dagger had a half-moon and grooved shape and was small. The Indian dagger was larger with a straight blade and a conical handle. Both the knife and dagger were embossed and embellished on both handle and blade and were worn in the sash. The scabbard was made of braided material (*qeitan*) and gold brocade (*zarbaft*).[919]

Poniard: Soldiers also used the poniard, the double-edged so-called *qammeh* or *qaddareh*. It was typical for those soldiers originating from the Caucasus (Cherkes, Georgian, Armenian) where also the best poniards were made. The scabbard was of metal and only embellished on one side with braided silver and/or gold thread. The handle was usually of bone, sometimes of jasper.[920]

Spear/Lance: Soldiers were armed with a lance.[921] The spear or lance was referred to by terms such as *neizeh* and *senan*. Not much has been written about them. We know that the cavalry used a lance which was not longer than five ells long.[922] The spears could be quite heavy such as a

---

[911] Dhoka, p. 200.
[912] Montazer-Saheb, pp. 154, 233.
[913] Adle, p. 471.
[914] Andersen, p. 160. For pictures of maces see Zygulski, pp. 213-38.
[915] Montazer-Saheb, pp. 384, 409. For pictures and detailed discussion see A.S. Melikian-Chirvani, "The tabarzins of Lotf'ali", in Elgood, pp. 117-35; also Zygulski, pp. 213-38; Welch, *Persian Painting*, p. 58 (fig. 13); Loukonine & Ivanov, nr. 248.
[916] Mervi, pp. 44, 130, 606.
[917] Mervi, p. 127.
[918] Rumlu, p. 468; Adle, p. 473; Mervi, pp. 144, 185, 229, 470; Welch, *A King's Book*, p. 146.
[919] Dhoka, p. 198. A. Ivanov, "A group of Iranian daggers of the period from the fifteenth century to the beginning of the seventeenth with Persian inscriptions", in Elgood, pp. 64-77; see also Loukonine & Ivanov, nrs. 165, 179, 220, 249, 250-1.
[920] Dhoka, pp. 198-200; Loukonine & Ivanov, nr. 180.
[921] Don Juan, p. 50.
[922] Berchet, p. 288. For miniatures see Welch, *A King's Book*, p. 136 (fig. 102);

silver spear weighing four *mann*, which may have been more for show and ceremony than for real use.[923] Often spears were painted.[924]

Sling: The sling or *sang-e qollab* is also mentioned as being in use by Safavid cavalry.[925]

Bow: "The Mahomentans delight much in archery" and took great pride in it.[926] They therefore seldom rode without bow and arrows, and, albeit some think incomparable in execution to a gun, yet time has been they have with that in many parts of Asia obtained memorable victories.[927] Ideally, bows were made of *khadang* wood, but, generally they were made of plane tree wood or *chub-e channar*, mixed with horn and tree bark, and with sinews bound around them.[928] The Persian bow or *kaman* was short but strong, painted and varnished. "Their Bows are shorter than our, not made of Wood, but glutinated Horn, which being not so long, makes them more servicable on Horseback; but being made of Horn, they are less fit for Rainy Weather."[929]

"The Persian Bows are the most valued of all the East: The Matter whereof they are made is Wood and Horn laid over one another, and cover'd over with Sinews, and over that with the Skin of a Tree very sleek and smooth; the Paint them afterwards, and Varnish them so admirably well, that one may see one's self in those Bows, and the colour of them is a bright as possible. The Goodness of a Bow, as the Persians say, consists in this, viz. That a Bow be hard to bend till the Arrow be half laid over it, and then that it be soft and easy, till the end of the Arrow be fixed in the String: The Bow-strings are of twisted Silk of the bigness of a first Quill."[930]

The bow was kept in a leather quiver (*tarkesh*), either worn aside or at the back, with many shafts.[931] The quiver and case were often wrought

---

Ibid. *Persian Painting*, p. 60 (fig. 40); Gray, p. 128.

923 Natanzi, p. 506. There were also iron lances or *neizeh-ye fuladi*. Afshar, '*Alamara-ye Tahmasp*, p. 220.

924 Membré, p. 30. For a picture of a soldier with a lance or *neizeh* see Dhoka, p. 187 (plate 122).

925 *Travels to Tana*, part 2, p. 207.

926 Herbert, p. 60.

927 Herbert, p. 235.

928 Bacqué-Grammont, *Les Ottomans*, p. 125, n. 511; Richard, vol. 2, p. 154.

929 Fryer, vol. 1, pp. 336, 349; Herbert, p. 235. For a discussion of the use of the bow as a weapon see J.D. Latham and W.F. Paterson, "Archery in the lands of Eastern Islam", in Elgood, pp. 78-87.

930 John Chardin, pp. 270-1. how the bow was carried see Welch, fig. 225, p. 152, 146. For more historical background see Purdavud, "Zein abzar - kaman va tir", *BT* 2, pp. 29-46; Abu'l-Qasem Jennati 'Ata'i, "Kamandari va tirandazi dar adabiyat-e farsi", *BT* 5/1, pp. 113-35; BT 6/2, pp. 242-76.

931 Dhoka, p. 195; *Travels to Tana*, part 2, p. 207. For miniatures see Gray, p. 128, 134; Welch, *A King's Book*, pp. 110 (fig. 30); Ibid., *Persian Painting*, p. 51 (fig. 9), 58 (fig. 13).

and cut very artificially.[932] These quiver coverings also could have another use. At one occasion, when Homayun found that, when he alighted from his horse to pay his respects to Tahmasp I, there was no place for him to sit, because Tahmasp I sat on a very small carpet. One Moghul attendant, "having cut off the cover of his quiver, spread it for His Majesty to sit on."[933] The expensive quivers were made of gold or silk embroidered leather.[934]

The arrows or *tir*, made by *tirgar*s, were long and well-headed and made of rattan reed (*kheizoran*) and had a sharp metal point, though sometimes gold embossed ones also were made.[935] The arrows were dangerous projectiles, because they were able to pierce protective armor.[936] Arrows for target practice were not equipped with sharp point, but with blunted iron tips.[937] In general, the war arrows were painted.[938] Important commanders and famous soldiers carved their names on the arrows to claim the kill of an important enemy, if it so happened that their arrow had the required effect.[939] In one case seven combattants claimed to have killed the enemy's champion, which after examination proved to be true. In the end it did not make a difference for all claimants had already the rank of khan.[940] The names were also written on arrows for divining purposes (*zalmun*), though this explicitly forbidden in the Qoran. In 1544, Homayun had some acrimonious words with Tahmasp I when the subject came up of Homayun having marked 12 of his best arrows and 11 inferior arrows with Tahmasp's name.[941]

To protect their thumb Persian archers used a *zeh-gir* or bow-string holder, and "on their thumb commonly wear a ring of horn, which makes the arrow go off both strongly and easily."[942] They drew their bows with the thumb armed with a horn ring, which was a method "not after the same manner as our Archers do."[943] The ring or *zeh-gir* was usually made of agate, jasper or marble.[944]

---

932 Herbert, p. 235.

933 Jouher, p 72.

934 John Chardin, pp. 270-1.

935 Herbert, p. 235; Richard, vol. 2, p. 154 "long as a water pump-handle". Dhoka, p. 195.

936 Savory, *History*, vol. 1, p. 89; Monshi, vol. 1, p. 54.

937 Richard, vol. 2, p. 154.

938 Shirley, p. 153.

939 Savory, *History*, vol. 2, p. 942; Monshi, vol. 2, p. 750.

940 Mar'ashi, *Tarikh-e Khandan*, p. 242. For another case where blood-money was claimed based on the identification of the owner of the arrow see Savory, *History*, vol. 2, p. 942; Monshi, vol. 2, p. 750.

941 Jouher, p. 69.

942 Herbert, p. 60. The string was also referred to as *chelleh*. Richard, vol. 2, p. 154.

943 Fryer, vol. 3, p. 57; Ibid., vol. 1, p. 336, and vol. 2, p. 60.

944 Dhoka, p. 195; *Travels to Tana*, part 1, p. 56; for picture see Loukonine &

Cross-bow: The cross-bow (*takhsh-andaz* or *navak-andaz*) is also mentioned among the military hardware used by Persian troops throughout the 16th century.[945] "They also had a certain kind of crossbow, made like bows of horn, but made on purpose stronger than those which are drawn by hand, and have a handle, with a contrivance like ours for bending them, and are without nuts, but instead of them they have a bit of iron. Their bolts are long, about half the length of an arrow, and slender; they are feathered, and have points like the Turkish arrows, and go a great distance. Of these crossbows there were about twenty in one of the castles."[946]

Arquebuses and Match-locks: The first guns were the match-locks, which, during the last quarter of the 15th century were considerably improved through the introduction of the snap matchlock, and later by another improvement which led to its large scale military use. The new, cheap and easy to make matchlock consisted of "a long sear lever pivoted vertically inside the lockplate under pressure of a mainspring. To one of this was linked the serpentine or match-holder and on the other end was an extension lever which served as a trigger." From the beginning of the 16th century the match-lock co-existed with the wheel-lock and later the snaphaunce. But because of its simplicity and easiness of operation the matchlock continued to be the main military application of ignition systems. The earliest term for these guns was arquebus. The musket, bastard musket (short barreled form of musket) and the caliver all appeared during the later half of the 16th century. The musket was the largest gun, and needed the aid of a forked rest when fired. The true flint-lock was developed in the 17th century and superseded the matchlock at the end of the 17th century.[947]

The Safavids used two types of guns: the match-lock (fuse) or *fatileh*, and fire-flint or *chakhmaq* guns. The matchlocks were equipped with rifling (*khan*) and muzzle (*sarpar*), and used pellets or shot (*sachmeh*). The flint guns required the use of a piece of cotton to relay the flame. This cotton wad was called *qu* (*gou*), which after having been soaked in ash-water, was dried and kept by the soldiers in a small box called *qulaq*.[948] Persian guns, of course not those handled by the common musketeers, were heavily decorated, embossed and inlaid, and even decorated with jewels, such as those given as a present to Homayun.[949] Arquebuses made of fine patterned steel were known as *tofang-e jouhardar*, while European

---

Ivanov, nr. 178.

[945] Natanzi, p. 294; Adle, pp. 476-7.

[946] *Travels to Tana*, part 2, p. 153.

[947] De Witt Bailey et alii. *Guns & Gun Collecting.* London 1972, pp. 10-11. [Ian Hogg, Geoffrey Boothroyd, Frederick Wilkinson).

[948] Dhoka, p. 204. with pictures pp. 202-5.

[949] Savory, *History*, vol. 1, p. 164. and the *tofang-e khass* which 'Abbas II presented to the Indian ambassador. Vahid Qazvini, p. 85, see also p. 205.

arquebuses were referred to as *tofang-e ferangi*.[950]

The arquebus, and later improvements, was called *tofak*, an onomatopoeic, formed from the sound "*tof*" and the suffix "*ak*". The term tof refers to the sound of air being forcibly expelled from the mouth by blowing pellets out of a tube. The term *tofak* refers to a wooden tube or blow-pipe, the length of a spear which was used to shoot clay pellets at small birds. The term *tofak* turned into *tofang* in the 16th century, though the term *tofak* also continued to be used. The term *tofang* is the result of the Persian habit of adding the sound "n" before "k", which also had the effect of turning the "k" into a "g" sound. The same phenomenon occurred, for example, with the equally onomatopoeic term *feshak* (from the sound *fesh* made by the burning fuse or projectile) which became *feshang* (cartridge).[951] The arquebus also was termed *bunduq* (projectile) and its operator *bunduqchi*.[952] The guns used lead pellets or shot (*sachmeh*) as well as stones for bullets (*geluleh* or *galileh*).[953]

In 1618, the Persian army still did not have muskets with a springlock, for when della Valle showed Persian cavaliers his musket, they were much surprised by the rapidity and ease with which he operated his musket, and admitted that a man armed with such a musket would be a match for four times his number.[954] "The Persians do not make use of a Flint to their Guns, nor to strike Fire with. They have a Wood which serves them instead of Steel and Flint, and has the same Effect."[955] It is not exactly known when flintlock guns were introduced in Safavid Persia. By the end of the Safavid period they were in wide use and generally referred to, and in distinction to the *tofang*, as *dur-andaz* or *dur-andaz-e chakhmaq*.[956] To better aim their muskets the Persians used a tripod of 80 cm length which turned on a pivot. When they fired the gun was about 50 cm from the ground.[957] The *shamkhal* was a heavy gun that was carried by two men. It shot bullets of 25 mm. It had to be operated from a seated position. Therefore they were mostly used on the walls of fortresses and cities and barricades. The barrel, hammer, and flint of the *shakhmal* as of other guns was gold embossed, fretted, inlaid with *khatamkari* or with

---

[950] Monshi, vol. 1, p. 99; Ibid., vol. 2, p. 656. For minatures showing guns see Welch, *Persian Painting*, p. 108 (fig. 39); Hillenbrand, p. 66 (fig. 147).

[951] On the term *tofak* see Yahya Zoka, "The Tofang and its Antecedents in Iran", *BT* 1 (1971), pp. 53-59; Ahmad Kasravi, "Dar Peiramun-e Tofak", pp. 434-7, in *Karvand-e Kasravi*, ed. Yahya Dhoka (Tehran 1352/1973).

[952] Adle, p. 653; Savory, *History*, vol. 1, pp. 489-90.

[953] *'Alamara-ye Safavi*, ed. Yadollah Shokri, Tehran 1350/1971, pp. 88, 90.

[954] della Valle, p. 14.

[955] John Chardin, p. 164.

[956] Mervi, pp. 106, 118, 172, 194f. A *dur-andaz-e sha'ban* is also mentioned. Ibid. p. 668.

[957] Chardin, vol. 5, pp. 320-1.

mother-o'-pearl.[958]

In addition to the arquebus and flint-lock, soldiers carried with them all kinds of equipment to operate the guns such as *dabbeh-ye barut* (powder-horn), *qulaq, suzan* (pricker; firing needle), rod (*mileh*), *sonbehha-ye gunagun* (gun-stick), *sang-e chakhmaq* (flint stone), *vazneh-ye barut* (powder weight or -flask), *sachmeh-dan* (pellet sack) etc.[959]

Classification of 16th-17th guns is difficult, because contemporary writers do not use standardized terms to refer to them. However, in 1630 the standard sizes for English military long arms ranged from 3 feet overall for a arquebus and a petronel to 5 feet and 2 inches for a musket.[960] Persian arquebuses had a barrel of 6 to 7 spans long and carried a ball less than 3 ounces in weight, around 1580.[961] According to Sherley "harquebusiers which bare long pieces, half a foot longer than our muskets, slightly made, the bullet of the height of caliver [caliber] which they use well and certainly."[962] According to Herbert "their harquebus is longer than ours, but thinner; they use that very well, but detest the trouble of cannon and such pieces as require carriage."[963] However, according to della Valle the musketeers fought with "guns somewhat similar somewhat smaller than our muskets, with matchlocks, which have a fork fastened by a cord to the stock, by which, when they dismount, they have a rest to take aim by."[964] How well trained and used Persian troops were to arquebuses is clear from a contemporary report. "They use them [arquebuses] with such facility that it does not hinder them in drawing their bows, nor in handling their swords, keeping the latter hung at their saddle-bows till occasion requires them. The arquebus then is out away behind the back, so that one weapon does not impede the use of another."[965]

Not only did they handle guns well, "The Persians make also very well, the Barrels of Fire-Arms, and Damask them as they do the Blades, but they make them very heavy, and cannot avoid it: They bore and scower them with a Wheel, as we do, and forge and bore them so even that they almost never burst. They make them alike strong and thick all along, saying that the Mouth of the Gun being weak, the Report shakes it, and communicates the wavering Motion to carry the Shot further and straighter, the Soder the Breech of the Barrel with the heat of the Fire, and reject Screws, saying that a Screw Breech going in without Stress, may be thrust out by the Violence of the Powder, and is not to be rely'd on. They do not understand very well how to make Locks or Springs; those they put

---

958 Dhoka, p. 205.
959 Dhoka, pp. 205-6.
960 De Witt Bailey, p. 14.
961 Berchet, p. 181; *Travels to Tana*, part 2, p. 227.
962 Sherley, p. 232.
963 Herbert, p. 243.
964 Della Valle, vol. 7, p. 79.
965 *Travels to Tana*, part 2, p. 227.

to their Fire-Arms, are very unlike ours; for they have no Steel, the Pan is very fast, being all of a Piece with the Barrel, the which moves along a small rough Iron Branch, that comes out of the Inside of the Gun, and moves backward, that it toward the But-End, on the Pan, but quite contrary to it; the Pan is usually no bigger than the little Finger Nail, without Snap-haunce; and most Pans are rough within, like a File, that the Prime may stick the better to it. They do not understand how to Mount Fire-Arms, and do not observe the Rules of Staticks, but make the But-End small and light, which is the Reason that their Guns are light at the Breech, and heavy at the Muzzle."[966] The gunstocks, which were not fit for a man's shoulder, were made of juniper wood from the *ghiz* tree.[967]

The terminology to refer to the firing of modern arms ranged from *goshad kardan, shelik kardan, beh atesh, atesh dadan, atesh kardan* to simply *dadan*.[968] *Kamandari* to refer to firing is also extensively used.[969] This also resolves the meaning of puzzling terms such as *tofangchiyan-e kamandar* and *tupchiyan-e kamandar*.[970] Pistols were also used by Safavid officers who wore them in the belt.[971] They were also given as presents to dignitaries by foreign visitors.[972]

Cannon: The term *tup* is the generic name for cannon which shot a ball in a direct line.[973] There were several types of cannon, both small (*khord*) and big (*kalan*) cannon.

Large cannon: The large cannon was known by its generic term of *qal'eh-kub* or the fortress-smasher. This was either a large siege gun or a large mortar. It fired a projectile in a parabolic angle.[974] It was probably the same type of cannon referred to as *badlij* or *balmiz*.[975] The term *balmiz* is a bastardization of the Ottoman word *balyemaz* (meaning, he who does not eat honey), which itself is a turcization of the German word *faule metze*. The *badlij* was also used in siege operations.[976] The *balmiz* was a large cannon. For example, Barkhvordar Beg, the *tupchi-bashi*, was ordered to cast two heavy large cannon and one extraordinary heavy siege

---

966 John Chardin, pp. 270-1; according to du Mans the quality of work by the Persian gun-smiths or *qondaqgar* was not as good as that of his European counterpart. Richard, vol. 2, p. 160.
967 della Valle, p. 101.
968 Montazer-Saheb, pp. 74, 77, 79; Qomi, vol. 1, p. 182; Mervi, pp. 382, 724f.
969 Yusef, p. 150; Mervi, pp. 190, 358, 383f.
970 Vahid Qazvini, p. 232; Valeh Esfahani, p. 349.
971 Dhoka, p. 206; Mervi, p. 374.
972 Foster, 1651-54, p. 173.
973 As suggested by Adle, p. 546, this may be concluded from Monshi, vol. 2, p. 905; Savory, vol. 2, p. 1121.
974 Adle, p. 548.
975 Molla Jalal, p. 255 mentions the two types of cannon as separate types of ordinance. Mervi, pp. 85-6, 138, 215, 285 only mentions the *badlij*.
976 See article "Balyemez" in *EI-2*.

gun (*balyemaz*).[977] The biggest Persian cannon, known as *kalleh gush*, was of the *ra'd-khorush* type. It was used during the siege of Tabriz to fire (*kamandari*) at the battlements. Half of the tower was blown away by this cannon whose balls weighed 15 *mann*.[978] Don Juan, who was present at the siege, writes: "One of the best siege guns, a famous piece dating from the time of Shah Tahmasp I, which hurled a ball weighing fifteen *mann* (about 97.5 lbs.). During a sortie, its crew was dispersed, ropes were tied to its wheels and dragged into the fort." These cannon really made an impression, for Don Juan singled them out in his account of Persia. During the siege of the Ottoman fort in Tabriz in 1585 "two immense siege-guns were set in position, and these were of so huge a calibre as never before had been seen in Persia. These two cannon were of such a size that the bore of each at the mouth spanned a yard a cross, the length of the barrel being five yards."[979]

Usually, the *qal'eh-kub* cannons were of a smaller size. In 1051/1641, Morad Khan, the *tupchi-bashi*, hastened to Mashhad, there he cast (*andakht*) in a short time five cannon of the *bal-e namir* (?) type, each ball weiging 10 *mann-e* Tabriz and 12 *mann-e* Tabriz. Each cannon had a name, viz.: Emam, Aslan, Simin, Azhdha, Babrbiyan and Ilderim.[980] Another famous cannon was called *hrt* (?).[981] In 1057/1647, the *tupchi-bashi* was at Qandahar with two *tup-e* *qal'eh-kub* cannon known as Azhdha and Babrbiyan (probably the same ones as cast in 1641) under the command of Mohammad Beg and a group of European gunners.[982] These may have been the same cannon seen by Andersen, a German gunner, who had signed up for the Qandahar campaign. He wrote that he found in the Mashhad arsenal "five big metal cannon which had been cast in Mashad. I have never in my life seen such large metal [pieces]. The two largest ones shoot iron balls of 90 pounds; two smaller ones of 64 pounds and the fifth one [a ball] of 48 pounds of iron."[983] Usually, the cannon used in fortresses was of a smaller type. The cannon used in Bandar 'Abbas were able to shoot 8-12 lb. balls. Of the 8 cannon in the Persian fortress next to that of the Dutch had 8 pieces, one of which was a German heavy cannon.[984]

Whether small or large, all cannon were transported on carriages, called *'arabeh* or *'arradeh*. By 927/1521, Esma'il I had 100 of these carriages which each held two or three cannon, some of which were very

977 Savory, *History*, vol 2, p. 997.
978 Valeh Esfahani, p. 739.
979 Don Juan, pp. 188-9.
980 Shamlu, p. 258.
981 Esfahani, p. 215.
982 Shamlu, p. 352.
983 Andersen, p. 155.
984 Andersen, p. 71.

big.[985] Hasan Rumlu also mentions the use of *'arabeh* loaded with *zarbzan* and *zarb-e ferangi*.[986] The *'arabeh*s were hauled by oxen or buffaloes and were operated by *'arabehchi*s.[987] When an artillery battery moved it was accompanied by a number of specialists. For example, in 1044/1634-5, three pieces of cannon, of the *balmiz-e qal'eh-kub* type, were moved to Erivan, together with pioneers (*bildaran*), musketeers (*tofangchiyan*), carriage-makers (*'arradeh-sazan*) and foundry-men (*haddadan*).[988] It is likely that these specialists were responsible for, respectively, build a artillery platform and protective pallisades, provide protection against attacks and sorties, build, repair and move the gun-carriage or *'arradeh* on which the cannon rested, and to repair or recast the cannon in case of need. In 988/1580-1, a force was sent to Georgia accompanied by Morad Beg, the *tupchi-bashi*, with cannon founders and all materials for the casting of cannon.[989]

Small cannon: The *zarbzan* probably was the (light) field gun of the Persian army. The Ottomans also had them in various sizes, ranging from a small 962 gram/300 *derham* ball; a medium type of one *oqqa* or 1,28 kg and a big one of 2 *oqqa*s or 2,56 kg. There also existed a *zarbzan-e sheikha-ye bozorg* with a ball of 36 *oqqa*s or 46 kg.[990] Another kind of cannon was the *saf-puzan* which was in use at the end of the Safavid period.[991]

Casting of cannon: To make a cannon one needed (i) a mould (*tanureh*) which determined the size of the outside of the jacket; (ii) the core (*mil*), which was made of clay and was put in the center of the mould to make the barrel after its removal; and (iii) the breech (*sendan*), which closed the mould. The mould was the most important element for canon-casting. First a wooden form (*chub-e qaleb*) was made, which also allowed for the placement of the various projecting parts of the cannon, including the trunnions (*bazu*), the axis on which the cannon turned. Moulds were made in steps. First, a special clay was prepared. Then a furnace (*kureh*) was made of bricks with an opening below for feeding the fire and a hole on top. One end of the wooden form (*qaleb*) would be put in this hole of the furnace (*beh kureh bordeh*). The other end was fixed on a gallows-like structure, whose upright parts were fastened at each side of the furnace. The entire mould consisted of smaller moulds (*tanureh*) put on top of one another, their number being determined by the required length of the cannon. After the wooden

---

[985] Amoretti, pp. 469, 534, 546.
[986] Rumlu, pp. 214, 451; the word *'arabeh* is a bastardization of *arradeh*. See further the articles 'arabeh, arradeh, balyermez, and barud in *EI2*.
[987] Amoretti, p. 125; Andersen, pp. 154-5; Monshi, vol. 2, p. 620.
[988] Esfahani, p. 214.
[989] Savory, *History*, vol. 1, p. 390.
[990] Adle, p. 546; Mervi, pp. 261, 280f.
[991] Mervi, pp. 292, 563f.

mould had been consumed by the fire the small moulds were removed from the furnace. Now the actual mould was made by assembling the small moulds in a pit. The breech and the core were then put in place, while the mould was surrounded and reinforced by a brick sleeve. Then molten metal (100 parts copper, 10 parts tin, 8 parts brass) was poured in the ready-made mould. After a few days the spindle was taken out of the mould, and the cannon was ready for use. The breech was made by pouring molten metal in a sand mould, which had been formed through the use of a wooden form (*ruye sendan avardeh*). [992] The same mould appears to have been used many times. For example, the *tupchi-bashi* started casting cannons using the moulds which had been constructed at Bargoshat. [993] The barrel of the cannon had no sight, but it had been equipped with a *dastgireh* (handle), *mehvar* (axle), *magasak* (little fly), and *shekaf* (fuse hole). [994] The other way to cast a cannon, viz. in one piece rather using an assembly of smaller moulds, was also known in Iran, for around 1500, a young Armenian cast a mortar in the Turkish manner - all in one piece. [995]

Despite the regular use of modern artillery the Persians were never very good at its manufacturing. During siege of citadel of Tabriz [in 1585] it "had taken two months to assemble the necessary materials and personnel. Because of the severe cold and the lack of sunshine the mold did not set properly and retained some moisture. When the molten brass was taken from the furnace and poured into the mold, it boiled up over the sides and spilled in all directions." The new *tupchi-bashi*, Barkhordar Beg, assembled new materials in six weeks, and cast a gun that hurled a ball of 25 *mann*.[996] From this example it is clear that unless all the required inputs had been gathered and planned beforehand the casting of cannon took a long time. But even when their casting had been planned it usually took one month to six weeks to make a cannon. In 1598, two cannon were cast within one month, the weight of the ball (*geluleh*) was for the one 40 *mann-e sang* and the other 32 *mann-e sang*.[997] Barkhordar Beg made a number of cannon in 45 days, one of which had balls of 25 *mann*.[998]

Very large European types of cannon Persian craftsmen were unable to make. "The cannon captured at Bahrein used iron balls which had a weight varying between 3-8 *mann* each. The expert masters were unable to copy these, because the iron did not melt enough to be able to cast it, moreover a cannon of 7 *gaz* or ell, which weighed 2,000 *mann* could not

[992] Bayani, Khanbaba. "Mo'arrefi-ye yek noskheh-ye khatti," *BT* 6 (1350/1971), pp. 139-54; Molla Jalal, p. 332.
[993] Savory, *History*, vol. 2, p. 902.
[994] Dhoka, p. 202.
[995] *Travels to Tana*, part 2, p. 153.
[996] Savory, *History*, vol. 1, pp. 452-3.
[997] Molla Jalal, p. 154.
[998] Valeh Esfahani, p. 740.

be taken to the furnace and to make it in a mould was impossible.[999] Apart from making cannon on the spot at siege operations there were also cannon made for defensive and other purposes in the arsenals. Lar, according to Le Bruyn, was reputedly the town where "the best cannons in all Persia are cast."[1000]

Cannon balls: The balls were rocks, but they also were made of metal. Vechietti and Eskander Monshi mention that the Persians were firing "big stone balls" at the citadel of Tabriz.[1001] Olearius also maintains that the cannon balls were of marble stone.[1002] Andersen however mentions that the balls were made of iron.[1003] Sometimes, instead of balls they shot *namad va latteh* (felt and linen rags) which were set on fire and shot at windows and rooftops. In 1722, the Afghans fired clay balls covered with a thin layer of lead into Isfahan. [1004]

Zanburak: Because arquebuses were sometimes ineffective in mobile warfare "the Qezelbash used a zanburak, the balls were of a metal alloy (*mefragh*) and weighed one *sir* (70 grams) and caused damage to the Kurds, where the guns could not penetrate the wooden redoubt (*sabiyeh*).[1005] Treetrunk-houses (*kalleh-khaneh* or *saqnaq*) also were invulnerable to guns.[1006] The name *zanburak* probably refers to the twang of the crossbow at the moment of discharge.[1007] *Zanburak* is a Turkish diminutive from the Arab *zanbur* meaning 'hornet' much as the term musket comes from 'mosquetta'. The *zanburak* was a small light gun that could be turned around an axis. It was usually placed on camels, who served as a kind of carriage to fire from. These swivel-guns or falconets were probably already introduced to the Safavid army by 926/1520. Venetian reports mention the use of "falconeti et cannoni de 50 numero XX" and the Persian gunners gave a demonstration of their expertise.[1008] *Zanburak*s were also mentioned as being in use by the Uzbegs at the beginning of the 16th century.[1009] Molla Jalal mentioned them in

---

[999] Molla Jalal, p. 332.

[1000] Le Bruyn, vol. 2, p. 69.

[1001] Tuuci, pp. 154, 156; Monshi, vol. 2, p. 905. The Moghul army also used rocks. Zahiru'd-Din Muhammad Babur Padshah Ghazi. *Babur-nama (Memoirs of Babur)* tr. A.S. Beveridge (New Delhi 1921 [1989]), p. 571.

[1002] Olearius, p. 478; Laheji, p. 88 *zarb-e sang*; Rumlu, pp. 230 (*sang-andazha*), 450, 477, 582.

[1003] Andersen, p. 155.

[1004] Floor, *Afghan Occupation*, p. 113 (April 12).

[1005] Molla Jalal, p. 407.

[1006] Qomi, vol. 1, p. 56. also Mar'ashi, *Tarikh-e Khandan*, p. 240-1.

[1007] Raschid-Eldin, *Histoire des Mongols de la Perse*. ed. E. Quatremère (Paris 1836), p. 285-6. The first time it is mentioned is in 1187, as a cross-bow, during the siege of Tyre. Reynaud, "De l'art militaire chez les Arabes au moyen âge", *Journal Asiatique* Ser. IV, vol. XII, p. 211-13.

[1008] Amoretti, p. 546.

[1009] Mukminova, *Ocherki*, p. 122.

1019/1610-11.[1010] *Zanburak*s were also given as a parting gift to a Moghul prince on his way back to take the throne in 1107/1696-97 as well as used in regular warfare.[1011] There existed eventually a corps, the *zanburak-khaneh*, under a *zanburakchi-bashi*,[1012] who was in charge of a 3,000 strong *zanburak-e shotor* corps towards the end of the Safavid period.[1013]

Mortars, Grenades and Rockets: The *qazqan* or cauldron were used as mortars to bombard a fortress in 958/1551-52.[1014] The use of *qazqan* or cauldron also prevailed among the Moghol and Ottomans armies. The *khompareh* was already used prior to the Safavids. They were made of strong clay earthenware in the form of a wine-jar, hence the name. These pear-shaped, large jars had a hole in which the fuse was put.[1015] Because the *khompareh*s were a kind of hand grenade, these were also known as *khompareh-ye dasti*. They were handled by specialists known as *khomparehchi*s.[1016] By the end of the Safavid period the *tupchi*s and the *khomparehchi*s numbered 3,000 men.[1017] Rockets or *mushak* also were used by the Safavid army to which end it employed *mushak-sazan* or rocketeers.[1018] Du Mans, mistakenly, states that the Persians did not have bombs and grenades.[1019]

Training: The usually careful observer Kaempfer maintained that "There were no maneuvers or training."[1020] Kaempfer, also remarked that "Persian words for military orders were unknown,"[1021] which given the fact that the military language was Turkic is not surprising. The order for "forward" was, for example, *suren*.[1022] He, however, was wrong, for the Persian army hardly could acquire military skills in the use of bow, sword, lance and musket, its standard armament, without having trained in their use. The Carmelites remarked on the attention that 'Abbas I spend on the readiness of his troops and their arms and equipment. 'Abbas I spent whatever time "is left over for him from military practices he spends on

---

1010 Molla Jalal, p. 407.

1011 Nasiri, *Dastur*, pp. 119, 279.

1012 Asaf, p. 100.

1013 Daneshpazhuh, "Amar", pp. 396-423; Mostoufi, pp. 146, 181. Also massively used in the 1730s. Brosset, *Collection*, vol. 2, p. 273.

1014 Rumlu, pp. 450-1, 477 (the *tup* and cauldron were loaded with rocks). The *ghazghan* was used against the walls. Afshar, *'Alamara-ye Tahmasp*, p. 205.

1015 Dhoka, pp. 206-8.

1016 Mervi, pp. 131, 600, 953.

1017 Danesh-pazhuh, p. 423.

1018 Mervi, pp. 78, 164-5.

1019 Du Mans, vol. 2, pp. 119, 158.

1020 Kaempfer, *Am Hofe*, p. 75-6; and so does du Mans, Richard, vol. 2, pp. 117, 285.

1021 Kaempfer, *Am Hofe*, p. 75-6.

1022 Monshi, pp. 54, 80, 107, 511, 622; Afshar, *'Alamara-ye Tahmasp*, pp. 181, 187, 198, 214; Mervi, p. 261f. The term also means 'battle cry; loud and frightening shrieking and yelling'.

seeing his armaments, cleaning weapons - which he does by his own hand."[1023] Various observers attest to the Persian skill at the various arms that they used, even when military prowess was not a high priority anymore in Persia. "They also know well how to use the bow, dart, scimitar, gun, and javelin."[1024] In fact, there was even a court official whose task it was to teach the royal pages and the court staff in general how to shoot. This official was known as *oumajdar*.[1025] Della Valle mentioned a butt on the *meidan* of Qazvin where people were wont to shoot as a mark with arrows.[1026] In June 1652, the Dutch embassy observed the training of soldiers who had been recruited for the Qandahar campaign. "They are busy to test the experience in handling a musket of anyone who has come to present his services. They do this by having them hit a target twice that was at a distance of 30 paces from them, by which [feat] they were accepted and received the king's shilling."[1027] Games such as *qebeq-bazi*, which required the participants to hit a target strung on a pole with an arrow, while galloping past it on horseback, also honed the soldiers skills. The same was true for polo or *chugan-bazi* and *jarid-bazi* or javelin throwing in which Persian horsemen practiced regularly.[1028] In 1717, Bell observed that on a plain, half a mile outside of Isfahan, "the Persians every evening exercise their horses in riding, and accustom them to the discharge of fire-arms. They also shoot at butts with bows and arrows, and throw blunted darts at one another: at which they appear very dextrous."[1029]

Chardin has given us a detailed description of the training in the use of the bow, the sword and the horse by the Persian military, though he also admits that apart from the army review there were no manoeuvres or military exercises.[1030]

> First of all, to bend the Bow, the Art of which consists in holding it right, bending of it, and letting the Cord go with ease, without letting the Left-hand which holds the Bow, and which is stretched out at length, nor the Right-hand, which handles the String, stir the least in the World. They teach 'em at first, to bend it easily, and then harder by Degrees. The Masters of these Exercises teach 'em to bend

1023 Carmelites, vol. 1, p. 286, see also p. 160.
1024 Herbert, p. 243.
1025 Olearius, p. 673.
1026 della Valle, p. 75.
1027 Hotz, p. 328. see also Tavernier, p. 228.
1028 E.g. Herbert, p. 50; John Chardin, p. 87; Chardin, vol. 3, pp. 181-2; *Travels to Tana*, part two, p. 201; della Valle, p. 73; Shokri, pp. 140, 145 (*neizeh-bazi*).
1029 Bell, p. 307.
1030 Chardin, vol. 5, p. 317. The dexterous use of the horse and weapons was referred to as *salahshur* or *asleheh-shuri*. Mervi, p. 374.

the Bow before 'em, behind 'em, and side-ways, up and down; and to be short, a hundred several ways; and always quick and easy. They have Bows that are very difficult to bend; and to try their Strength, they hang them against a Wall to a Peg, and they tie Weights to the Cord of the Bow, at the Place where they put the notch of the Arrow: The stiffest of 'em will bear five hundred weight before they will bend. When they can handle an ordinary Bow, they give 'em others to bend, which they make heavy by putting a great many thick Rings of Iron upon the Cord: There are some of these Bows that weigh an hundred Weight; they can handle them, they bend them, they unbend them, as I have said, as they are Jumping, Tossing and sometimes Running: The clattering of the Rings make a troublesome Noise: This is to get more Strength. They judge that they perform that exercise well, when, in holding the Bow in the Left-Hand stretch'd out very stiff, fast, and without shaking, they bring the Cord or String with the Thumb of the Right-hand to their Ear, as if they were to hang it upon it. .....When they are very well skill'd in handling the Bow, their first Exercise is to let fly the Arrow in the Air, and who shall make it fly highest, they account him a clever Archer, and the Bow the best, that throws an Arrow to the elevation of forty-five Degrees, which is as far as the Bow will bear. The next Exercise is shooting at the Mark; and it is not only the shooting into it, but the Arrow must be thrown firm, and without shaking, into it. They afterwards learn to draw it with Strength and Weight. They Exercise themselves that way after this manner; They make about four Foot high, a Frame of about two Foot Diameter, sloping, about five or six Foot deep, fill'd with wet and fine Gravel, like the Frame of a Founder for Casting. They take their Bow and Arrow without Squares, and when they are ready to shoot, there comes a Servant with a great Flint-stone in his Hand, and strikes home just in the middle of the Frame, which is more to hinder them from making their Aim where to shoot, than to harden the Gravel. They shoot into it with all their Strength, and the Arrow generally sinks half-way into it. They draw it out, and shoot again into the Place, till such a time as the Arrow is buried in it. They succeed in that Exercise according as they bury the Arrow at fewer or more times, and that falls out as they shoot strait to the same Point. These Exercises are to teach 'em to shoot the Arrow, the Art of which, in a Word, consists in shooting a great way, in shooting true, and in shooting stiff and strong, that the Arrow may enter and pierce through. They learn to say, at shooting the last Arrow, Tir a ker derdil Omar; May the Arrow, this last Bout, enter the Heart of

Omar: And this is to keep up the aversion and hatred they have for the Sect of the Turks, whereof Omar is the second Pontif after Mahammed. It is to be observ'd, that the Arrows for these Exercises, have a round piece of Iron, small and obtuse, whereas their Arrows for Battle have Iron like the point of a Lance, or like our Lancets.[1031]

To keep in practice and remain an expert in the use of arms the individual Persian soldier probably followed the example of Nader Shah, who every day shot five arrows into the *khak-e toudeh* in his camp. The *khak-e toudeh*, or frame as Chardin referred to it, "is a Heap of fine Mold, well fitted, and beat strongly in betwixt two stone Walls. 'Tis five Foot high, three Foot thick, and from three to four Foot broad. The Front of it very smooth and even, beat hard with a heavy Trowel. One who is well skilled, can shoot his Arrow into it quite to the Head; whereas one that shoots ill (be he never so strong) can't put a third Part in. The Arrows for this Exercise have the Iron part quite round, about four Fingers long, of the Size of the Reed, until near the Point, where they are somewhat thicker, from which Part they taper gradually to a sharp point. The Length, from the thickest Part to the Point, is from ¾ to 1 Inch."[1032]

The second Exercise is to handle the Sabre; and this art consists in having a strong Wrist and very pliant, they teach the Youth to handle the Sabre with two Weights in their Hands, in turning them up and down, before and behind, quick and strong: And in order to make their Joints the more pliabale, and the Nerves the more supple, they put, during the Exercise, two other Weights upon their Shoulders made like a Horse-shoe, that it may not hinder their Motion. This Exercise is good for Wrestling, as well as to make 'em use the Sabre as well.[1033]

The third Exercise is that of the Horse, which consists in Mounting well, to have a good Seat, to gallop with a loose rein without stirring; to stop the Horse short in his Gallop, without moving one's self, and to be so light and active upon a Horse, as to tell, upon the Gallop, twenty Counters upon the Ground one after the other, and to take 'em up at their return, without slackening their Speed. There are People in Persia that sit so Firm and Light upon a Horse, that they stand straight on their Feet upon the Saddle, and make the Horse Gallop in that manner with a loose Rein. The Persians ride a little Side-ways, because they turn

---

[1031] John Chardin, pp. 198-9.
[1032] Fraser, James, *The History of Nadir Shah.* (London 1742 [1970]), p. 143.
[1033] John Chardin, p. 200.

themselves so in performing their Exercises on Horse-back, which are three Sorts, to play at the Mall, to draw the Bow, and to throw the Javelin. Their play at the Mall ....The Exercise of the Bow on Horse-back is perform'd by shooting at a Bowl or Cup behind one, put upon the end of a Mast or Pole about twenty-six Foot high, where they get up by little Ribs of Wood nailed to it, and which serve as Steps. The Gentleman takes his Career towards the Pole with his Bow and Arrow in his Hand, and when he is gone by it, he bends himself backwards either to the Right, or Left; for they must know how to do it both Ways, and lets fly his Arrow. This Exercise is common to all the Towns of Persia. Even the Kings, Exercise themselves that way. .... The Javelin, which they use in these exercises, and is call'd Gerid, as much as to say, the Bough of a Palm-Tree, is much longer than a Partizan, and very heavy, insomuch as it requires a very strong Arm to dart, or throw it. There are People in Persia so well made, and so Skillful at this Exercise, that they will throw a Dart or Javelin, six or seven hundred Paces.[1034]

Although we haven no description thereof, it is clear that neither guns nor cannon could be used without training. Venetian documents mention or infer training in the use of these modern arms, but given the cost, this must have been limited in scope. Kaempfer and du Mans are right that large scale manoeuvres appear not to have been held. However, a similar occasion for training, which was the only exercise that came close to large scale maneuvering of troops, was the hunt. Thousands of troops were used who had to collaborate to ensure a positive outcome of the hunt.

War
When the shah learnt of a foreign army approaching his borders with ill-intent, or when he himself wanted to invade a neighboring country or suppress a rebellion he raised an army.[1035] Mobilization orders (*sanad*) were served on the great emirs, bidding them to report to the royal camp with their men. Sometimes, a general mobilization order was given, but for smaller operations only part of the forces were called upon.[1036] It was

---

[1034] Chardin, p. 200. The shooting of arrows at the pole was known as *qebeq-bazi*. *Travels to Tana*, part 2, pp. 111, 201; Monshi, vol. 1, pp. 59, 298; Sanson, p. 34. For the Qezelbash practicing *jerid-bazi* see also Herbert, p. 50; on *jerid-bazi* see Floor, Willem. "Two communications (*naqibu'l-mamalik* and *jaridbazi*)", *Zeitschrift der Deutschen Morgenländischen Gesellschaft*, 123 (1973), p. 82.
[1035] Shah Khodabandeh held a council of war. Savory, *History*, vol. 1, p. 374; see also 1, p. 423, 439.
[1036] Qomi, vol. 2, p. 882; Savory, *History*, vol 1, p. 479; vol. 2, pp. 682, 794, 809, 1113.

usually the *qurchi*s that were sent to deliver the mobilization orders.[1037] They, or the army musterers (*tovachiyan*), went to all parts of the country and proclaimed (*jar zadand*) the mobilization.[1038]

The various provincial governors-emirs were responsible to field the required number of troops, when called upon, and to see to it that their cavalry was properly equipped. "Every *mir* (chief) who had only a few *molazem*, horsed or on foot, with gun, even a digger (*bildar*) or a tunnel digger (*qumesh*), was told to come to the Khorasan campaign and got an order (*sanad*)."[1039] According to Don Juan, who wrote from his own experience, "The manner of mustering the troops is for the chief of each of the [32 Qezelbash] noble families [*uymaq*] to call out eight, ten or twelve thousand horseman of his clan and a like number of foot-soldiers armed with their arquebuses."[1040] This manner of mobilization is confirmed by Venetian documents which report that "Each *soltan*, of which there were 70, was supposed to supply 300-500 horsemen and footmen."[1041] After the military reforms of the 1590s, the provincial governors had a preponderant role in mobilizing the army.[1042]

Both for military and financial reasons records were kept of the number of men that could be mobilized. This was done at the central level by the viziers of the different army corps. But "the elders of each tribe were [also] ordered to make detailed lists of the families in their tribe resident in Azerbaijan and Iraq, so that, as required by religious zeal, every group might have ready for service the number of *yasaq* troops compatible with its means, whether they were actually called to the colors or not. All these men were to report for duty early in spring and the *qurchi*s were instructed to see to it that these orders were carried out.[1043]

Failure to show up could be explained as treason and was punished accordingly. Therefore, a review was held to check the muster rolls with those actually present as well as to see whether every man was able-bodied and adequately armed. Tahmasp I held review of his troops before marching to Turkestan.[1044] Alpan Beg went to Isfahan to collect 15,000 infantry (*piyadeh*), where he held a review and then completely armed presented them to shah.[1045] 'Abbas I also held reviews prior to marching. "After spending three days reviewing his troops at Bestam [in 1004/1595-6], the Shah marched."[1046] Those of the khans, *soltan*s, *qurchi*s,

---

1037 Savory, *History*, vol. 2, p. 809.
1038 Rumlu, pp. 151, 275; Qomi vol. 1, p. 178.
1039 Qomi, vol. 2, pp. 882, 1019.
1040 Don Juan, p. 51.
1041 Berchet, pp. 9-10, 13, 287.
1042 Olearius, p. 666.
1043 Savory, *History*, vol. 2, p. 861.
1044 Afshar, *'Alamara-ye Tahmasp*, p. 347.
1045 Natanzi, p. 573.
1046 Savory, *History*, vol. 2, p. 683.

lashkariyan were not present had their revenue assignments (*teyul*s) and salaries (*mavajeb*) cut and revoked.[1047]

It was the task of the *tovachiyan-e lashkar* or the army muster-masters to check that the soldiers that had been called to arms came properly armed and equipped. Also, to make sure that the soldiers were properly ordered and ready, regiment-wise, for the royal inspection. To facilitate inspection the troops were lined up in rows.[1048] After the review, the *monadi* or herald cried loudly that all those in the royal army who was unable, because of weakness or inadequacy of equipment, to join the punitive expedition to the *dar al-marz* was excused.[1049] It would seem that under 'Abbas II this task had been given to officials who were named *mohasselin*, a term usually reserved for tax collectors.[1050] Under Soltan Hosein, the role of *tovachiyan* and *jarchiyan* in mobilizing troops is mentioned around 1109/1697-8, but the term *mohasselin* is also used in the same text in 1107/1695-6.[1051] Given the fact that military service was part of the fiscal burden of the tribes the term *mohassel* for the muster-masters was not inappropriate. For that reason, each clan and tribe had to know exactly how many soldiers it had to have at readiness.[1052] Once the army had been assembled it waited for orders to move. For the time being the army, awaiting further orders, was quartered in the homes of the urban population and/or in tents outside the city. This measure, known as *nozul*, was not popular with the population, of course.[1053] Once the shah decided to have the army march, the order was immediately made public by criers in every quarter of the city. This order was further made know through notices that were stuck in every part of the city.[1054]

The Tovachi-bashi

The official in charge of the mobilization and review of the troops was the *tovachi-bashi*. We know very little about this official beyond the fact that he was in charge of the mobilization and review of the troops and that he was always chosen from among the Qezelbash. The function also existed in the administration of the two dynasties that the Safavids replaced, viz. the Timurids and Aq-Qoyunlu. Under the Timurid Soltan-Hosein Baiqara, there was a *divan-e a'la* in charge of both civil and military matters, for Turks and Persians. For Turkish interests there was a *divan-e bozorg-e emarat* headed by the *divan-begi*, assisted by *bakhshi*s or secretaries. The

---

[1047] Natanzi, p. 567.

[1048] Qomi, vol. 1, pp. 178, 198; Yusef, pp. 151, 214.

[1049] Adle, p. 480.

[1050] Vahid Qazvini, p. 215, and p. 278 (to mobilize beaters for a major hunting event).

[1051] Nasiri, *Dastur*, pp. 104, 305.

[1052] Tavernier, p. 228.

[1053] On the fiscal aspect see Floor, *Fiscal History*.

[1054] della Valle, p. 74.

tovachi divani probably was a section of this *divan-e bozorg*. For Persian and civil matters there was part of the *divan-e a'la* headed by a vizier, assisted by *nevisandegan-e tajik* or Persian clerks. The *divan-e mal* or finance department was part of this section.[1055] The function also existed under the Aq-Qoyunlu where its holder also occupied a high station. There was also a *divan-e tovaji*, while the *tovaji-bashi* also had the task of organizing the army's review. The *tovaji*s shouted the commands to the troops, and indicated the locations the detachments had to occupy.[1056] The formation taken by the troops during the review was in rows, most likely in the form of a circle, which was referred to as *yasal*.[1057]

Under the Safavids the *tovachi-bashi* remained an important official. Whenever the *tovachi-bashi* at court is mentioned he is identified by name and mentioned as "one of the principal officers of state."[1058] Esma'ilqoli Khan, the *tovachi-bashi*, who held the title of *yuldash* (comrade), was even empowered to affix his seal to divan documents and letters of appointment.[1059] The *tovachi-bashi*, a title that disappeared from the texts in the 1640s,[1060] was later referred to as the *jarchi-bashi*. Apart from organizing the mobilization of troops and their review the *tovachi-bashi* also had to see to it that army orders were passed on while on march and during military operations. The *tovachi-bashi* was also charged to announce the shah's orders at public places with a loud voice, or through his underlings, so that everybody would be informed.[1061]

Some of these officials made quite an impression on their contemporaries. "Malek 'Ali Beg Taji-buyuk, the herald... on occasions when he placed on his head the unique jeweled headgear which was his special prerequisite, and wore his jewelled earrings dangling on both sides of his face, and came to court with his Taji-buyuk retainers, all of whom were clad in special and unusual costume, everybody trembled, he died in 1023-4/1614-6."[1062] Neither function is mentioned in the DM or in the TM. The *jarchi-bashi* does figure among the courtiers mentioned by Asaf

---

[1055] Roemer, p. 169, n.3, p. 170.

[1056] Minorsky, "Military Review", pp. 154-5, 161, 163; Khunji, Fazlollah b. Ruzbehan. *Tarikh-e 'Alamara-ye Amini*. ed. Woods J.E. (London 1992), p. 388; Doerfer, vol. 1, p. 133.

[1057] Minorsky, Military Review, p. 161.

[1058] Savory, *History*, vol. 1, p. 365; see also Qomi, vol. 1, p. 49, 83; and Valeh Esfahani, p. 140.

[1059] Savory, *History*, vol. 1, p. 479.

[1060] Yusef, p. 213; also mentioned in an *ensha* manual of the 1630s quoted by Röhrborn, *Provinzen*, p. 21. Esfahani, pp. 86, 205, 213 still mentions the use of *tovachi*s. Nasiri, *Alqab*, pp. 33-34 also mentioned the *tovachi-bashi*, but lists it as an office that had been abolished by 'Abbas I.

[1061] Kaempfer, *Am Hofe*, p. 87.

[1062] Savory, *History*, vol. 2, p. 1101-2; Hosein Beg Qur Dhu'l-Qadr the chief herald in 1013 [1015-16]. Ibid., vol. 2, p. 908, 941; Malek Beg, *jarchi-bashi*, Astarabadi, p. 207;

and thus appears to have been a part of the Safavid court fixtures.[1063]

Table 3.10 List of *tovachi-bashi*s

'Abdi Beg Shamlu *tovachi-bashi*[1064]	907/1501
Zeinal Beg Shamlu	920/1514
Durmish Khan Shamlu[1065]	920/1514
?	
Kepeg Soltan[1066]	933/1527
Hamza Beg *tovachi*[1067]	933/1527-8
Qoduz Soltan *tovachi*[1068]	935/1528-9
?	
?	
Safi Vali Khalifeh-*ye tovachi*[1069]	982/1574
Soltan Hosein Khan[1070]	985/1577
Esma'ilqoli Khan[1071]	988/1580
'Ali Khan[1072]	989/1581
Ommat Khan *tovachi-bashi*[1073]	990-999/1582-90
Bonyad Beg *tovachi-bashi*[1074]	999/1591

Local rulers such as Malek Safi al-Din of Seistan had a complete military staff, including a *tovaji*, at their disposal.[1075] One of them was a qadi, who was at the same time *tovaji* and *saff-ara* (organizer of the battle order) as well as *sepahsalar* of Malek Jalal-al Din Mahmud.[1076] The Uzbegs also had a *tovachi-bashi*.[1077] In addition to his task of *tovachi-bashi*, this

---

1063 Asaf, p. 100.
1064 Qomi, vol. 1, pp. 49, 83; 'Abdi Beg Shamlu *tovachi-bashi* was mentioned as one of the famous emirs; see also Valeh Esfahani, p. 140; Rumlu, p. 106 [in 909/1503].
1065 Aubin, "Soufis", p. 14, n. 155-56.
1066 Qomi, vol. 1, pp. 170, 176.
1067 Qomi vol. 1, p. 176;
1068 Qomi vol. 1, p. 180;
1069 He was governor of Seistan for three years had held the function of *tovachi*. Seistani, p. 162.
1070 Savory, *History*, vol. 1, p. 365.
1071 He was appointed as *tovachi-bashi* with the rank of khan and given him permission to kill his predecessor in 988/1580-1. Savory, *History*, vol. 1, p. 382. He was also governor of Qazvin. Qomi, vol. 2, p. 613 [here *beg*], 763, 808.
1072 Horst, "Ein Immunitätsdiplom", p. 290, document dated Rabi' II 989/May 1581; he was also *emir al-omara* of Fars.
1073 Qomi, vol. 2, pp. 736, 801.
1074 Qomi, vol. 2, p. 918.
1075 Seistani, p. 205.
1076 Seistani, p. 319. One of the Seistani elite members was Malek 'Ali Soltan *jarchi-bashi*. Ibid., p. 404.
1077 Qomi, vol. 1, p. 288.

official usually also held other functions. 'Ali Khan and Ommat Khan *tovachi-bashi* also commanded, as governor-general of Fars, the emirs of Fars and Kuhgilu.[1078]

Military Tactics

It has been remarked by students of Safavid history as well as contemporary European authors that the Safavids, despite their familiarity with modern arms, never really made them part of their army and military strategy. Various arguments have been advanced such as the difficulty of getting the raw materials to make gunpowder and to cast cannon as well as the absence of roads and wheeled carriage.[1079] While there is some truth in all these arguments it would seem that the real situation is more nuanced.

Safavid military strategy was based on mobility, the judicious use of the ambush and the scorched earth tactic. Consequently, a strategy of static defensive options such as walled cities was not pursued at all. This choice was a deliberate one, for de Chinon remarks that "this country has a unique advantage with regard to its power and defense in having mountains surround it on all sides as well as having abundant deserts which are almost waterless."[1080] Persian strategy therefore was based on capitalizing on its natural defenses (difficult mountain passes; hostile countryside and inclement weather) thus making an invasion a logistical nightmare. The results for the invading force, usually, were heavy casualties, food, fodder, water and transport problems, which were aggravated by illness.[1081]

Therefore, in case of an invading army the tactic was the use of burnt earth and attacks from ambushes (*kamin, bosqu*).[1082] In 921/1515, Esma'il I had created a kind of no-man's land between Tabriz and Anatolia where nobody lived at all.[1083] Shah Tahmasp I dispatched reliable men to lay waste the entire area between Tabriz and the Ottoman frontier so that no trace of grass remained. The people of Tabriz blocked up the underground water channels so that no drinking water could be found. Similarly, measures were taken to deny the enemy all forms of food. The shah

---

[1078] Qomi, vol. 2, p. 736, 801, see also p, 918. (Qazvin), pp. 763, 808; (Seistan), Seistani, p. 162.

[1079] See on this issue in general Matthee, Rudi. "Unwalled Cities and Restless Nomads: Firearms an Artillery", in Ch. Mellville, *Safavid Iran* (London 1996), pp. 389-416.

[1080] de Chinon, *Relations*, p. 69. Chardin and Bell make the same point. Chardin, vol. 5, p. 293; Bell, p. 295.

[1081] Richard, vol. 2, pp. 118-9, 289. For results of lack of food for the Ottomans see Rumlu, p. 426.

[1082] Kaempfer, *Am Hofe*, p. 76; see also Don Juan, pp. 116, 174; Chardin, vol. 5, pp. 318-9; Mervi, pp. 115, 124, 154, 194.

[1083] Bacqué-Grammont, *Les Ottomans*, p. 153.

disposed his forces all around the Ottoman army, and they were not left in peace during day or night, and suffered casualties. As a result the Ottomans could not go outside the camp to search for food. Driven by starvation they were forced to retreat.[1084]

The shah also sent couriers out in all directions to move the rural population out of harm's way; his officers had instructions not to leave any food supplies on the Ottoman line of march. Any peasant who was not able to remove his own supplies of grain was instructed to leave them to be transported into the fort, and to draw payment from the divan at the current market price. ... the civilian population left the city, taking with it all stocks of food.[1085] In 1605, when the Ottomans began their counter offensive 'Abbas I totally emptied Armenia and drove the entire population to the province of Ararat. The result was that there nothing to eat for the Ottomans, and nothing to return to for the Armenians.[1086] In 1618, 'Abbas I had the territory around Tabriz completely inundated by emptying a river so that the Turkish cavalry could neither advance nor return.[1087] The 'burnt earth' policy was still practiced in Chardin's time for he reported "that the Persian even uprooted trees, detoured rivulets and rivers; they do everything to deny the enemy anything. The destruction was total over a six day journey."[1088]

The opposing Safavid forces, in so far these were not with the main defense force, were housed in fortresses commanding strategic positions, which were well-stocked with food and arms.[1089] In case the shah was the attacker himself he normally took care that sufficient supplies were available for the army to do its job, although at times the supplies were not adequate and military operations had to be broken off.

Thus, Safavid military strategy was based on having the enemy not only fight its military forces, but also its natural ones. The Safavids decided against the use of walled cities, which had to be protected against

---

[1084] Savory, *History*, vol. 1, pp. 118-9; Monshi, vol. 1, p. 71; Rumlu, p. 424 in 955/1548; *Travels to Tana*, part 2, p. 227; the shah decided to lay waste the Erzerum-Van area to deny provisions to the Ottomans. Savory, *History*, vol. 2, p. 1138; Monshi, vol. 2, p. 921; Yusef, p. 165 in 1045/1636.

[1085] Savory, *History*, vol. 2, p. 1028; Monshi, vol. 2, p. 822. The shah send a force to burn all the crops along the probable line of the Ottoman advance, to ensure that there should not be one *mann* of wheat, straw, or hay to be had within a distance of ten days' march of Erivan. Savory, *History*, vol. 2, p. 1022; Monshi, vol. 2, p. 818. It had been deliberate policy to leave the Erivan region uncultivated until such time as Azerbaijan was once more firmly under Safavid control, in order to deny food supplies to Ottoman armies operating in the area. Savory, *History*, vol. 2, p. 930; Monshi, vol. 1, p. 740.

[1086] Chamich, vol. 2, p. 349.

[1087] della Valle, p. 86; Brosset, vol. 2, p. 64-5.

[1088] Chardin, vol. 5, pp. 319-20. Gives also examples of snow storms and rains reducing Ottoman forces.

[1089] Valeh Esfahani, p. 170; Natanzi, p. 449; Chardin, vol. 5, p. 318.

invading forces. They preferred to have the difficult geographical and climatological circumstances work for them. The invading force paid by having to be burdened with an unwieldy baggage train to bring all its food and fodder. The long difficult passage was rendered more difficult by ambushes and other harassing tactics. Once the enemy had been softened up the Safavid army was ready to offer battle and force the issue. Irrespective who won or lost, the invading force with few exceptions could not stay and had to withdraw, because it had suffered too many casualties in men and beasts to be able to stay.[1090] Even when the invading force stayed it was relatively easy dislodged again once the Safavids were able to mount an effective force that was free from internal dissension.

This strategy of mobility was a cheaper alternative and more effective than building walled cities. After all, the enemy was interested in killing the Safavid army, not the urban population. If the latter acquiesced in the rule of the new power the urban population was left alone. If they defended the town or in any other way proved to be a hindrance drastic measures were taken. Therefore, the Persian army could have its pudding and eat it as well, if it could hold out long enough in the citadel and wait for reinforcements to oust the hostile army, or harry the opposing force long enough so that it ran out of steam (food, fodder, healthy soldiers). Also, the army often suffered from a lack of provisions after too long a campaign in areas with little to support an army without previous preparation. "On the return march the army lost many horses, mules and camels because of lack of fodder."[1091] Also, "they did not have enough donkeys to pull their heavy guns .... vast quantities of arms abandoned by the retreating Ottomans.[1092]

The option of making expensive investments in heavy city walls that could withstand an artillery bombardment was abandoned by the Safavids. This decision was probably taken for various reasons. Most importantly, in my view, was the fact that the Safavid army could fight its battles the way it wanted. That is, either a pitched battle or a sudden attack from an ambush. Even the better armed and trained Ottoman army was never able to force its tactical will on the Safavid army. The Ottomans, who knew city fortification first-hand through their European conquests, did not bother to invest too much in them in those Persian cities that they held for a long time. This probably is due to the same reason why the Safavids did not do it either. Namely, the building materials and techniques were inadequate, and it was very expensive to make less pregnable fortifications on a city scale. Herbert remarks on the effect of torrential rains on the mud brick walls. "For albeit the King .... has raised at every three miles' end a wall or castle, yet by unstable foundation, in March and

1090 della Valle, pp. 86, 88.

1091 Savory, *History*, vol. 2, p. 688; Monshi, vol. 1, p. 512.

1092 Savory, vol, 2, p. 1271; Monshi, vol. 2, p. 1050.

September, in despite of their best props, it is piecemeal torn asunder, that little or no remains appear of their late standing."[1093] The cost of doing so was also high, reason why Persian military based their strategy on strong citadels in cities. This was already true for the period prior to the use of guns and cannon.[1094]

Given the fact that Safavid Persia was not a wealthy country it was an intelligent decision not to concentrate on building expensive city walls to have them blown away at the next siege. It comes therefore as no surprise to observe that most cities, which in the 16th centuries still had a wall, had none anymore in the 17th century. Sieges, therefore, were not waged against cities, for "The city-wall is of no force against cannon: but of use against horse, and shock of lance."[1095] The object of a siege therefore was always the fortress or citadel of the city, never the city itself.[1096] On hearing news of the arrival of the Uzbegs, the Qezelbash started to reinforce the fortress, not the city of Herat.[1097] Shah Khodabandeh told the population of Tabriz to make peace with the Ottomans and surrender. The Qezelbash meanwhile destroyed the city of Tabriz before the arrival of Farhad Pasha.[1098] Sometimes, the population was ordered to leave to ensure that the enemy could find no spoils at all.[1099]

We therefore also note that the shahs invested in building strong forts and/or reinforcing existing ones. The manner in which this was done also demonstrates one of the underlying reasons for not building city walls, viz. the lack of modern building techniques and materials. Chardin commented that in the Middle East people had no knowledge of the modern arts of fortification.[1100] This is also clear from the rather make-shift fashion, and with non-professional labor, in which some of the forts were constructed. For example, 'Abbas I decided to repair the fort of Mobarakabad and divided this task among his troops: Allahverdi Khan and the *gholam*s the western part; the Qezelbash the southern part; the divan officials and scribes the northern part; and the *qurchi*s with the workers (*qologhchiyan va 'amalat*) of the royal workshops (*boyutat*) the eastern part; whilst those close to the shah did the inner part or *narin*. A fortress had an outer-wall or *hesar-e shir-hajji*, which consisted of towers or *borj*, and connecting walls or *bareh*. Inside the walls was the *ark* or *narin* in which the defenders could withdraw when the outer-wall had

[1093] Herbert, p. 143.

[1094] Mar'ashi, *Tarikh-e Khandan*, pp. 64-5, 240-1, 246.

[1095] Herbert, p. 131.

[1096] Rumlu, p. 66 (attack on Baku, not on city but on its fortress) for the case of Kerman in 1719 and 1721 see Floor, *Bar Oftadan*, and Ibid., *Afghan Occupation*, chapters 1 and 3.

[1097] Rumlu, p. 222. Don Juan, p. 182.

[1098] Natanzi, p. 205; Don Juan, p. 201; Sanson, p. 76.

[1099] della Valle, p. 88.

[1100] Chardin, vol. 5, p. 292; Richard, vol. 2, p. 120.

been breached. The *narin* was held by the fortress commander, the *kotval* or *qal'ehdar*.[1101] It was of course necessary to stock the fortresses with food, fodder and supplies. If not the defenders were forced to starve and eat unedibles and/or finally surrender.[1102]

This did not mean that at times cities were not attacked or defended by the army. However, in these cases, street fighting rather than siege-works, were characteristic for military operations. "To defend cities the emirs erected barricades in the street, and hand to hand fighting took place at the barricades."[1103] The commander did not place his sole reliance of the citadel, but barricaded all the streets in the outlying parts of the city. Behind every barricade he stationed seasoned officers, with gunners and musketeers. Battles raged at the barricades but the Uzbegs failed to storm a single barricade.[1104] The Ottomans when faced with these kind of barricades blew them away with cannon.[1105] In some cases the population did not want to stay, but wanted to flee. This the governor then tried to prevent by giving orders that on pain of death the population had to stay and assist him in defending the city.[1106]

Food and Fodder
Although the provisioning of the army was the commander's task, to feed and cloth each individual was the soldier's responsibility. "The troops have each to take care individually for their food and clothes, even after battle."[1107] That is, the shah or his commanding general saw to it that, if he was a good general, that sufficient supplies were available in the army camp to feed both men and animals. Esma'il I saw to it that roads and bridges were repaired and had supplies ready at each halting place.[1108] He gave strict orders not to oppress peasants when his army was passing

---

[1101] Adle, pp. 450, 493; Valeh Esfahani, pp. 135, 137-8, 743. *borj va bareh-ye hesar*. Ibid., p. 216. Each section (*pareh*) of the brickwall was called *mohreh* in Seistan. Seistani, p. 260.
[1102] Rumlu, pp. 256, 349.
[1103] Savory, *History*, 1, p. 93; Monshi, vol. 1, p. 57 (Mashad against the Uzbegs in 935/1528-9).
[1104] Savory, *History*, vol. 1, p. 155; Monshi, vol. 1, p. 93. For similar occurence in 1520s including watering streets to make them freeze over. Valeh Esfahani, p. 229; Rumlu, p. 182 in 919/1513-4; barricades erected in the streets of Qazvin and placed musketeers and archers at each. Savory, *History*, vol. 1, p. 468; Monshi, vol. 1, p. 333.
[1105] Savory, *History*, vol. 1, p. 442; also Valeh Esfahani, p. 716.
[1106] Floor, *Bar Oftadan*, pp. 43, 75; Ibid., *Afghan Occupation*, pp. 43, 73.
[1107] Kaempfer, *Am Hofe*, p. 75; they only received their arms and ammunition, Chardin, vol. 5, p. 318. According to Tavernier, p. 228 the infantry had a mule between three or four soldiers to carry their food and luggage.
[1108] Montazer-Saheb, pp. 335, 337, 356; *soyursat* for the army in the 1630s. Yusef, p. 249.

through Ottoman territory to Diyarbekr in 1507.[1109] Prior to the 1512 Transoxianian campaign, the "*ordu-bazariyan va sarkaran va sudagaran*" brought grains and provisions.[1110] 'Abbas I, when marching on Balkh carried four years of provisions with his troops.[1111] Tahmasp I estimated the food needs at two *mann* per person and his donkey per day, which translated in substantial logistical problems.[1112]

To guard against any shortage of supplies of grain or the army the shah ordered the divan officials to indent for 20,000 *kharvar*, each of 100 *mann*, to be provided by those areas in Azerbaijan which had an abundance. This had to be transported to the royal camp by the peasants using their own donkeys .. price was paid for grain and for transport... special collectors were appointed and dispatched to see to this task.[1113] When food supplies ran low, the shah to alleviate a shortage of barley send all horses and transport and riding donkeys not needed for the siege to the alluvial plain."[1114] The responsibility to ensure that supplies were available for the army's well-being was given to the *sursat-bashi* or purveyor-general, a function that is mentioned towards the end of the Safavid dynasty, who was assisted by *sursatchiyan*.[1115]

'Abbas I's army moved quietly and efficiently. "Their march is a blessing, for people from all around come with supplies, for everything is paid for. Unlike in many countries of Europe, its march is a blessing instead of a curse for the countries through which it lays." Consequently abundance reigns in the army, while the Shah punished those that did not pay.[1116] This was all the more remarkable, because the army train was often larger than the army itself. "As all the officers and principal persons take their servants and family with them, the number of the army is swollen prodigiously; yet the greatest abundance constantly reigns in the camp during its march, so much so as to make it a saying in the country, 'That the army of the King is one of the finest and best provided cities in Persia'."[1117] Although there is no detailed similar description for the Safavid army, there is one for that of Uzun Hasan, which gives interesting information about the composition of a Persian army and thus its logistical implications. Uzun Hasan in 1474, "set out with his troops, the number

---

[1109] *Travels to Tana*, part 2, pp. 53-4, 196; Bacqué-Grammont, *Les Ottomans*, p. 22.

[1110] Khvandamir, vol. 4, p. 528.

[1111] Adle, p. 542.

[1112] Shah Tahmasp. p. 51.

[1113] Savory, *History*, vol. 2, p. 901; Monshi, vol. 2, p. 708.

[1114] Savory, *History*, vol. 2, p. 921; Monshi, vol. 2, p. 732, glut of animals in army camp. Savory, *History*, vol. 2, p. 879; Monshi, vol. 2, p. 688.

[1115] Asaf, p. 100. On *sursat* or *soyursat* see Floor, *Taxation*.

[1116] della Valle, vol. 7, p. 80.

[1117] della Valle, vol. 7, p. 80. Though the number of servants was less than was normal in France. Pacifique de Provins, p. 258.

being twenty-five thousand foot-soldiers, eighteen thousand country-people, three thousand tents, six thousand camels, thirty thousand baggage mules, five thousand women, three thousand boys and maid-servants, and many animals of different kinds. This was his standing army; I leave you to judge of the number he could levy on an emergency."[1118] According to du Mans to field 50,000 combatants at least 400,000 non-combatants were required. These consisted of camel drivers (*sarban*), tent pitchers (*farrash*), water carriers (*saqqachi*), valets (*shater*), grooms (*mehtar*) and multitudes of pack and riding animals.[1119] The large number of horses and servants were not a luxury, but served a real and necessary purpose. For example, a horse could be shot or otherwise disabled, or it grew tired, then it was the task of the cavalarist's servant (*yadak-kesh* or *asbdar*) to bring his master a new horse.[1120]

The food and fodder itself, for which the men received payment, was provided by sutlers, referred to as *ordubazariyan*, or as *dokkandars* (shopkeepers), and *baqqal* (grocers), etc.[1121] An army on the march counted on the people of the *ordu-ye bazar* and the well-wishing merchants from the nearby regions to bring the necessary supplies, especially when foraging became difficult and supplies were expensive.[1122] The soldiers did not carry food or water with them as did European and Ottoman troops.[1123] The Portuguese observed under Esma'il I that half a league from the shah's camp "there is continually another camp of pleasing tents, in which are found many merchants whom bring all [kinds of] merchandise: to wit, garments made of silk in costly linings, caparisons for horses, and well made saddles; wheat, barley, and meats, butter, and fruits, and rice, and cooks who sell all [kinds of] food very well cooked. They call this camp: *ordubuzar*, which means encampment of [the] market place, where many Moors are continually, and it appears like a great fair. This camp provides for that of the Sufi."[1124] The situation was not different under Tahmasp I. "At the beginning of the said urdu is the piazza with all the craftsmen and merchandise, and kitchens for food, all together with their tents."[1125]

To cook, usually a small ditch was dug, surrounded by two or three stones on top of which a grill was put. Fuel normally was brushwood and

---

1118 *Travels to Tana*, part 2, p. 94.

1119 Richard, vol. 2, p. 119.

1120 Mar'ashi, *Tarikh-e Khandan*, pp. 295, 326.

1121 Chardin, vol. 5, p. 318; Richard, vol. 2, p. 118.

1122 Valeh Esfahani, p. 218; Afshar, *'Alamara-ye Tahmasp*, p. 201.

1123 Richard, vol. 2, p. 287.

1124 Smith, p. 76.

1125 Membré, p. 23; della Valle, p. 89 (in 1618). The situation under Nader Shah in the 1740s was quite like that 200 years earlier. Hanway, J. *An Historical Account of the British Trade over the Caspian Sea*. 3 vols in one (London 1743), vol. 1, pp. 247-8.

in particular camel dung. As to bread making, some baked it on a iron plate, with fire under it. The dough was spread out over the plate using a roll. Others, in particular the more important people in the army, had a portable oven. It consisted of two iron cones, each [the size of] a half-quart, which were equipped with large nails to hold the clay with which they have been covered. These two parts fitted together and thus formed one quart. They were narrower at the top than at the bottom. A large fire was made in it, over which they put the dough in the form of a round tart which stuck to the lining of that oven.[1126] This oven, when used, was round and dug into the ground. An entire sheep also could be roasted in it. When the army moved the clay was broken off and the two semi-cones were loaded on the back of a beast of burden, one part on each side of the animal.[1127]

If the *ordu-bazar* failed to have the necessary supplies soldiers were sent in foraging parties to find food and fodder.[1128] Pacifique de Province extols the efficient Persian system whereby each governor saw to it that provisions were available at each site where the army struck camp. Therefore, camel caravans were moving day and night to ensure food security for the army.[1129] During the 1649 Qandahar campaign Andersen also observed the sutlers and merchants following and provisioning the army.[1130]

The merchants, in the hope of profit, followed the army with their wares,[1131] which included not only foodstuffs and drinks,[1132] but also materials to take care of repairs or replacement of equipment such as leather and horse irons.[1133] For rather than a public sector operation the provisioning of the army was in the hands of sutlers, who sold whatever was required. However, under later shahs soldiers were not well paid and they were allowed, by necessity, to obtain credit. If the soldiers had no money and could not get credit they had to steal and rob.[1134]

Women also followed the army,[1135] for these were always in short supply, except when a town or fortress had been taken, when, young women, girls, and boys became the property of the conquering army.[1136]

1126 Richard, vol. 2, p. 118.

1127 Bastiaaensen, pp. 132-3; John Chardin, p. 272. For a picture of this oven in the Turkish *Surnameh* (ca. 1720-25) see R. Ettinghausen, *Turkish Miniatures* (UNESCO 1965), pl. 27.

1128 Valeh Esfahani, p. 219; Rumlu, p. 124.

1129 Pacifique de Province, p. 258.

1130 Andersen, pp. 154, 156.

1131 Savory, *History*, vol. 2, p. 886; Monshi, vol. 2, p. 695.

1132 Rumlu, pp. 173, 420; Savory, *History*, vol. 2, p. 673; Monshi, vol. 1, p. 499.

1133 Floor, *Hokumat*, pp. 25, 48, 58-9; Natanzi, pp. 82-3.

1134 Kaempfer, *Am Hofe*, pp. 75-6; Richard, vol. 2, p. 287.

1135 Amoretti, p. 105.

1136 Monshi, vol. 2, p. 746; Savory, *History*, vol. 2, p. 937; Mervi, p. 82; Andersen, pp. 158-9; Floor, *Bar Oftadan*, p. 53; Ibid., *Afghan Occupation*, p. 50.

The army market, or *ordu-bazar*, was a simple affair such as one saw "at the gate of the caravansarai was a bazar, or tent (like sutlers in armies) for money furnish passengers with provision."[1137] To keep order in the army market there was an official referred to as *ordu-begi* or *mir-ordu-ye bazar*.[1138] The *ordu-bazar* also followed the royal court when it travelled for other purposes than military campaigns. Such a move had important consequences for trade in the capital where the shah usually resided. A lengthy absence of the shah from the capital city had a downward effect on sales of especially luxury goods. It further removed thousands of people from the capital, while the *ordu* constituted a drain on the provinces where it temporarily stayed or passed through. Also, the cost to the elite of moving along with their retinue of servants, horses, tents etc. impoverished them and reduced their purchasing power considerably.[1139] When the court returned to the capital city sales and prices grew and merchants were happy once again.[1140] For the population of Isfahan could double according to Chardin.[1141]

On the March
According to della Valle the Persian army "Whenever [it is on the march], the greatest silence and regularity takes place, neither trumpets or drums beat," and "in their march they keep no ranks, but each goes as he pleases, uniting in body only when in suspected places or near the enemy's army. Baggage and women are placed in the rear."[1142] However, from Persian sources it is clear that the army marched according to a clear well-thought plan and that musical signals were given. The various army units may not have kept perfect cohesion such as European armies may have practised, but as della Valle also observed that in case of danger army unity was re-established.

Before giving his marching orders the shah placed his troops in battle order or *yasal*. The constituent parts of the army on the march were the following: In front of the army was a screen of scouts (*pish-qaravol* or *pish-ravaneh*) for both the left and right parts of the army.[1143] These were followed by the *charkhchi*s or skirmishers. Then followed the van-guard

---

1137 Herbert, p. 51.

1138 Utar Khan was *ordu-begi*, Yusef, p. 240; *ordu-begi*, Molla Jalal, p. 172; *mir-ordu*, Qomi, vol. 1, p. 270; *mir-ordu-ye bazar*, Qomi, vol. 2, pp. 1033, 1044.

1139 *ARA*, VOC 1307, 1/8/1676, f. 669r.

1140 *ARA*, VOC 1246, 8/2/1664, 774; voc 1241, 15/2/1664, f. 573v; voc 1307, 28/3/1676, f. 634r.

1141 Chardin, vol. 10, pp. 2-4; see also *ARA*, VOC 1747, 6/10/1706, f. 279 where the shah's pilgrimage to Mashhad reduced the size of the population.

1142 della Valle, pp. 80, 95.

1143 Montazer-Saheb, pp. 55, 181; Nasiri, *Dastur*, pp. 200, 226; Mervi, p. 142. *Qaravol*s were also put out to scout for raiders as against the Baluch in the 1690s. Nasiri, *Dastur*, p. 72.

(*qaravol*), which had a separate commander or *talayehdar-e sepah*.[1144] The vanguard was often also split in a left and right group (*javangar* and *berangar*), which was backed by the center of the army. Normally the center was split up in a left and a right center (*qalb-e sul* and *qalb-e saq*), and between them the main center (*qalb, tip*). Flanking scouts (*bogrekchi*), usually *yuz-bashi*s and *qurchi*s, covered the left (*meisareh*; *dast-e chap*) and right wing (*meimaneh*; *dast-e rast*) and the main body of the army (*qalb-e sepah*), at about half a *farsakh* (3 km) distance, which followed the vanguard slowly under the grand-vizier with the *ordu*, the baggage, the remainder of the troops, the *'arabeh* (carts), cannon, and muskets.[1145] Often the army was divided into parts called *tip*, sometimes as many as four, which were under *qul-begis*.[1146] Behind the center was the rear-guard, variously referred to as *jondavol*, *choghdavol* or *saqeh*, which also doubled as the reserve. The rear-guard was under a separate commander, the *jondavol-bashi*.[1147] At the very end was the army train of camp followers and the *ordu-bazar*.

Spies were used to be aware of the enemy's movements and strength.[1148] Before marching the shah would also gave orders to spread disinformation with regards to his real objective. For example, 'Abbas I ordered Dhu'l-Feqar Khan, *vali* of Ardabil, in 1012/1603 to spread rumors that he would march to Mazandaran, while at the same time informing the *vali* about his real objective and precise marching route.[1149]

When the army was set into motion the shah sent staff, known as *baladchi*,[1150] who were familiar with the terrain, to reconnoiter and report which route had the best supplies of water and to obtain intelligence and to harry the enemy at every occasion.[1151] "The shah stationed squadrons of cavalry in front and on each side of the advancing Ottomans to furnish him with up-to-date information."[1152] These skirmishers were under "the

---

[1144] Montazer-Saheb, pp. 427, 357, 508; Shokri, p. 132, 299, 374, 468; Mervi, p. 129, 173, 178f.

[1145] Adle, p. 467; Savory, *History*, vol. 2, p. 815, 819; Monshi, vol. 2, p. 624, 628; Astarabadi, p. 173; Rumlu, p. 64, 92, 158, 284, 335, 430, 496; Mervi, p. 85.

[1146] Nasiri, *Dastur*, pp. 228-9; della Valle, p. 89. It also means regrouping. Mervi, pp. 23, 35, 45, 61f. (*tip resanidan; sakhtan*).

[1147] Valeh Esfahani, p. 780; Mervi, p. 530; Adle, p. 492; Rumlu, p. 413; Monshi, pp. 20, 38.

[1148] Seistani, p. 364; Uzbeg spies acting as religious mendicants (*qalandars*) were in the fortress. Ibid., p. 388; spies used on army movements. Valeh Esfahani, p. 285; Natanzi, pp. 142, 481; Don Juan, p. 137; Brosset, vol. 2, p. 62.

[1149] Papaziyan, 1959, doc. 1; see also Bacqué-Grammont, *Les Ottomans*, pp. 48, 75.

[1150] Montazer-Saheb, pp. 185, 217. Were these the same as the *balad-bashi*? Mervi, pp. 59, 65, 615, 635.

[1151] Savory, *History*, vol. 2, p. 815; Monshi, vol. 2, p. 624.

[1152] Savory, *History*, vol. 2, p. 860; Monshi, vol. 2, p. 669; Rumlu, pp. 336-7, 427, 430, 484; Nasiri, *Dastur*, p. 158.

command of his most experienced and brave officers. They licked their fingers in anticipation of Ottoman loot."[1153] Also, the advance-guard or *monqelay* which was send ahead of the army (or even the van-guard) often moved at speed march or *ilghar*.[1154] Also, at regular intervals the patrols, skirmishers, and flankers were relieved as were their commanders (*omara-ye charkhchi*).[1155]

As practice showed scouts and skirmishers were really needed to receive advance warning against enemy action. "The *qurchi*s learned that Talesheeh Kuli [in 1002/1593-4] had moved and had blocked the roads with trenches and barricades of tree trunks (the local term for these barricades is *bona-bor*) ... with musketeers stationed behind them. The *qurchi*s stormed them and routed the troops.[1156] The Gilani army blocked the road through a narrow valley, and behind this barricade they stationed musketeers and skilled archers.[1157] The Lors, in 988/1580-1, ambushed Khalil Khan in a mountain valley, and they hurled large rocks down from the tops of the hills, and fired arrows and muskets.[1158]

Another important element of army organization were the *yasaqi*s, who regulated the march of the army and guarded the roads. Their insignia were arrows, stuck in their turbans, their chief, known as *yasaqchi-bashi*, wearing a golden arrow.[1159] From the military point of view it seems that the *yasaqchi-bashi* was in charge of the mobilization of the auxiliaries.[1160] However, it is not clear in what way this function was subordinate to the *tovachi-bashi*.[1161] From the limited textual evidence it is clear that the *yasaqchi*s operated in conjunction with other groups which had a regulating function such as *qurchi*s and *yasavol*s.[1162] According to

---

[1153] Savory, *History*, vol. 1, p. 129; Monshi, vol. 1, p. 78.

[1154] Rumlu, pp. 253, 324, 326, 449, 472, 505.

[1155] Astarabadi, p. 173.

[1156] Savory, *History*, vol. 2, p. 636; Monshi, vol. 2, p. 462.

[1157] Savory, *History*, vol. 1, p. 185, Monshi, vol. 1, p. 112; see also Savory, *History*, vol. 1, p. 470 troops blocked in narrow defile. Tahmurath mobilized his cavalry and infantry and constructed a strong defensive position in the forests, making barricades of tree trunks. Ibid., vol. 2, p. 1082; Monshi, vol. 2, p. 869; Don Juan, p. 214.

[1158] Savory, *History*, vol. 1, p. 403; Monshi, vol. 1, p. 273. In Shirvan palisades (*chapar*) were erected. Rumlu, p. 422.

[1159] Della Valle, p. 71. One of the brothers of Qara Khalifeh wore an arrow upon his turban-cloth, and was Bahram Mirza's *yasaqi*. Membré, p. 19. For a picture of a *yasaqi* see Welch, *A King's Book*, fig. 14. Sobhan Verdi Beg was *yasaqchi-bashi* in 1043/1633-4, Astarabadi, p. 250.

[1160] Molla Jalal, p. 220.

[1161] Sobhan Verdi Beg, *yasaqchi-bashi*, Yusef, p. 149, Astarabadi, pp. 250, 207; Shah Nazar Beg, the *yasaqchi-bashi* died, his kisman Yadegar Beg succeeded him. Savory, *History*, vol. 2, p. 1101.

[1162] *Yasaqchiyan va qurchiyan*. Esfahani, p. 83. *tovachi va yasaqchiyan va yasavolan-e qur*. Ibid., p. 87.

Bayani so-called *nasaqchiler* were responsible for keeping order in the army. However, Krusinski stated clearly that the role of the *nasaqchis*, who were under a *nasaqchi-bashi*, was to engage the enemy, then they would withdraw to the rear, "where the form a Rear Guard, which is only to force those whom they have engaged with the Enemy to fight, and to hinder any Body from falling back." To that end they even killed soldiers who did not quickly returned to fight. This is confirmed by contemporary Armenian sources, who add that it was their role to police the army camp, to relay messages to the troops, to carry out the shah's orders, and like the public criers pass on orders in large gatherings.[1163]

To keep contact with the events elsewhere in the country and officials who had not joined the army use was made of messengers, Arabs, on fast dromedaries or *jammazeh*.[1164] If a message had to be send quickly this had to be done *chaparvar* or post-haste.[1165] These royal messengers were recognizable by a white silken band which was wound around their neck, which was fastened cross-wise around over their breast and back and in the form of a knot in front. "On pain of corporal punishment the messenger is not allowed to undo the knot until he has arrived at his destination where he has to deliver his letter. This is done, partly so that the messenger can be recognized as the royal mail, partly so that he will not tardy too long en route to freshen up."[1166] The *chapars* could take a better or less fatigued horse from anyone that they met underway, whether this person was a khan or not. In theory, the horse would be later restored to the owner.[1167]

In case of a retreat the emirs who normally constituted the vanguard were ordered to the rear, with instructions to maintain constant guard and at night to camp half a *farsakh* from the main camp.[1168] If the army met obstacles such as a river, the army crossed first and the baggage came later. "The shah therefore crossed over with his men by boat, leaving the baggage to be floated across later on rafts constructed of wood and reeds. The horses and camels were driven into the river and forced to swim across.[1169] Similarly, during forced marches (*ilghar*) the army waited at a predetermined location so that stragglers could rejoin the main force. Allahverdi Khan waited 2-3 days to allow stragglers to join, which they

1163 Bayani, KhanBaba, *Tarikh-e Nezami-ye Iran - jangha-ye doureh-ye Safavi*, Tehran 1353/1974, p. 75; Mervi, pp. 267, 278f; who were under a *nasaqchi-bashi*, pp. 534, 697, 769; Krusinksi, vol. 1, pp. 149-50; Brosset, *Collection*, vol. 2, pp. 268, 282, 293, 299.

1164 Adle, p. 461; 300 *jamazeh-ye savar-e tofangchi*. Seistani, p. 376.

1165 Afshar, *'Alamara-ye Tahmasp*. p. 350; *beh-rasm-e chapari*, Astarabadi, p. 256.

1166 Andersen, pp. 148, 151.

1167 Andersen, p. 149.

1168 Savory, *History*, vol. 2, p. 817; Monshi, vol. 2, p. 627.

1169 Savory, *History*, vol. 2, p. 920; Monshi, vol. 2, p. 731.

did coming in small groups, after having crossed the Dasht-e Lut.[1170] Prior to a forced march various necessary measures were taken such as the shodding of the horses.[1171] In Gilan horses were of little use, so the entire army had to go on foot, on which they wore "shoes made of cow-hide known as Charuk. The king himself wore these to set an example, marching at the head of his troops, we all following in his footsteps."[1172]

The following description by Eskander Beg gives an excellent picture of the army on the march.

> 300 cannon, with gun carriages, chains, and other equipment were available and the shah marched ... Qarchaqay Beg was placed in command of the artillery and the musketeers; a regiment of *gholam*s of the royal household was placed at his disposal; and he was charged with the supervision of the artillery whenever the army pitched camp and struck camp. The vanguard, was under Hosein Khan Shamlu and of other emirs, and numbered 12,000 men and it marched half a farsakh in front of the main body. According to a daily roster, one of the emirs of the van led his men out on patrol. Immediately behind the vanguard came the artillery with 10 musketeers stationed between every pair of gun carriages, making in all a force of three thousand musketeers, who marched on foot behind the chains of the gun carriages. Behind the artillery came the officer in charge, with the rest of the musketeers, marching in good order behind the guns. A number of qezelbash emirs were also detailed to support the artillery. Behind the regiments of musketeers came the shah and the main body composed of high-ranking emirs, troops of the royal household and the *gholam*s of the royal household forming the right and left wings. The whole army amounted to 40,000 regular troops and 10,000 musketeers, a total of 50,000 men. In addition, the number of servants, camel drivers, commissariat personnel, and other hangers-on all over the place was legion. Because of its size and the abundance of horses and pack animals, so much dust was raised by the army on the march that each man could scarcely see his neighbor. Twelve trumpets sounded constantly from the rear, so that the troops of the royal bodyguard and the *gholam*s could maintain station and not get separated from the center, where the shah was positioned. A number of emirs guarded the rear from

---

[1170] Adle, p. 444.

[1171] Adle, pp. 468, 471, 491; Valeh Esfahani, p. 666; *beh rasm-e monqelay* they went to Marv. Rumlu, pp. 152, 253, 324, 326.

[1172] Don Juan, p. 214.

surprise attack. Since it was not prudent to march by night in hostile country, the army marched by day. But because of the extreme heat, neither men nor animals, could travel more than two or three *farsakh*s a day; the size of the supply train accompanying the army also precluded rapid movement.[1173]

According to du Mans and Kaempfer, there was no order when the army pitched camp, anyone put his tent where he wanted it. Though, guards were posted to give warning against the enemy's approach.[1174] However, Membré states that "And at the place where the King's pavilions are pitched, they all lodge themselves according to their rank; some lodge near the court, some at a distance, according to their quality."[1175] This also seems to agree with the plan we have of Nader Shah's army camp that creates the impression of order and hierarchy. Hanway also remarks "In placing the camp a general regularity is observed, as far is agreeable to the size and shape of the ground; it being a rule constantly pursued, to place the tents of certain principal ministers and officers in the front, or to the right or left of the SHAHS's quarters."[1176] Also, hills and the like, were usually chosen as the site of the camp, because these provided a good defensive position. Moreover, the hill would be surrounded by a wall of rocks of about six cubits high, which was called a *matras* (pl. *mataris*).[1177] Thus, while the order may have seem to be chaotic to a European observer there was some order nevertheless.

When the army had caught up with the enemy it was of course vital to get reliable information about his strength.[1178] To that end skirmishers were sent, who had to ride up right to the enemy's camp and make prisoners to get information, which was called *zaban-giri*. Also, harrying the enemy and keeping him on its toes and giving him no rest was also part of the objective.[1179] Whenever prisoners were taken this was also considered to be a good omen for the coming battle. To sow doubt among the enemy's troops these prisoners were often released again and escorted through the lines to their own camp.[1180]

On the eve of battle the army set out patrols and guards (*pasdari, talay, qaravol*) and prepared their arms for the next day.[1181] Each soldier had a

1173 Savory, *History*, vol. 2, pp. 810-11; Monshi, vol. 2, pp. 619-20.

1174 Kaempfer, *Am Hofe*, p. 75; Richard, vol. 2, pp. 118, 287; Tavernier, p. 227.

1175 Membré, p. 23.

1176 Hanway, vol. 1, p. 245.

1177 Brosset, vol. 2, p. 271.

1178 Savory, *History*, vol. 1, p. 89; vol. 2, p. 887, 1217; Monshi, vol. 1, p. 54; vol. 2, pp. 695, 994.

1179 Rumlu, p. 414; Savory, *History*, vol. 2, p. 683; Monshi, vol. 1, p. 508; Natanzi, p. 569; Shah Tahmasp, pp. 56, 58.

1180 Savory, *History*, vol. 2, p. 1217; Monshi, vol. 2, p. 994.

1181 Valeh Esfahani, p. 128; Qomi, vol. 1, p. 70.

tent, those better equipped also had servants that looked after them, their arms and horses. This also held true, of course, for the officers and emirs. As pointed out above, the army baggage train offered everything that the soldiers needed. When a commander was not watchful and made merry the enemy might attack and take him unawares. For example, 'Aliqoli Khan did not believe his sentries and found himself prisoner.[1182] Also, when a commander did not set guards at all his army could be the target of a surprise night-attack (*shabikhvun*).[1183]

Rules of War
Sometimes a battle could be avoided and a single combat would take place between two champions. In fact, Don Juan states "The Persian method of fighting is by challenging to single combat, with a trumpet sounded or a king-at-arms send forward, and no ambush is allowed..... Yet it may be affirmed in clear terms that the Persian way of fighting is now in open combat, in hand-to-hand battle; and as to their artillery, they mask it or hold it in reserve."[1184]

If battle was given, some rules were supposed to be respected. For example, "As is the custom with us Persians they immediately send their heralds to the prince to challenge us. We accepted their challenge, and the signal was given to attack."[1185] Further, "it was contrary to protocol for emirs to give battle to kings."[1186] It was also expedient sometimes, because the shah was protected by a strong force, including the reserves. Therefore a commander when seeing the shah's parasol decided "let us not give battle, because the shah is there."[1187] For when the shah's standard and the prince's parasol came in sight, followed by the serried ranks of the royal army, 'Aliqoli Khan knew the contest was hopeless.[1188] The sight of the royal standards caused the Ottoman resistance to weaken, and many turned to flee.[1189]

This right to attack the shah belonged to the ruler of the opposing

---

[1182] Savory, *History*, vol. 1, p. 415; Monshi, vol. 1, p. 284.

[1183] Rumlu, p. 419; Afshar, *'Alamara-ye Tahmasp*. p. 357; Shokri, pp. 79-80, 115, 143, 361, 374; Don Juan, pp. 125, 151. Even when there were guards these were not always awake. della Valle, p. 88. The result of such an attack see Welch, *A King's Book*, fig. 241, pp. 156-9 which also shows the details of an army camp with its tents. Welch, *Royal Persian Manuscripts*, p. 88, plate 28 with tents.

[1184] Don Juan, p. 52; see also e.g. Montazer-Saheb, p. 154. For a miniature depicting a single combat see Welch, *A King's Book*, p. 164 (fig. 341); for a description of such a single combat see Boxer, pp. 74-5.

[1185] Don Juan, p. 199.

[1186] Savory, *History*, vol. 2, p. 617; Monshi, vol. 1, p. 444.

[1187] Savory, *History*, vol. 1, p. 114.

[1188] Savory, *History*, vol. 1, p. 415; Monshi, vol. 1, p. 284.

[1189] Savory, *History*, vol. 2, p. 831; Monshi, vol. 2, p. 641.

army,[1190] who, however, sometimes did not want to avail himself of that opportunity. An exasperated Shah 'Abbas declared [in 1004/1595-6] "This time, the [Uzbeg] Khan's reputation for valor demanded that he stand and fight like a man, so that God's will might be fulfilled and God's people spared the injury resulting from careless passage of armies."[1191] The Ottomans clashed with one of his patrols, and although it is contrary to the accepted rules of warfare to engage enemy patrols in strength, Mohammad Tekellu did so.[1192] However, rules are, if not to be broken, certainly to be bend, and therefore "although it was not appropriate for the shah to engage in battle in person with a mere Ottoman commander in chief, nevertheless the Shah kept himself in reserve to assist any of his army groups which might need the shelter of his kingly umbrella.[1193]

The same practice applied to the army commander, who had to command, not necessarily fight. "Although it is not normal military practice for a commander in chief to lead his men into battle in person, Emir Guna did so on this occasion, because he feared that his troops might suffer defeat."[1194] Although the Safavid army was initially a mainly tribal army, where soldiers obeyed their tribal chiefs rather than unknown line officers discipline prevailed in the Safavid army. The shah, or the army commander, really was in command. For "without express orders from the Shah Qarchaqay Khan was not allowed to give battle to the Ottomans.[1195]

Battle Formation
The standard battle formation or *yasal* was in the form of a half-moon with a center (*qalb*),[1196] left and right wings, a van-guard (*yazak* or *pish-qaravol*)[1197] with skirmishers (*charkhchis*) out ahead, a rear-guard (*chaghdavol*), and cannon and musketeers stationed a suitable points.[1198] Between the *charkhchis* and the main army there was usually another protective layer, called the *muchis*, who had to absorb the shock in case of an eventual breakthrough by the enemy, when the *charkhchis* failed to hold the line.[1199] The center and the wings were under the great emirs, while smaller army groups, *qul* or *tip-e sepah*, were under subordinate emirs, later known as *qul-begi*.[1200] In front of the army center wagons were

---

1190 Bacqué-Grammont, *Les Ottomans*, p. 36, n. 56.
1191 Savory, *History*, vol. 2, p. 682; Monshi, vol. 1, p. 507.
1192 Savory, *History*, vol. 2, p. 867; Monshi, vol. 1, p. 677.
1193 Savory, *History*, vol. 2, p. 888; Monshi, vol. 1, p. 696.
1194 Savory, *History*, vol. 2, p. 1023; Monshi, vol. 2, p. 818.
1195 Savory, *History*, vol. 2, p. 1151; Monshi, vol. 2, p. 932; one of the commanders said taking the fortress of Qandahar was difficult and that the shah had not given orders to that effect. Seistani, p. 409; della Valle, p. 90.
1196 Valeh Esfahani, pp. 739, 780; Afshar, *'Alamara-ye Tahmasp*, p. 163.
1197 Valeh Esfahani, p. 202; *yazakdaran*, Nasiri, *Dastur*, pp. 28, 109.
1198 Savory, *History*, vol. 2, pp. 885; 756.
1199 Amini, p. 31; Rumlu, p. 144-5.
1200 Valeh Esfahani, pp. 238, 739.

placed on which Frankish light cannon were mounted.[1201]

The army wings were traditionally distributed among the Qezelbash tribes according to a standard order, although there were variations on the theme. Usually, the Shamlu led the right wing, and the Ostajalu the left wing. The other major Qezelbash tribes were usually placed as follows: The right wing: Shamlu, Turkoman, Rumlu, Tekellu, Akrad and the left wing: Ostajalu, Dhu'l-Qadr, Afshar, Qajar.[1202] Later, beginning under Shah 'Abbas I the role of the Qezelbash troops was diminished and their traditional place in the wings was partly taken over by the *gholam*s and *qurchi*s. The *qurchi*s were on the right side of the shah, the *gholam*s on the left side[1203]

The *tovachi*s were in charge of putting the army in proper battle order, which was referred to as *saff-ara, tasviyeh-e sofuf* and *ta'biyeh-ye lashkar*. Sometimes all the camels were brought together and chained together so that they would not take to their heels.[1204] Elvand Mirza put his camels at the back of his army and fastened them with chains to prevent his soldiers from fleeing.[1205] "At the hour fixed both armies were set in array, the first, second, and third columns being al in order by the break of the day."[1206] A Persian source confirms this three line battle formation. "There were three rows of mounted and foot riflemen at a distance of one farsakh; there were also three rows of cavalry, and in the center, which is the shah's place, were all the *sardaran, aqayan, yuz-bashiyan* and magnates of Iran."[1207]

The *tupchi*s and *tofangchi*s (usually) were placed in front of the first row (*saff*), the gunners before the musketeers.[1208] Because of their exposed position on one occasion the *tofangchi*s came to see the emirs saying that they could not defend the army if no measures were taken to protect them through barricades.[1209] The Shirvan-shah placed his foot in front of his cavalry, which were put into disorder through the shooting of arrows by the enemy. He could not contain himself any longer and gave his cavalry

---

1201 Savory, *History*, vol. 1, pp. 89-90; Monshi, vol. 1, p. 54-55. For the armament, fighting tactics and various functions of the Mazandarani army see Mar'ashi, *Tarikh-e Khandan*, pp. eighteen-twenty one. Bayani, *Tarikh-e Nezami-ye Iran*, offers a detailed tactical discussion with maps of all major Safavid battles.

1202 Haneda, p. 60. For details on half moon battle order and who was in charge of wings, center and rear- and van-guard see Haneda, pp. 60, 75-6 and Adle, p. 492.

1203 Savory, *History*, vol. 2, p,. 756; Monshi, vol. 1, p. 571; Nasiri, *Alqab*, pp. 13, 16.

1204 Valeh Esfahani, pp. 117-8, 219, 224, 255; Natanzi, p. 80 the *qurchi*s on one side, in the manner of [*beh rasm*] *tarh* put themselves in *saff-ara*. Valeh Esfahani, p. 236; Rumlu, pp. 92, 281.

1205 Qomi, vol. 1, p. 71; Montazer-Saheb, p. 525.

1206 *Travels to Tana*, part 2, p. 181.

1207 Seistani, p. 443.

1208 Rumlu, p. 284; Nasiri, *Alqab*, p. 24.

1209 Rumlu, p. 290. *Kucheh-bandi* or barricading was effective against Uzbeks. Ibid., pp. 443-4.

order to attack. These rode down their own foot which thus could not support them with their arrow fire.[1210]

Usually there was a battle plan complete with wings and proper placement of troops. For example, "Most of these reinforcements of Hamzeh Mirza were auxiliary troops and few were fully equipped .. their horses were poor, therefore placed in the center to create an impression of numbers."[1211] Sometimes, however, the commander preferred not to have one and "to attack at once, without waiting to form in proper battle order, to prevent the enemy from forming an accurate estimate of the size of their force."[1212] It seldom occurred that to shore up courage, soldiers were given to drink alcohol just prior to the battle. I have come across such an event only once, and that in the pre-Safavid period.[1213] Although at the eve of the Chaldiran battle in 1514, all the Persian commanders, including Esma'il I, were so drunk that an Ottoman spy could walk through their camp and observe this encouraging phenomenon, this does not seem to have been a case of shoring up courage.[1214] Aubin has made a good case that this was a case of Turkic shamanistic ritual rather than just getting plastered.[1215]

The shah adorned the center with other important emirs and officials.[1216] This was not necessarily a safe place, in particular when the battle went bad for the shah's own side. Those high-ranking officials (grand vizier, sadr) that were with Shah Esma'il I during the battle of Chaldiran were all killed, for example.[1217] At another battle, Mir 'Abd al-Karim, the motavalli of Mashhad, who was stationed at the foot of the standard, was slain by unknown assailants.[1218] The royal center was recognizable by the gilded ball on top of the royal standard known as the chatr-e zarnegar which was visible from afar.[1219] The gilded globe that surmounted the shah's own personal standard was distinguished from other royal standards and was known as yukruk meaning "swift courser."[1220] The royal standard was held by a chatrdar.[1221] In late Safavid times, this officer was called chatrdar-bashi.[1222]

1210 Qomi, vol. 1, p. 60.

1211 Savory, *History*, vol. 1, p. 472; Monshi, vol. 1, p. 335.

1212 Savory, *History*, vol 2, p. 852; Monshi, vol. 1, p. 661.

1213 Mar'ashi, *Tarikh-e Khandan*, p. 41.

1214 Shah Tahmasp, p. 29; Qomi, vol. 1, p. 232; Bacqué-Grammont, *Les Ottomans*, p. 47.

1215 Aubin, "L'Avènement", pp. 46-7.

1216 Savory, *History*, vol. 1, p. 69; Monshi, vol. 1, p. 42.

1217 Savory, *History*, vol. 1, p. 70; Monshi, vol. 1, p. 43.

1218 Savory, *History*, vol. 1, p. 379; Monshi, vol. 1, p. 257.

1219 Valeh Esfahani, pp. 667, 777, 186; Savory, *History*, vol. 1, p. 79; Monshi, vol. 1, p. 47. Tahmasp Mirza's golden parasol was visible. Savory, *History*, vol. 1, p. 473; Monshi, vol. 1, p. 337.

1220 Savory, *History*, vol. 1, p. 114; Monshi, vol. 1, p. 69.

1221 Shahqoli Beg *gholam*. Valeh Esfahani, p. 780.

1222 Asaf, p. 100.

"When the king of Persia personally goes out on campaign, the fact is advertised to all by his standard, which is then carried before him. Further, the umbrella of state is seen held over the king and his horse as he rides, and the umbrella is adorned with precious stones, so that it glitters in splendour like the very sun."[1223] Apart from the royal golden parasol the shah's center also often had various standards (*'alam*) and/or banners (*parcham*). Shah Esma'il I had a triangular green banner with the half moon, although the lion-sum emblem had been in use since Sheikh Joneid.[1224] Ebrahim Mirza with the *sadr* and the *sheikh al-eslam* were in the center next to the banner, which carried the text: *nasr^{un} min Allah* or *nasr^{un} min Allah va fath^{un} qarib*.[1225] In 1539, "in front go the banners, which they call 'alam, which are lances covered with red broadcloth, with two points, and on top of the lance a circle, and, inside the said circle certain letters of copper, cut out and gilded, which say, '*Ali wali Allah la ilah illa Allah*; *'Ali wali allah wa Allahu Akbar*. They are carried in the hand on horseback. As many standards go as there are kingdoms, and below the said letters are armozeens of red silk with double points."[1226] In the 1670s, the Persian banner is described as "A Bloody Sword with a double Point, in a White Field, and is always carried next the Emperor's Person."[1227]

According to Chardin many colored triangular flags were used in battle with prayers or Qoran verses,[1228] which may be the same as the *parcham-e rangarang a'lam-e saltanat* mentioned in early Safavid times.[1229] In addition, banners with the Dhu'l-Fiqar sword and the lion-sun emblem were also used.[1230] The shah, of course, also had a special official or ensign (*'alamdar*) to hold the standard.[1231] This official was also known as *tuqchi* in 1516, of whom there could be more than one at the same time as is clear from the army review in 1516 amongst whom figured Khan Turmish Tukchi, emir of Qom and Soltan Chelebi Tukchi, emir of Shiraz.[1232] This official was also referred to as *'alamdar-bashi*.[1233] The

---

1223 Don Juan, p. 51.

1224 Dhoka, p. 208; the royal *'alam-e azhdar-e peikar.* Valeh Esfahani, p. 194.

1225 Montazer-Saheb, pp. 521, 537; Dhoka, p. 209.

1226 Membré, p. 24. For miniatures depicting banners see Welch, *A King's Book*, p. 138; Gray, p. 135; Hillenbrand, p. 66 (fig. 147).

1227 Fryer, vol. 3, pp. 55, 60. He refers to Dhu'l-Feqar, the sword of 'Ali, the fourth caliph. See for a picture Dhoka, p. 210; see also Nasiri, *Dastur*, p. 100 with similar Qoran texts on banners.

1228 See picture in Dhoka, p. 209; Chardin, vol. 5, p. 321.

1229 Valeh Esfahani, p. 117.

1230 Chardin, vol. 5, p. 321; see picture Dhoka, p. 207.

1231 Shah Tahmasp, p. 40; Abu'l-Qasem kholfa-ye Qajar *'alamdar-e khasseh.* Qomi, vol. 1, p. 312; Ghaffari Qazvini, p. 296. Daneh Moh. Soltan father of Akhi Soltan 'Alamdar. Montazer-Saheb, p. 351.

1232 Bacqué-Grammont, *Les Ottomans*, p. 182; Doerfer, vol. 2, p. 642.

1233 Chardin, vol. 5, p. 321; Dhoka, p. 209; Montazer-Saheb, pp. 351, 353.

bannner of the *qurchi-bashi* was green, that of the *qollar-aghasi* was white, and of the *tupchi-bashi* was green with a white border. Other officials also had colored banners that were peculiar to them.[1234]

Being highly visible was a double-edged sword, especially if you were loosing. This is what Hamzeh Mirza almost experienced when things went bad for him during battle. Fortunately for him, "The dust of battle obscured the prince's [Hamzeh Mirza] parasol, so that the rebel troops passed right by the prince's center without realizing it and returned to their own lines."[1235] Each of the emirs had as a standard piece of their accoutrements also a standard or *'alam*. We know little about them, but it seems they also had distinctive functions. For we find mention made of a skirmishers' banner (*parcham-e 'alam-e charkhchiyan*).[1236] Since Farhad Khan did not have with him his corps commander's standard, which would have provided a rallying point for the Safavid skirmishers, their retreat became a rout.[1237] According to Don Juan the number of troops present in the army was exactly known by the number of standards that were seen, for with every thousand men present a separate standard was unfurled. He claimed to have counted 200 standards displayed.[1238] The adverse side of the ruler's standard was that when the standard-bearer would ride off with the colors if the shah was dead, or believed to be so. This happened in 1734, when Nader Shah had his horse killed under him and it took a while before he could get remounted. As a result, the standard-bearer left the field, which alarmed the Persian army, which panicked and fled.[1239]

Charkhchis

The Persian army, like its traditional opponents, first send its skirmishers, *charkhchis*, *sharbasharan*, or *haraval*[1240] ahead and when they got sight of the advance patrols or skirmishers of the enemy they attacked.[1241] This was also called *be rasm-e qaravoli*.[1242] The idea was to scatter these advance troops, cause panic in the ranks of the troops that were stationed behind them, and to put them to flight, thus cluttering the enemy's battle formation and making it difficult for the enemy to maneuver. If the skirmishers were successful in doing so they usually would attack the enemy's center. The Persian commander seeing that his skirmishers had caused panic and driven a wedge in the opposing army's formation would

---

1234 Nasiri, *Alqab*, pp. 13, 16, 19.
1235 Savory, *History*, vol.1, p. 474.
1236 Valeh Esfahani, p. 777.
1237 Savory, *History*, vol. 2, p. 756; Monshi, vol. 1, 571.
1238 Don Juan, p. 51.
1239 Fraser, *Nadir*, p. 110.
1240 Ben Khvandamir, p. 412; Mervi, pp. 97, 130f.
1241 Montazer-Saheb, p. 549.
1242 Natanzi, pp. 78, 167.

attack either by ordering his wings or the center to charge as well.[1243] This tactic could, of course, work both ways. The Uzbeg victory over the Persian army in 952/1545 was ascribed by Rumlu to the fact that the Persian army had started the battle without *charkhchi*s and *muchi*s.[1244] But all armies concerned continued with this opening move, because sometimes an even small, but a fearless attack by the *charkhchiyan-e ateshbar*[1245] could lead to the defeat of the enemy. "Soltan Soleiman flew in a rage when he saw that his troops were defeated by a small force of skirmishers and advance patrols in 941/1534-5.[1246] At one time, (against the Dhu'l-Qadrs) the *charckhi*s consisted of 1200 men.[1247] The *charkhchi*s also were used to lure the enemy in a trap as happened in 1618, when the fleeing Persian skirmishers drew the Ottoman army into the Persian army train. The Ottoman troops started to plunder the *ordu-bazar*. At that moment, the Persian reserve attacked routing the Ottoman troops, which had to withdraw completely routed.[1248]

Charkhchi-bashi

The *charkhchi-bashi* was in charge of the advance patrols. In the 1630s, he is even referred to as *charkhchi-bashi-ye 'askar-e Iran*.[1249] We know practically nothing about this official beyond the fact that he was supposed to lead the charge.[1250] The function was usually held by a mid-level official, but one with promise.[1251] In the 1630s, the appointment of Khalaf Beg, the *sofreh-bashi*, to the function of *charckhchi-bashi* was considered a promotion.[1252] Often this official also had other functions such as provincial governor.[1253] To become a *charkhchi* was in itself noteworthy, for the various Safavid chroniclers make a point of it to mention such an event not only of the appointment of the *charkhchi-bashi*, but also of those of the leading military that were appointed as *charkhchi*. For the selection of those that were to be *charkhchi* often appears to have

---

[1243] Savory, *History*, vol.1, p. 126-7; 351, 473; Monshi, vol. 1, pp. 76, 236, 336.

[1244] Rumlu, p. 404; Savory, *History*, vol. 2, p,. 756; Monshi, vol. 1, p. 571.

[1245] Montazer-Saheb, p. 76.

[1246] Savory, *History*, vol. 1, p. 114; Monshi, vol. 1, p. 69.

[1247] Valeh Esfahani, p. 163.

[1248] della Valle, pp. 88-9.

[1249] Shamlu, p. 473.

[1250] Yusef, p. 216.

[1251] Qomi, vol. 2, p. 739.

[1252] Yusef, pp. 179, 277.

[1253] Beiram Khan *charkhchi-bashi* Montazer-Saheb, p. 426; Emir Aslan son of Vali Khan Ostajalu Qomi, vol. 2, p. 739; Nazar 'Ali Khan, *hakem* of Ardabil. Shamlu, p. 473. Vali Soltan Ostajalu Qomi, vol. 2, p. 674, 688; Khalaf Beg Yusef, p. 216

Mehrab Khan *charkhchi-bashi* Shamlu, pp. 335, 429, 473; he also was *begler-begi* of Qandahar.

been made during the formation of the army prior to its march toward the battle field rather than it being a regular function. I.e. this year's *charkhchi*s need not to be last year's or next year's *charkhchi*s.[1254]

When the battle began there arose on all sides the rousing war cry "*Allah, Allah*" which was characteristic for the Qezelbash.[1255] These battle cries were not as characteristic as they may seem for in pre-Safavid times soldiers cried "*al-Aman*, or *Allah* and *Allah al-akbar*".[1256] In the 17th century the battle cry was: "*Yuru, yuru*, or march, forwards."[1257] The horsemen tried to ride to the gun carriages and the barricade, and with blows of the sword to sever the chains linking the gun carriages. Then the protective cover of the musketeers was hacked to pieces. Both heavy artillery, light cannon (*zarbzan*) and muskets were such that smoke blotted out the brightness of the day.[1258] When the cavalry had insufficient room to wield their lances, they began to fire a volley of arrows at the opposing forces.[1259]

Increasingly, the use of modern arms was used to overwhelm the enemy. Nader Shah made good use of his modern arms. In his battle against the Abdali Afghans in 1729 Tahmaspqoli Khan (the later Nader Shah) kept his men close, and being posted on a rising ground, played upon them with some small field-pieces, causing considerable damage among the enemy. He only ordered his troops to discharge their small-arms until the enemy was within forty yards, which caused such havoc among the Abdalis that they retreated. This allowed the Persian arquebusiers to reload and repeat the same manoeuvre several times, followed by a general engagement. The result was a resounding victory for the Safavid troops.[1260]

During battle, orders from the chief commander to his sub-commanders were communicated by messengers, often *qurchi*s and *nasaqchi*s, while orders within each regiment or detachment were loudly cried by criers or *jarchi*s.[1261] Nevertheless, once the battle was engaged, it looked to European observers that "The Persians observe no order in fighting; the different khans, sultans etc. mixing their fuzileers with their bowmen and such as fight with lances indiscriminately. The Persian

---

[1254] Qomi, vol. 1, pp. 77, 92; vol. 2, pp. 787, 791, 820; Shamlu, p. 334; Yusef, pp. 58.

[1255] Afshar, '*Alamara-ye Tahmasp*. p. 376; Savory, *History*, vol 2, p. 891; Monshi, vol. 2, p. 699; Valeh Esfahani, p. 163; Natanzi, p. 14; the "*sufiyan-e lashkar* cried *allah, allah* and *salavat*s". Qomi, vol. 2, p. 966; or also "'*Ali, 'Ali*". Astarabadi, p. 196.

[1256] Mar'ashi, *Tarikh-e Khandan*, pp. 50, 180.

[1257] Kaempfer, *Am Hofe*, p. 76. According to du Mans they cried "*yeri, yeri*." Richard, vol. 2, p. 289.

[1258] Savory, *History*, vol. 1, 70; Monshi, vol. 1, p. 42.

[1259] Savory, *History*, vol. 1, p. 476; Monshi, vol. 1, p. 339.

[1260] Fraser, *Nadir*, p. 93.

[1261] Valeh Esfahani, p. 784; Montazer-Saheb, p. 304; Brosset, vol. 2, p. 293.

archers they retreat rather than run away, like the Parthians, they turn their back to the enemy as they draw the bow to shoot with greater power. The fuzileers copying them, after having fired their piece.[1262] However, the commanders' standards served as rallying point.[1263]

Fleeing troops, generally had to expect no quarter, for usually the attackers stopped to finish off even wounded soldiers.[1264] The wounded of the winning side were cared for in a field hospital, which e.g. 'Abbas I visited to show his appreciation.[1265] The dead were left to rot, while the heads, if the shah was in the battlefield himself, were stacked up in the form of a pyramid.[1266] The reason was that a large number of stuffed heads of enemy soldiers would bring them a royal reward. Also, the soldiers were wont to adorn themselves with the ears of their enemy.[1267] In fact, only important officers, or someone who had put up a valiant fight, could hope to be spared. In the former case, such a person could hope to be ransomed, to be taken into enemy service, or to be sent back to his own lines with presents. The brave soldier usually was honored by the enemy and send back. If a very large number of troops were involved prisoners were also made, many of whom could even join the ranks of the conquering army. "Of those in the fort a number were registered as employees of the divan and received wages; others preferred military service."[1268] However, others were less fortunate and were beheaded, or shackled and shown-off with the booty. When Elvand Mirza was defeated, part of his troops taken prisoner and shackled, others beheaded and with other spoils of victory triumphantly shown off.[1269]

Soldiers therefore did their utmost not to be caught by the enemy. When put to flight, if you could not outrun the enemy, you tried to put up a running fight to escape, or if all else failed die a honorable death. "Mostafa Beg, realizing that he was in a tight spot, ordered his men to dismount and use their horses as cover to protect them from the Uzbeg arrows and musket fire. In this way, he conducted a fighting retreat on foot for about four farsakh in 1001/1592-3. Qarchaqay Beg formed his men up, dismounting from their horses and using them as protection

---

1262 della Valle, vol. 7, p. 95;

1263 della Valle, p. 95; Savory, *History*, vol. 2, p. 756; Monshi, vol. 1, p. 571.

1264 Savory, *History*, vol. 1, p. 91; Monshi, vol. 1, p. 56; della Valle, vol. 7, p. 89.

1265 Molla Jalal, p. 303.

1266 Qomi, vol. 1, p. 61.

1267 Sherley, p. 210; della Valle, p. 58.

1268 Savory, *History*, vol. 2, p. 933; Monshi, vol. 2, p. 743.

1269 Valeh Esfahani, p. 116. Many important people were taken prisoner, but others, including emirs, were killed. Valeh Esfahani, p. 163, 166. Prisoners taken, Valeh Esfahani, p. 188. Many were taken prisoner, part of whom were beheaded. Natanzi, pp. 109, 504; della Valle, p. 58. For picture of a Turkoman prisoner see *Rahnama-ye Ketab* 7 (2), 1343/1964, p. 279; see also Don Juan, p. 226.

against the musketballs flying in all directions. [1270]

Role of Music

An emir was a lord of the standard ('alam) and kettledrum, for music played an essential and important role in military life. The standard equipment for a battle group was a karnas (trumpet), nafir, luleh, shahiq, zafir-e Shirvaniyan (various types of flutes and trumpets), kus (kettle drum) and naqqarehs (drums).[1271] The Gilani troops sounded trumpets, fashioned from concha veneris.[1272] The sounding of golden trumpets, was the prerogative of the royal family.[1273] To play one's military band and to sound them in frontier areas, was sometimes done by emirs, in the hope that the enemy would hear of them and that his prestige would correspondingly increase.[1274]

Consequently prior, during, and after a battle the air rang with the sound of trumpets, fifes, tympani, and kettledrums.[1275] "With such thundering of trumpets, kettle-drums carried upon camels, and suchlike instruments of war, that a man would have thought heaven and earth were tilting together. Their trumpets being all straight, some two yards and a half in length, having such a deep, harsh, and horrible voice that it would amaze a man to hear them, if he never heard them before."[1276] Music was also played during the siege of a fortress during attacks.[1277]

Kaempfer, in the 1680s, commented that there is military music (long horns, kettle drums) in the Persian army, but it does not serve to signal or give orders or even to encourage the soldiers to fight.[1278] However, Persian sources give a different impression. First, commanders such as Shah Esma'il I ordered the drums to sound for breaking camp,[1279] and also to keep flanks in line. When the army was on the march "twelve trumpets sounded constantly from the rear, so that the troops of the royal body guard and the gholams could maintain station and not to get separated from the center, where the Shah was positioned."[1280] Also, with the

---

[1270] Savory, History, vol. 2, pp. 629, 889; Monshi, vol. 1, p. 456; Ibid, vol. 2, p. 697.

[1271] Rumlu, pp. 159, 282; 422; the nafir-e karna and na'reh-ye hendi-daray accompanied the start of battle. Valeh Esfahani, p. 194. Also Natanzi, p. 202.

[1272] Savory, History, vol..1, p. 396; Monshi, vol. 1, 268.

[1273] Savory. History, vol. 1, p. 429; Monshi, vol. 1, p. 298?.

[1274] Savory. History, vol. 1, p. 429; Mar'ashi, p. 128.

[1275] Savory, History, vol. 2, p. 831; Monshi, vol. 2, p. 641; Valeh Esfahani, p. 194; Natanzi, p. 202; Richard, vol. 2, p. 287.

[1276] Sherley, p. 117.

[1277] Afshar, 'Alamara-ye Tahmasp, p, 181. see also Qomi, vol 1, p. 60. For a picture of the "military band" during an attack see Welch, A King's Book, pp. 136 (fig. 102), 138 (detail); Gray, pp. 128, 134-5.

[1278] Kaempfer, Am Hofe, p. 76.

[1279] Savory, History, 1, p. 61; Monshi, vol. 1, p. 37.

[1280] Savory, History, vol. 2, p. 810; Monshi, vol. 2, p. 621.

Shamlus, the shah sent several trumpeters and another detachment of troops from the right wing.[1281] The *naqqareh*s and *karnas* were beaten and blown, the standards were unfurled and the army engaged the enemy.[1282] Each wing of the Seistan army had a number of *karna* (trumpets),[1283] these would be sounded as soon fresh troops entered into battle, according to plan.[1284] It is also mentioned that the drum of departure (*tabl-e rahil*)[1285], and of retreat or return (*tabl-e moraje'at*) was beaten,[1286] and finally to announce victory.[1287] The Persian signals may have been rudimentary by comparison with European ones, but they were signals and they were effective, and that was all that counted.

Siege Operations

If an ambush or a pitched battle, the preferred military tactic of the Safavid army, was not possible or brought no solution, because the enemy force was able to withdraw in a fort of fortified town, there was no choice but to conduct siege warfare.[1288] Siege operations made warfare different, longer lasting, and logistically more difficult. In fact, without proper preparation to ensure that the siege would be supported by sufficient supplies of food, fodder, and fire power, the siege was likely to fail. The siege of Baku in 988/1590 was raised due to shortage of supplies.[1289] Also, the Persian army had not been very successful at siege warfare. "To capture a fort from the Ottomans was usually reckoned to be an impossible task," according to Eskander Monshi.[1290] Consequently, a siege was not something that the Persian military liked, and often the smaller provincial armies were not even equipped to do so. For when Kustandil, *begler-begi* of Shirvan, laid siege to Shamakhi he did not have adequate equipment for this purpose. He therefore "asked the shah to send him materials for casting cannon, lead, gunpowder, and a number of gunners. In response, the shah sent a gunner named Abu Torab Beg, with a team of workmen and the necessary materials."[1291] When it was clear from the beginning that a military action would lead to a siege the shah saw to it that the expeditionary force was properly equipped for this type of work. For

---

1281 Savory, *History*, vol 2, p. 890; Monshi, vol. 2, p. 699.
1282 Seistani, p. 283.
1283 Seistani, p. 346, 300.
1284 Mar'ashi, *Tarikh-e Khandan*, p. 227.
1285 Nasiri, *Dastur*, p. 98.
1286 Rumlu, pp. 173, 295; *tabl-e baz-gasht; -jang*, Afshar, *'Alamara-ye Tahmasp*, p. 214.
1287 Mar'ashi, *Tarikh-e Khandan*, p. 243-4.
1288 Savory, *History*, vol. 1, p. 61; Monshi, vol. 1, p. 37; for a miniature picture of a siege around 1500 see F. Rosen, *Persien in Wort und Bild* (Berlin 1926), p. 240.
1289 Valeh Esfahani, p. 622.
1290 Savory, *History*, vol. 2, p. 835; Monshi, vol. 2, p. 645.
1291 Savory, *History*, vol. 2, p. 872; Monshi, vol. 2, p. 681.

example, "Farhad Khan provided with musketeers and siege guns commenced the siege of the fortress of Larejan."[1292] 'Abbas II, when he decided to lay siege to Qandahar, had cannon, balls and gun-powder brought from allover Persia months before the actual siege took place (Erivan, Isfahan, Hormuz, and Mashhad) to be used for that siege.[1293]

In 1006/1598, 'Abbas spent therefore a month collecting provisions, which was important, because the Uzbegs hid behind the walls of their forts, which invariably had forced the Persian forces in the past to retreat due to lack of food and fodder.[1294] After besieging the fort for 18 days the Qezelbash were forced to abandon the siege on account of the shortage of supplies and the destitution of the population in the area.[1295] Things were invariably better if the local population had enough supplies and could support the additional burden of feeding a voracious army, or when appropriate measures were taken to ensure that sufficient supplies were available to sustain a long campaign. During the siege of the fortress of Baghdad peasants from allaround brought supplies (food and fodder) to the Qezelbash.[1296] At the start of the Khorasan campaign in 1591, the army's orders were to camp in the Bestam plain until the crop had been harvested and, if the Uzbegs launched any raids, to march against them; they were also to collect military intelligence from all parts of Khorasan. After the crops had been harvested and safely stored in the forts.[1297]

The major part of the siege operations, apart from outright assault, was to build breast-works and gradually push these forward right up to the walls. This allowed the besiegers to put siege guns (cannon and cauldron) to be put in place and to play on the towers and battlements and to shake the foundations of the fortress.[1298] The shah divided among his emirs the responsibility for the various aspects of the siege operations.[1299] The troops took up positions among the cultivated areas and walled gardens around the fort. Each group erected high palisades on the side of their tents which faced the fort to protect them from enemy fire.[1300] Either the troops were ordered to dig a narrow trench across the open space in front of the fortress, where a detachment of troops, including musketeers of the royal stirrup, were stationed, with the object of preventing anyone from

---

[1292] Savory, *History*, vol. 2, p. 697; Monshi, vol. 1, p. 522; see Don Juan, p. 218 for an amusing story.

[1293] Andersen, pp. 151, 153, 155.

[1294] Adle, p. 434.

[1295] Savory, *History*, vol. 1, p. 388; Monshi, vol. 1, p. 263, see also Natanzi, p. 504.

[1296] Yusef, p. 64.

[1297] Savory, *History*, vol. 2, p. 712; Monshi, vol. 1, p. 533.

[1298] Savory, *History*, vol. 1, p. 128; Monshi, vol. 1, p. 77; Rumlu, p. 450, 477; Afshar, *'Alamara-ye Tahmasp*, p. 205.

[1299] Savory, *History*, vol. 1, p. 413; vol. 2, p. 811, 835; Monshi, vol. 1, p. 282, vol. 2, pp. 622, 645; Rumlu, p. 477; Afshar, *'Alamara-ye Tahmasp*, p. 181.

[1300] Savory, *History*, vol. 2, p 834; Monshi, vol, vol. 2, p. 644-5.

emerging from the gates of the fort,[1301] or a blockhouse was built facing the main gates of the fort and manned with musketeers and *gholam*s to deny the defenders ingress and egress.[1302] These protective measures also served to protect the digging and tunneling operations.[1303] During the first week or so, usually no shot was fired for the army would be busy making palisades (*sabiyeh*).[1304]

Trenches (*jar*) were dug on all sides of the fort; mining operations proceeded apace; and ditches were dug to drain off the water from the moat.[1305] Spring mudslides and rocks were used to fill the moat,[1306] or other means were applied to do so.[1307] A special officer, a so-called chief of the pioneers (*bildar-bashi*), was in charge of the tunneling operations.[1308] The digging operations were done by foot soldiers, or by the local population who were drafted for that purpose, with spades (*bil*) and pick-axes (*keleng*).[1309] But even the cavalry (*qurchi*s, *gholam*s and others) were used to dig. For example, Eskander Monshi reports that "the *qurchi*s, mindful of their reputation as crack troops, labored day and night at the tunnel."[1310]

However, usually, local workgangs or *hashar* were commandeered for this type of work. In 993/1585 the emirs began to construct breastworks around the citadel of the Tabriz, the work was divided among the emirs, but they had not enough troops to encircle the citadel. "A levy of men with spade and pick-axes was made throughout Azerbaijan and siege guns were cast under the supervision of Morad Beg, *tupchi bashi*. The mosque of Uzun Hasan was chosen as the starting point of a mine, and sappers started to work." .... breastworks were carried forward step by step, and only after making sure that the rear was secure and one was covered by musket fire, in case of sorties.[1311] Usually, the men started digging trenches, commencing at a point a considerable distance from the fort. Every few yards a towerlike structure was erected, with a ditch around it, and in these defense points musketeers, archers, and crack troops were stationed to protect the men who were digging the trenches. In this way,

---

[1301] Savory, *History*, vol. 2, p, 835; Monshi, vol. 2, p. 645.

[1302] Savory, *History*, vol. 2, p. 903; Monshi, vol. 2, p. 710.

[1303] Natanzi, p. 500.

[1304] Seistani, p. 443.

[1305] Savory. *History*, vol. 2, p. 811; Monshi, vol. 2. p. 622.

[1306] Valeh Esfahani, p. 110.

[1307] Rumlu, p. 530, see also pp. 67, 103.

[1308] Elzebar Beg, *bildar-bashi*, a *gholam-e khasseh* who became governor of Abivard, Yusef, p. 199; Asaf, p. 101.

[1309] Valeh Esfahani, pp. 650, 679; Natanzi, p. 203; Rumlu, p. 230.

[1310] Savory, *History*, vol. 2, pp. 939, 906; Monshi, vol. 2, pp. 748, 715.

[1311] Savory, *History*, vol. 1, p. 451; Monshi, vol. 1, p. 317; see also Natanzi, p. 203, 237.

the trenches were pushed forward.[1312] Probably for this reason a special officer was put in charge of the trenches, the so-called *seibeh-bashi*, whose task, undoubtedly, was to see to it that they were properly constructed, maintained and manned.[1313]

Quantities of earth were brought from elsewhere, if need be, and the siege works went on day and night.[1314] The troops moved forward their breastworks by means of avenues of baskets. Night and day the men worked to bring up the materials, and the basket weavers worked flat out to produce more baskets. Other men fetched earth and clay to fill the baskets, carrying it considerable distances. A thick screen, faced with iron and mounted on a gun carriage, was constructed so that the workmen could continue without danger from enemy bullets and mortars; in this way, working at night and standing guard during the day, they inched their way forward.[1315]

The besieged did not remain idle either and put up a stout defense and threw up counterworks to enable them to make sorties.[1316] The defenders also made efforts to destroy the work that had been done during the day by night. The Safavid musketeers, aiming by the light of torches, repelled them, every night there were casualties on both sides.[1317] Because duty at the pallisades was arduous and boring oftentimes, the soldiers had their vulnerable moments. They sometimes took to drinking, which during the 1512 Uzbeg campaign led to a night-attack by the Uzbeg garrison who killed 300 *qurchi*s. The enemy tended to attack, in particular "when the night guard gone off duty and the daytime guard had not yet come."[1318]

Part of siege work entailed tunneling, and "the Persian are very expert miners and engineers, in which qualities they surpass any other nation" a Portuguese report observed.[1319] For this kind of work *naqqaban* or tunnelers were used.[1320] May be they were under the command of the *moqanni-bashi*, a court official mentioned at the end of the Safavid era.[1321] Master well diggers began tunneling operations. As far as the soil extend, those digging trenches, when they reached the area of solid rock, they wove baskets and dividing the night into two shifts, carried soil from a considerable distance, filled the baskets, and stacked them on top of

---

1312 Savory, *History*, vol. 2, p. 922; Monshi, vol. 2, p. 73.
1313 Shamlu, p. 394.
1314 Savory, *History*, vol. 1, p. 480, 497; Monshi, vol. 1, pp. 343, 359; Natanzi, p. 236.
1315 Savory, *History*, vol. 2, p. 1011; Monshi, vol. 2, p. 808.
1316 Savory, *History*, vol. 1, p. 413; Monshi, vol. 1, p. 282.
1317 Savory, *History*, vol. 2, p, 1000; Monshi, vol. 2, p. 799.
1318 Savory, *History*, vol. 1, p. 452; Monshi, vol. 1, p. 318.
1319 Boxer, p. 46.
1320 Rumlu, pp. 67, 144, 417 (*naqqabanchi*).
1321 Alternatively, this official also may have been involved in irrigation activities on *khasseh* land. Asaf, p. 101.

another to form a protective avenue of approach to the fort.[1322] Calculations were made as to the distance from the point of entry to the inside of the fortress. At the end an exit shaft was dug, after which a party of soldiers would exist sound their trumpets as a signal for a general assault from the breastworks. Sometime there were miscalculations as the length of the tunnel as in 1585.[1323]

Tunneling operations had to be protected, because often, despite its subterraneous nature, the enemy got wind of what was happening and would take counter-measures. "After the welldiggers had been working for several days, the Kurds got wind of what they were doing. The reason for this was that the welldiggers, to maintain the correct alignment of their tunnel, made a hole through to the surface every few paces and inserted a marker... the Kurds launched attacks against the tunnel every night and clashed with the musketeers who had been detailed to guard the tunnelers.... the vazir's own troops, who were particularly diligent in their conduct of sieges.[1324] Sometimes the debris that fell down from the fortress as a result of the artillery bombardment covered the soil and thus "prevented the besieged [to see] what earth was being thrown up from below by the men who were digging the mine."[1325]

Another danger was treachery which caused the location of a tunnel to be revealed and its workers to be attacked. "Because of treachery such a tunnel also could be used by the besieged to mount a counter-attack as happened in 1585 in Tabriz. The Persians were forced to make holes in the roof of the tunnel and push straw through, and set fire to it to smoke the Ottomans out. Finally, they were even forced to pour water into the tunnel as a result of which it caved in.[1326]

Meanwhile, while the construction of breastworks, the digging of trenches, the making of tunnels, was going on "The emirs applied themselves to bombard the forts with cannon, light artillery, and heavy siege guns to breach the walls and toppling the towers.[1327] The shah either sent for siege-cannon, if there not enough with the army, or he had new ones cast on the spot.[1328] In the case of the siege of Tabriz in 1585, "the gunners busied themselves with casting cannon.... by the time the cannon had been cast, the breastworks had been pushed forward to the edge of the ditch where the guns were to be placed, and protective earthwork were

---

[1322] Savory, *History*, vol. 2, p 998; Monshi, vol. 2, p. 798; on the extent of tunneling during the siege of Hormuz castle see Boxer, p. 157.

[1323] Savory, *History*, vol. 1, p. 453; Monshi, vol. 1, p. 319.

[1324] Savory, *History*, vol 2, p. 999; Monshi, vol. 2, p. 799; see also Boxer, p. 157, n. 1.

[1325] Don Juan, p. 189.

[1326] Savory, *History*, vol. 1, p. 454; Monshi, vol. 1, p. 320; Don Juan, p. 191.

[1327] Savory, *History*, vol. 1, p. 138; Monshi, vol. 1, p. 83.

[1328] Savory, *History*, vol. 2, p, 835; Monshi, vol. 2, p. 645; see also section of *tupchi*s.

constructed... in the fourth month of the siege, a number of heavy siege guns went into action and began to make an impression on the towers and walls.[1329] In the absence of artillery, the Safavid army under Esma'il I bombarded the besieged fort with arrows and rocks, and if available arquebuses.[1330] Andersen reported that during the daytime the cannon played on the walls of the fortress to make a breach, while during the night musket fire kept the defenders on their feet and at bay.[1331] At night, the artillery remained always silent.[1332]

After some weeks, the palisades were creeping closer to the walls, the breastworks were being strengthened and the besieged were being penned down.... the besiegers now began mining operations.[1333] The fire of the heavy siege guns, which projected a shot weighing 30 *mann*, was beginning to make breaches in the walls. The sappers by that time had penetrated beyond the ditch and had tunneled under the walls.[1334] For, if it was difficult to gain entry into the fortress it was tried to blow up the fortress walls. "Sappers dug a mine beneath one of the towers and filled the mine with gunpowder. One evening they exploded the mine and caused a breach in the walls, though which some 300 to 400 Uzbegs poured. Mir Fattah and his musketeers lit torches and poured a heavy fire on the Uzbegs. They fled into the city where they were picked off by the Rumlu *ghazis*, the musketeers and the townsmen."[1335] However, du Mans, writing in 1660, states that the Persians army did not mine walls, but only dug them out to bring the foundations down.[1336] This undoubtedly refers to a period when Persia was not involved in any major military conflict.

Other weaknesses in the construction of a fortress also were taken advantage of. In addition to rocks and earth, timber was used to make up a fortress' skeleton. Around 1503, during the siege of Darband, having no artillery, Esma'il I ordered two mines to be made, "neither of which succeeded. At last they made a large mine under a tower, digging out all the foundations, and supporting it with beams of wood; then filling the hollow with dry wood they set fire to it hoping that when the beams were burnt the tower would fall. The dry wood soon burnt and flames soon poured out of the hollow, but had little effect as they were choked in the cavern. But the governor fearing greater damage and the loss of the place" offered to yield the fort.[1337] Some 90 years later, the technology had not

---

1329 Savory, *History*, vol. 2, p. 905; Monshi, vol. 2, p. 714.
1330 Valeh Esfahani, pp. 146, 180; Afshar, *'Alamara-ye Tahmasp*, pp. 78, 181, 205.
1331 Andersen, p. 158.
1332 Richard, vol. 2, p. 119.
1333 Savory, *History*, vol. 2, p. 923; Monshi, vol. 2, p. 733.
1334 Savory, *History*, vol. 2, p. 937; Monshi, vol. 2, p. 746.
1335 Savory, *History*, vol. 2, p. 638; Monshi, vol. 1, p. 464.
1336 Richard, vol. 2, p. 119.
1337 *Travels to Tana*, part 2, pp. 204, 114.

changed. In the course of the bombardment, a considerable part of the sun-dried brick of the towers had been smashed, and some of the interior timbers had been exposed. At dead of night, a small patrol of *qurchi*s crept up to the walls and set fire to these timbers. The defenders cried for quarter... the greater part of the Kojur troops were killed; the survivors were enrolled among the shah's servants.[1338] Or when troops had been successful in excavating about 500 cubits of the actual foundations of the fort and in shoring up the walls with timbers. They then set fire to the timber, and the wall above came crashing down. The defenders rushed to repair the breach but the Safavid musketeers prevented them from doing so.[1339]

Once sappers were busy constructing mines beneath the base of the towers the assault troops were put in position in the trenches, which were overflowing with men.[1340] For when the tunneling and mining were successful a direct assault of the walls was called for. This usually began by setting fire to the fortress gates. Those troops that had been able to do so "stood there with their shields over their heads, hoping a gap would appear through which they could pour into the fort.... the gates were soon half-consumed, and a crack appeared through which the *gholam*s, with their shields over their heads and their chain mail and jerkin protecting their chest, charged into the fort."[1341]

Because of the casualties that the troops suffered the army commander also could have recourse to a movable wooden tower borne on a platform running on wheels "which 200 pioneers were to work up to the edge of the outer ditch, where it then would overtop the cavalier or bulwark. [It was protected by] bags filled with earth nailed on the outside; and it had an upper work so high that from it the square inside the fortress might have been overlooked; and from this upper piece a drawbridge with ropes could, at the proper moment, be let down over the parapet of the fortress wall. The whole of this machine was planked and protected by sandbags adjusted to serve their purpose. [The attack was to be made at dawn to surprise the sentinels.] "although the axles of the wheels under the platform had been well greased, and the tyres had been cased in cotton to muffle the sound, and the lights from the matchlock fuses, and priming horns, and cannon-vents had been all carefully masked, yet the Turks heard us coming."[1342] This wooden platform is possibly the same as is referred to by Marvi as the *havaleh*.[1343] In 1603, 'Abbas I had the fortress

---

1338 Savory, *History*, vol. 2, p. 716; Monshi, vol. 1, p. 536.

1339 Savory, *History*, vol. 2, pp. 906, 1011; Monshi, vol. 2, pp. 715, 808; see also Rumlu, p. 451.

1340 Savory, *History* vol. 2, p. 843-4; Monshi, vol. 2, p. 653. auxiliary troops, Savory, *History*, vol. 2, p. 849; Monshi, vol. 2, p. 799.

1341 Savory, *History*, vol. 2, p. 719; Monshi, vol. 1, p. 539.

1342 Don Juan, p. 191.

1343 Shamlu, p. 354; Mervi, pp. 82, 195, 358.

of Erivan encircled by several bastions (*qal'ehcheh*) made of wood and clay which were higher and stronger than the walls of the fortress itself. From behind the protection of these bastions the Persian troops were able to shoot at the Ottoman defenders. 'Abbas II did the same in the case of Qandahar in 1650, using both *havaleh*s and *qal'ehcheh*s. [1344]

Pressed by time, or when the fortress seemed to be a ripe fruit to be plucked after the walls had been pounded and breaches started to occur the commander would give the orders for a general assault using scaling ladders (*nardoban*), which was not always successful. Don Juan mentioned that after 6 days such an attack was beaten off with substantial loss of life.[1345] The attackers used their broad shields over their heads to protect themselves and used various means to pass the moat, breach the wall, or reach the top of the wall.[1346] To protect the attackers against the "powder pots", a kind of hand grenade, that the Portuguese used in large quantities during the defense of Hormuz castle, the Persian general sent for "Coates and Jackets made of Leather, which indeed are nothing so subject to take fire as are their Callico Coats bombasted with Cotton wooll." Each soldier among the assaulting troop was covered by two musketeers (*tofangchi*s) and archers (*kamandari*s).[1347] The troops "shouldered their scaling ladders. Musket fire rained down like hail .. those who reached the walls and ascended them were hurled down by the defenders with blows from blacksmith's hammers and iron war maces, and with thrusts from spears and pikes."[1348] In addition to arrows and musket fire, the defense of a fortress was also carried out with other means. For example, fire balls, pots of naphtha, sacks of gun-powder, heavy rocks, and bags filled with nail and gun-powder were dropped on the attackers. The rocks stunned or killed people, while the sacks and pots, when lighted or exploding, set them on fire and/or seriously wounded them.[1349] To that end there were arrow-slits on top of fortress walls to shoot at enemy. Under them there were triangles at larger distances through which the defenders could throw hot sand or boiling water on the enemy. To protect the defenders against throw-javelins nose-like protectors stuck out over these openings.[1350] To reduce casualties the Safavid army reportedly also forced members of the local population, who had been made prisoners, "to advance to each assault in front of his [the shah's] troops, where they fell

---

[1344] Gulbenkian, Roberto. *L'ambassade en Perse de Luis Pereira de Lacerda* (Lisbon 1972), p. 99.

[1345] Don Juan, p. 190. These frontal assaults could be very costly in terms of loss of human life. Andersen, pp. 158-9.

[1346] Valeh Esfahani, p. 108; Savory, *History*, vol. 1, p. 143; Monshi, vol. 1, p. 86.

[1347] Boxer, p. 273; Seistani, p. 357.

[1348] Savory, *History*, vol. 1, p. 480; Monshi, vol. 1, p. 343.

[1349] Montazer-Saheb, p. 224; Rumlu, p. 103; Don Juan, p. 192; Savory, *History*, vol. 2, p. 906; Monshi, vol;. 2, p. 715.

[1350] Kaempfer, *Am Hofe*, p. 155.

by the arrows and other missiles discharged by their own countrymen."[1351]

Once a decision to a general assault had been given the soldiers were basically given a free hand in what they did once they had scaled the walls and were successful in taking the fortress. Often when the defenders refused to surrender the order for 'no quarter' (*in sha' allahdad*) was given which usually resulted in a general slaughter or *qatl-e 'amm*.[1352] According to Eskander Monshi, "the rules governing the storming of castles and conquests permit killing and plundering, and in fact it is impossible to prevent it" and to distinguish between military and innocent civilians.[1353] Andersen reported that after a fortress had been taken that all the men were killed, while the women and children were enslaved.[1354] If a fortress or town had decided to surrender in exchange for the besiegers to spare their lives[1355] and a payment of an attractive sum of money or *mal-e amani*, the town was divided among the various military groups. "The total sum was divided between the *gholam*s and *qurchi*s, officers at court, musketeers and each detachment was allotted a certain number of people on the register from whom they could collect the appropriate sum. If anyone complained that the sum was too much or too little, the *qurchi-bashi* of Gilan would reach a settlement."[1356] Once the surrender had been formalized, the defenders would come out of the fortress with their swords hanging around their neck as a sign of submission. Another form of submission was that the officers had "a towel round his throat which reached to his knees (sign of captive noblemen in nearly all the East, whereas those of lower degree come without their turbans and wearing the towel with a knot tied in it)."[1357]

The Army's Homecoming

At the end of each campaign, which usually lasted up to six months, but during the reconquest of Azerbaijan (1011-16/1602-07) lasted five years, the shah and/or his commanding generals held a review of the troops. The idea was to keep record of all those that were there, how they had given account of themselves, and who needed to be rewarded in particular. Deeds of heroism were recorded under the soldier's name to be sure that he would receive a proper reward. The muster rolls then were handed over the comptrollers of the army, in particular to the *mostoufis* responsible for

---

1351 Chamich, vol. 2, p. 346.

1352 Qomi, vol. 2, pp. 753 (Sabzavar), 815-6 (Qazvin); Valeh Esfahani, p. 138; Mostoufi, p. 181.

1353 Savory, *History*, vol. 2, p. 937; Monshi, vol. 2, p. 746. For a miniature depicting the sack (*allahdad*) of a town see Hillenbrand, p. 67 (fig. 148).

1354 Andersen, pp. 158-9; see also Floor, *Bar Oftadan*, p. 53; Ibid., *Afghan Occupation*, p. 50.

1355 Andersen, p. 159.

1356 Savory, *History*, vol 2, p. 943; Monshi, vol. 2, pp. 750, 413-4, 766.

1357 Boxer, p. 57, 52.

the different army corpses. Having completed the review the army was dismissed and returned to its various localities.[1358] In case of proven courage common soldiers were promoted to the rank of khan of which Olearius gives several examples.[1359] The review of the troops, before sending them on leave, was usually done by the *qurchi-bashi* or the *tofangchi-aghasi* jointly with the *ishik aghasi-bashi*.[1360] Sometimes, when hostilities had only ceased because of the approach of the winter season the shah sent on leave all his troops except a number of emirs, *qurchi*s, *gholam*s, musketeers and others, while he sent out patrols to find out which point the enemy general was aiming at.[1361]

During the triumphal entry of 'Abbas I in Isfahan...."After those who carried the heads came young men dressed like women richly decked, who danced in a manner and with movements which we had never seen elsewhere, throwing their arms about and extending them above their heads even more than they raised their legs from the ground, to the sound of atabales [*tabl, atbal*], flutes and certain instruments which are provided with strings, and to the sound of a song composed on the victory which they had gained, this being sung by four old women. ... [followed by acrobats and courtesans] .... On either flank of the cavalry, and in the first ranks there were four trumpeters who played on certain trumpets and sackbuts of extraordinary dimensions, which gave a bitter and broken sound very alarming to hear."[1362]

Quite a frightening sight were some of the spoils of war, such as horsemen "carrying heads of men on their lances, and some having the ears of men put on strings and hanged about their necks; next after these came the trumpeters, making a wonderful noise; because they are contrary to our English trumpets, these trumpets being two yards and a half in length, with the great end big, and so much compass as a hat. Next after them came the drummers, their drums being made of brass, and carried upon camels; then after them came six standard bearers."[1363] The heads of important enemies were wrapped in a silk turban; the others were bare, but all were thrust through with a lance.[1364]

1358 Savory, *History*, vol. 2, p. 948; Monshi, vol. 2, p. 755; see also DM.

1359 Olearius, p. 667. It was the role of the *lashkar-nevis* to record such feats of courage. DM, p. 92.

1360 Savory, *History*, vol. 2, p. 1217; Monshi, vol. 2, pp. 994-5; Yusef, p. 81, 238, 243.

1361 Savory, vol. 2, p. 858; Monshi, vol. 2, p. 666.

1362 Sherley, p. 155.

1363 Sherley, p. 210; in Seistan not only the head was cut off, but also a finger of Malek Heidar. Seistani, p. 200. See also Rumlu, p. 198 where the head and the signet ring (*angoshtarin*) of Morad Mirza the Aq-Qoyunlu were brought to Esma'il I. For a miniature depicting the post-battle situation with prisoners see Hillenbrand, p. 68 (fig. 152).

1364 della Valle, p. 58.

Conclusion

The army under the Safavids consisted of regular levies, mainly composed of Turkoman tribesmen, who were supported by Georgian and other non-Turkoman groups. In addition there were irregular auxiliaries. The crack troops were formed by the shah's household troops, the *qurchi*s, who were mainly recruited from among the Qezelbash tribesmen. The regular troops were led by the tribal leaders, who paid them out of the fiefs assigned to them by the shah. Tahmasp I aimed to decrease his reliance on the Qezelbash forces by increasing the strength of his household troops as well as that of the role played by non-Turkoman forces, in particular royal slaves, which were entirely dependent on the him. On the death of Tahmasp I in 1576 these changes were not yet strong enough to prevent civil war breaking out among the Qezelbash (1576-87). Therefore, when 'Abbas I became shah in 1587, he formalized and reinforced the changes that his grandfather had instituted. He also reduced the unity of the Qezelbash by breaking the direct link between their leaders and the tribal clansmen. The effect of the creation of a serious countervailing force (the *gholam*s) and the economic weakening of the Qezelbash proved to be an effective solution, both military and politically. Whereas in the 16th century military command had been almost exclusively in the hands of the Qezelbash as of 1590 there was power sharing between the Qezelbash, the *gholam*s and the Tajik forces, the arquebusiers. The Qezelbash were able to hold the exclusive rights to the function of *qurchi-bashi*, who became the leader of all the Qezelbash forces in the 17th century, the *gholam*s after an initial exclusive hold on the function of *qollar-aghasi* had to share it later with the Qezelbash. The same power sharing took place in case of the function of *tofangchi-aghasi*. This power-sharing and co-habitation in the military sphere reflected the situation in the political arena. It did not mean, of course, that there was no jockeying for power between the various commanders. In fact, there was often fierce rivalry, but this was a personal, individual competition, and was not the expression of social cleavages.

The size of the Safavid army was rather modest. Though the shah could mobilize more than 100,000 men this did not mean that he could all arm, feed, and field them over a long period. Usually, military operations were limited to 10,000 – 30,000 troops. Only in the case of well-prepared major operations under 'Abbas I was the number of combattants three times larger. With the passage of time, and the absence of external military threats, combined with the neglect of martial skills and lack of esprit de corps, the preparedness of the Safavid troops declined. This situation led to the total defeat of the ill-prepared, ill-armed, ill-paid, and unmotivated troops at Golnabad in 1722 against a numerically inferior Afghan force.

Although modern arms (arquebuses and cannon) were known to the Safavids from the beginning of their reign they only started to make use of these weapons on a systematic scale under Tahmasp I. Under 'Abbas I significant increased use of modern arms occurred, which development contributed to his successful campaigns against the Ottomans and Uzbegs. These developments demonstrate that the use of cannon and arquebuses was a home-grown affair and that Europeans had little to do with their introduction or production in Safavid Persia. This did not mean that their technical assistance was not appreciated or sought by various shahs, but these requests were marginal issues. Nevertheles, the Persian cavalry (the bulk of the army) felt more comfortable with their traditional arms (lance, bow, mace) and after the 1660s the role of the arquebusiers and gunners was reduced significantly. At the peak of their military might the Safavid forces were well trained in the use of both modern and traditional arms. Though they seemed a motley crowd, with no organization or order (whether camping, on march, or in battle), the Safavid army followed a battle order, had a tactical plan, used signals, and proved to be a formidable force that was able to defend the state's borders. Though the Safavid army was not good at sieges and preferred a pitched battle or sneak attack, it nevertheless developed sufficient technical competence to successfully take strongholds the slow and methodological way.

AFTERWORD

This study has tried to show that there was a shift in political and military power in the Safavid state, for which the basis was laid in the mid-16th century. The shift itself was formalized after 1590 through the reforms initiated by 'Abbas I. The changes took two different forms.

First, the monopoly on military power of the Qezelbash tribes was broken by severing the direct ties between the Qezelbash leaders and their clansmen. This was achieved by dislodging the Qezelbash leaders from their traditional fiefdoms and appointing them as governor in other areas. Furthermore, captured or bought slaves (*gholams*) were trained to serve both as a military countervailing force as well as to serve the shah in the country's administration. The power shift did not mean that the Qezelbash elite was ousted from power. It did mean however that their monolithic hold on power was broken as was their oligopoly of military might. For henceforth they had to share power with the *gholams*. The *qurchi-bashi*, the military leader of the shah's household troops, became the leader of all Qezelbash forces. Although he became the most important military leader his powers were checked by those of the *qollar-aghasi*, the commander of the *gholams*. The latter sometimes also held simultaneously other powerful central government functions such as that of *tofangchi-aghasi* and *divan-begi*. The former function had been traditionally held by Tajiks and the latter by Qezelbash. However, the *gholams* did not have an exclusive hold on any of these three functions for throughout the 17th century and the beginning of the 18th century these functions were also held by Qezelbash emirs.

However, there were also other contenders for power. The Tajiks who traditionally had held mainly the highest administrative functions now, as part of the power shift, also lost exclusive hold on those functions where traditionally they had held a monopoly. This held not only for functions such as that of *nazer-e boyutat* or the steward of the royal palace, but also for lower ranking administrative functions. The biggest loss that the Tajiks suffered was their exclusive claim on the function of grand vizier, which as of 1669 was held almost uninterruptedly by Qezelbash officials till the end of the regime.

The *gholams* and Tajiks were not the only social group that vied for a piece of the power pie. The harem inmates increasingly also wanted to have their say. Royal women had always played a role behind the scenes in Safavid politics in the 16th century, while at occasion they even tried to hold outright power directly (sister of Tahmasp II; wife of Khodabandeh). Generally, however, the royal women could not play a direct role in the administration of the country, but their fellow harem inmates, the eunuchs, could. They were the only ones, apart from the shah, who had direct contact with them and they could hold office. We therefore see that the eunuchs, apart from trying to influence state policy from behind the harem walls, also participated directly in the administration of the country. For example, as of the 1680s eunuchs held functions such as that of *nazer-e boyutat*, which had been a Tajik prerogative until the 1650s, and of *jabbehdar-bashi*, which always had been held by the Qezelbash.

It is clear that while the new configuration of power-sharing between the contending members of the elite was to the advantage of the shah, because the various opposing forces held each other in check. It meant, however, that the political decision-making process became more difficult. It finally led to paralysis when Shah Soltan Hosein came to power. He was so weak that he agreed with every last person that talked to him. Rather than allowing one's opponent to have his way, even when it would be in everybody's interest, the opposing elite members preferred that nothing happened at all to avoid that the other might gain political or other advantage of having his way.

Secondly, there was a shift in power between those officials who managed the *mamalek* or state lands and those who managed the *khasseh* or household lands. Because of the growth of the size of *khasseh* lands the officials in charge of those properties saw their role and importance increase. This was but a logical outcome of the reduction of power of the Qezelbash, whose economic power base had been their governing all of the *mamalek* lands. The change in the number and size of *mamalek* lands reduced their ability to finance troops and thus diminished their military might. Because of the growth of the *khasseh* lands in the 16th century, which were governed mainly by royal viziers, and the revenues of which were remitted directly to the royal court, the powers of the managers of the *khasseh* lands increased accordingly. We see therefore that invariably those officials, whose importance had been subordinate to that of their *mamalek* colleagues during the 16th century, reversed that role during the 17th century. For example, the *monshi al-mamalek* had to yield to the *majles-nevis* and the *sadr-e mamalek* to the *sadr-e khasseh*. Only the *mostoufi-ye khasseh* still remained subordinate to the *mostoufi-ye mamalek*, though he played a more important role. This change in circumstances was also reflected in administrative procedures. Whereas in the 16th century the *neshan* and *parvaneh* (both *mamalek* documents) had been predominant, in the next century it was the *raqam*, a *khasseh* document. Also, whereas the former required the counterseal of the Keepers of the Seal (a function held by Qezelbash), the latter was sealed by the shah.

Thirdly, apart from the changes there also was considerable continuity in that both the function of the shah and the grand vizier remained constant. The position of the shah, who enjoyed enormous legitimacy, was never seriously challenged. The shah's means to exercise power, through the growth of his hold on the means of production in the country, had increased considerably, however. The elite therefore tried to undermine the position of the shah's main agent, the grand vizier. For it was the grand vizier who continued to hold the purse strings and the keys to political influence from the beginning to the end of the Safavid reign. Whereas in the 16th century the Qezelbash emirs tried to impose themselves on the grand vizier (*vakil*), in the 17th and 18th century they were joined by the *gholams*, Tajiks and harem inmates. This shows that there was significant continuity in the authority of the grand vizier, but that the game had remained the same, and that only the composition of the players had changed. The fact also that a *gholam*, between 1655-61, and Qezelbash officials as of 1669 regularly held the office of grand vizier not only demonstrates their absorption into the Tajik dominated bureaucratic system, but also that the players rather than trying to beat the system had decided to join it. It was of course still possible to weaken the position of the grand vizier, but it was only temporary gain, for the shah, if he did not dismiss the grand vizier, when push came to shove always backed his own man.

Bibliography

(Books or articles cited only once are not listed here).

Archives

Algemeen Rijks Archief (General State Archives, the Hague, the Netherlands) cited as *ARA*.
a. Incoming letters *VOC* or *KA* (there is a concordance in the ARA for conversion from the old *KA* to the new *VOC* numbering system)
b. Collectie Geleynsen de Jonge, nr. 100

Published Books and Articles

Adle, Chahryar. *Siyaqi-Nezam – Fotuhate Homayun – "Les Victoires augustes", 1007/1598.* (unpublished thesis Sorbonne – Paris 1976)
Afshar, Iraj ed."Chand farman marbut be Yazd", *FIZ* 11 (1342/1963), pp. 169-74.
_____, "Farmani az Shah Soltan Hosein", *Rahnama-ye ketab* 17 (1353/1974), pp. 406-08.
_____, "Seh farman va yek hokm marbut beh Yazd" *FIZ* 25 (1361/1982), pp. 396-405.
_____, *'Alamara-ye Shah Tahmasp* (Tehran 1370/1991)
Allen, W.E.D ed. *Russian Embassies to the Georgian Kings (1589-1605),* 2 vols. Hakluyt Society (London 1970 [1972]).
Amoretti, Biancamaria Scarcia. *Shah Isma'il I nei <<Diarei>> di Marin Sanudo* (Roma 1979).
Andersen, Jürgen und Iversen, Volquard. *Orientalische Reisbeschreibungen in den Bearbeiting von Adam Olearius.* (Schleswig 1669 [Tübingen 1980]).
Anonymous. *A chronicle of the Carmelites in Persia and the Papal mission of the seventeenth and eighteenth centuries,* 2 vols. (London 1939).
Anonymous. "2500 sal dar hemayat-e shahanshahi-ye Iran", *Zamimeh-ye majalleh-ye Hur beh monasabat-e 2500 sal-e shahanshahi-ye Iran.* (Tabriz 1350/1971).
Ardalan, Khosrou b. Moh. b. Manuchehr. *Lobb al-Tavarikh - Tarikh-e Ardalan* (Tehran 2536/1977).
Asaf, Mohammad Hashem. "Rostam al-Hokoma", *Rostam al-Tavarikh*, ed. Mohammad Moshiri (Tehran 1348/1969).
Astarabadi, Sayyed b. Morteza Hoseini. *Az Sheikh Safi ta Shah Safi*, ed. Ehsan Eshraqi (Tehran 1364/1985).

Atabay, Badri. *Fehrest-e Ketabkhaneh-ye Saltanati, fehrest-e tarikh, safarnameh, siyahatnameh*, etc. (Tehran 2537/1977).

Aubin, Jean. "Révolution chiite et conservatisme. Les soufis de Lahejan, 150-1514 (Etudes safavides II)", *Moyen Orient & Océan Indien* 1 (1984), pp. 1-40.

_____, "Chiffres de population urbaine en Iran occidentale autour de 1500", *Moyen Orient & Océan Indien* 3 (1986), pp. 37-54.

_____, "L'Avènement des Safavides reconsiderée" (Etudes Safavides III), *Moyen-Orient et Océan Indien*, 5 (1988), pp. 1-130.

Bacqué-Grammont, Jean-Louis. *Les Ottomans, les Safavides et leurs voisins* (Leiden 1987).

Bafqi, Mohammad Mofid Mostoufi-ye. *Jame'-ye Mofidi*. 3 vols. ed. Iraj Afshar (Tehran 1340/1961).

Bardsiri, Mir Mohammad Sa'id Moshizi. *Tadhkereh-ye Safavi*, ed. Ebrahim Bastani Parizi (Tehran, 1369/1990).

Bastiaensen, Michel ed. *Souvenirs de la Perse safavide et autres lieux de l'Orient (1664-1678)*. (Brussels 1985).

Bedik, Petro. *Cehil Sutun seu explicatio utriusque celeberrisimi, ac pretiosissimi theatri quadriginta columnarum in Perside Orientis* (Vienna 1678).

Beiburdi, Hosein. *Tarikh-e Arasbaran* (Tehran 1346/1968).

_____, "Panj farman-e tarikhi", *BT* 4 (1348/1969), pp. 2-3, 67-80.

Bell, John. "Travels from St. Petersbug in Russia to Various parts of Asia in 1716, 1719, 1722, &c.", in John Pinkerton, *A General Collection* 17 vols. (London 1808-14), vol. 7.

Ben Khvandamir, Amir Mahmud. *Iran dar Ruzgar-e Shah Esma'il va Shah Tahmasp*, ed. Gholam Reza Tabataba'i (Tehran 1379/1991).

Ben Khvandamir Amir Mahmud, *Tarikh-e Shah Esma'il va Shah Tahmasp Safavi*. ed. Mohammad 'Ali Jarrahi (Tehran 1370/1991).

Berchet, Guglielmo. *La Repubblica di Venezia e la Persia* (Torino 1865 [1976]).

Bidlisi, Sharaf Khan. *Cherefnama ou Histoire des Kourdes*, publiée par V. Veliaminof-Zernof, 2 vols. (St. Petersburg 1860-62).

Bosworth, C.E. *The History of the Saffarids of Sistan and the Maliks of Nimruz (247/861 to 949/1542-3)* (Costa Mesa 1994).

Boxer, C.R. ed. *Commentaries of Ruy Freyre de Andrade* (London 1930).

Brosset, Marie-Félicité. *Histoire de la Géorgie depuis l'antiquité jusq'au XIX siècle*. 2 vols. (St. Petersburgh 1849-58).

_____, *Collection d'Historiens Arméniens*. 2 vols. (St. Petersburg 1874-76 [Amsterdam n.d]), [2 vols. in one].

Bushev, P.P. *Istoria posol'stv i diplomaticheskikh otnoshenii russkogo i iranskogo gosudarstvo v 1588-1612 gg* (Moscow 1976).

Busse, H. *Untersuchungen zum islamischen Kanzleiwesen* (Kairo 1959)

Careri Giovani, Gemelli, *Voyage du Tour du Monde*. 6 vols. (Paris 1727)

Chardin, Jean. *Voyages*, ed. L. Langlès, 10 vols., (Paris 1811)

Chardin, Sir John. *Travels in Persia 1673-1677* (London 1927 [1988]).

Chinon, Gabriel de. *Relations nouvelles du Levant* (Lyons 1671).

Daneshpazhuh, Mohammad-Taqi, " Amar-e mali va nezami-ye Iran dar 1128, *FIZ* 20, pp. 396-423.

Da'udi, Hosein. "Asnad-i khvandan-i kalantari-ye Seistan", *BT*, 4 (1348/1969), pp. 1-34.

Della Valle, Pietro. "Extract of the Travels of Della Valle", in John Pinkerton, *A General Collection of Voyages and Travels*, (London, 1811), vol. 9.

Dhabihi, M. and Setudeh, M. *Az Astara ta Astarabad*, 10 vols. (Tehran 1354/1975).

Dhoka, Yahya. *Artesh-e Shahenshahi-ye Iran az Kurosh ta Pahlavi* (Tehran 1350/1971).

Dickson, M.B. and Welch, S.C. Introduction. *The Houghton Shahnameh*. 2 vols. (Cambridge 1981).

Don Juan of Persia, a Shi'ah Catholic 1560-1604, tr. G. le Strange (London, 1926).

Dorn, B. *Geschichte Shirwans unter den Statthaltern und Chanen von 1538-1820* (Beiträge zur Geschichte der Kaukasischen Länder und Volker, vol. 2, Mémoires de l'Academie etc. (St. Petersbourg 1840).

Du Mans, Raphael. *Estat de la Perse*. Ed. Ch. Schefer (Paris 1890).

Efendiev, O.A. *Obrazovanie Azerbaidzhanskogo Gosudarstva Sefevidov v natsale XVI veka* (Baku 1961).

Elgood, Robert ed. *Islamic Arms and Armour* (London 1979).

Esfahani, Mohammad Ma'sum b. Khvajegi. *Kholaseh al Siyar*, ed. Iraj Afshar. (Tehran n.d. [1992]).

Fekete, Lajos. *Einführung in die persische Palaeographie. 101 persische Dokumente.* Aus dem Nachlass des Verfassers herausgegeben von G. Hazai (Budapest 1977).

Floor, Willem. *Bar Oftadan-e Safaviyan va Bar Amadan-e Mahmud Afghan* (Tehran 1365/1987).

_____, *Bar Takhtegah-ye Esfahan* (Tehran 1366/1987).

_____, *Commercial Conflict between Persia and the Netherlands 1712-1718*, University of Durham Occasional Paper Series no. 37 (1988).

_____, "The rise and fall of Mirza Taqi, the eunuch grand vizier (1043-55/1634-45)", *Studia Iranica* 26 (1997), pp. 237-66.

_____, *The Afghan Occupation of Safavid Persia 1721-1729* (Paris 1998)

_____, *The Fiscal History of Safavid and Qajar Persia* (New York 1999).

_____, *The Persian Textile Industry 1500-1925* (Paris 1999).

_____, "The *sadr* or head of the Safavid religious administration, judiciary and endowments and other members of the religious institution", *ZDMG* 150 (2000), pp. 461-500.

_____, "The Secular Judicial System in Safavid Persia," *Studia Iranica* 29 (2000), pp. 9-60.

Fragner, B. "Ardabil zwischen Sultan und Schah. Zehn Urkunden Schah Tahmasps II." *Turcica* 6 (1975), pp. 177-225.

Fryer, John. *A New Account of East India and Persia Being Nine Years' Travels, 1672-1681*, 3 vols. (London, 1909-15) (Hakluyt Second Series).

Fumeni, 'Abd al-Fattah. *Tarikh-e Gilan dar vaqaye'-ye salha 923-1038 hejri qamari*, ed. Manuchehr Setudeh (Tehran 1349/1970).

Gerber, Johann Gustav. "Nachrichten von ..." in Müller, *Sammlung Russischer Geschichte*, 9 vols. (St. Petersburg 1732-64), vol. 4.

Gilanetz, *The Chronicle of Petros di Sarkis Gilanetz*. ed. Caro Owen Minasian (Lisbon 1959).

Haneda, Masashi. *Le Chah et les Qizilbash. Le systeme militaire safavide* (Berlin 1987).

Herbert, Thomas. *Travels in Persia, 1627-1629*, ed. W. Foster. (New York 1929).

Hinz, Walther. *Irans Aufstieg zum Nationalstaat im fünfzehnten Jahrhundert* (Berlin - Leipzig 1936).

_____, "Die persische Geheimkanzlei im Mittelalter", im: *Westöstliche Abhandlungen. Festschrift für Rudolf Tschudi* (Wiesbaden 1954), pp. 342-54.

Honarfar, Lotfollah. *Ganjineh-ye athar-e tarikhi-ye Esfahan* (2nd. ed.). (Tehran 1350/1971).

Horst, H. "Ein Immunitätsdiplom Schah Muhammad Khudabandahs vom Jahre 989/1581", *ZDMG* 105 (1955), pp. 290-2.

_____, *Iran unter der Horezmshahs und Gross-seljuqen* (Wiesbaden 1956).

_____, "Zwei Erlasse Shah Tahmasps I. Von Persien", *ZDMG* 105 (1961), pp. 301-09.

Hotz, A. *Reis van de gezant der O.I. Compagnie Joan Cunaeus naar Perzië in 1651-1652* (Amsterdam 1908).

Jahanpur, F. "Faramin-e padeshahan-e Safavi dar muzeh-ye Britaniya", *BT* 4 (1348/1969), pp. 223-64.

Janabadi, Mirza Beg Hasan b. Hosni. *Rouzat al-Safaviyeh*. ed. GholamReza Majd Tabataba'i (Tehran 1379/1999)

Jouher, *Private Memoirs of the Moghul Emperor Homayun*. tr. Charles Stewart (Calcutta 1832 [1975]).

Kaempfer, Engelbert. *Am Hofe des persischen Grosskönigs (1684-85). Das erste Buch der Amoenitates exoticae in deutscher Bearbeitung*, hrsg. v. Walter Hinz. (Leipzig 1940).

_____, *Amoenitatum Exoticarum. Fasciculi V, Variae Relationes, Observationes & Descriptiones Rerum Persicarum* (Lemgo 1712 [1976]).

Khatunabadi, Sayyed 'Abdol-Hosein al-Hoseini. *Vaqaye' al-senin va a'lam* (Tehran 1352/1973).

Khonji, Fazlollah b. Ruzbehan. *Ketab-e Soluk al-Moluk.* ed. Mohammad NizamudDin (Hyderabad/Deccan 1386/1966).

Khvandamir. *Habib al-Seyar,* 4 vols. ed. Mohammad Dabir-Siyaqi. (Tehran, 1362/1983 [3rd. ed.]).

Kroell, Anne. *Nouvelles d'Ispahan 1665-1695* (Paris 1979).

Krusinski, [Judasz Tadeusz]. *The History of the Late Revolutions of Persia* (London 1740 [1973]).

Kutelia, Tinatin. *Catalogue of the Iranian Copper Coins in the State Museum of Georgia* (Tiflis 1990).

Laheji, 'Ali b. Shams al-Din b. Hajji Hosein. *Tarikh-e Khani,* ed. Manuchehr Setudeh (Tehran 1352/1973).

Lambton, A.K.S. *Landlord and Peasant in Persia* (London 1953).

Lang, D.M. *The Last Years of the Georgian Monarchy* (New York 1957).

Le Bruyn, Cornelius. *Travels into Moscovy, Persia and part of the East-Indies,* 2 vols. (London 1737).

Lockhart, L. *The Fall of the Safavid Dynasty* (Cambridge 1958).

Mar'ashi, Teimur. *Tarikh-e Khandan-e Mar'ashi-ye Mazandaran,* ed. M. Setudeh (Tehran 2536/1977).

Matthee, Rudi. *Politics and Trade in Late-Safavid Iran: Commercial Crisis and Government Reaction Under Shah Solayman (1666-1694)* (Ph.D. dissertation UCLA, 1991)

_____, "The Career of Mohammad Beg. Grand Vizier of Shah 'Abbas II (r. 1642-1666)", *IS* 24 (1991), pp. 17-36.

_____, "Administrative Stability and Change in Late-17th-Century Iran: The Case of Shaykh 'Ali Khan Zanganah", *(IJMES* 1994), pp. 77-98.

Membré, Michele. *Relazione,* ed. G.C. Scarcia (Rome, 1969). English translation see Morton, A.H.

Mervi, Mohammad Kazem. *Tarikh-e 'Alamara-ye Naderi,* 3 vols. ed. Mohammad Amin Riyahi. (Tehran 1369/1990 [2nd. ed.]).

Minadoi, John-Thomas. *The History of the Warres betwen the Turkes and the Persians* (London 1595 [1976]).

Minorsky, V. "A Soyurghal of Qasim b. Jahangir Aq-qoyunlu (903/1498)", *BSOS* 9 (1937-39), pp. 926-60.

_____, "A Civil and Military Review in Fars in 881/1476," *BSOS* 10 (1939), pp. 141-78.

_____, *The Tadhkirat al-Muluk, A Manual of Safavid Administration.* London 1943 (reprint Cambridge 1980)

_____, *Calligraphers and Painters. A treatise by Qadi Ahmad, Son of Mir-Munshi (circa A.H. 1015/A.D. 1606)* (Washington 1959).

Mir Ja'far, Hosein. "Seistan dar 'Asr-e Safaviyeh", *BT* 12/4 (2536/1977), pp. 49-67.

Mirza Rafi'a, *Dastur al-Moluk.* ed. Mohammad Taqi Daneshpazhuh. Zamimeh-ye shomareh-ye 5 va 6 sal-e 16 Majalleh-ye Daneshkadeh-ye Adabiyat va 'Olum-e Ensani (Tehran 1347/1967).

Mo'aseseh-ye pazuhesh va motale'at-e farhangi, *Farmanha va raqamha-ye doureh-ye Qajar* (Tehran 1371/1992).

Mofakhkham, Mohsen. "Asnad va mokatebat-e tarikhi", *BT* 2 (1346/1967), pp. 361-6.

Mohaddeth, Mir Hashem (ed). *Tarikh-e Qezelbashan* (Tehran 1361/1982).

Modarresi Chahardehi, Morteza. "Mosha'sha'iyan", *BT* 12/6 (2536/1977), pp. 149-88.

Molla Jalal al-Din Monajjem, *Ruznameh-ye 'Abbasi ya Ruznameh-ye Molla Jalal*, ed. Seifollah Vahidniya (Tehran 1366/1967).

Monshi, Eskander Beg. Tarikh-e 'Alamara-ye 'Abbasi. Iraj Afshar ed. 2 vols. (Tehran 1350/1971). For English translation see Savory, R.M.

al-Monshi, Mahmud al-Hoseini. *Tarikh-e Ahmad Shahi.* ed. Dustmorad Sayyed Muradof 2 vols. (Moscow 1974)

Montazer-Saheb, Asghar ed. *'Alamara-ye Shah Esma'il* (Tehran 1349/1970).

Morton, A.H. *Mission to the Lord Sophy of Persia (1539-1542)* (London 1993).

Mostoufi, Mohammad Mohsen. *Zobdat al-Tavarikh.* ed. Behruz Gudarzi (Tehran 1375/1996).

Mukminova, R.G. *Ocherki po istorii remesla v Samarkande i Bukhare v XVI veke* (Tashkent 1976).

Müller, G.F. *Sammlung Russischer Geschichte*, 9 vols. (St. Petersburg 1732-64).

Musavi, Mamad Taqi. *Orta asr Azarbaijan tarikhina dair fars dilinda jazymysh sanadlar* (Baku 1965).

_____, *Baky tarikhna dair orta asr sandalari* (Baku 1967).

_____, *Orta asr Azarbaijan tarikhina dair fars-dili sanadlarXVI-XVIII asrlar* (Baku 1977).

Nasiri, Mirza 'Ali Naqi. *Alqab va mavajeb-e doureh-ye salatin-e Safaviyeh* ed. Yusef Rahimlu (Mashhad 1371/1992).

Nasiri, Mohammad Ebrahim b. Zein al-'Abedin, *Dastur-e Shahriyan.* ed. Mohammad Nader Nasiri Moqaddam (Tehran 1373/1995).

Natanzi, Mahmud b. Hedayatollah Afushteh-ye. *Naqavat al-athar fi dhekr al-akhyar*, ed. Ehsan Eshraqi. (Tehran 1350/1971).

Neves Aguas ed. *Viagens por terra da India a Portugal* (Lisbon 1991).

Olearius, Adam. *Vermehrte newe Beschreibung der moscowitischen und persischen Reyse*, ed. D. Lohmeier (Schleswig, 1656 [Tübingen 1971]).

Pacifique de Provins, P. *Le Voyage de Perse.* ed. Godefroy de Paris & Hilaire de Wingene (Assisi 1939).

Papaziyan, A.D. *Persidskie dokumenty Matenadarana* (Erivan 1956).

_____, *Persidskie Dokumenty Matenadarana I, Ukazy, vypusk vtoroi (1601-1650)* (Erevan 1959).

Payandeh, Mahmud. *Qiyam-e Gharib Shah Gilani mashhur beh 'Adelshah* (Tehran 1357/1978).

Petruchevshi, I.P. *Ocherki po istorii feodal'nikh otnoshenij v Azerbaidzhane i Armenii v XVI-nachale XIX vv.* (Leningrad 1949).

Purchas, Samuel. *Hakluytus Posthumus or Purchas His Pilgrims.* 20 vols. (Glasgow 1905).

Puturidze, V.S. *Gruzino-Persidskie Istoricheskie Dokumenty* (Tiflis 1955).

_____, *Persidskie istoricheskie dokumenty v knigoxraniloshchax Gruzii,* 4 vols., (Tiflis 1961; 1962; 1965; 1977).

Qa'em-Maqami, Jahangir. *Yaksadupanjah sanad-e tarikhi az Jala'iriyan ta Pahlavi* (Tehran 1348/1969).

_____, *Moqaddameh'i bar shenakht-e asnad-e tarikhi az Jala'iriyan ta Pahlavi,* (Tehran 1350/1971).

Qarakhani, Hasan. "Buq'eh-ye Ayyub Ansari dar Takab - faramin-e shahan-e Safavi dar bareh-ye mouqufat-e an", *BT* 9 (1353/1974), pp. 71-122.

al-Qazvini, Yahya b. 'Abd al-Latif al-Hoseini. *Lobb al-Tavarikh.* ed. Sayyed Jalal al-Din al-Qazvini (Tehran 1314/1935).

Qazvini Ghaffari, Qadi Ahmad. *Tarikh-e Jahanara* (Tehran 1343/1964).

al-Qomi, Qadi Ahmad ibn Sharaf al-Din al-Hosein al-Hoseini. *Kholasat al-Tavarikh,* 2 vols., ed. Ehsan Eshraqi. (Tehran 1363/1984).

_____, *Golestan-e Honar.* ed. Soheili Khvonsari, Ahmad. (Tehran 1351/1972) (translated by Minorsky as Calligraphers q.v.)

Richard, Francis ed. *Raphael du Mans, missionnaire en Perse au XVIIe s.* 2 vols. (Paris 1995).

Röhrborn, Klaus-Michael. *Provinzen und Zentralgewalt Persiens im 16. und 17. Jahrhundert* (Berlin 1966).

_____, "Staatskanzlei und Absolutismus im safawidischen Persien", *ZDMG* 127 (1977), pp. 313-43.

_____, "Regierung und Verwaltung Irans unter den Safawiden" in Idris, H.R. & Röhrborn, K. *Regierung und Verwaltung des Vorderen Orients in Islamischen Zeit* (Handbuch der Orientalistik) (Leiden 1979).

Roemer, Hans Robert. *Staatsschreiben der Timuridenzeit. Das Sharafnama des 'Abdallah Marwarid in kritischer Auswertung* (Wiesbaden 1952).

Ross, Denison E. "The Early Years of Shah Isma'il, Founder of the Safavi Dynasty" *Journal of the Royal Asiatic Society* (1896), pp. 249-340.

Rumlu, Hosein Beg. *Ahsan al-Tavarikh.* ed. 'Abdol-Hosein Nava'i (Tehran 1357/1978).

Sam Mirza, *Tadhkareh-ye Tohfat-e Sami.* ed. Rokn al-Din Homayunfarrokh (Tehran n.d.)

Sanson, M. *The Present State of Persia* (London 1695).

Savory, Roger M. "The Principal Offices of the Safawid State During the Reign of Isma'il I. (907-30/1501-24)", *BSOAS* 23 (1960), pp. 91-105.

_____, "The Principal Offices of the Safawid State During the Reign of Tahmasp I. (930-84/1524-76)", *BSOAS* 24 (1961), pp. 65-85.

_____, "Some Notes on the Provincial Administration of the Early Safawid Empire", *BSOAS* 27 (1964), pp. 114-28.

_____, *History of Shah 'Abbas the Great* (translation of Monshi) 2 vols. (Boulder 1978).

_____, "The Office of Sipahsalar (Commander-in-Chief) in the Safavid State", in Bert G. Fragner et alii, *Proceedings of the Second European Conference of Iranian Studies* (Rome 1995), pp. 597-615.

Sazman-e Asnad-e Melli-ye Iran, *Fehrest-e Rahnama-ye Asnad* (Tehran, n.d.).

Schillinger, F.C. *Persianische und Ost-Indianische Reis* (Nürnberg 1707).

Schimkoreit, Renate. *Regesten publizierter safawidischer Herrscher-urkunden.* (Berlin 1982).

Seistani, Malek Shah Hosein b. Malek Ghayath al-Din Mohammad b. Shah Mahmud. *Ehya al-Moluk.* ed. Manuchehr Setudeh (Tehran 1344/1966).

Semsar, Mohammad Hasan. "Farman-nevisi dar doureh-ye Safaviyeh", *BT* 3 (1), pp. 61-83.

_____, "Du farman va-mohri tazeh az padeshahan-e Safaviyeh va Zandi-yeh", *BT* 8 (1352/1973), pp. 77-94.

Setudeh, Manuchehr. "Raqamha-ye divani-ye begler-begi-ye Astarabad", *FIZ* 26 (1365/1986), pp. 388-93.

Sha'bani, Reza. *Hadith-e Nader Shahi* (Tehran 2536/1977).

Shah Tahmasp, *Tadhkereh.* ed. 'Abdol-Shokur (Berlin 1343/1925).

Shamlu, Valiqoli b. Da'udqoli. *Qesas al-Khaqani*, 2 vols., ed. Hasan Sadat Naseri. (Tehran, 1371/1992)

Sherley, Sir Anthony and his Persian adventures. ed. Sir Denison Ross (London 1933).

Shirazi, 'Abdi Beg. *Takmeleh al-Akhbar*, ed. 'Abdol-Hosein Nava'i. (Tehran 1369/1990).

Shushtari, Mir 'Abd ol-Latif Khan. *Tohfat al-'Alam* ed. Samad Muhed. (Tehran 1363/1984).

Sumer, Faruk. *Safevi Devletimin Kurulusu ve Gelismesinde Abadolu Turklerinin Rolu* (Ankara 1976) tr. Ehsan Eshraqi and Mohammad Taqi Emami, *Naqsh-e Torkan-e Anatoli dar Tashkil va Touse'eh-ye Doulat-e Safavi.* (Tehran 1371/1992).

Tavernier, Jean-Baptiste. *Voyages en Perse et description de ce royaume* (Paris 1930).

Tehrani, Abu Bakr. *Ketab-e Diyarbekriyeh*, ed. Faruk Sumer and Nejati Lughal, 2 vols. in one (Tehran, 2nd. 1356/1977).

Tehrani, Mohammad Shafi'. *Tarikh-e Nader Shah.* ed. Sha'bani, Reza (Tehran 1349/1970)

Teixera, Pedro. *The Travels.* tr. William F. Sinclair, Hakluyt Society (London 1902 [1991]).

Thevenot, J. de. *The Travels of M. de Thevenot into the Levant* (London, 1686 [1971])

Travels to Tana and Persia by J. Barbaro and A. Contarini, (ed) Lord Stanley, Hakluyt no. 49, 2 vols. in one, (London 1873).

Valeh Esfahani, Mohammad Yusef. *Khold-e Barin*. ed. Mir Hashem Mohaddeth (Tehran 1372/1993).

Vahid Qazvini, Mohammad Taher. *'Abbasnamah*. ed. Ebrahim Dehgan (Arak 1329/1950).

Valentijn, F. *Oud en Nieuw Oost-Indien* 5 vols. (Dordrecht-Amsterdam 1726).

Welch, S.C. *A King's Book of Kings. The Shah-nameh of Shah Tahmasp*. (New York 1972 [1976]).

_____, *Persian Painting. Five Royal Safavid Manuscripts of the Sixteenth Century* (New York 1976).

Woods, John E. *The Aqquyunlu. Clan, Federation, Empire* (Minneapolis 1976).

Yazdi ,Taj al-Din Hasan b. Shehab. *Jame' al-Tavarikh-e Hasani*. Iraj Afshar and Hosein Modarresi Tabataba'i eds. (Karachi 1987).

Yusef, Mohammad. *Dheil-e Tarikh-e 'Alamara-ye 'Abbasi*, ed. Soheil Khvonsari (Tehran 1938).

Zdzislaw Zygulski Jr. "Islamic weapons in Polish collections and their provenance", in Robert Elgood ed. *Islamic Arms and Armour* (London 1979), pp. 213-38.

INDEX